THE IMAGE BEFORE
THE WEAPON

THE IMAGE BEFORE THE WEAPON

A Critical History of the Distinction between Combatant and Civilian

Helen M. Kinsella

CORNELL UNIVERSITY PRESS   ITHACA AND LONDON

First published 2011 by Cornell University Press
First printing, Cornell Paperbacks, 2015
Printed in the United States of America

Library of Congress Cataloging-in-Publication Data

Kinsella, Helen
    The image before the weapon : a critical history of the distinction between combatant and civilian / Helen M. Kinsella.
        p. cm.
    Includes bibliographical references and index.
    ISBN 978-0-8014-4903-1 (cloth : alk. paper)
    ISBN 978-1-5017-0067-5 (pbk. : alk. paper)
  1. Combatants and noncombatants (International law)   I. Title.
    KZ6515.K56 2011
    341.6'7—dc22   2010052642

Cloth printing   10 9 8 7 6 5 4 3 2 1
Paperback printing   10 9 8 7 6 5 4 3 2 1

This book contains a revised version of "Discourses of Difference: Civilians, Combatants, and Compliance with the Laws of War," *Review of International Studies* 31, no. S1 (2005): 163–85, reprinted with the permission of Cambridge University Press, and "Gendering Grotius," *Political Theory* 34, no. 2 (2006): 161–91, reprinted with the permission of Sage Publications.

For my ever-lovin' family:
roots mansion that's where we'll be.

For my father:
Who taught me that I could and expected that I would.

For my son:
Whose participation began when, unbeknownst to me, he decided all the materials collected for what would become this book—papers, notes, files, drafts, and so forth—needed to be re-sorted according to his unique two-year-old logic. He continues to astound me in every way.

Contents

Acknowledgments   ix
Abbreviations   xi

1. Gender, Innocence, and Civilization   1
2. Martial Piety in the Medieval and Chivalric Codes of War   24
3. Civilization and Empire: Francisco de Vitoria and
      Hugo Grotius   53
4. General Orders 100, Union General Sherman's March
      to Atlanta, and the Sand Creek Massacre   82
5. The 1899 Martens Clause and the 1949 IV Geneva
      Convention   104
6. The Algerian Civil War and the 1977 Protocols Additional   127
7. The Civil Wars of Guatemala and El Salvador   155
8. Responsibility   187

Notes   199
Index   255

Acknowledgments

Friends and family are a solace and a delight, a formidable redoubt against the common miseries and elations of writing. This first book is a testament to their fortitude and patience, as well as to their admonitions and stern encouragements. It would be folly to believe I can thank them sufficiently for their interest in and support of this book, or for the love and kindness they have shared. So, let this appear as simply the first of many expressions of gratitude.

Thank you to...

...my professors at the University of Minnesota-Minneapolis who created a community marked by such intellectual and personal generosity: Mary Dietz, Lisa Disch, Bud Duvall, Sally Kenney, Richard Price, and Kathryn Sikkink.

...Bob Hammarberg and Dan Kelliher for putting it all in perspective.

...faculty and students of the University of Minnesota-Minneapolis, University of Wisconsin-Madison, and Stanford University MacArthur Consortium Interdisciplinary Program on Peace and International Co-operation for an introduction to the joys of interdisciplinary research and community.

...Adam Sitze, in whose debt I will happily, and hopefully, ever remain. And to Adam and Mary Strunk for a visit that brought immeasurable comfort.

...the writing group, Rachel Estroff and Rene Wilson, led by Lisa Disch.

...readers of incomparable merit and spirit: Kristin Fitzgerald, Petrice Flowers, Bahar Rumelli, and Ann Towns.

...Diane Elam and Kim Savo, whose critical gaze corrected more than a few errors.

...Anne Orford and Sarah Sewall, who arrived at a perfect time.

...Carol Cohn; the Boston Consortium on Gender, Security, and Human Rights; the Women and Public Policy Program; and the Belfer Center for Science and International Affairs at the John F. Kennedy School of Government, Harvard University.

...cohorts at the Center for International Security and Cooperation, who cared for Matthew and me with such grace and humor, especially Tarak Barkawi, Alex Downes, Page Fortna, Elizabeth Gardner, Ron and Laura Hassner, Tracy Hill, Colin Kahl, Lien-Hang Nguyen, Tonya Putnam, Scott Sagan, Karthika Sasikumar, and Carola Weil.

...Lynn Eden for everything and more.

…Terrell Carver, Kevin Kinneavy, Jo Lee, Patricia Owens, V. Spike Peterson, Laura Sjoberg, Joe Soss, Maria Stern, Ann Tickner, Mary Vavrus, Jolie von Suhr, and Marysia Zalewski for being there when called.

…Ann Shaffer for her precision, intelligence, and enthusiasm.

…the indomitable women of Hillington Green; you rock!

…Mark, doxology.

…Jess Clayton, Meredith Keller, and Julie F. Nemer for their discerning read.

…my colleagues at the Department of Political Science, University of Wisconsin-Madison, for their generous support and kind encouragement. And, for reading a version of this, I am indebted to Mark Copelovitch, Jimmy Casas Klausen, Nils Ringe (good effort!), Howard Schweber, Nadav Shelef, and Scott Straus.

…Roger Haydon, Christian Reus-Smit, and Ward Thomas for providing clarity.

Every other expression of gratitude will be over drinks and dessert—Matthew's buying!

Abbreviations

AAAS	American Academy of Arts and Sciences (United States)
AID	Agency for International Development (United States)
ALN	Armée de Libération Nationale, Army of National Liberation (Algeria)
CCW	Committee on the Conduct of War (U.S. Congress)
CEBs	Comunidades Eclesiales de Base, Christian Base Communities (Latin America)
CEH	Comisión para el Esclarecimiento Histórico, Historical Clarification Commission (Guatemala)
CIA	Central Intelligence Agency (United States)
CIIDH	Centro Internacional para Investigaciones en Derechos Humanos, International Center for the Investigation of Human Rights (Guatemala)
CONAVIGUA	Coordinadora Nacional de Viudas de Guatemala, National Coordination of Guatemalan Widows (Guatemala)
CUC	Comité de Unidad Campesina, Peasant Unity Committee (Guatemala)
EGP	Ejército Guerrillero de los Pobres, Guerrilla Army of the Poor (Guatemala)
FDR	Frente Democrático Revolucionario, Revolutionary Democratic Front (El Salvador)
FLN	Front de Libération Nationale, National Liberation Front (Algeria)
FMLN	Frente Farabundo Martí para la Liberación Nacional, Farabundo Martí National Liberation Front (El Salvador)
GAM	Grupo de Apoyo Mutuo, Mutual Support Group (Guatemala)
ICC	International Criminal Court
ICRC	International Committee of the Red Cross
ICTR	International Criminal Tribunal for Rwanda
ICTY	International Criminal Tribunal for the Former Yugoslavia
IGO	intergovernmental organization
ISAF	International Security Assistance Force
LWP	*The Law of War and Peace* (*De jure belli ac pacis libri tres*), by Hugo Grotius (Amsterdam, 1625)

MINUGUA	United Nations Verification Mission in Guatemala
NACLA	North American Congress on Latin America
NATO	North Atlantic Treaty Organization
NGO	nongovernmental organization
NOAB	*The New Oxford Annotated Bible* (New York, 1973).
OAS	Organisation de l'Armée Secrète, Organization of the Secret Army (France in Algeria)
OAU	Organization of African Unity
OEF	Operation Enduring Freedom (United States in Afghanistan)
ONUSAL	United Nations Observer Mission in El Salvador
ORDEN	Organización Democrática Nacionalista, Nationalist Democratic Organization (El Salvador)
ORPA	Organización Revolucionario del Pueblo en Armas, Organization of People in Arms (Guatemala)
PACs	patrullas de autodefensa civil, civil defense patrols (Guatemala)
PLO	Palestine Liberation Organization (Palestine)
REMHI	Proyecto Interdiocesano, Recuperación de la Memoria Histórica, Recovery of the Historic Memory (Guatemala)
SJC	Socorro Júridico Cristiano, Christian Legal Assistance (El Salvador)
SWAPO	South West Africa People's Organization (South Africa)
UN	United Nations
UNICEF	United Nations Children's Fund
URNG	Unidad Revolucionaria Nacional Guatemalteca, Guatemalan National Revolutionary Unity (Guatemala)
USSR	Union of Socialist Soviet Republics, Soviet Union

THE IMAGE BEFORE
THE WEAPON

GENDER, INNOCENCE, AND CIVILIZATION

> **Law is a rule or measure of action by which one is led to an action or restrained from acting. The word law (lex) is derived from ligare, to bind, because it binds one to act.... [Therefore] a rule or measure is imposed by being applied to those who are to be ruled and measured by it. Wherefore, in order that a law obtain the binding force which is proper to a law, it must needs be applied to the men who have to be ruled by it.**

—Thomas Aquinas, *Summa Theologica*, Question 90

Since the start of the ground wars in Afghanistan (2001) and in Iraq (2003), the distinction between combatant and civilian has remained a significant referent of engagement and standard of judgment guiding the operational strategy of the U.S. military and allies. In 2001, referring to operations in Afghanistan, General Richard Myers said, "the last thing we want are any civilian casualties. So we plan every military target with great care."[1] Charles Allen, deputy general counsel for the U.S. Department of Defense, stated in an interview on December 16, 2002, "with regard to the global war on terrorism, wherever it may reach, the law of armed conflict certainly does apply...in the sense of the principle of distinction."[2] Active military operations in both Afghanistan and Iraq conformed to the laws of war insofar as targeting decisions were evaluated with regard to the distinction to be made between combatant and civilian.

On September 16, 2008, in his capacity as commander of the North Atlantic Treaty Organization–International Security Assistance Force (NATO-ISAF), U.S. Army General David D. McKiernan averred, "NATO and American officials in Afghanistan believe that one civilian casualty is too many."[3] This statement followed the release earlier in the month of a tactical directive reviewing procedures for using lethal force, the singular purpose of which was reducing civilian casualties. Both the directive and the general's statement were in response to widespread condemnation of civilian casualties resulting from an air strike in the province of Herat. A week later, the UN Security Council extended the NATO-ISAF mission in Afghanistan, but only after issuing explicit cautions about moderating civilian casualties. This followed specific changes in NATO-ISAF and Operation Enduring Freedom (OEF) tactics in Afghanistan in 2007 that included delaying attacks when civilians might be harmed. Furthermore, as Lawrence Wright reported in the June 2008 issue of the *New Yorker,* events of the previous year revealed that even organized networks of violence such as Al Qaeda are not unified in their acceptance of civilian casualties as a necessary normative and strategic dimension of armed conflict. In July 2009, the Taliban, under the directive of Mullah Omar, issued a new code of conduct for the Afghanistan Mujahedeen that specifically instructed them to "do their best to avoid civilian deaths and injuries and damage to civilian property."[4]

These actions suggest that the protection and defense of civilians during armed conflicts are an elemental strategic and normative commitment on the part of the majority of states and organized militaries and insurgencies; moreover, they have been for some time. Beginning with his September 1999 "Report to the Security Council on the Protection of Civilians in Armed Conflict," Kofi Annan, former UN secretary-general and Nobel laureate, repeatedly stated that "the plight of civilians is no longer something which can be neglected, or made secondary, because it complicates political negotiations or interests."[5] The centrality of the civilian was evident in the conduct of the 1999 NATO intervention in Kosovo. General Wesley K. Clark, supreme allied commander of NATO during the Kosovo war, writes, "Both we and the Serbs realized at the onset how critical this issue would be. It was the most pressing drumbeat of the campaign: minimize, if not eliminate, civilian casualties."[6]

Significantly, it is not only the United Nations, the United States, and NATO that, in increasingly rare agreement, hold the principle of protection of and respect for civilians in great regard. Signed and ratified by a diverse array of states, the mandate of the International Criminal Court (ICC) explicitly reiterates the essential distinction between combatant and civilian, criminalizing intentional actions against civilians. In addition, the statutes of both regional criminal tribunals for Rwanda and the former Yugoslavia preceded the ICC in their acceptance of this distinction as definitive of the laws of war. Notably, these institutions were created soon after, or in the midst of, conspicuous transgressions of the laws of war. Consequently, in regard to the protection of and respect for civilians, the striking congruence of political and legal convictions suggests that the civilian is an essential concept and category of international law and international relations and a crucial referent by which conflicts and conduct are judged. Perhaps Alberico Gentili, the seventeenth-century Italian publicist, said it best: "He is foolish who connects the laws of war with the unlawful acts committed in war."[7]

Juridically, formally distinguishing between combatants and civilians is known as the *principle of distinction.* The principle of distinction is one of three elements composing the principle of discrimination; the other two are distinguishing between civilian objects and military objectives and directing attacks only toward combatants and military objectives. The principle of distinction is a peremptory obligation of international humanitarian law; it requires universal observance from which no derogation is permitted.[8] The principle is expressed in both customary and codified international humanitarian law and, as such, is both a positive and necessary precept for establishing the protection of civilians.[9] Moreover, it is a central category of contemporary human rights and humanitarian discourses. The principle prescribes respect for and protection of civilians in times of armed conflict and "forms the basis of the entire regulation of war."[10]

What does it mean to say that the principle of distinction forms the basis of international humanitarian law? International humanitarian law is the oldest and most highly codified system of international law. It reflects and regulates the customs and practices of war among and, less extensively, within states.[11] In accordance with the formal classification of armed conflicts as either international or non-international, international humanitarian law articulates material and conceptual limitations on the actions of states, militaries, combatants, and noncombatants. As a result, international humanitarian law is a primary referent for the training and disciplining of those entities and, more recently, for the peacekeeping troops of the United Nations.

* * *

Nonetheless, at the same time as it serves as one of the foundations of contemporary law and politics, the principle of distinction, taken on its own terms, has proved to be remarkably frail. Contemporary armed conflicts, marked by a "mixture of war, crime and human rights violations," are nasty, brutish, and increasing in duration and devastation.[12] The quintessential characteristic of the majority of these conflicts is the blurring of the distinction between combatant and civilian. The debasement of this distinction poses formidable challenges for the enforcement of international humanitarian law and dramatically discloses its limitations.

Scholars and historians of international humanitarian law agree that the principle of distinction is "recognized as the fundamental principle upon which the entire notion of 'humanity in warfare' rests." Yet it is equally acknowledged as "the most fragile."[13] Indeed, the ragged conflicts in the former Yugoslavia, in Rwanda, and in the Sudan have been scored by the extremity of both the deliberate, determined persecution of civilians and the haphazard, wanton destruction of civilians, resulting from a concerted military strategy or its absence altogether.[14] There is no doubt that these internal conflicts are marked by what many scholars and essayists term a "particular savagery."[15] But to ascribe violations of the principle of distinction to the location of a war is highly misleading, if not also an effect of a particular conception of civilization. Certainly, sophisticated military technologies in ostensibly less ragged wars render the conceptual distinction equally absurd—if not more so.[16]

In both instances, the most striking result is a consistent and terrifying indifference to the classic distinction between the elemental categories of international humanitarian law—combatant and civilian are to be identified and distinguished at all times. Let me be clear: I do not claim that international humanitarian law outlaws the killing of civilians. That would be a patent misreading of the law. Although the principle of distinction is the predicate of the potential protection of civilians, it is not an obligation of absolute protection. Instead, it confers responsibility on military commanders and their forces, as well as on civilians in positions of authority, to refrain from directly attacking civilians and civilian objects, to take reasonable precautions to avoid and minimize civilian deaths, and to avoid and minimize the destruction of civilian property and objects necessary to civilian survival. The laws of war have admitted the possibility of collateral or unintentional damage since Thomas Aquinas first wrote of an act "beside intention."[17] Thus, it appears that the foundation of international humanitarian law—the principle of distinction—actually *allows* the death of civilians in war and that the robustness of positive and customary law is not reflected in an equally robust compliance.[18]

Is this a paradox? Yes, if *paradox* is defined as an "unresolvable proposition that is true and false at the same time."[19] But, within the increasingly functionalist mapping of the role of laws and norms by scholars attentive to both, a *paradox* is taken to be a simple contradiction that can and should be resolved once behavior is aligned with the norm in question. Indeed, the practical work of international organizations and institutions both rely on and reify this interpretation. For example, consider a discussion of the UN Security Council on the topic of the protection of civilians: insofar "as civilians have become the primary victims and often the very objects of war," the proper response is to encourage and solidify "full compliance with the rules and principles of international law" and to promote, in the words of one participant, no less than the "civilianization of conflict."[20] According to this logic, the appropriate response is to buttress the principle of distinction through increasing compliance and enforcement.

Likewise, regardless of the increasing acknowledgment within international relations of the importance of law to regulate world politics, the paradigmatic approach to the study of international law and international relations is consistently restricted to the study of the dimensions of compliance,[21] which in turn only "implicitly examines the foundations of international institutions and international order."[22] This framing excludes an analysis of the very politics that informs and produces international institutions and creates international order. In addition, as Martti Koskenniemi observes, this focus on compliance "silently assumes that the political question—what the objectives are—has already been solved."[23] Further, this focus on compliance necessarily presumes that its foundational concepts—the combatant and the civilian—are secure. Ironically it is exactly this presumption that is proved false in the conduct of armed conflicts.

* * *

Within armed conflicts the "dividing line between combatants and civilians is frequently blurred"—this is a consistent refrain voiced by both witnesses and participants, and sounded repeatedly throughout the numerous statements and debates within the UN Security Council regarding the protection and treatment of civilians in war.[24] To suggest, as one scholar of international law does, that the definition of the *civilian* (which he calls a "term of art") should be determined within the "context of international and non-international armed conflict" presupposes a clarity of conflict reminiscent of the ideal of set battles.[25] After all, as another international lawyer acknowledges, the empirical and juridical categories of combatant and civilian are "not quite so neatly separable" as implied and were rarely so.[26] Indeed, international humanitarian law itself admits the imprecision of the distinction, stating that "in case of doubt whether a person is a civilian, that person shall be considered to be a civilian."[27] Doubt, then, becomes an integral attribute of the category itself as well as the basis for the injunction to extend the category.

If doubt and indeterminacy are integral and evident characteristics of the categories combatant and civilian and, significantly, of the difference between them, what are the implications for responding to the violation of the principle of distinction? Foremost, the concepts and categories of combatant and civilian cannot be taken as self-evident either within international humanitarian law or in conflicts. Therefore, they must be produced; in other words, the significance and strength of the categories of combatant and civilian are provisional and, as such, must be consistently reiterated to ensure their status and grant them sanctity.[28] Thus, the move toward increasing compliance with and enforcement of international humanitarian law presumes (and necessarily so) that which the atrocities of conflict so brutally belie—that the combatant and civilian are coherent and determinant categories. Put another way, although the laws rest on a seemingly self-evident categorization—you are either one or the other, combatant or civilian—it is not that simple. As any soldier in Baghdad or Herat can attest, errors lead not simply to the deaths of Iraqi and Afghani civilians mistakenly killed but also to the deaths of U.S. soldiers who mistake Iraqi or Afghani combatants for civilians. Even in the laws of war, to which we refer to clarify the difference, the combatant and the civilian are not as distinct as implied.

Consequently, the distinction between combatant and civilian, which should ostensibly mark the triumph of international humanitarian law, instead signals its most radical crisis. While remaining accountable to the evidence of its violation, I specifically engage the challenges raised by the indeterminacy of the principle of distinction. I ask: What is a combatant? What is a civilian? Who is a combatant? Who is a civilian? How do we know? Who is to judge, and on what grounds?

In focusing on the civilian, I alter a primary preoccupation of international humanitarian law—the question of who should be legitimately considered a combatant. I ask, instead, who should be legitimately considered a civilian. Although the concepts of civilian and combatant are irrevocably linked in international humanitarian law, as the concept of the civilian is inseparable from the distinction that should be made between combatants and civilians, it is the combatant who has been its primary subject. Indeed, not until 1949, in the Geneva Convention Relative to the Protection of Civilian Persons in Time of War (IV Geneva Convention), did the civilian formally become a subject of treaty law. And not until 1977, in the Protocols Additional to the 1949 Geneva Conventions, was *civilian* formally defined within international law.[29]

Approached in a conventional way, a civilian (a concept presumed to be so clear that "everyone has an understanding of its meaning") is simply one who is *not* a member of the armed forces.[30] What I find intriguing about the reliance on this negative definition (in which *civilian* is defined through a simple lack of combatancy) is the way that it prohibits consideration of the significance of the concept of civilian itself. How do we begin to understand and effectively respond to the dissolution of the principle of distinction if we lack a prior understanding of the very concept and category that it is said to protect?

I contend that we can no longer ask what difference international humanitarian law makes without also asking *on* what differences international humanitarian law is made. I suggest that the principle of distinction does not so much rest on a categorical difference between combatant and civilian as produce it. The principle of distinction is a relationship that, in Michel Foucault's terms, "puts into operation differences that are, at the same time, its conditions and its results."[31] To understand these differences produced by the principle of distinction, I begin a genealogy of the principle of distinction focusing on the concept of the civilian.

* * *

What would it mean to write a genealogy of the principle of distinction? For one, a genealogy helps us to understand how fixed oppositions (here civilian versus combatant) mask the degree to which their meanings are, in fact, a result of an established rather than an inherent contrast. Moreover, a genealogy expressly engages the hierarchical interdependence of the opposed terms, whereby the combatant is invested with primacy and thus is responsive to the operation of power.[32] As Foucault succinctly states, a genealogy is a form of history that transforms the "development of a given into a question."[33] A genealogy illustrates how that which is taken to be universally necessary and necessarily universal (here, the civilian) has come to be understood and institutionalized as self-evidently so. It opens the possibilities of rethinking the concept of the civilian and, in turn, of rethinking what we are doing.

To begin this project, however, the comfort of preconceived categories must be relinquished and the familiarity of this venerable norm must be made strange—even though either seems like the very last thing we can or should do. Hannah Arendt indicates the reason for this counterintuitive move: "Adherence to conventional, standardized codes of expression and conduct have the socially recognized function of protecting us against reality, that is against the claim on our thinking attention that all events and facts make by virtue of their existence."[34] Perhaps the brutal events of recent armed conflicts have already done both by clearly denoting the breach of the principle of distinction, as Foucault puts it, as a "breach of self-evidence," in which the construction of the principle and its constitutive elements, the combatant and the civilian, can be made visible rather than simply automatic.[35]

What I want to insist upon is that the abrogation of the principle of distinction is also an opening, providing a space for reviewing the principle and its core concepts without retreating to a reflexive, unthinking acceptance of its status and significance. The gravity of this move is matched by the centrality of the principle of distinction itself; what remains evident even in its breach is the importance of the principle as a means of regulating and systematizing interactions among and within states and of establishing individual and international security. It is a protocol of international order.

My point is not that a distinction *cannot* be made; indeed, both practically and juridically, the distinction is made every day. Nor is it that the distinction *should not* be made; on the contrary, the distinction has many purposes and uses. Rather, recognizing the contingent presence of the principle of distinction imposes the question of its origins and emergence, which in turn underscores the intricacy of its form. It suggests that how, when, and for whom the distinction is constituted are precisely what affects if it is made at all.[36] It reminds us that every norm possesses a history, the marks of which remain.

I trace throughout this book a series of discourses—gender, innocence, and civilization—that, like red threads, mark the history of the principle of distinction.[37] It is this series of discourses, each of which is itself composed of a confluence of political, moral, and legal judgments, that conditions the appearance of the civilian and the combatant and invests the distinction with a seemingly indisputable gravity and authority.

I use here Foucault's concept of a series to denote the relationships among these three discourses. Foucault highlights the diffusion rather than the unity or distinctions of discourses. Put another way, this series is not braided tightly throughout but may unravel and fray as often as it knots at particular historical moments. In his words, "discourses must be treated as discontinuous practices, which cross each other, are sometimes juxtaposed with one another, but can just as well exclude or be unaware of each other."[38] In this book, I document how these discourses converge at particular junctures to produce the combatant and the civilian, demarcating the difference between them. My historical claim is that, in each of the moments I analyze, this series is a necessary element in the production of the distinction. But I am not risking the transhistorical claim that in each instance the principle appears (or appears only) as an effect of this series. Accordingly, my choice of this series is neither whimsical nor exhaustive; it derives from listening to "popular language in which words…are daily used as political clichés and misused as catchwords."[39]

Perhaps the best example of the power of this series is found in the common metonymy *innocent civilian,* in which *innocent* signifies civilian such that a *guilty civilian* appears oxymoronic. Another example is the equivalence of *women and children* with *civilian* such that all women and children are civilians and that civilians are, in part, women and children. The formidable material effects of these substitutions are captured in a 1982 interview with the spokesman for Guatemalan General José Efraín Ríos Montt. When asked about the massacres of civilians, including women and children, the spokesman replied, "And then it would be said that you were killing innocent people. But they were not innocent, they had sold out to subversion….No…Guatemalan general could order the death of an innocent."[40] Ríos Montt, who was indicted for his role in the Guatemalan civil war, subsequently confirmed this claim, insisting that "no Guatemalan general could order the death of an innocent."[41]

This invocation of the principle of distinction poignantly illustrates how those denied recognition as civilians were, and would continue to be, massacred without compunction. But surely the statements by Ríos Montt and his spokesman raise more questions than they answer. After all, the two men strategically and sequentially repudiated the marks of the civilian without ever rejecting the centrality of the concept itself. If we were to allow this to claim our thinking attention, might not questions such as these follow: Why were the massacres and deaths of civilians defended with reference to their lack of innocence? Is innocence a necessary attribute of civilians? If so, exactly what is innocence? Or, put differently, of what is a civilian innocent? And if, continuing to follow the General's logic, we agree that a civilian is innocent of subversion, does this not simply raise further questions about how we would recognize subversion or judge a person innocent of it? Moreover, it appears that the massacre of women and children signals a worse crime than the massacre of civilians. Conceivably, then, women and children cannot (or cannot easily) be accused of subversion. Is this because women and children are innocent? But, if we set aside the question of innocence, even the conjunction of women and children prompts its own confusions. Does innocence result from the relationship *of* women and children? Or is it from the relationship of women *and* children? To pose these questions is to recognize the "profound instability" each question identifies and the "enormous responsibility" each entails for it is on the answers that, as General Ríos Montt demonstrated, lives depend.[42]

Slowly, there appears to be a growing recognition that compliance with the principle of distinction, to "prevent the progressive widening of the scope of violence," must be attentive to its "legal, political, historical, and sociological nature."[43] Particularly noteworthy about this statement is that its author represents the International Committee of the Red Cross (ICRC), an organization dedicated to improving compliance through the increased institutionalization, implementation, and enforcement of international humanitarian law. Clearly, as Simon Chesterman writes in response to the crisis of distinction, more than a "reliance on rules" is needed.[44]

* * *

What are the rules of war? What is their history? Before answering these questions, I first clarify my use of the term *laws of war,* address the possible tension in the chronological ordering of the chapters of the book and a genealogy, and provide a brief overview of the conventional history of the laws of war.

The ICRC promulgated the term *international humanitarian law,* as opposed to *laws of war,* after the Kellogg-Briand Pact and the 1945 United Nations Charter outlawed and cautioned against, respectively, resorting to war. It was Jean Pictet, as the vice president of the ICRC, who introduced the use of *humanitarian law* in the early 1970s.[45] Critics of the use of the term *humanitarian* to describe the laws of war argue that it denies the role of states and militaries in determining the application of the rules of war and minimizes the limitations of the law to check the brutality of war. Furthermore, as Judith Gardam notes, the term *humanitarian* mistakes the standard figures of the law (the combatant and the civilian) as neutral images. In fact, she argues, both are modeled on a male norm and, furthermore, it is the male combatant who is the central concern of international humanitarian law.[46] Because of this and because much of this book is concerned with the period that precedes the introduction of humanitarian law, I use the term *laws of war*. This substantial debate over the proper name underlines how war—our practice and conduct of it, and our interpretations and responses to it—is "politically constituted and bounded."[47]

As mentioned, there is a possible tension between the chronological order of this book and genealogy's refusal of the historicist claim of the necessity of such an unfolding of time (e.g., that the principle of distinction emerged from these contexts, where *context* is defined historically and geographically). Still, I am working within the extant narrative of the principle of distinction as created by scholars and historians to demonstrate how this (chronologically ordered) narrative is governed by and made possible through the discourses of gender, innocence, and civilization. To a degree, I write a genealogy of an Enlightenment, Christian, and Western narrative; and insofar as one undermines the other, that will remain an acknowledged tension throughout the book. I engage the authors of this narrative critically, illuminating their unacknowledged reliance on discourses of gender, innocence, and civilization to stabilize their claims of a progressive development of the concepts of combatant and civilian. Part of my purpose is to rewrite this conventional narrative of international humanitarian law. Before beginning, however, let me provide an overview of the history with which my work engages.

* * *

The laws of war draw from a concordance of narratives of divine law (developed in the Christian jurisprudence of ecclesiastical writings on the just war and made possible by the existence and idea of the Holy Roman Empire), natural law (which held that the expression and dictate of right reason reveals moral principles universal to all), and the law of nations (the customs, practices, and usages found, first, among the *civitas maxima* and, later, among the society of states).[48] The laws of war have two areas of emphasis. The first is the *ius ad bello,* which considers the right to resort to war, and the second is the *ius in bello,* which restrains the means and methods of war. It is principally the *ius ad bello* that occupied the earliest works on the laws of war due to the persistent disputes over the role and obligations of Christians participating in war. As conventionally understood, the conclusion of the Peace of Westphalia in 1648 precipitated the steady diminishing of the importance of Christian thought, specifically its scholarly teachings and debates on *ius ad bello,* or just war.[49]

Beginning in the early eighteenth century, which was marked by the emergence of secularizing nation-states and the conceptualization of war as an instrument of state formation and practice, the laws of war shifted primarily to concerns about the *ius in bello*. Therefore, the evaluation of the justness or right of resorting to force no longer determined the restraints on the means and methods of war. In other words, the *ius in bello* developed as a standard independently of the reasons for or justice of the war itself. This was an important development in the laws of war because it required that each belligerent, specifically understood to be a sovereign state, obey and uphold the laws of war irrespective of a determination of the just or unjust nature of its cause.

In the nineteenth and early twentieth centuries, the *ius in bello* was further divided between the Law of the Hague and the Law of Geneva. The Law of the Hague describes the "law of warfare proper, that is, the means and methods of war."[50] Within the laws of war, the protection of the civilian derives from two interdependent tenets. The first, articulated in the preamble to the 1868 St. Petersburg Declaration, is that "the only legitimate object which States should endeavor to accomplish during war is to weaken the military forces of the enemy."[51] Therefore, as further developed in Article 22 of the 1899 and 1907 Hague Regulations (Respecting the Law and Customs of War on Land), the right of each belligerent to injure enemies is not unlimited. Excessive harm to and superfluous or unnecessary suffering (harm and suffering deemed inessential to the strategic pursuit of military success) of combatants or civilians are prohibited, and civilians are not to be treated as enemies. Each of these precepts owes its formulation to the propositions put forth by Jean-Jacques Rousseau a century earlier. He believed that war was not a relationship between one man and another but a relationship between one state and another— a relationship that conferred no "right that is unnecessary to its purpose," which is ultimately peace.[52]

It was primarily the Law of Geneva, within the *ius in bello*, that progressively developed and delimited the protection of and respect for civilians in the twentieth century. The Law of Geneva promotes and provides for the respect for and protection of noncombatants, civilians,[53] and civilian objects as far as the requirements of military necessity and the maintenance of public order allow. In the twenty-first century, the Law of Geneva is rooted in both customary and codified law, bound by the four Geneva Conventions of 1949 and the two Protocols Additional of 1977.

Although distinct, humanitarian law and human rights law are frequently invoked together to underscore the essential concept of human dignity on which each holds itself to be founded. This mutual reference is grounded in a relationship between the two forms of law clearly articulated in the turbulent decolonization decades of the 1960s and 1970s—as is well illustrated in the UN General Assembly Resolutions of 1968 and 1969 addressing "Respect for Human Rights in Armed Conflicts." Drawing from the rubric of human rights, these statements define the essential principles of humanitarian and human rights that are applicable in all armed conflicts—international or internal—and underscore the necessity of the further development of international humanitarian law to respond to violations in internal armed conflicts.

The concerted effort to expand the purview of international humanitarian and human rights law, and to link their field of application, was a direct result of the contentious conclusion of two decades of wars of decolonization and national liberation. A similar pattern is notable in contemporary endeavors to further the complementarity of the two branches of law to better respond to the forms of warfare found in recent armed conflicts. For example, international human rights and humanitarian law increasingly converge in the rulings of regional criminal tribunals, in the declarations of the UN General Assembly and Security Council, in the individual reports of special rapporteurs to the United Nations, and in the work of nongovernmental organizations (NGOs).[54] During the 1960s, human rights spurred the development of international humanitarian law; today it is international humanitarian law that is undergoing its own complex renaissance.

Even before the U.S.-led war on terror, and after a lull of almost twenty years, there had been a dramatic increase in the invocation of and reliance on international humanitarian law. Most visibly, the statutes of both the International Tribunal for Rwanda (ICTR) and the International Tribunal for the Former Yugoslavia (ICTY), as well as the Statute for the International Criminal Court, set forth the competence of each to prosecute violations of international humanitarian law. The rulings of the first two tribunals are explicitly founded on international humanitarian law, both the treaty law as set forth in the Geneva Conventions and the 1977 Protocols Additional I and II and the recognized customary laws of war.[55] The ICC presides over genocide, crimes against humanity and war crimes as set forth in international humanitarian law and relevant UN treaties. In addition, the 1989 UN Convention on the Rights of the Child recognizes the specific obligations of states to observe their responsibilities under international humanitarian law. Furthermore, legal efforts to prosecute former heads of state (e.g., General Augusto Pinochet of Chile, President Slobodan Milosevic of Serbia, General Ríos Montt of Guatemala, and Thomas Lubanga Dyilo of the Democratic Republic of Congo) and volatile conditions of conflict and occupation in many regions of the world, not the least of which is the U.S.-led "war against terror," have drawn international humanitarian law into a newfound currency. It is in this way that, as Theodor Meron, eminent jurist, observes, "international humanitarian law/ law of war and the corresponding institutions have thus become central to the protection of human rights."[56]

As a result, legal scholars and practitioners specializing in other forms of law now argue that international humanitarian law provides additional resources to strengthen and clarify the applicability of other bodies of international law. In the case of refugee law, for example, "recourse to international humanitarian norms should not only be an essential step in civil war and armed conflict cases…[but it can also] help ensure that refugee law does not become an isolated *lex specialis* on the outer margins of public international law."[57] Moreover, both legal scholars and practitioners argue strongly that adequate responses to contemporary conflicts require the dissolution of the traditional threefold partition of international human rights law, refugee law, and humanitarian law to establish an integrative humanitarian framework. Therefore, international humanitarian law offers a means for strengthening individual branches of international law. And, as the primary corpus of international law arising from and applicable to armed conflicts, it is an essential component of all international law.

This momentum, potentially accelerated by the September 11, 2001, attacks, refutes the oft-made claim that international humanitarian law is irrelevant to the ordering and conduct of international relations and challenges the broad belief that in times of war the law is silent. Rather, as Hugo Grotius, seventeenth-century publicist, argued in his Prolegomena to *De jure belli ac pacis* (1625), "Let the laws be silent, then, in the midst of arms, but only the laws of the State, those that the courts are concerned with, that are adapted only to a state of peace….between enemies…unwritten laws are in force, that is, those which nature prescribes or the agreement of nations has established."[58] As Grotius illuminates, those laws of war, written or not, consistently inform the practice of war. It is as much a mistake to argue that the laws of war are superfluous to war as it is to argue that the laws of war pertain only to its practice.

To better understand the relationship among this series of discourses, the production of the combatant and the civilian, and the material treatment of those designated as civilians, I consider the concepts of combatant and civilian within the conditions and conventions of armed conflicts. This approach helps identify and map the complex relations of change and continuity. By focusing on what Richard Price calls "defining moments" in customary and positive laws of war and armed conflict,[59] I illuminate the indebtedness of the concept of civilian to the discourses of gender, innocence, and civilization. Such a situated reading guards against a rudimentary misreading of the civilian as nothing but a fiction whose effects are no more than ephemeral. Thus, this work is conceived, in the words of Arendt, as an "exercise in political thought as it arises out of the actuality of political incidents." The purpose of my exercise is not, however, as Arendt might have it, to "discover the real origins of traditional concepts"[60] but, instead, to think within and against the narrative and institutionalization of the laws of war.

* * *

I employ the terms *principle of distinction, combatant,* and *civilian* in describing the logic and findings of each chapter. I do so simply for ease of explanation; these terms—with the exception of *combatant,* which has been in use since the early twelfth century—are anachronistic. *Civilian* entered common parlance in approximately late eighteenth century and *principle of distinction* in roughly the twentieth century. A fuller discussion of the evolution of these concepts is found in chapter 2.

Chapters 2 and 3 engage the paradigmatic history of the laws of war as recounted in the work of James Turner Johnson, a just war theorist; Theodor Meron, an international lawyer and scholar; and Michael Walzer, a political theorist. Each of these scholars is renowned in his field and has contributed immeasurably to the study of the laws of war. In chapter 2, I analyze what is generally considered to be the first manifestation of the principle as it appears in the early Christian texts of Thomas Aquinas and Augustine, but I specifically concentrate on the formulation of the principle of distinction in Christian canon law and the chivalric codes of the High to Late Middle Ages (eleventh to fifteenth centuries). I do so because as Maurice Keen, a prominent historian of the Middle Ages, writes, it is possible to identify the "existence in the middle ages of some sort of prototype of the Geneva Convention, a branch of international law governing the conduct of war."[61] I recognize that it may be difficult to imagine that the medieval codes of chivalry and the canons of the Christian Church are still pertinent to the structure and practice of international relations and international law. But this difficulty may be dramatically lessened by current debates in which the concepts and categories of just wars, unlawful and lawful combatants, and honor are consistently referenced. Recall that President George W. Bush believed that the United States was called to no less than a "crusade" against "evil-doers" in its war in Afghanistan.[62] The medieval Crusades remained outside the parameters of the extant doctrine of just war, achieving the signal status of wars waged without immunity; in this way, they were much like Bush's war against terrorism, in which "no immunity is possible."[63]

By rereading the original works of Thomas Aquinas, and Augustine, of Christine de Pisan, and Honoré Bonet, I deconstruct the paradigmatic history of the laws of war put forth by contemporary writers. I demonstrate how discourses of gender, innocence, and civilization worked in various ways and at various times to secure the distinction between combatant and civilian. A close reading of these texts identifies the ambiguities and inconsistencies in the arguments put forward for the existence of the distinction itself but overlooked by contemporary authors. By historicizing these texts, relating the formulation of their arguments to the sociopolitical practices and events of the time (e.g., the Crusades and the medieval peace movement, the Peace of God), I further document the multiple origins and purposes of this distinction.

A central finding of chapter 2 is the significant role of the Christian virtues of mercy and charity in informing the distinction. To spare someone who is in one's power is to exercise these much-desired virtues. Although I was already aware of the emphasis that the ICRC places on *caritas* in its own work, I underestimated the centrality of these concepts in justifying the exercise of discrimination by sovereign entities.[64] In the writings from the medieval era to the nineteenth century, mercy is clearly identified as both regulating sovereign power and, specifically, constituting a civilized sovereign.

What I find provocative is the way this concept of mercy is taken to contrast with, or be subsumed by, the concept of rights in the conventional narrative of the laws of war. For example, Hugo Slim suggests that the concept of civilian is invoked to "cradle and preserve the ancient idea that mercy, restraint, and protection should have a place in war."[65] According to Walzer, civilians are no longer spared by a combatant's merciful action; rather, being spared is a right of civilians, and indeed, the recognition of this right is a hallmark of civilized society.[66] Yet, considering that the civilian has all too frequently been sacrificed in the defense of civilization, is mercy so surely replaced by rights? Suffice it to say that the relationship among this triad (mercy, rights, and the laws of war) points most suggestively to the power of the sovereign; a power that is, for Foucault, the power to decide life and death itself and also in Hegel's formulation the right to grant pardon.[67] It is hardly incidental that the Council of Clermont (in 1095) both proclaimed the Peace of God, one origin of the medieval concept of immunity, *and* launched the First Crusade.

Let me offer another example. In his discussion of the beginnings of the principle of distinction, Johnson argues that because "medieval weapons were heavy and cumbersome and required considerable strength on the part of their bearer, those who were physically too weak were natural noncombatants."[68] That is, the distinguishing variable determining who was a combatant and who was a civilian was physical strength. This conclusion is certainly logical enough, and it is an explanation still relied on today. But on closer scrutiny physical strength cannot be the pivot on which this difference turns. What Johnson fails to consider are the medieval debates, recounted in the works of Bonet and de Pisan, on the treacherous possibilities of the wise counsel of the elderly and the cunning and speed of the child who may act at the behest of others. Writing in the sixteenth century, Alberico Gentili warns, "one is often strong in council who has denied bodily strength, and the shadow of the old man is more potent than the sword of the youth."[69] Should those who are too old or too young to lift a weapon, but who are capable of decisive influence, be identified as combatants or as civilians? The answer to this question was not obvious, and arguably such a question continues to haunt us today. Significantly, the irresolution of these debates indicates that physical strength does *not* provide the distinction that Johnson presumes.

Returning to his statements, however, what do appear to inform the distinction are discourses of gender that establish sex and sex difference and, in turn, are taken to *naturally* distinguish combatants (men who carry arms) from others. Throughout this book, I consider how discourses of gender establish sex and sex differences, and how those differences fund and stabilize the distinction of combatant and civilian. I demonstrate that, even though children, women, and the elderly are consistently invoked as the paradigmatic civilian, only the category of women is accepted as always already civilian. Individuals in the other two categories, children and the elderly, are civilians momentarily, bounded by their chronological age; but women are civilians always, bounded by their sex. Thus it is sex and sex difference, as constructed through discourses of gender, that enable a distinction to be made between combatant and civilian.

* * *

In chapter 3, I continue to document the discourses of gender, innocence, and civilization, but here my primary stress is on discourses of civilization. This focus derives from the evocative history of the term. The definition of *civilian* as a "nonmilitary man or official" entered into common parlance in the nineteenth century, but its origins are attributed to its eighteenth-century definition, "one of the covenanted European servants of the East India Company, not in military employ."[70] The relationship this suggests among the institutions of colonization and practices of imperium (preeminently, the East Indies Company) and the elaboration of *civilian* is ignored in conventional histories of the laws of war, and in the disciplines of international relations and international law.

Referring to the discipline of international law, Martti Koskenniemi observes, "one of the most remarkable feats in the discipline's self-construction has been its overwhelming Eurocentrism."[71] He notes that "very little has been written on imperialism and international law. Not only does there seem to exist no full-length study of the matter, there is an almost complete silence on it."[72] Yet a relationship among these elements is quite literally embodied in Hugo Grotius, the purported "father" of international law and international relations. Scholars of the laws of war credit his great seventeenth-century treatises with secularizing and expanding the laws of war, but Grotius accomplished this supposed feat while *simultaneously* defending the imperial reach of the Dutch East Indies Company. Therefore, it is the task of chapter 3 to examine the effects of this relationship—that is, the laws of war as a function of the Christendom of Europe before and during its imperial expansion—on the formulation of the principle of distinction.

To do this, I analyze the writings of Grotius and Francisco de Vitoria. Vitoria, like Grotius, grappled with the scope and applicability of the laws of war to those designated outside the realm of Christian civilization while also responding to the demands and desires of imperial nations.[73] For both authors, the process of defining the categories combatant and civilian and distinguishing between them was inextricably intertwined with establishing and legitimating a specific social order. My analysis reveals the multiple effects of the discourses of civilization—from restricting the scope of the laws of war to wars among civilized nations, and identifying as civilized those entities capable of recognizing and implementing the laws, to negating any distinction between combatant and civilian among those said to be outside the bounds of civilization.

The contemporary laws of war, similar to international law, are consistently described as arising from a specifically European (Western) culture, and from a highly Christianized one as well. "The law created to govern the diplomatic, commercial, military and other relations of Christian states forming the Europe of that time [the sixteenth and seventeenth centuries]…provides the basis for the present law."[74] The ascendancy and hegemony of this particular system of authority and law, such that it now is called universal, did not result from the absence of other possible systems but from a complex history of colonization and imperium. Thus the principle of distinction and this law of Christian nations are mutually indebted, as my analysis of the wars of conquest, commerce, and colonization and of the establishment of an international order demonstrates.[75] Medieval Christendom dramatically influenced the concept of civilian, as is evident in the revival and reliance on just war theories. For this reason, although I reference other forms of law, for example, Islamic law, a complete braiding of these two strands is yet to be completed.

* * *

After these historical chapters, I explore the constitutive role of these discourses in specific armed conflicts. In both chapters 4 and 7, I compare two cases of civil wars. In chapter 4, I investigate the identification and protection of civilians during the American Civil War and the U.S.-Indian wars. In chapter 7, I analyze this concept during the civil wars of Guatemala and El Salvador.

In each chapter, the two wars being compared occurred more or less simultaneously. In the chapter on the American Civil War and the U.S.-Indian wars, I focus on the period 1861–1865. Specifically, I concentrate on General William Sherman's march to Atlanta in 1864 and compare the descriptions and justifications of it to those of the Sand Creek Massacre of 1864, in which over two hundred Indians were slaughtered. In the chapter on the civil wars of Guatemala and El Salvador, I concentrate on the 1980s, highlighting the pivotal years 1980–1983, in which the majority of deaths occurred. These foci provide me with a commensurate comparative period and a shared sociopolitical context within which to situate each comparison. Consequently, I can make sufficiently detailed assessments of the similarities and differences in the constitution and treatment of the civilian in each pair. In addition, the wars in first comparison precede the first formal codification of the laws of war, whereas the wars in the second occur after the last major positive treaty on the laws of war. This offers a broader historical perspective, from primarily customary law to highly developed positive law.

The American Civil War was a defining moment in the development of the laws of war because in the midst of this war the first modern code of war was written and promulgated. Francis Lieber, Prussian immigrant and political science professor, wrote General Orders 100, which marked the first time in modern history that the proper conduct of war was codified. General Orders 100 governed the behavior, expectations, and obligations of all parties to the conflict, and it was not formally replaced in the United States until 1956. General Orders 100 provided the basis for the Brussels Conference of 1874, which produced the (nonbinding) International Declaration Concerning the Laws and Customs of War. In addition, the code was adapted by the Prussian army and influenced the 1880 *Oxford Manual of the Institute of International Law.* All these documents were the principal sources of the 1899 and 1907 Hague regulations. Notably, although often overlooked, the foundation of the international laws of war was laid within an *internal* armed conflict, which makes the relative weakness of positive law governing internal armed conflicts (see chaps. 5–6) all the more puzzling.

The civil wars of Guatemala and El Salvador took place after the final codification of the laws of war in 1977. Yet the first application of Common Article 3 of the 1949 IV Geneva Convention (governing war within a state) was in Guatemala in 1954 during the overthrow of Jacobo Arbenz's regime. The civil war in El Salvador also marked a first; it was the first application of the 1977 Protocol II governing internal armed conflicts. The Salvadoran war was also a defining moment in the laws of war because it was one of the first conflicts in which international organizations, intergovernmental organizations (IGOs) and NGOs, proclaimed the applicability of Protocol II and actively worked to hold all parties to the conflict accountable to international humanitarian law. Furthermore, the insurgent Frente Farabundo Martí para la Liberación Nacional (FMLN; Farabundo Martí National Liberation Front) in El Salvador announced that it would accept and conform to the laws of war, much as the Front de Libération Nationale (FLN; National Liberation Front) in Algeria had done to great success in prior decades (see chap. 6). The diffusion and acceptance of the laws of war in El Salvador was a marked contrast to Guatemala. In the Guatemalan civil war, the laws of war were rejected as inapplicable by the Guatemalan government, and the insurgent Unidad Revolucionaria Nacional Guatemalteca (URNG; Guatemalan National

Revolutionary Unity) made no public attempt to recognize the laws of war. Thus, not only are these two conflicts critical cases in the history of the laws of war but they provide an important comparison of the conduct of the wars, the identification of the civilian, and the treatment of those so designated.

In chapters 4 and 7, I weave a narrative of the production and protection of the civilian into the history of the laws of war and the principle of distinction. I record how the discourses of gender, innocence, and civilization affected the identification and treatment of the civilian. In each comparative case, the acceptance of and conformance to the laws of war in one of the conflicts—El Salvador and the American Civil War—translated into significantly fewer violations of individuals, murders, and atrocities. This suggests that the principle of distinction is a significant factor in the protection of individuals. Nevertheless, the pivotal element is how the civilian is so identified and constituted. In each comparison, the discourses of civilization discriminated against individuals who otherwise would be accepted as civilians, as evidenced by the brutalities of the U.S.-Indian wars and the Guatemalan civil war. During the U.S.-Indian wars, even those who held that the Indians were not *all* incorrigible barbarians and that, therefore, the rules of civilized warfare should be considered nevertheless cautioned against their application. After all, "when civilization and barbarism are brought in such a relation…it is right that the superiority of the former should be asserted and the latter compelled to give way."[76]

Moreover, both the U.S. and the Guatemalan militaries effectively employed discourses of innocence to construe the American Indians and the Maya as collectively guilty, of bearing the constant potential for insurrection. (As we will see, this construction eerily resonates with Vitoria's first writings on both the immanent threat posed by the Indians and the proper consequences for those who, confirming the suspicions of the Spanish, resisted the progress of civilization; see chap. 3.) Indeed, after the American Civil War ended, the essential approach in the U.S.-Indian wars was that all Indians who resisted removal to reservations, regardless of age or sex, were legitimate targets.

Although the discourses of civilization may sound most loudly in chapters 4 and 7, distinguishing those to whom the laws of war apply from those to whom they do not, discourses of gender are also heard. Not unexpectedly, in each of these four wars women were identified as presumptive civilians. Yet, and again not unexpectedly, in the wars in which discourses of civilization triumphed, this presumption no longer held. The statements of General Sherman most vividly capture this point. In reference to the American Civil War, he argued, "war is at best barbarism, but to involve all—children, women, old, and helpless—is more than can be justified." In contrast, in the U.S.-Indian wars, he instructed his men to "act with vindictiveness against the Sioux, even to their extermination, men, women, and children."[77] To put it starkly, discourses of civilization trump those of gender in both the U.S.-Indian wars and the Guatemalan civil war. The killing of women and children—otherwise antithetical to the standards of civilization—is made intelligible when those same women and children are said to be outside of civilization and, in turn, pose a potential threat to it.

* * *

In this book, I concentrate on internal armed conflicts for three interrelated reasons. First, the conduct and characteristics of internal armed conflicts continue to deeply influence the laws of war. The 1949 IV Geneva Convention owes its existence not solely to the world wars but also to the debates and discussions sparked by the treatment of civilians in earlier wars, most notably the Spanish Civil War of 1931–1936. Likewise, the decolonization and liberation wars of the 1960s and 1970s prompted the 1977 Protocols Additional, which distinctly affected the articulation of the laws. Thus, internal armed conflicts matter greatly to the laws of war.

Nonetheless, relatively few studies address the relationship of the laws of war and internal armed conflicts. Instead, the laws of war are dismissed as irrelevant to internal armed conflicts because of the weakness in positive law.[78] But specifically in the case of the principle of distinction, customary law recognizes no distinction between international and internal conflicts, as confirmed by the 2005 ICRC study on customary law binding on all parties in all armed conflicts.[79] The NATO-OEF operations in Afghanistan are governed by Protocol I because of the mixed military operations that define that conflict, and Common Article 3 was held by the U.S. Supreme Court in the 2006 Hamdan decision to cover dimensions of the war on terror. Consequently, the foundation of the entire regulation of the laws of war remains operative, and the laws of war continue to be invoked in response to internal armed conflicts. Thus, the purposeful exclusion of such conflicts from the purview of the laws of war is a historical and political event worthy of analysis. In analyzing this exclusion, the discourses of civilization are paramount.

Moreover, the statues and rulings of the ICTR and ICTY, as well as that of the ICC, are slowly but surely unifying the applicability of the laws of war regardless of the location of the conflict. Finally, and perhaps most suggestive, these internal armed conflicts provide us with a wealth of information regarding the constitution and the treatment of the civilian in contemporary wars. As M. L. R. Smith points out, the tactics associated with internal armed conflicts, or guerrilla warfare, do not "intrinsically constitute a separate category of war" because these tactics and strategies are consistent across all wars.[80] Indeed, as I demonstrate in this book, the construction of the practice of internal armed conflicts as, to appropriate Stathis Kalyvas' phrase, "wanton and senseless"[81] is one effect of discourses of civilization, whereas the division of wars into internal and external owes it existence to a concerted defense of the sanctity of state sovereignty.

The emphasis of the Bush administration on reviewing former internal armed conflicts (e.g., in Algeria) further confirms the pertinence of my study to contemporary events.[82] After all, on July 16, 2003, U.S. General John P. Abizaid cautioned that the allied forces in Iraq were under attack from "a classical guerrilla-type campaign."[83] For all the initial insistence of the Bush administration that the war against terrorism is a war potentially requiring different strategies, it returned to the strategies of classic internal armed conflicts for information and guidance, suggesting that the difference is not altogether clear. Thus, the production of the combatant and the civilian in internal armed conflicts may just matter in the war against terrorism, especially given the primacy of the protection and security of civilians in the new U.S. joint services counterinsurgency field manual and in governing the renewed 2010 surge in Afghanistan.

* * *

I devote chapters 5 and 6 of the book to an analysis of the two treaties of the laws of war that were most influential for the principle of distinction: the 1949 IV Geneva Convention Relative to the Protection of Civilian Persons in Time of War (chap. 5) and the 1977 Protocols Additional to the 1949 Conventions (chap. 6). In both chapters, I pay special attention to the records of the preparatory conferences, as well as to the published articles and debates regarding the viability of continued codification of the laws of war. Obviously, the conduct of the wars that preceded each treaty—the Spanish Civil War, World War I, and World War II for the 1949 Conventions and the wars of decolonization for the 1977 Protocols—deeply affected the formulation of the treaties, as well as assessments of the power and purpose of the laws of war. Therefore, once again, I situate these treaties in the sociopolitical context of their times while simultaneously underlining how the principle of distinction is understood in relation to its past history.

These two chapters also highlight another significant transformation in the discourses of gender, innocence, and civilization. As I discuss in chapter 6, during the preparatory conferences for the 1977 Protocols, colonized peoples and insurgent movements from Algeria to South Africa successfully re-signified discourses of civilization to justify the wars fought against the colonial powers. By establishing their ability and desire to conform to the rules of civilized warfare, the insurgent movements legitimated their capacity to rule themselves. Furthermore, by appropriating discourses of civilization to indict the barbarism displayed by the colonial powers, they cast the wars of decolonization as necessary and logical responses to the rule of colonialism. Thus, the expropriation of the discourses of civilization by those previously unauthorized to claim its benefits, including self-rule, facilitated enormous change in the national and international order.

Nevertheless, this appropriation of the discourses of civilization did not significantly challenge the characteristics by which the distinction between civilization and barbarism was known. Rather, decolonization movements such as the Algerian FLN demonstrated their capacity and willingness to abide by the standards of civilization, for example, moderation and discrimination in war as demonstrated by their adherence to the principle of distinction. Instead of contesting the characteristics said to distinguish civilization from barbarism, the Algerian FLN proved that it possessed them and that the "civilized" French did not. Thus, the discourses of civilization were deployed to transform international hierarchies of colonization, but the characteristics that marked the distinction remained.

Similarly in my analysis of discourses of gender in chapters 5 and 6, I foreground how sex and sex difference were constructed and, in turn, informed the distinctions between combatant and civilian. In the 1949 and the 1977 treaties, the characteristics of sex and sex difference invoked to distinguish between combatant and civilian are, respectively, reproductive capability and sexual vulnerability—two attributes that only women are said to possess. This is a marked change from seventeenth-century discourses of gender, as found in the work of Hugo Grotius, which identified the inability to discriminate or reason as the essential difference between the sexes; nevertheless, sex and sex difference still founded the distinction to be made between combatant and civilian.

Tracing these transformations and continuities in the discourses of gender, innocence, and civilization offers new insights into the production of the categories of combatant and civilian, the persistence and power of these discourses, and the potential for change. Finally, this work suggests that the indeterminacy of the principle of distinction affects compliance with the principle. Although my approach may place me outside of their company, in this simple hypothesis I am in conversation with many international relations and international law scholars who specify the effects of indeterminacy on compliance.

* * *

Thus three interdependent elements are at play in this book. First, the recognition of the indeterminacy of the principle of distinction provokes critical and sustained analysis of its production—who and what is the civilian that this principle is ostensibly designed to protect? Second, this critical analysis of the production of the principle of distinction, a genealogy, inevitably leads us to inquire about the power of the principle, its presence and its effects, in international law and politics. Third, this inquiry returns us to the relationships of compliance and indeterminacy, forcing us to reconsider the multiple dimensions of compliance. In characterizing the ways in which these three elements interact, I can think of no better image than that of a "turning operation," in which each element bears on the others, shifting and changing its composition and, in turn, affecting the ways in which the other two are understood.[84]

MARTIAL PIETY IN THE MEDIEVAL AND CHIVALRIC CODES OF WAR

The passion for inflicting harm, the cruel thirst for vengeance, an unpacific and relentless spirit, the fever of revolt, the lust of power, and such like things, all these are rightly condemned in war.... Be peaceful, therefore, in warring.

—Augustine, *Contra Faustus* XXII

How does this series of discourses on gender, innocence, and civilization inform the conventional narrative of the development of the principle of distinction? I begin with the conventional narrative as presented by three of its most formidable authors: Theodor Meron, an international humanitarian lawyer, and Michael Walzer and James Turner Johnson, political theorists. I argue that this conventional narrative is flawed in three ways. First, it projects on to the past a prototype of the principle in which combatant and civilian stand in opposition to one another. Second, it proceeds as if this opposition were clear and well defined, thus eliding the contentious, unresolved debates over exactly what marks the difference between combatant and civilian. Third, it imposes an inevitability on that opposition, ignoring evidence of its flux and change. The narrative presents the principle of distinction as an inevitable product of enlightened, progressive development, arising from a select and identifiable origin, rather than recognizing it to be a contingent effect of multiple political claims.

In an effort to secure the principle of distinction against today's threats—that is, to confirm its moral and empirical certainty—Meron, Walzer, Johnson, and other scholars create a particular history of the past. Yet this history, invoked to strengthen the principle, may paradoxically weaken our comprehension of its faults. Foregrounding the use to which this conventional history is put and considering what satisfactions or services such a distinction provides and to whom will assist us in evaluating its purposes. For example, Johnson discerns in Augustine's writings the source of what he refers to as "noncombatant immunity," or the "concept of discrimination."[1] Yet Augustine wrote nothing specifically defending the innocent in war. This is highly significant when we consider that contemporary theorists of just wars repeatedly turn to Augustine for confirmation of the origins and clarity of the principle. In Johnson's case, Augustine's "concept of proportionality" and a "concern for the innocent in war" are held to be "the germs of what centuries later became the *jus in bello* of Western tradition on limiting war."[2] And, as Johnson also argues, our attention to this narrative of the development of the laws of war will show "what has been lost and what needs to be recovered for the sake of all people...for the development of governments without innocent blood on their hands, and for the maintenance of international order and the peace that it fosters."[3] Contemporary understandings of what is lost and what needs to be recovered, the maintenance of international order and the peace and the purity of governments, may be predicated on this conventional narrative—but to their detriment.

Writing in 1993, Louise Doswald-Beck and Sylvain Vité, scholars and practitioners of international law, one of whom was formerly the head of the legal division of the ICRC, suggested that a "perception of human rights" should be encouraged as the logical substitute for "the perception of honour." They held that, "if the chivalry of earlier times cannot be resurrected," then at least the perception of human rights will provide a "motivating force" similar to the role of honor.[4] Likewise, Robert Stacey, a historian, observes that, although "[I am] prepared to believe in the prospect of a better system [than the laws of war in the age of chivalry]...I have not yet seen it in practice."[5] Note the irony here: Stacey prefers to place his faith in a system that he has *never* seen in practice rather than in one he has yet to see. Meron adds his lament over the demise of chivalry, concluding, "we need to reinvigorate chivalry's concept and culture of values, especially the notion of individual honour and dishonour as motivating factors for the conduct of both warriors and citizens."[6] With this, he affirms Adam Roberts, who earlier wrote, "we have lost something: the sense that rules arise naturally out of societies, their armed forces, and their rulers on the basis of experience; the flexibility that came from their essentially customary character; and the value attached to honor, chivalry, and mercy."[7] Johnson shares in this nostalgic celebration of the virtues of mercy, charity, and justice conceptualized in the Middle Ages, identifying them as both the origins of modern principles of international humanitarian law and their aspirations.[8]

It appears almost disingenuous that each of these scholars is so ready to claim honor, chivalry, and mercy as the lost, although potentially retrievable, source of the contemporary premise of protection and respect in war. The ideals of honor, chivalry, and mercy as articulated in the Middle Ages were rarely only an antidote to atrocities; they were just as often also complicit in them. The conduct of the Crusades is the most glaring example of the ambiguity and complexity of these ideals. The rules of war did not arise naturally out of society, but were a result of the naturalization of a particular social order. The Peace and Truce of God, notable medieval efforts to restrain war, developed from the desire of the Church to protect its clerics and its property. When combined with the call for the Crusades, the Peace and Truce of God helped redirect the endemic violence of Europe away from Europeans and toward, primarily and initially, Muslims. Moreover, these chivalric and canonical codes did not clearly differentiate between those who were to be spared and those who were not. In fact, such decisions were complicated, relying on extensive and contested lists of individuals, property, and actions, and not on a single dichotomy.

The claim to have located a prototype of the modern distinction between combatant and civilian found in the 1949 Geneva Conventions premised on a consensus agreed on during the Middle Ages, as Maurice Keen and Johnson contend, is a misreading of the multifarious selection of these elements (individuals, property, and actions) as well as the irresolution of the debates that characterized the categorization as those who were to be spared and those who were not. In other words, these authors construe a particular relationship between the present and the past in which the principle of distinction gradually emerges cleanly and coherently from universal notions of humanity, mercy, and honor: its history is recounted descriptively, a simple documentation of its past. It is, as Hannah Arendt might suggest, an attempt to "escape from the grimness of the present into nostalgia for a still intact past."[9]

To illustrate my disagreement with these authors' construction of the past and present of the principle of distinction, I next examine the significance of medieval and canon law for the laws of war.

* * *

Scholars and historians of the Western laws of war trace the emergence of the principle of distinction to the Middle Ages, in particular to the teachings of the medieval Catholic Church and chivalric treatises, both of which drew on and incorporated Roman traditions of war. As Gerald Draper, a noted historian and practitioner of international law, writes, "the ideas of the medieval law of arms and their intimate association with the conception of military honour have lingered long and have not been without influence in determining the pattern of the customary, and later, conventional law of war as it emerged in the eighteenth and nineteenth centuries respectively."[10] The characterization of the 2001 U.S. military strikes against Afghanistan as an avenging war against evil derives its resonance from the distinguished debates that marked the Middle Ages, as does George W. Bush's assurance in January 2009 that U.S. military served a "cause" that "has always been just and right."[11] Not unlike the pundits of contemporary conflicts, publicists[12] of the Middle Ages debated the proper reasons for and conduct of a just war and the correct identification of those individuals who could not only lawfully wage war but to whom the protections of the laws of war applied.

In the eighteenth and nineteenth centuries, as armies professionalized (i.e., became organized and nationalized) the chivalric code of conduct was incorporated into ordinances of war promulgated by individual regents and, eventually, state militaries. The concepts of chivalry and honor still infuse the formal codification of the laws of war in the military training manuals used by the United States, Canada, and the United Kingdom.[13] According to the U.S. manual, the laws of war require "that belligerents refrain from employing any kind or degree of violence…not actually necessary for military purposes…and conduct hostilities with regard for the principles of humanity and chivalry."[14] In 2008, the U.S. army issued a new field manual (FM 3-21.75) that identified honor as fundamental to maintaining a "warrior ethos." As Stacey writes, "what had been a chivalric code of military conduct was thereby transformed into a code of conduct for officers."[15]

Official commentaries and individual statements by the ICRC, the authoritative body responsible for disseminating, strengthening, and securing the observance of international humanitarian law, explicitly refer to the basic tenets of chivalry as the underpinnings of international humanitarian law. During the Diplomatic Conferences for the 1977 Protocols Additional to the Geneva Conventions of 1949, delegates debated whether the wording of the Protocols reintroduced the medieval concept of just war; nevertheless, the delegates relied on chivalry as one possible "source of international humanitarian law."[16]

In addition, there is a pedagogical reason for looking at historical origins and sources that is explicitly pertinent to the study and practice of the laws of war. The laws of war are composed of both positive and customary law. The relationship between these two forms of law is complex, reciprocal, and generative; it is integral to establishing the general principles by which each is interpreted and implemented. Positive law is basically the law of treaties. Customary law is law that states accept as legally obligatory through consistent general practice and authoritative statements. Customary law not only advances and informs the resolution of positive law but may exist in its absence. Therefore, customary law not only is highly significant and influential on its own merits but also directly affects the exposition of treaty law itself. Furthermore, customary law creates obligations for all members, not merely states, of the international community.

The consequences of this relationship between positive and customary law translate into a requirement that we study both the customary and positive sources of the laws of war. When we review the history of the principle of distinction, we find that not only does its existence in customary law antedate that in the positive law of 1949 but also that the definition of *civilian* was not formally codified until 1977. Thus, it makes sense to begin my work not in the nineteenth century, when the first conferences on the laws of war were called, but in the eleventh century, when the first discussions were held regarding the distinction between those who were to be killed and those who were not, those who were to be spared and those who were not.

Let us clarify the meaning of the word *civilian* by examining its root. According to the *Oxford English Dictionary,* the term was first used in the fourteenth century to refer to someone who practiced civil law and was proficient in the study of Roman law. In this early sense, *civilian* is placed in opposition to *canonist,* one who practices canon law (the law of the Church), and not *combatant.* Canon law was a significant component of medieval thought and practice, and its reach within medieval Christendom was complete. Canon law was not simply a series of religious dicta but an extensive system of law that supervised and regulated all aspects of life. The distinction between those who practiced canon law and those who practiced civil law developed over time. In the twelfth century, these two forms of "learned laws" interdependently informed the "emergence and growth of a legal science." This emerging legal science habitually drew on and elaborated both canon and Roman law to address specific questions of medieval warfare. In other words, during this time the two forms of law "infused and shaped the language and conditions of political and philosophical inquiries" and reciprocally influenced the development of the laws of war.[17] It was not until the late thirteenth and early fourteenth centuries that a formal distinction was made between those who practiced civil law and those who practiced canon law.

As James A. Brundage, a distinguished historian of canon law, writes,

> the medieval laws of war depended in large part upon practices customary among military men, but these were changeable, often loosely defined, and not always and everywhere agreed upon. Men trained in canon and civil law saw this situation both as an intellectual challenge and as a practical problem of considerable significance. Canonists and civilians, accordingly, sought to impose order on…custom…to apply principles and analytical techniques from Roman civil law to fashion mechanisms for settling conflicting claims to property and compensation that warfare inevitably produced.[18]

Thus, although the original meaning of *civilian* was related to the laws of war, it had little to do with the modern understanding of *civilian.* Rather, the civilian was one who attempted to reason, create, and apply the laws of war, not one who was the direct subject of the laws of war. It was not until the nineteenth century that *civilian* meaning a "nonmilitary man or official" entered into common parlance. Significantly, this use developed from the eighteenth-century definition of *civilian* as "one of the covenanted European servants of the East India Company, not in military employ."[19] (See chap. 3 for a discussion of the writings of Hugo Grotius, who was employed by the East India Company.)

So, *civilian*, as the term is currently understood, is a product of the nineteenth century. In contrast, the meaning of *combatant* has not changed since its entry into common parlance in the twelfth century. Thus, the modern opposition of combatant versus civilian is not an entirely satisfactory indication of the origins of the distinction. Clearly, the civilian did not simply and miraculously appear in the nineteenth century, and the civilian was only gradually placed in contradistinction to the combatant.

To fully grasp the development of the concept of civilian, we also need to understand immunity, the concept to which later definitions of *civilian* refer. Conceptually and etymologically, *immunity* entails not only protection against but also lack of susceptibility to disease or infection. Significantly, it also refers to exemption from civil obligation. Indeed, the Latin root is *immunis*, meaning "exempt." Bear this in mind as I trace how scholars and practitioners of the laws of war have claimed that exemption from (military) service is the foundation of protection of civilians. As I show, although this exemption is a necessary part of the explanation, it is not sufficient. In fact, the recurrence of metaphors of disease in the justifications for killing those we might otherwise exempt not only from (military) service but also from violence demonstrates that the debt the concept of protection owes to immunity is greater than simple exemptions. This debt to immunity (disease) is of particular importance in the case of the Guatemalan civil war (see chap. 7). We also need to trace the formation of the civilian within particular social and political patterns and relationships that are neither necessarily constrained nor informed by the conventional binary.

Reflecting historical and contemporary perceptions of the proper consonance of politics and violence, the laws of war developed with a twofold purpose: to govern the resort to war and to establish what is right conduct in war. From antiquity, notations on the laws of war are found in Greek, Roman, Asian, and Islamic texts—perhaps the most quoted aphorism being "in time of war, the law is silent," attributed to Marcus Cicero (106–43 BC), a Roman. Writing on the contours of international law in ancient Greece and Rome, David Bederman, a legal historian, documents the existence and influence of formalized rules dictating the declaration of war and the conduct of hostilities. These "recurrent patterns of thinking and practice" not only set the parameters for the actions taken by individual polities but regulated interactions among them by establishing a basis for obligation and exchange.[20] As he puts it, "it was not just that ancient peoples had a sense of legal obligation in warfare. The Greek *to dikaion* and the Roman *ius ad bellum* and *ius in bello* had actual substantive content...as...all ancient States saw the need for limitations and immunities to be impressed on the conduct of warfare. These were the most specific, and literal, of the norms governing armed conflicts."[21] In other words, the laws governing the commencement and conduct of war regulate an intentional system of order within ancient societies. Similarly, in early Jewish thought, the Deuteronomic laws of warfare found in the Old Testament are frequently cited as an example of ancient requirements to curb the effects of war; they are mentioned as some of the first explicit prohibitions against the killing of women and children.

In both Greek and Roman texts, as well as in the Old Testament, the multivalent sources of obligation and restraint were at once sacred and secular. Informed by faith and determined by temporal considerations, the rituals of armed conflict—from declaration of war to truce and treaties—melded these two influences. The interweaving of the sacred and secular, which was intrinsic to the formalities of war, consistently marks the evolution of the laws of war. Later publicists of international law, particularly through the sixteenth and eighteenth centuries, relied on these texts as sources of obligation and restraint to debate the conduct of armed conflicts, the protections and immunities offered during war, and the proper mode of peace. In the broadest of readings, scholars of the laws of war identify these ancient texts as forming the outlines of a narrative of immunity from which arose the current concept of civilian.

* * *

These ancient narratives attest to a manifest concern with creating a political and military order within and among polities, an order that depended on a distinction between those who could be killed and those who could not, those who could be spared and those who could not. Nevertheless, these narratives of immunity were also fractured by differences of religion, status, and identity.

For example, in Deuteronomy, it is decreed that women and children are to be spared, along with the livestock, as booty to be enjoyed upon the capture of certain non-Canaanite cities, whereas all males are to be put "to the sword."[22] Indeed, upon capture, if "among the captives is a beautiful woman whom you desire and want to marry," it is appropriate to do so with the understanding that "if you are not satisfied with her, you shall let her go free and not sell her for money."[23] The passage is also clear that upon capture of Canaanite cities "you must not let anything that breathes remain alive....You shall annihilate them," including the women and children.[24] Women and children are offered immunity only as commodities; further, even this limited immunity is dependent on whether one is or is not Canaanite.

Indeed, in Numbers, Moses' response to the capture of women and children in the holy war against the Medians reiterates the predicates of protection: "Moses said to them, 'Have you allowed all the women to live?...kill every male among the little ones, and kill every woman who has known a man by sleeping with him. But all the young girls who have not known a man by sleeping with him keep alive for yourselves.'"[25] Again, the immunity of women is not absolute; instead, it is based on comeliness, economic contribution, and current sexual purity. In contrast, for males neither utility nor identity matters—only their sex matters. This holds even for the children, for among the little ones any male child is to be killed as well.

The gradations of distinction found in this passage in Numbers form the core of the immunity it describes and to which the laws of war are said to be indebted. Moreover, this passage describes a distinction between who may be killed and who may not. This persistent emphasis in these early writings is often translated as a distinction between who fights and kills (and thus who may be killed) and who does not fight (and, thus should not be killed), but there is not an exact correspondence in any of the early texts or, significantly, in the later writings.

Considering the richness and complexity of this passage from Numbers and its central importance in the conventional histories of the laws of war, it is puzzling that Walzer chooses not to fully analyze its consequences. After all, his argument in *Just and Unjust Wars*, canonical in its own right, begins with this passage.

Walzer does invoke the Deuteronomy passage regarding captive women as an example of the early recognition of the rights of individuals within armed conflicts. He interprets the numerous instructions regarding the proper treatment of the captive (i.e., the beautiful woman) as evidence of the care taken with such women. He writes that it "is clear that what is at work here is a conception of the captive woman as a person who must be respected, despite her capture; hence the month of mourning before she is sexually used, the requirement of marriage, the ban on slavery."[26] Perhaps. But does this passage not actually illustrate a conception of the captive as a possession, one degree removed from enslavement? Does a ban on slavery not suppose the imminent threat and practice of slavery? And, moreover, has this woman not been captured? Further, it is the beautiful woman, the aesthetically pleasing possession, who becomes both war trophy and war booty. The requirement of marriage merely formalizes ownership and possession. And, as Walzer admits only a page earlier, this indicates she is "not a person at all."[27]

Consequently, I find it difficult to accept that the observation of ceremonies before she is, in Walzer's words, "sexually used" implies that she "has lost some of her rights...but, not all of them."[28] Exactly which rights has she retained and on whose judgment? She has, at most, been granted the right to grieve as so directed, but this is by far too flimsy a scaffold to support the weight of Walzer's argument regarding the link between the recognition of personhood and the establishment of rights—as is evident in his struggle in these two pages of his book.

Nevertheless, he culls from this brief and formidable passage from Deuteronomy evidence that the immunity of noncombatants (as he anachronistically terms them) is premised on rights that are granted to individuals because they are so. In particular, noncombatants retain these rights and, in Walzer's terms, are innocent. They are innocent because "they have done nothing and are doing nothing that entails the loss of their rights."[29] But he is wrong. The caveats of immunity found in the international law of antiquity were premised not on a *universal* right of personhood but on distinctions of sex, age, and use. Certainly, the fact that it was not until the sixteenth century that religious and ethnic identities were formally rejected as a premise for war more than suggests that innocence had little to do with actual conduct during war and that immunity had even less to do with a respect for intrinsic rights.[30] The very choice of the language of rights, which presupposes a universal and absolute reach, is inconsistent with clear demarcations made in Numbers and Deuteronomy. The women of Canaanite cities, such as the Medians, did not possess what Walzer contends is the premise of immunity, that is "moral standing independent of and resistant to the exigencies of war."[31]

There remains a relatively unremarked error in Walzer's imputation of rights, specifically human rights, to a historical period when the concept was nonexistent. Although he briefly acknowledges this anachronism, he continues to ground his argument on it. Furthermore, in returning to what he takes as the origins of the principle of distinction, Walzer manufactures a clarity that is not supported by the text. In fact, Walzer's argument that noncombatant immunity (in his words) is founded on a theory of rights actually implicity depends on discourses of gender. In other words, discourses of gender lend clarity and stability to the principle of distinction not otherwise found there. Walzer holds that there are "limits" that "correspond to our sense of what is right." In turn, these limits reflect and reify the "theory of rights" that he takes as informing the principle of distinction.[32] But in introducing and justifying these limits (which evolves into a broad discussion of immunity), his theory of rights does little work.[33] Instead, a particular theory of gender does the work.

To cite one instance, Walzer constructs an analogy of war among states, specifically its conduct and conventions, as a family feud—an analogy that already indicates reliance on gender. In this family feud, the "occasional killing of a father or a grown-up son, an uncle or a nephew" continues through the years and "so long as nothing more happens, the possibility of reconciliation remains open." But, should someone "kill a woman or a child, the result may well be a massacre or a series of massacres." This, he reasons, is at least "similar to intermittent war among states."[34] From this he extrapolates that there must be certain limits among states that are commonly accepted if there is eventually to be peace among the belligerents. What are those limits? Namely, they are the killing of women and children.

What is confusing about Walzer's theory is his suggestion that rights set the limits of war. In fact, it appears that it is the moral recoil incited by the killing of women and children that sets the limits of war. Consequently, discourses of sex and sex difference produce this limit and constitute our sense of what is right in war. In other words, rights are not the source of what Walzer calls our "moral vocabulary"; rather, it is defined by a particular discourse of gender.[35]

In each of Walzer's discussions of noncombatant immunity (founded in a theory of rights), it is the treatment of women and children that demarcate the limits of war: the rape of the Italian women; the enslavement of the women of Canaan; and the setting adrift the women and children after the sinking of their ship, the *Laconia*. These examples involve a particular interpretation of gender in which women are largely, and naturally, irrelevant to the practice and politics of war, except as incentives, booty, or victims. The treatment of women sets a limit on war because women are presumed to be incidental to its conduct.

He returns to this theme in his discussion of guerrilla warfare, in which he notes that men who are not "moral monsters"[36] recognize that old men, women, and children are not the enemy. For Walzer, the immunity of old men, women, and children is not itself a moral state. Instead, it is the ability to respect and recognize these limits that makes a man moral. In these statements he appears to be making a claim similar to the one so boldly advanced by John Keegan, a military historian, who writes, "Warfare is, nevertheless, the one human activity from which women, with the most insignificant exceptions, have always and everywhere stood apart....Women...do not fight....if warfare is as old as history and as universal as mankind, we must now enter the supremely important limitation that it is an entirely masculine activity."[37]

I began this section with a discussion of the earliest citations of the laws of war and then moved to the particular use to which Walzer has put these citations. But when we examine Walzer's theory of rights, which is taken to inform our moral vocabulary in regards to immunity, what we see is a discourse of gender at work. To discover those rights, their existence, and implementation, Walzer relies first on an analogy between war and a family feud (conjuring not only an implicit homology between the two but reestablishing a relationship between family and state reminiscent of Aristotle) in which women and children embody immunity.

He continues to premise his argument for the protection of these innocents on the disavowal of rape, both in his discussions of the rape of the Sabine women and of Deuteronomy. These examples, so he argues, illustrate the distinct human capacity to restrain utter violence and decide immunity in war.

* * *

The concept of immunity, as well as our more general and juridical notions of what is acceptable in warfare, evolved within a profoundly Christian culture and was codified during the Middle Ages. Premised on the writings of Augustine (fifth century), the enumeration of Thomas Aquinas (thirteenth century), and the commentaries of Christian canon law, these traditions significantly influenced the context and content of restraint in war. In particular, the just war traditions developed in answer to the question of whether it was ever right for Christians to participate in war. Thus, the just war traditions established restraints on war while at the same time maintaining the justice of war itself and legitimating Christian participation in war.

Although Augustine is considered the founder of the just war tradition, he did not write extensively or consistently on the subject.[38] Rather, his essential contributions, "brief, scattered and unsystematic," justified Christian participation in wars of defense undertaken to rectify injuries and to remedy injustice and vice.[39] As scholars of Augustine note, there is a "deep irony" in Augustine's vaunted association with the just war tradition—his statements were intended in fact to legitimate, not restrain, war by Christians.[40] His only comment regarding the possibility of moderation in warfare occurs when he says that "cruelty, bloodlust, or desire for vengeance" may not motivate wars because war should be motivated by a love for justice and is a form of service not unlike prayer.[41] Phillipe Contamine, a medieval historian, details this brief invocation of love for justice in the service of war:

> The justice of a war thus rests on the disposition of the spirit and the motivation of the conscience. That is why one keeps one's word to an enemy, avoids needless violence, profanation of churches, atrocities and reprisals, for behavior which is too cruel would be a sign of a war waged because of a taste for murder and not because of love of justice, and betrays a wicked intention.[42]

Nevertheless, throughout the Middle Ages the practice of penance and mandatory repentance for acts committed in war demonstrates an understanding that in war mistakes of intent and practice were made and that the separation between killing because of a love of justice and needless violence was none too secure. Indeed, the ever more elaborated and juridical definitions of *just war* during the Middle Ages are evidence of the continuing fragility of the boundary between just and unjust warfare and its need for consistent reinforcement. The fragility of this boundary encouraged a Christian soldier to fight according to his conscience and faith to ensure that he would not be guilty of the same, or greater, injustices—a taste for murder and aggression—against which his war was fought. Therefore, as Johnson points out, "the Christian warrior must feel a hand on his shoulder and a cautioning voice in his ear, even though he believes he is right to have taken up arms."[43] In Augustine's felicitous phrase, quoted by Aquinas, there must be "peace in your warring."[44]

Johnson then takes his interpretation one step further, thereby putting himself out of step with other scholars of Augustine and just war traditions. Johnson discerns in Augustine's writings a "concept of proportionality" and a "concern for the innocent in war, the germs of what centuries later became the *jus in bello* of Western tradition on limiting war."[45] Here Johnson locates the source of what he later calls "noncombatant immunity" or the "concept of discrimination."[46] Yet, Augustine wrote nothing specifically defending the innocent in war, much less clearly establishing grounds for noncombatant immunity. As a scholar of these traditions states, "one finds virtually no constraints against individuals participating in war, provided only that they do so without otherwise forsaking God and without feelings of revenge, cruelty, and so forth."[47] Richard Hartigan, another scholar of just war traditions, concludes even more definitively: "Augustine presented no clear cut argument for the protection of the innocent, especially for the civilian innocent or noncombatant, in time of war."[48] Indeed, the attribution of innocence or guilt was incumbent on the state of the soul and heart of the *warrior*. Thus this attribution was primarily an interior (assessing the soul) rather than exterior (assessing the action) ruling. For Augustine, it is "not what the man does [that] is the thing to be considered; but with what mind and will he does it."[49]

In fact, Augustine is clearly more concerned with the innocence of the soldier than with the innocence of the one who may be killed. First, any soldier commanded to war remains innocent because he has a duty to obey authority. Second, to have peace in the warring further absolves the soldier of any guilt in killing (of murder). Finally, as Frederick H. Russell, a medieval scholar, writes, "the subjective *culpa* or guilt of the enemy merited punishment of the enemy population without regard to the distinction between soldiers and civilians."[50] That is, simply being the enemy was sufficient to establish prior guilt, which remained regardless of the specific deeds committed by individuals. Therefore, the "objective determination of personal guilt was not only unnecessary, but irrelevant."[51] Thus, within the teaching of Augustine, we find little formulation of a principle of immunity and only the broadest distinction between those who fight and those who do not. According to Augustine, innocence is possessed by the one who obediently and charitably wages war for peace under the command of his superior and of God.

Thomas Aquinas (thirteenth century) details the standards of a just war more completely in his massive Aristotelian synthesis of Christian theology, the *Summa Theologiae*. Aquinas only briefly attends to the relationship between just wars and innocence by focusing on when the innocent may be killed. Strikingly, his comments on the killing of innocents are in answer to the larger question of homicide and are addressed in that chapter, not under the heading of war. For Aquinas, although there is "simply no justification for taking the life of an innocent person," such killing is acceptable if God, as the sovereign authority over life and death, so commands it.[52] In his exposition on war (which is largely derivative of the approach taken by Augustine), Aquinas devotes *no* time to considering those killed, focusing instead on who may do the killing and under what conditions. It is only in his advocacy of right intention in war and the avoidance of the "savageness of fighting on" that he (like Augustine) can be interpreted as offering a standard for restraint in war that may bear on the conduct of war itself.[53] Russell offers this curt assessment: "it is thus difficult, if not impossible, to attribute to Aquinas a clear doctrine of noncombatant immunity."[54]

Neither Augustine nor Aquinas is terribly explicit about the concept of immunity. They both accept moderation in victory as discussed in Deuteronomy, agreeing that women, children, and trees should not be wantonly destroyed because of the potential they possess for use—sex, reproduction, labor, and sustenance—by the victors. They also agree about the injunction to war peaceably and justly. Decidedly, however, neither draws a link among innocence, immunity, and noncombatancy. Thus, if it is from these beginnings that the principle of distinction and the concept of the civilian arose, as assumed by the conventional narratives, it is a startlingly ambiguous and flimsy legacy—perhaps more suggestively shaped by contemporary interpreters than written by these two Christian saints.[55]

Aquinas parses Augustine's concept of right intention, arguing that even with right intention (i.e., to wage war peaceably and justly) it is possible that a person's actions may create unintended consequences. These unintended consequences (which Aquinas refers to as consequences that are beside intention) are not so much unforeseen as they are simply not intended. This doctrine is now termed the doctrine of double effect, and it is more familiarly employed to excuse the unintended killings of civilians as collateral damage.

In the writings of both Aquinas and Augustine, the supposed founders of the just war traditions, there is the barest attention paid to the specifics of conduct within wars. Although Aquinas does consider who may participate in war and on which days war may be fought, his attention to the means of war simply addresses the question of fraud and ruses (an inheritance identifiable in contemporary laws of war, specifically in defining perfidy). What Aquinas introduces, then, is *not* a means of distinguishing between those who fight and those who do not; that would be a sharp and distinct distinction. Rather, he is concerned with complex standards of who may be killed, who may be spared, by whom, and when. Absolute immunity is not discussed. Any reference to moderation is understood within a concept of constraint in war deriving from the virtues of love, charity, and mercy. Citing Augustine, Aquinas writes "for the good would even wage war with mercy."[56] Mercy, according to Aquinas, "involves giving from one's abundance to others, and, what is more, relieving their needs, a function especially belonging to a superior."[57] Thus, even if immunity were deduced from the practice of these virtues, it would be dependent on the proper exercise of each by individual combatants and their commanders. Mercy, the mercy recalled nostalgically by Meron and Roberts, is granted to the weak at the will of the strong; it requires inequality for expression. Furthermore, it is a mercy burnished in an avenging violence against the enemy. And it is in response to an avenging war that the Catholic Church formulates its own indulgences.

* * *

The specific influence of the Catholic Church on the development of the laws of war in the Western world was pronounced throughout the Middle Ages.[58] One particular development of the tenth century, the peace movement, continued to exist in some form through the thirteenth century. The work of the peace movement made the concept of immunity integral to the establishment of right order as understood in Christian Europe and among Christian lords.[59] First led by Christian ecclesiastics, and eventually secularized, the peace movement was composed of two initially distinct efforts to moderate the endemic warfare of the Middle Ages: the Peace of God and the Truce of God. The Peace of God signified a perpetual suspension of hostilities against particular consecrated individuals (e.g., clergy), in particular consecrated places (e.g., churches), and at particular times (e.g., on Sunday). The Truce of God was a temporary suspension of hostilities, but included a broader range of individuals (e.g., merchants) and places (e.g., castles). The clergy declared both the Peace and Truce of God, often after great ecumenical council meetings, but the Peace and Truce of God also became moments of active popular participation in protest against unregulated violence. The peace movement itself began in France in the tenth century, in part in response to persistent aristocratic feuding and the disintegration of effective peacekeeping after the decline of specific kingships. It soon extended across Europe.

Johnson claims that this movement "forms one of the roots of the doctrine of noncombatant immunity in later just war doctrine and in international law from Grotius to the present day."[60] Russell refers to the Peace of God as a "medieval expression of noncombatant immunity."[61] And Contamine singles out the Peace of God as specifically helping "to release the notion of the *natural* immunity of non-combatants and their possessions."[62] The last description of the Peace of God as releasing a natural immunity (releasing it from what, we might ask; he does not provide an answer) is more than misleading. An analysis of the Peace of God illustrates, if anything, the degree to which any notion of natural immunity is caught in and by the specific feudal hierarchy of the Middle Ages, suggesting such immunity is not natural at all but highly constructed. This hierarchy relied on the labor of peasants, animals, and merchants to exist, appealing to the authority of the Church and nobility to govern. Johnson's use of the Peace of God relies perilously on the claim voiced by Contamine.

The Truce of God (*treuga dei,* eleventh century) started the movement, and it is now the inclusive phrase by which both movements are referred. It decreed that all fighting was to cease between Wednesday evening and Monday morning and during all great Church feasts. It was only in effect in wars among Christians; the Truce of God did not need to be observed in wars against infidels and heretics.[63] The punishment for violating the Truce of God could be as severe as excommunication, yet it was infrequently observed. It did have some influence, however, and created a specific limit on waging war that some scholars claim contributed to later beliefs about the importance of truces.[64]

The earliest canons of the Peace of God (*pax ecclesiae*) are from the late tenth century. The Peace of God was an attempt to thwart, with the threat of divine punishment, the rising power (and increasing plundering) of the knights (*milites*) and secular lords. It was a move by the Christian church to gain and retain ecclesiastical dominance in a shifting sociopolitical order by developing canons and dictums that distinguished between licit and illicit violence. Although every particular council of peace drew up its own specific legislation and codes of conduct, there was considerable interchange among them.[65]

The councils of peace were essentially great open-air gatherings incorporating oaths, rituals, veneration of relics, and religious revivals. The clergy attending the councils debated and legislated the appropriate conduct of feudal wars. "There—surrounded by clerical and lay magnates, by saints, and by their social inferiors—members of the warrior elite took oaths of peace, framed in a context that mobilized what a modern observer might call popular opinion."[66] This "challenge to aristocratic violence essentially based itself on at least a momentary alliance between the clergy and the peasantry."[67] The premise on which immunity was granted was concerned with the fragility of that alliance but more centrally with the restoration and sanctity of the Church. As one medieval historian writes, "these clerics had a dual interest since, as unarmed lords, they were victims of this violence. Still, as lords of justice, clerics had much to gain from these new developments."[68]

Thus, led by the Church, the peace councils sought to limit and suppress the quotidian violence of the early Middle Ages by setting aside certain goods, people, and sites as specifically protected and defended against feuds and plunder. The list of protected people and goods was defined primarily in relation to the possessions of the Church; that is, "the Peace and True legislation was conceived to defend the Church's landed and material wealth just as much as to protect the *ordo* of labourers."[69] As John France, a historian, points out, the "Church inveighed against the horrors of war, and doubtless this had some influence, but it was the economics of landowning that really mitigated the horrors of war."[70] After all, the Church (seconded by the nobility) was the largest landowner of the time and, consequently, needed to ensure that agriculture and trade would continue uninterrupted and that private property would be defended.

Accordingly, those protected were "clerics, monks, friars, other religious, pilgrims, travelers, merchants, and peasants cultivating the soil. The animals and goods of such persons were also protected as well as the peasants' lands."[71] Like the equally protected domestic animals, under the peace legislation of the Second Council of Elne in 1065 those who toiled the land were considered instruments of labor not of war. In fact, Hans W. Goetz, a historian, argues that the Peace of God protected the land, animals, and person of the peasant only insofar as was necessary for the production of food and maintenance of resources. Analyzing the legislation of numerous councils, he writes that the defense of the peasantry "was closely associated with the protection of cattle…mentioned between the dispositions concerning domestic and pastured animals…and (sometimes)…animals and peasants joined in a particular clause."[72] Peasants were not protected for who they were or for what they did or did not do in war but for their utility for war.

Distinct from the peasantry, the clergy was protected as an extension of the sanctity of the Church. Yet not all clerics were to be equally protected or protected at all. In some of the canons, only unarmed clerics were to be protected, whereas in others, the protection of the clergy was less important than the restriction of the types of weapons allowed to the clergy.[73] Furthermore, the protection of the clergy took on a wider significance as the scope of the peace movement broadened to include ecclesiastical reform. Both protection and reform were meant to prevent the further estrangement of the clerics from their spiritual duties and to further distinguish the clergy as the rightful, and righteous, custodians of the spirit and property of the Church. In other words, the material protection of the clergy and the Church was founded on the identification and creation of the clergy as a distinct and distinctively sacred category. Ecclesiastical purity, as well as ecclesiastical property, was to be protected by binding the clergy from the laity through the prohibition of certain clerical practices. Thus, strictures prohibiting clergy from carrying arms, shedding blood, accepting money for the sacraments (simony), and engaging in sexual intercourse were integrated into the legislation of the peace councils to protect the clergy. The purification and the protection of the clergy became interdependent. Once again, regulation of sexuality and regulation of protection occur together (in this case, the regulation of clerical sex). Of course, the clergy was not thrilled about all these strictures. As one eleventh-century observer wrote, while "the priests were ready enough to give up bearing arms but even now they are loathe to part with their mistresses or lead chaste lives."[74] The twin prohibitions against harming (unarmed) clerics and against clerics' participating in war are spelled out by the eleventh-century canons, as well as by the twelfth-century decretum of canon law.[75] The participation in wars by clerics could jeopardize the legitimacy of the war itself, increasing the incentive for both clerics and nobles to ensure that clerics relinquished their arms.

The immunity of both the clergy and the peasantry from war was not, as Contamine claims, a "natural releasement."[76] On the contrary, there was nothing natural about it. It was a complex social movement that challenged and transformed one social strata of the Middle Ages while strengthening others. Distinguishing the clergy from the knights, the peasantry from the clergy, and the landed aristocracy from the peasantry, as well as creating distinctions within each order, the Peace of God was an effort at social differentiation and regulation that, as historians of the period emphasize, "helped to form and cement the division of society into three orders…and to lay the foundation for the feudal order."[77] Moreover, the granting of immunity reified the desired social order promulgated by the Church because its enforcement depended on the complex relationship between the Church and the knights, the interwoven sacred and secular powers of the medieval hierarchy.

The second premise of just war scholarship is also now open to challenge. This premise assumes that immunity was predicated on the belief that the people deemed immune from violence "are all types of persons who, because of their social function, have nothing to do with warmaking; thus they are not to have war made against them."[78] There are two reasons why this is not true. First, as we have seen, immunity is *not* a natural releasement but an artifice. Second, immunity does not rest, as Johnson supposes, on the simple binary distinction between those who have nothing to do with warmaking and those who do have something to do with it; that is, it is not because they have nothing to do with warmaking that certain people are not to have war made against them. For peasants, this distinction is based on their utility in tilling the land and preserving the resources of the Church. The peasantry was absolutely integral to the possibility and desirability of making war—they tilled and preserved the wealth of the land over which war was fought and provided the sustenance for those who did fight. In other words, they had everything to do with warmaking. For the clergy, their immunity is an effect of their being sacralized and distinguished from the laity by relinquishing arms, women, and money. (Note that money and women were intricately connected; by outlawing clerical sex and marriage, the Church prevented any possible offspring from inheriting Church land.) One of the earliest (sixteenth-century) definitions of *immunity* draws on the definition of *ecclesiastical distinctiveness* so desired by the reformers of the Peace of God. It specifically exempts clergy and clerical property from lay jurisdiction and secular taxation and, significantly, protects the sanctuary from invasion—the goals sought by the reformers both to restrain war and to privilege/sanctify the Church by keeping it free from the contagions of simony and sex. The regulation of simony and sex was simultaneously the regulation of violence.

Contrast this with Johnson's phrasing, which renders a conflicting and complex interdependency, ambiguous and contradictory, into an unanimous and coherent dichotomy that is more reminiscent of its desired form than of its historical expression. The relationship of the Church and chivalry made the formulation of the distinction between who may be killed and who may not all the more precarious, because now the distinction became entangled not only with just war traditions but with the secular customs of chivalry and both of these traditions were now directed specifically toward war against the infidels.

* * *

The relationship between Christianity and chivalry was complex and contentious, as befits a relationship of two distinct yet interdependent sources of strategic and social power. As the Peace and Truce of God illustrate, the Church tried mightily to directly intervene in the conduct of war. Furthermore, beginning in the eleventh century, the Church altered its stance on the inherent illegitimacy of warfare; the "spiritual legitimacy and social function of the warriors" was transformed from a state of sin to one of possible grace (in the service of the Church).[79] Strategically, military service at the behest and benefit of the Church became a means for the Church to redirect warfare away from the Church itself, its properties and possession, and toward the infidels and heretics who also threatened the power of the Church. It is of no small interest that the Council of Clermont (in 1095) simultaneously proclaimed the Peace of God and called the First Crusade.[80] The prohibition against harming clergy and peasantry in the Peace of God was itself premised on the injunction to war against all pagans, infidels, and heretics in pursuit of grace.[81] In particular, as Christopher Tyerman notes, "however important the just and holy war against enemies of the church in general, the highest justification for knighthood was the battle against the infidel, against Islam."[82]

At this interstice, the Church and the noble knights found themselves working in a powerful alliance, although for competing purposes. For one, the Crusades offered a means for the Church to assert its sacred authority and to reclaim the Holy Land, and for the other, the Crusades presented a means to reconcile the warring way of life, without which the concept of chivalric knights would be meaningless, with spiritual renewal and grace—as well as to gain substantial economic and social rewards. The Crusades were also a telling example of the differentiation inherent in both the chivalric and canonical injunctions of immunity. It was in the contentious and competitive interplay of chivalry and Christianity that immunity was further elaborated.

Symbolically the power of the Church was recognized in the blessing of the swords of knights who accepted the principles of honor, fidelity, and brotherhood that formed the core of the chivalric code.[83] The right to wage war was reserved primarily for knights and princes in the form of public wars, and the strictures on their conduct were formalized through a noble code that limited the degree and direction of force against certain individuals as a matter of personal honor and redemption. Matthew Strickland, a historian of the Crusades, writes that there was "increasingly explicit expression and conscious clerical sponsorship of the concept that knighthood constitutes a discrete ordo[,] entry into which conferred not simply distinction but a defined set of moral responsibilities."[84] These responsibilities not only included, as their pinnacle, participation in the Crusades but also detailed expectations for the knights' conduct.

Yet, although from the twelfth century on this knightly order of professional soldiers was thoroughly and intimately Christian, chivalry possessed in addition its own formative codes of conduct and identity that were never fully subordinated to ecclesiastical authority. In particular, medieval scholars highlight the secular concepts of honor, prowess, loyalty, and courage—each of which was defined and won through acts of war—as informing the code of conduct for knights. These concepts, as elaborated and embellished in the chivalric and courtly literature, ruled the specific order of knighthood and, specifically, its warfare.[85] Fundamentally, chivalry was an aristocratic martial code of arms derived from a potent mix of secular and Christian beliefs. It was a heroic ideal supported by a bellicose belief in the "proper exercise of violence," by those allowed to engage in it; it was a "most ambivalent" kind of force.[86] Chivalry had limited success in curbing violence among noble knights. It fundamentally found its resonance and significance in the conduct of war; therefore, when the exigencies of war competed with the restrictions of the code, the former was the consistent victor.

The honor of knights, to which contemporary scholars so wistfully refer, was an honor founded in individual violence, exercised in patronage, and easily relinquished in times of stress. I do not disagree that it functioned to discipline knights, to encourage them to conduct themselves in accordance with the code of chivalry. But the code of chivalry was itself bounded and graded according to noble status and privilege; "as a code, chivalry had next to nothing to do with ordinary people at all."[87] Thus, when contemporary scholars seek to "restore" the "loss" they willfully elide the select and discriminatory origins of the contemporary "principles of humanity" founded in and revealed by chivalry itself.[88] To restate, chivalry is not the basis for a universal code; it is the basis for a highly selective differentiation, part of a complicated attempt to institute public order, promulgated among the nobility through treatises, manuals, popular romantic writings, and hearings before the High Court of Chivalry. Moreover, chivalry was forged *in* war, so why do modern scholars now call on it to *moderate* war? Recall that it is Meron who believes that we need to "reinvigorate chivalry's concept and culture of values."[89]

Maurice Keen's analysis, and that of most medieval scholars, stresses the importance of reading the writings of chivalry as attempts to regulate a particular order in a time of seemingly unending disorder.[90] As with the Peace of God, chivalry distinguished between those who fought—strictly limited to the knights themselves—and those who did not. In binding themselves to the code of chivalry, knights vowed to protect the poor, the widowed, the orphaned, and the clergy—those identified as in need of defense and protection. These categories, whose vague outlines are discernible in the later proclamations of the peace movement, remained at the core of the code of chivalry. Nonetheless, during the later thirteenth and fourteenth centuries the list of those protected expanded to include, for example, students, peasants, doctors, merchants, noblewomen, and unarmed knights on certain days.[91] Note that, first, the number of categories multiplied; this, as scholars of both the Peace of God and of chivalry claim, was because the logic of immunity and protection was deeply intertwined with the politics of the social order and the concern for social reform. Second, the code of chivalry introduced an explicit concern for and attention to special categories of women—namely widows and ladies—as deserving particular protection.

Keen notes that the institution of courtly love (the highly elaborated romantic complement of martial chivalry) in the twelfth to fourteenth centuries provided the "traditional, ancient obligation of all knights to come to the defense of the widow, the orphan, the weak and the defenseless—the last two being categories in which womankind has come, under its influence, to be included—with a new charged emphasis."[92] Courtly love was the extremely scripted veneration of a noble lady, displayed in words and deed both poetic and martial. Reversing the gendered hierarchy of medieval society through mimicry of the economic hierarchy, the lady became the superior of the knight—as a lord to a serf—and the knight sought to serve and honor her through his protection and prowess. The defining mark of this ornate relationship, and one that some scholars argue places it in interesting comparison to the worship of the Blessed Virgin, is an all-consuming but unconsummated passion.

I venture that this charge, which Keen identifies, is not simply the charge of unquenched passion but the recognition of the precarious position occupied by a lady so venerated. The charge was a potential threat held in check only by the silken cords of courtesy. The prowess of the knight was most frequently demonstrated in the protection of his lady from the advances of other knights. Indeed, one scholar of the period writes that "even when idealized or adored, women seem to have been considered property in much chivalric literature, prizes to be won by knightly prowess or to be defended against the prowess of another."[93] This is similar to Deuteronomy, in which women are regarded as prizes, possessions, and property. In fact, this scholar ventures, the commentary of such texts is more preoccupied with the honor of the knight *vis-à-vis* another knight than with the protection of or service to the lady herself. This highlights another dimension of the secular value of honor so cherished by contemporary scholars: honor is due to a knight in competition with, but among the *ordo* of, other knights for the skillful protection and defense of property—be it land, wealth, or ladies. Honor is a thing of violence and masculinity—"the ultimate vindication of honour lies in physical violence."[94] The fact that knightly honor was such a volatile concept makes the current nostalgia for chivalry, as "an ideal form of manly perfection"[95] advocated by contemporary scholars, troubling.

Keen's comment effectively introduces a gendered conception of chivalry, one that remains overlooked by these contemporary scholars seeking to resurrect its conceptual values. Because their purpose is to resurrect chivalry, this remains, of course, a necessary oversight; yet the importance of gender is betrayed in the very words of the scholars themselves. For example, Keen's phrasing flags the necessity of interpreting chivalry as a gendered and gendering code of conduct. Recall that, for him, chivalry is the *means* by which womankind has come to be included in the categories of the weak and defenseless, and the *means* by which such an extension of protection is charged. Thus, the identification of women as weak and defenseless required effort, concerted effort made visible in the gilded codes of martial and courtly chivalry. The recognition of this process denaturalizes the protection of women and allows us to consider how particular women, the widows and noble ladies, are created as being in need of and worthy of protection.

In turn, it assists us in identifying how this protection is simultaneously a threat in that it is premised on the subordination of these particular women, and the absence of protection for all other women.

The significance of this analysis is heightened by the claims made by Johnson that chivalry produced a "concept of noncombatant protection that went well beyond what the Church was willing to attempt in the twelfth and thirteenth centuries."[96] Notably, he contends that the relationship between noble knights and noble ladies, which he describes as a "relation of condescension," produced this advancement.[97] Recollect that Walzer conceded the murder and rape of women to introduce his concept of noncombatant immunity. In a similar way, Johnson is proposing here that the advancement of conceptions of immunity was dependent on a relationship of condescension in which women were undeniably subservient or, regardless of its dependence on the subservience of women, chivalry was still an advance. In either case, the relationship is naturalized as if it were premised on an incontrovertible materiality of the female body—for Walzer as potentially and always rapeable and for Johnson as physically weak.

The position of, and perspective on, women in the Middle Ages was highly complex, varying according to decade, status, and estate. In summarizing it, Peter R. Coss, a historian, begins appropriately with the statement: "as daughters of Eve, women were portrayed as temptresses as embodiments of sin...but also portrayed as personifications of virtues as well as vices."[98] Another commentator observes that the female sex "was aligned with corporeality and sensuality in order to justify the claims about women's social, juridical and psychological inferiority to men."[99] Brundage makes clear that in the profoundly hierarchical society of the Middle Ages, the laws of the Church reflected and reified the subordinate and subservient position of women. The influential *Decretrum of Gratian*—the decree that exempted women, pilgrims, monks, clerics, and the unarmed poor from violence—also established "that women were in general subject to men and that husbands in particular had charge over their wives."[100] Yet the cult of the Blessed Virgin Mary, which paralleled the rise of courtly love, suggested that the superiority of women stemmed from the transcendence of the corporeality of her sex. Thus, women were simultaneously viewed as superior and subservient but also as fundamentally distinct due to their material sex. Furthermore, the limitation of their materiality placed women firmly, as Brundage writes, "subject to men."[101]

Johnson accepts this logic of the Middle Ages when he writes that women were granted immunity because they were physically incapable of bearing arms and, thus, required male protection from violence. Yet consider the actual phrasing of Honoré Bonet, the fourteenth-century Benedictine monk whom Johnson chooses, along with Christine de Pisan (Bonet's pupil), as one of the representative synthesizers of canonical and chivalric immunities. Bonet's authoritative treatise, *The Tree of Battles,* was widely read and studied throughout the later Middle Ages, and in 1949, it was touted as the "oldest doctrinal monument to the legal discipline of international law."[102] Bonet writes, "I hold firmly, that according to ancient law, and according to the ancient customs of good warriors, that it is an unworthy thing to imprison either old men taking no part in the war, or women, or innocent children. Certainly it is very bad custom...as it is common knowledge that they can have no part in war, for the former lack strength and the others knowledge." Earlier in this passage, Bonet states that a "child is innocent of the war and that neither by person nor counsel can he render help or succour in it." He also states that an old man is not to be imprisoned unless "he has given counsel and help for the conduct of war" because old men are no longer capable of rendering military service. Note that Bonet does not take this lack of virility to mean senility because an old man is frequently "of more avail by his counsel than ten soldiers."[103]

When we read these passages, it is difficult to ascertain to which category women belong. As a problematic intermediate term, women are located literally and metaphorically between childlike innocence and physical incapacity. Thus the reason why women are not to be imprisoned, and are to be treated as distinct in war, is, contra Johnson, not at all clear.

Compounding this uncertainty is Bonet's statement, that "women should not be compelled to go to war, even though they were wise, rich and strong,"[104] which suggests that women *are* capable of warring mentally, economically, and physically. This is further supported by his longer example of "a lady, a widow possessing fine lands, who has continually made war against a very proud knight [who]...has pressed the lady so hard that she is in strong need of help...but she does not ask for help, or call upon anyone."[105] In this passage, Bonet certainly acknowledges not simply the belief, accurately reflecting the times, that noblewomen could and should manage and defend their estates; he also introduces the idea that this lady was the adversary in warfare. Given this, it is extremely difficult to maintain the logic that women were physically incapable of warring, much less any sense that women were innocent (either in its meaning of ignorant or harmless) of war itself.

Likewise, the work of Christine de Pisan (1408), immediately contradicts the supposition of ignorance. In her influential military manual of the early fifteenth century, the *Book of Deeds,* de Pisan specifically notes that intelligence is more important than physical prowess. Her book contains technical details regarding siege warfare, armaments, and provisions, as well as cultural details of chivalric honor, and was used extensively in the late fifteenth century. Furthermore, de Pisan is notable for her rejection of female passivity, weakness, and subordination and renowned, in both her time and ours, for her spirited defense of women against her contemporaries' denigration and disgust and, some argue, for inaugurating the long-standing tradition of debate (*querelle des femmes*) about the role of women in society.[106] Thus, far from needing the protection of chivalrous knights, women, as de Pisan demonstrates, possessed attributes (capacity for counsel and knowledge of strategy) that, in the calculus of forces, were worth more than "ten soldiers."[107]

Overall, the problem with Johnson's characterization is not solely that he attempts to base the advancement of the concept of noncombatant immunity on a relation of gendered condescension or that he contends that such a relationship is only logical considering the physical weakness of women or that this assessment of the physical capacity of women is linked to their nonparticipation in war; the problem is that he maintains this syllogism, disregarding evidence and debates that clearly propose the contrary.

My fundamental concern here, however, is not Johnson's intimation that women did not or could not participate in war; as Meron writes, this position is "clearly rebuttable."[108] Instead, my focus is on Johnson's interpretation of immunity as founded on the essentialization and naturalization of women. He accepts this as complete and absolute—despite his paradoxical acknowledgement of the artificiality of immunity. In fact, as we have seen, the development of immunity was contingent on an extant perception of the subordination of women already made coherent within the context of Christianity and chivalry.

From the fact that "medieval weapons were heavy and cumbersome and required considerable strength on the part of their bearer," Johnson infers that "those who were physically too weak were natural noncombatants." He continues, "this was not true, however, of those named in the canon. They were after all, men; they were physically capable of carrying arms."[109] Johnson seems to forget that the peasantry, pilgrims, and merchants who were protected under canon law were both male and female. Moreover, as John Lynn, historian, notes, camp women (as followers of the armies, whores, wives, and laborers, were known) were full "participants" in military campaigns; they "suffered its hardships and faced its dangers...and their labor both maintained and defined the changing nature of warfare."[110] He repeatedly underscores that women performed hard, muscular tasks. Therefore, like Contamine, Johnson naturalizes and embodies immunity when, paradoxically, he also writes that immunity is an effect of a particular hierarchical order, "the social ideal of the secular warrior aristocracy of the west European Middle Ages." In this ideal, "the social and legal inferiority of women to men in the Middle Ages exemplifies the dominance and control that men of the knightly class sought to exercise over all of Christendom."[111] Again, there is a disquieting blindness to the ways in which immunity is bound to a particular concept of gender; in the case of Crusades, as we will see, immunity is also bound to a concept of civilization.

The narrative, as constructed by Johnson and Walzer, relies on and reifies a particular notion of the physicality of women. But further, Johnson neglects to consider the ramifications of the differentiations made among women. If the fundamental logic of chivalric immunity was founded in the (lack of) physical strength of women, why then were only *particular* women singled out for protection? The extension of immunity was intimately concerned with the construction of sex and sex difference, while the differences among women, the gradations of gender, were premised on the estate itself. Meron relies on Johnson's interpretations and, therefore, also founders in his attention to the role of gender. In essence, he writes that chivalry required the protection of those defined by "weakness and innocence," including women, children, and the aged. It is fascinating that Johnson (drawing from Russell) and Meron (drawing from Johnson) find it absolutely striking that the Peace of God did not specifically extend immunity to women, children, and the aged, who by all accounts must be noncombatants. Johnson and Meron conclude that this must be because the chivalric codes extended immunity to those individuals. But this presumption of the complementarity of canon law and chivalry overlooks the proprietal interests of the Church; after all, the Church had little to gain from protecting women, children, and the aged. Furthermore, at the same moment, both scholars note that indeed, canon law did, on occasion, protect particular women (widows, for example).

These scholars' strange struggle to align and cohere the categories of immunity falters because the placement of specific individuals in either category (to be killed or not killed) is never steadfast. The complementary opposition that these authors strive to make is troubled by the flux of differentiation both within and across the distinction itself. For example, if knights are the combatants and clerics immune, how do we explain clerics who wage war and knights who must be protected? Why is the extension of knightly protection so highly conditional? As one medieval scholar writes, "the duty to defend the weak and defenseless was not a universal injunction, but one which applied only to one's own dependents."[112] Thus, it is not *all* women who are granted immunity—it is only noblewomen and widows. This ties immunity, once again, to a reciprocal relationship of hierarchical privilege among nobility and the Church, reconfirming the social and legal inferiority of women found in each and justifying it with an imperative premised on the easily disproved ignorance or harmlessness of innocent women. Moreover, this protection was only extended as a form of patronage when it burnished the ideal form of knightly masculinity.

Let us examine the warring lady mentioned by Bonet. If a knight offers assistance to this warring widow—whether she desires it or not—he has thereby demonstrated his "vain glory and the valour and prowess of his person" and furthermore shown "that he can perform feats of arms before ladies."[113] We see here the implied threat of chivalry; the widow, who was considered to be easy prey for sexual violence, has neither requested nor accepted the knight's offer, a fact irrelevant to the evaluation of his performance. It is irrelevant because that performance is for his fellow knights, not for the lady herself. Bonet's writings further underscore the manner in which knightly prowess, courage, and honour are fundamentally self-referential, having less to do with the actual value of those defended. For example, in scorning those who would imprison women, old men, and children, he remarks that it would "show no great courage to do so, for all gentleman should keep them from harm," whereas those who do not are no better than common pillagers.[114] That is, his derision is directed at the lack of courage, not the actual act of imprisonment.

Likewise, the violation of the prohibition against the rape of women—a principal form of protection within chivalry—would, somewhat paradoxically, emasculate and dishonour the offender. Rape was a transgression that was simultaneously a trespass against the chivalric code, which bestowed, through its ornate oaths of obligations, recognizable masculinity as well as nobility. This dimension of rape was layered on the extant legal code, in which women remained the property of men; therefore, rape was considered a crime against property. These discourses of gender are fundamental to the concept and conduct of chivalry and to the conception of immunity found therein. The honor of chivalry— that is, the honor of the knight—provided a conditional patronage not so subtly disguised as a physical threat for only those deemed to be within the knight's sphere of responsibility. The relationship between protection and obedience, or among protection, utility, and subservience, was fundamental. And the absence of this proprietary protection is starkly observed in the conduct of Crusades.

* * *

In the Middle Ages, "it is clear that Christianity and war, the church and the military, far from being antithetical, on the whole got on well together."[115] Nowhere was this relationship more evident than in the conduct of the Crusades, in which the knightly duties and obligations of respect and protection were quickly discarded in the war against infidels and heretics. Participation in the Crusades, understood to be wars commanded by God and waged by Christians to punish these enemies, bestowed special religious and divine favor on those who participated, regardless of their conduct during them. As Keen notes, canonists interested in preserving the power of the Church over the nobility and controlling knightly violence in the service of the Church, effectively cast participation in the Crusades as a holy activity that exculpated sins. The call to the Crusades at the peace council of Clermont in the eleventh century sanctified violence against heretics and infidels as it sanctified the role of the clergy and knights as the sacred and secular authorities on violence. By defining the exceptions—heretics and infidels—for whom the restraints of the peace movement did not apply, papal authority reasserted itself, affirming that otherwise prohibited acts of violence were permitted. Thomas Asbridge writes, "within the context of a holy war, in which the Franks were conditioned to see their enemy as sub-human, Christian piety prompted not clemency, but, rather, an atmosphere of extreme brutality and heightened savagery."[116] And, certainly, there was a strong historical background for such a call. The fathers of the Church, Aquinas and Augustine, were equally willing to condemn barbarians, infidels, and heretics to the might of the sword. Throughout the Middle Ages, Jews were subject to repeated pogroms and assaults, and Muslims were specifically excoriated.[117]

Service in the Crusades was associated with increased social and economic status on the knight's return.[118] In fact, the Crusades provided an opportunity for chivalry and Christianity to meet in the service of the Lord, gaining equal spiritual and material benefits for knights, the spiritual benefits of the Crusades being in the form of penance accomplished. Keen writes that a knight "may not only save his soul but win as well things that are...very desirable in this world, social identity, privilege and recognition among his own kind."[119] Hence, in reading the protections granted under the auspices of both chivalry and the Church, it is imperative to recognize that the establishment of immunity derived not only from the differentiation within the desired social order of medieval Christendom but also from the differentiation between Christians and the Islamic infidels. Pope Urban II reputedly "exhorted his listeners to be especially moved by the fate of the Holy Selpuchre of Our Lord and Saviour which is in the hands of unclean races."[120] Without the external distinction made between proper Christians and others, the internal differentiation of the European social order would lose a primary justification. That order relied fundamentally on the distinctions among the knighthood, whose *raison d'etre* was violence; the Church and canonists, who supervised that violence in the service of the Church; and the peasants who tilled the land.

More suggestively, the correspondence of the peace movement and the call for the First Crusade points to the inextricable relationship of the Crusades to the burgeoning concept of immunity—insomuch as the immunity of certain individuals was made possible, it relied on the impossibility of immunity for others. The immunity of those within Europe was created and consolidated *vis-à-vis* the guilt of those against whom the Crusades were waged because the assumption of prior guilt was fundamental to a just war. Bloody war and sacred grace became reconciled through the authorial papal ruling of the enemy's guilt.

The question, then, must be at least contemplated: What sort of concept of immunity might have developed outside the conduct of the Crusades? The question is worthwhile because it recasts the relationship of immunity and the Crusades as intrinsically, but not necessarily, intertwined. It also highlights the significance of the broader discourses of civilization in the establishment of immunity because the beginnings of immunity were fully compatible with and complicit in the demarcation of civilized, heathen, infidel, and pagan societies.

Meron acknowledges this to a degree when he writes, "chivalry's norms were fully applicable regardless of nationality between knights and nobility, those who had the right to wage war, but did not protect commoners and peasants and were not applicable to non-Christians."[121] France notes, "in principle, Christians felt that they could behave much as they pleased in war with non-Christians and something approaching total war did sometimes occur."[122] Moreover, both France and Strickland show that non-Christians were not the only ones subject to something approaching total war. Encouraged by the Church, war was waged not only against the infidels in the East but in Europe against those categorized as barbarians or heretics. France observes, "crusade and conquest in the European experience were justified by religious exclusiveness, and produced a savagery that was otherwise reserved for heretics, and those who were perceived of as disturbing the social order."[123] France's and Strickland's arguments illustrate not just that the chivalric codes and canonical prohibitions were, for the most part, unobserved in wars against barbarians (e.g., the Celts of the British Isles) and Islamic infidels but that they did not, indeed could not, apply to all those deemed outsiders.

Why? The laws of war were premised, both internally and externally, on the grant of an exception determined not only by spiritual but also secular authorities. The distinctions of civilization and religion (which did not necessarily coincide) were fundamental to the scope and concept of the laws of war. As Strickland summarizes, "the Muslims too possessed a…concomitant set of "chivalric" values.…Yet, these shared military and social factors that encouraged the limitation of war were crucially offset by the religious dimension of the hostilities between Christian and Muslim." In contrast, "the fact that the Welsh, Irish, and Scots were co-religionists had virtually no positive effect on their treatment at the hands of Anglo-Normans. Here, behavior was determined by racial animosity that stemmed from pronounced cultural and linguistic differences, reinforced by the Celtic methods of war."[124] Augustine, the father of the just war tradition, was moved to write in defense of Christianity and against the pagan defeat of Rome, so it should be no surprise that his erstwhile inheritors of the Christian traditions remained recognizably allied with that cause.

This discussion of the Crusades helps us to discern the relationship between immunity and civilization. In the next chapter, I focus on the Crusades as they evolved into the early wars of colonization. "Crusading, far from an anachronism, provided one impetus for the European age of discovery."[125] Meron, clearly aware of the formative influence of the Crusades, states, "in medieval wars, honour, chivalry, and knighthood enhanced any existing compliance with humanitarian norms and strengthened protection for noncombatants. The idea that chivalry requires soldiers to act in a civilized manner is one of its most enduring legacies."[126] But we must ask: How can acting in a civilized manner be so clearly distinguished from acting against or for a particular conception of civilization? Was not one of the fundamental calls of chivalry to wage war against those identified as scourges to the Christian civilization? Is one of chivalry's most enduring legacies not also that it requires soldiers to act in a *civilizing* manner? Suffice it to say here that the chivalry of the knights in the conduct of the Crusades was precisely the "civilized manner" in which a Christian Europe sought to impose its order and beliefs on the pagan East.

Yet, in an argument that diverges radically from mine, both Johnson and Meron rely on the discourses of civilization to argue for the progressive, as well as protective, potential of the laws of war. Johnson writes that absent "common ideology, or morality, no common civilization with its inherited traditions...it follows that emphasis in regard to noncombatant immunity should be upon defining what civilization requires *even if somewhat arbitrarily,* so that all can see and judge."[127] I find this conclusion disturbing because that is exactly what the bloody Crusades achieved—the arbitrary imposition of a conception of immunity of a particular civilization. Moreover, I question whether it is from that particular inheritance that the protective and progressive potential of the laws of war devolve. I return to Johnson's injunction in the next chapter.

Without tracing the differentiation of immunities, the ambiguities and the tensions that plagued its formulation and implementation, the authors of the conventional intellectual genealogy of the laws of war fail to understand the complex history of this principle. In particular, they miss considering how social orders are formed and transformed through the designation of immunity and how, in turn, the designation of immunity informs the social order. Furthermore, by rereading the canonical texts and returning to the beginnings of immunity, I have demonstrated the productive power of gender, innocence, and civilization in establishing relations of inequity and difference, which simultaneously enable a concept of immunity.

At the very least, this genealogy should force us to reconsider the value of chivalric honor as a worthy source of present-day constraints. "Any assessments of just war theories are bound to be ambivalent, as were the theories themselves, for they were an unstable compound that was always in danger of splitting into its component parts and destroying the delicate balance."[128]

CIVILIZATION AND EMPIRE
Francisco de Vitoria and Hugo Grotius

> **No sooner had they [the Amerindians] been granted the status of human beings than the privileges and protections of such a classification were abrogated.... they had lost the right to ethical treatment that would normally be afforded to human beings, or more precisely to morally adequate, civilized human beings.**
>
> —Sankar Muthu, *Enlightenment against Empire*

The period between the late fifteenth and seventeenth centuries was a tumultuous time of discovery, conquest, travel, and transformation. As one commentator noted, "even more than other history the Age of Discovery is men come upon strangeness and traveling it mostly in dream."[1] Yet, although this period is often referred to as the Age of Discovery, it would perhaps be more aptly named the Age of Colonization. This period encompasses the colonization and conquest of the Americas and Africa, the expansion of commerce and trade, and the nascent theorizing of sovereignty within a network of slowly individuating states. Significantly, the Peace of Westphalia in 1648 formally ended the religious wars between Catholics and Protestants. Within the disciplines of international relations and international law, the conventional interpretations of the Peace of Westphalia hold that it marked the origin of an international system of independent sovereign and equal states, and augured the end of vagaries of religious rule.

During this period, in which war was as endemic as the plague, there were revolutionary changes in the size, discipline, and organization of Western European militaries. The details of this transformation and the exact timing of what is termed the military revolution are not the topics of this book; nevertheless, the consequences are notable for the several reasons. First, from the start of the sixteenth century to the end of the eighteenth century, rapid growth in the size of armies funded by and in the service of the state sparked questions about moral and military discipline, loyalty, and professional and personal training that had hitherto been answered by the social distinctions of the feudal order, the code of chivalry, and the traditions of nobility. Specifically, an increasing reliance on selective conscription, native troops, and the use of infantry, as well as the spread of brutal wars, created a surge in military service of commoners who were unfamiliar with the noble traditions of conduct in combat. Not only did the membership and professionalization of early modern European state armies change, so too did the methods of combat, which became arguably more indiscriminate, deadly, and comprehensive in range.

Second, these military and social transformations in membership, weaponry, and discipline spurred publicists and practitioners to assess the reasons for and restraints on war. Publicists and philosophers recognized it was "necessary and possible to imagine a 'law of war and peace' as a compendium of the minimal conditions of coexistence," and commanders and kings imagined a more regular, rational science of war.[2] Thus, and third, the laws of war continued to reflect as well as inflect the practice of war.

Notably, the concept of the just war, a complicated and debated set of protocols by which war was proclaimed and fought, became more elaborate. These protocols of conduct multiplied, with highly detailed military manuals becoming more common. Paralleling this trend, these manuals also shifted in emphasis, with the putative universalism of natural law replacing the particular aristocratic codes as the fount of both moral and legal reasoning about war. Wilhelm Grewe comments on this sedimentation of rules and reasoning, noting that it "drew on the intellectual tradition of the Christian Middle Ages and a natural law which was firmly anchored in the divine world order, and which was always either the basis, or at least the final legitimation, of the law of nations and the binding force of its rules."[3] Because the laws of war were one of the common means of justifying imperial expansion, commerce, and aggression, these laws had to account for not only wars waged within Europe, among European peoples, but also wars undertaken in the New World and against its inhabitants. Thus, to understand the laws of war, and the relationship of civilian and civilization, the history of European imperialism and the grant of immunity conceptualized therein must be addressed. I contend that immunity is an expression of charity and mercy—an indulgence of sorts—granted by individuals and states invested with sovereignty through discourses of civilization. In highlighting the discourses of civilization, however, I do not minimize the importance of the discourses of innocence and gender—far from it. Discourses of civilization are woven through the conception of immunity while discourses of gender and innocence ravel and knot the design.

Two scholars in particular greatly influenced the articulation of the laws of war as they themselves struggled to grasp the significance of, and adapt to, these changes and to conceptualize the relationships among the peoples of Europe and the New World. The first is Francisco de Vitoria, the sixteenth-century Spanish

Scholastic and Dominican friar who wrote *De indis noviter inventis* (On the Indians Recently Discovered) in 1532 and *De jure belli* (On the Laws of War) seven years later; the second is Hugo Grotius, the seventeenth-century Dutch lawyer and diplomat who wrote *De jure pradae* (On Prize Laws) in 1604 and *De jure belli ac pacis libri tres* (On the Laws of War and Peace) in 1625.

James T. Johnson refers to Vitoria as "one of the most impeccable sources for just war theory, perhaps the single most important figure in the development of that theory from its medieval to its modern form."[4] Legal and international relations scholars contend that "the issues that Grotius addressed, the concepts and language he used, even the propositions he advanced, have become part of the common currency of international debate about war in general."[5] In addition, the works of both Vitoria and Grotius are fertile ground for contemporary theorists of international law and international relations seeking to reseed current dilemmas in the practice of these disciplines. Scholars of international law and international relations have engaged in detailed documentation and refutation of the varying assessments of the contributions made by each of these men to the founding of their disciplines. Wearing thin, this debate over the proper fathering of international law and international relations has rightly been discarded in current discussions; I, too, am uninterested in pursuing the now hackneyed argument about to whom paternity should legitimately be granted.

Rather, their importance derives from their engagement with the transformation of both war and politics in a newly modern world of emerging states, proliferating transits of trade, and discoveries of the other. Their writings provide important insights into the way the world was newly imagined and newly conquered. Certainly, each is heralded for his enlightened and secularized interpretations of the relations among sovereigns and nations, and both are lauded for their considerations of the laws of war. Yet those who praise their work fail to consider the ways in which the discourses of civilization and barbarism inform their writings.

Despite the constitutive relations between the defining moments of the laws of war and the emergence of colonization as an integral part of the modern nation-state, contemporary scholarship remains governed by its failure to think through this relationship. For example, Johnson reads the discussions of imperialism and colonization, framed in the discourses of barbarism and civilization, as simply descriptive applications of the theoretical commitment of each author. He does not contemplate either works as constitutive of theoretical disquisitions. Instead, as he writes, "Vitoria's insistence on the natural law source of just war limits on belligerents meant that he could apply the received doctrine to the *special case* of the Spanish war on the Indians."[6] And Charles H. Alexandrowicz remarks in a representative statement referring to the works of Vitoria, Alberico Gentili (the Italian jurist), and Hugo Grotius: "it is remarkable how some of the classic writers anticipated the progress of the Family of Nations which (aside from the 19th century interlude of colonialism) went steadily ahead with endowing all its member communities with statehood and sovereignty."[7] This parenthetical dismissal of colonialism as if it were simply a jarring note in an otherwise pleasant symphony is all the more ironic considering that its author is among the most notable historians of the role of non-European countries in the development of international law. After all, an effect of the established discourses of civilizations was the creation of a particular system of international law.

For example, from the fifteenth to the seventeenth centuries, Spain and Portugal, as the preeminent colonial powers, attempted to restrict the application of the law of nations to specifically designated geographical areas. They did this to ensure their continued colonial monopoly on trade and "restrict the political relations and the rules of the game of their State system to Europe."[8] Consequently, when the imperial powers conducted imperial business within their colonies, the law of nations was suspended. The lines of amity "separated the European sphere of peace and the law of nations from an overseas sphere in which there was neither peace nor law."[9] This conception of the law of nations also helped to clarify the internal identity and external boundaries of the (civilized, Christian) society of states. The question of what civilization requires—of whom and in relation to whom—is one that lies at the foundation of international law. During this period, the discourses of civilization were predicated on the exclusion of barbarians, to whom the law was said not to apply.

Perhaps this is less than surprising; after all, the etymology of civilization (to make civil) refers foremost to a transformation within law. In the seventeenth century, *to make civil* or *to civilize* was the act of transforming a criminal matter into a civil one. *To civilize* was to recognize civil authority but also to polish, domesticate, tame, and make moral. *To civilize* also meant to subject to and be subject to a range of strictures, codes, and laws touching on moral, social, and legal comportment. Lacking any positive content of its own, when transferred to "'make civil' in other senses," the term *to civilize* signifies bringing "out of a state of barbarism, to instruct in the arts of life and thus elevate in the scale of humanity."[10] Thus, *to make civil* referred to a distinct yet related set of behavioral norms and a particular legal status. That is to say, *to civilize*, or *to make civil*, is to encode a complex set of regulative and productive strictures in the process of making one a subject and, significantly, making one a subject of the law.

By the eighteenth century, the term *civilization* was widely accepted to have two definitions: (1) "a law or act of justice or judgment which renders a criminal process civil" and (2) the opposite of barbarity or savagery.[11] It is commonly agreed that Jeremy Bentham was the first writer in the late eighteenth century to have "used the term civilization in the context of international law."[12] Bentham is also credited with introducing the phrase *international law*. Thus, it would appear that civilization and international law were brought jointly into being.

Therefore, when Vitoria and Grotius began their work, there were specific social hierarchies within which nations and peoples were configured and to which the laws of nations conformed. One of the major transformations during these centuries was that, through its imperial conquests, the "Christendom of Europe...came gradually to define itself as 'civilized.'"[13] Indeed, by the nineteenth century, scholars held that "public law, with slight exceptions, has always been, and still is, limited to the civilized and Christian people of Europe or to those of European origin."[14] Note that the discourses of civilization demarcate static differences most frequently bounded by territorial distinctions. Yet these discourses also denote processes of transformation—from barbarism to civilization—which immediately undermine the presumption of static or stable differences. The force of discourses of civilization, which both set the limits of law (civilization vs. barbarism) and occasion the exercise of the law (from barbarism to civilization), was brought into relief in the dictate of the Requirement.

* * *

In the sixteenth and seventeenth centuries, barbarism acquired specific meaning in relation to the discovery of the Americas. As Anthony Pagden details in his study of the term, *barbarism* has always signified inferiority because it presumes an inability to speak the language of those who are self-defined as the representatives of humanity. The inability to speak is not simply a benign difference because, according to the logic of the Greeks, from whom the term *barbarism* is inherited, the inability to speak signifies an inability to reason and, therefore, to be fully human. Further, as Pagden explains, "the ability to use language, together with the ability to form civil societies—since these were the clearest indications of man's power to reason—were also the things that distinguished man from other animals."[15] These elements, the ability to use language and to reason, as well as the distinction of man from animals, are central to Vitoria's work.

During the sixteenth century, discourses of civilization and barbarism conditioned the development of the law of nations through the processes of colonization and conquest carried out by the Catholic Iberian monarchies.[16] Spain, after all, dominated the burgeoning sphere of international relations, and the theologians and scholars of Spain "led the way in discussing problems of the laws of nations," not only making fundamental contributions to its development but also introducing the possibility of its existence.[17] The prevailing discourses of civilization and barbarism defined and defended the Spanish imperial reach, and the essential justification of its conduct was framed in the laws of war. If, as the

Spanish queen was famously told, "language is perfect instrument of empire,"[18] then law is the instrument that most perfectly advanced the Spanish empire itself. The nascent colonial project of Spain was distinct in its reliance on the law as the fundamental means of articulating and legitimating possession and conquest.

The most notable of these instruments of law and language was the Requirement (Requerimiento), which was read to the natives when they were "discovered" by the conquistadors. Written in 1513 by a legal scholar, it summoned the natives to recognize and submit to the twin superiority of the divine empire of Christianity and the temporal empire of Spain. As imagined by the rulers of Spain, the Requirement was a legal convention of conquest that, when read aloud to the newly found Indians, was held to legitimate the conquest. Equally, it was nothing less than a "fully ritualized protocol for declaring war" because, if the Indians refused to accept the Spaniards as the rightful bearers of the one true faith destined and designated by papal bull, the Spaniards had the right to subdue the "barbarous nations."[19] To refuse finding only a stupendous irony in the Requirement—read aloud in a language unknown to the Indians, often from great distances, in anticipation of an immediate assault, and by Spanish militia armed and girded for battle—is to begin to comprehend the tragedy that followed its recitation.

A highly specific "ultimatum for Indians to acknowledge the superiority of Christianity or be warred upon," the Requirement effectively fabricated the juridical and moral justice of the Spanish conquest.[20] And yet why did the conquistadors, possessing such superior force, supplement this force with this protocol? Any answer points most suggestively to the construction of the power of the sovereign. What I want to identify within this declaration is the presence of a pardon, an act of mercy, a gift of civilization on the part of the Spaniards that leads to an exemption of the Indians from violence. As absurd as this sounds, the Requirement also presented a pardon to those who willingly (and, yes, the irony is obvious) submitted to the superiority of Christianity and its "most faithful servants," the "subduers of the barbarous nations."[21] That is, if the natives—asked and required to "consider what we [the conquistadors] said"—accepted the king and queen of Spain as their lords and kings, they would "do well" and be received in "all love and charity."[22] Moreover, the conquistadors would "leave your wives and your children, free without servitude."[23] As articulated in the Requirement, sovereign power is not just the power to decide life and death itself but also the right to grant pardon.

But the proffered love and charity, as well as the promise of economic gain, was given only if the Indians recognized themselves as subordinate to and subjects of the king and the queen. If the natives rejected the superiority of Christianity and its faithful servants, if the natives "wickedly and intentionally delay[ed] to do so," the conquistadors "with the help of God shall forcibly enter into your country

and shall make war against you in all ways and manners that we can[,] …sub-
ject you to the yoke and obedience of the Church[,] …and take you and your
wives and your children and dispose of them."[24] The Requirement continued at
this threatening pace until its conclusion, at which point the Spanish, ever aware
of the intricacies of the law, asked the natives to sign as witnesses to the reading
of the Requirement—which was then notarized. Within the context and content of the Requirement, the possibility of peaceful resistance or rejection, debate
or dissension, was unrealizable. Those summoned possessed but one (putative)
choice of "their own free will" and could exercise but one act as identified by the
Spanish—to submit and become vassals of the empire. Without that acquiescence, nothing remained but outright slavery and slaughter.

What, then, did the Requirement really offer? On the one hand, there was
the promise of immunity found in the acceptance of the grace of God, extended
quite clearly as an exemption from war and made manifest through love and
charity. Within the Christian faith, mercy was intimately linked to charity, one
of the four theological virtues identified by Aquinas and the avowed foundation
of just war traditions. Moreover, as I explained in chapter 2, it is to this Christian
mercy that contemporary scholars of the laws of war return, believing that those
laws are its progeny. And, certainly, those natives who submitted, who surrendered and were made subject to the Spanish, were given "many privileges and
exemptions," not the least of which was the right to possession, property, and life
itself.[25] But these privileges and exemptions were not given freely. There was also
the specific qualification of conversion, to be converted from barbarian to subject, where this conversion was but the first step toward eventual civilization. The
refusal of this qualification, however, resulted in condemnation, both divine and
temporal, specifically a slaughter from which no one was immune and for which
only the natives themselves were responsible. "The deaths and losses which shall
accrue from this are your fault, and not that of their Highnesses, or ours, nor of
these cavaliers who come with us."[26] Here is the explicit conjunction of immunity with conversion and civilization (with the Spaniards as the embodiments
of a Christian civilization). The right to exempt, or pardon, one from violence
was invested in a sovereign, and herein only a Christian, civilized sovereign. Immunity remained a gift, an expression of mercy, an exemption from violence
extended from sovereign to vassal; it was (to return briefly to Walzer) not a right
but a gift that was not given freely. After all, immunity found its presence in relations of inequity and obligation.

* * *

I turn now to the writings of Vitoria, in particular to his two works, *On the
Indians Recently Discovered* (1532) and *On the Laws of War* (1539). Reading these

works in tandem, we can untangle how the demand for the Indians' conversion to Christianity—the first predicate for immunity—became at the same time a demand for the Indians' conversion to a particular civilization.

Vitoria is important for at least three reasons. First, Vitoria is credited with loosening the grip of divine law articulated and enforced in papal Rome as the primary standard by which international law was interpreted and legitimated. He did so by emphasizing international law as rooted in the common body of self-evident principles, known as natural law, which, he argued, were recognized and obeyed by all rational men. His formulation of the relationship between the law of nature and the law of nations opened the possibility that all men of reason, "irrespective of the local legislative convictions, beliefs, and customs of individual communities, or indeed their place in time" could be subject to and subjects of the law of nations.[27] That law was defined as "a set of precepts enacted by the power of the 'whole world, which is in a sense a commonwealth.'"[28] He can thus be credited with laying down the foundation for modern law as a secular law (one that was universal rather than particular) derived from the relations among a community of nations (the *jus gentium*).[29]

The second reason is that he accomplished this, in part, through a direct philosophical and on occasion infuriated engagement with the "affairs of the Indies" (the ongoing and contentious debates over the legitimacy of the Spanish conquest and conversion of the Americas). These events sparked his most famous disputations and also informed his exegesis on dietary laws and the laws of war.

Third, Vitoria turned to the laws of war to defend his interpretation of the affair of the Indies and the authority of all concerned. And through this engagement with the laws of war, he effectively transformed them.[30] In the words of Grewe, "it was his doctrine of *bellum iustum* which lay at the root of his judgment on the colonial question."[31]

The affairs of the Indies occupied the denizens of Europe and the New World from its first challenge (issued from the colonial pulpit in Hispaniola in 1511) to the famous debate at the Spanish University in Valladolid in 1550, at which two of its prime movers, Juan Ginés de Sepulveda and Bartolomé de las Casas, presented their opposing arguments before a committee of theologians and jurists. Spain, as the self-appointed guardian and representative of a universal Christendom, had an intimate and professed investment in acting in accordance with Christian principles, thus the centrality of the ritual legitimation of the conquest (i.e., reading the Requirement).[32] This is why interpreting the Requirement as a fictitious document, as an exercise of material force, or as evidence of unquestionable hubris misses its importance as a constitutive act through which Spain secured and legitimated its own sovereign reach and its identity as the Christian, civilized state.

Recall that during the sixteenth century the laws of war were primarily the collection of strictures and norms developed and refined during the Middle Ages (see chap. 2) under the auspices of defining just war. The core tenet of the just war during the sixteenth century was that it be waged as a war of defense; a just war was one that sought to avenge injury and right wrongs. In keeping with its Christian inheritance, just war was fought solely for the purposes of achieving peace and establishing proper order, both divine and temporal. Yet, because Vitoria held that the newly discovered Indians were in full possession of their lands and affairs and had not, by simple virtue of their "barbaric" existence or refusal to be forcibly converted, committed any injury against the Spaniards, a different ground for conquest and conversion had to be found.[33]

In a passage that lends credence to his celebrated title as the defender of the Indians, Vitoria sharply dismisses any suggestions that submission under the terms of the Requirement validated the rule of Spain. First, there was no semblance of choice in the options presented by the Requirement. Submission and acceptance is a false decision, he writes, because it is made "in fear and ignorance, factors which vitiate any freedom of election, but which played a leading part in this particular choice and acceptance. The barbarians do not realize what they are doing; perhaps indeed they do not even understand what it is the Spaniards are asking of them. Besides which, the request is made by armed men who surround a fearful and defenceless crowd."[34] In addition, the Indians already "had their own true masters and princes [and] ... cannot without reasonable cause seek new masters."[35] Thus, "by what right were the barbarians subjected to Spanish rule?"[36] His question, perhaps more academic than agonized, no doubt echoed the first charge issued in 1511 from the pulpit by his fellow Dominican, Antonio de Montesinos, who cried out, "by what authority have you waged such detestable wars?"[37]

The answer Vitoria gives is complicated and contradictory—in part because it simultaneously *counters* the legitimacy of papacy in extending its authority to temporal matters and the current mode of colonization but also *corroborates* the intrinsic truth of the conquest by Spain. Although Vitoria does recoil in embarrassment and shock from the atrocities of colonization, he does not "dispute the emperor's right to conquer the Indies."[38] In this, he foreshadows the work of individuals who did not declaim against colonization or imperialism per se but, instead, against the means by which it was conducted and the assumptions on which it was premised.[39] Vitoria did not suggest that the Spanish possession of the Americas was unjustified or unwarranted. Nor did he argue that Spain should relinquish its holdings. Rather, his intent was to clarify "some matters of doubt" about the ways in which Spain could legitimate its actions.[40] Here, the overall architecture of Vitoria's argument begins to appear.

To explain the Spanish conquest, Vitoria must first make clear that the matter before him, the rights by which Spain subjected the barbarians to rule, pertained not solely to human or natural law but was fundamentally derived from divine law. As a "case of conscience, it is the business of the priests, that is to say, of the Church to pass sentence upon it."[41] Coupled with his vehement rejection of the validity of the Requirement, his insistence that the Indians were in full possession of their lands and could not be forced to submit to the Spaniards, and his contention that war could not be waged against them because of their refusal to convert to Christianity, it is certainly right, as many do, to admire his critical stance. In the context of his time, when obedience to both temporal and sacred authority was expected—especially by a Dominican monk subject to both—these were no innocuous assertions.

Nevertheless, Vitoria's criticism had its limits. As he himself notes, his intent was merely to demonstrate and not to defy. Vitoria rails against the way the Indians were conquered and the rational for that conquest; he does not rail against the conquest itself. The order of things had been disturbed not by the manifest injustice of imperialism but because the Spanish imperialist enterprise was out of order. By the close of his two disputations, which were complementary arguments, Vitoria has ceded to Spain the rights and responsibilities of the conquest by re-inscribing the rights granted to Christian nations into the ledger of rights granted to civilized nations in the *jus gentium*. As a result, Vitoria can be credited, in the words of Peter Fitzpatrick, with both "getting international law off to an aptly exalted start…with his universalist humanitarian espousal of the interests of the Indian during the Spanish colonization of the Americas" and providing a "consummate legitimation for one of the most spectacularly rapacious imperial acquisitions."[42]

Before we can understand the specifics of Vitoria's argument, we need to fully understand the importance of the concept of natural law that informs the logic of Vitoria's disputation. We also need to understand the concept of innocence in his work. Vitoria accepted Thomas Aquinas's definition of *natural law* as the "participation in the eternal law by rational creatures." Composed of a body of "self-evident principles implanted by God…'in the hearts of men,'" natural law, as defined by Aquinas, is ordained for the common good not only "because it should be so, but because if it were not so it would cease to be law."[43] According to Aquinas, it therefore follows that natural law is "the efficient cause which underpinned man's relationship with the world about him and governed every practice within human society."[44] Hence, as a testimony to the intimacy of man and God, and as the text of the relationship of man to man, natural law is the fundamental arbiter of the rights by which the Spanish claimed possession. Further, natural law and the law of nations (*jus gentium*) bear a remarkable resemblance and had a special relation to each other. For Vitoria, the order of things among nations (*jus gentium*) was indebted to the proper order of things (natural law), understood in the most comprehensive sense of what is right. "To speak, therefore as something belonging to divine law is to imply that the thing is intrinsic to the whole structure of the creation. If the Indian question was to be considered as a part of divine law, then it became, by definition, a matter touching on the very nature of man and the metaphysics of social order."[45]

In his writings, Vitoria imagines a relationship between the metaphysics of the social order, the proper arrangement of both temporal and divine hierarchies, and the nature of man. This relationship illuminates his image as the defender of the Indians. By touching on the very nature of man, Vitoria was forced to establish, contradicting the dominant arguments of his time, that the Indians were people; that is, they were rational creatures of God and not natural slaves. The Indians were neither mad nor insensate; therefore, they could not simply be refused recognition as rational creatures of God. Moreover, the absence of a belief in Christianity or the commission of sins could not, in Vitoria's view, bar them from recognition as such.

Vitoria's willingness to consider the Indians as men is highly significant, although like all matters of significance it is subject to competing interpretations. Even though Vitoria believed the Indians to be barbarians, he did not indulge in a simplistic dichotomy of men versus beasts. He was preoccupied with the degree to which the Indians were men. Vitoria eventually concluded that the Indians were members of the family of man and, therefore, of international society; however, within the family of man, they were children. That is, the Indian was but a child of reason, whereas the Spaniard was a man of reason. Only through reason could one be privileged to define or identify natural law. The Indians were therefore obligated to turn to the Spaniards for tutelage and guidance in all things. Thus, although Vitoria established the common humanity of the Indians and Spaniards, he did so through individuating the two in a relation of inequity. The universality of natural law and the common humanity of all men were established through the assignment of subordinate status to the Indian. It seems that it was the business of priests to pass sentence on the conquest but that the grammar of their sentencing, highly indebted to the lexicon of natural law, allowed for a generous ruling in favor of the Spaniards.

Vitoria imagined a relationship between natural law and the law of nations in which the latter "either is or derives from natural law."[46] In this way of thinking, the hierarchy of imperialism remained secure. Indeed, one result of his conclusion was that Indians must possess only partial or limited dominium over their property and affairs, incapable of full exercise until properly tutored. We are easily reminded of the Requirement in the assignation of partial membership in the

Spanish crown: as neither "citizens nor slaves, but as an people indentured in not only in body, but mind as well—mere vassals of the Emperor."[47]

Vitoria believed the recognition and acceptance of this natural law, as enacted in the establishment and promulgation of the law of nations, was to be found in fullest flower in the law of nations as practiced in civilized, Christian, European states. It is difficult to maintain, as James Brown Scott wrote in 1934, that "the philosophy of Vitoria was, however, for an occasion, or rather to bring a concrete situation—arising from the discovery of the New World—within the law of Christendom, thus universalizing it."[48] Rather, Vitoria effectively transformed the "rules...particular and relevant only to Christian peoples into universal rules endorsed by the jus gentium."[49] The specific rules of Christian Europe were nominated as the universal rules of the society of nations, even though, or even as, the foundation of the *jus gentium* was to be found in natural law, whose principles were potentially self-evident to all. As a result, whatever claims the Spanish crown had could only be made in natural law and "by demonstrating that the native population had forfeited [their claims] by their own actions."[50] This was not difficult to do. All that was required was evidence that the Indians had forfeited their rights through a rejection or transgression of the law of nations, and because the Spaniards were the one who professed and policed that law, they could easily hold the Indians to be in violation.

Once the Indians were judged to be in violation, either by contesting or preventing the Spanish from the full exercise of the rights forming the presumptive foundation of the law of nations—the rights of travel, communication, and trade—the Spaniards had every right to wage war against them as "really harmful and offensive enemies" and "treacherous foes." The Spaniards were allowed everything necessary in war to fully defend and secure these rights. The only prerequisite was that before waging such a war the Spanish must "by reasoning and persuasion" convince the barbarians, who were "by nature cowardly, foolish, and ignorant," that the Spanish had come peaceably among them or, in the words of Stephen Greenblatt, that they had come to "give a great gift."[51]

Consider the terms of this gift to the Indians. First, the Indians must understand that the Spanish had come peaceably among them; they must also be persuaded of and by the reason of the Spanish. This supposition is more than slightly ironic because Vitoria had already established that the Indians possessed only an immature reason; how were they to be capable of understanding the superior reasoning of the Spanish? Here Vitoria imposed on the Indians an expectation no less incongruous than that put forth by the Requirement, demanding that the Indians consider the words of the conquistadors. Furthermore, the context in which these requests were issued remained fundamentally the same— the Spaniards were in the process of violently colonizing and conquering the

New World. Nonetheless, Vitoria persevered in presenting the possibilities for a considered exchange.[52]

Once they had heard the Spanish, to demonstrate that indeed they understood and were persuaded by the Spanish, the Indians must accept both the presence (because Christianity carried the gift of civilization, perhaps it was a present) and preaching of the Spanish. If they did not eventually accept this (unlike the Requirement, Vitoria was very willing to acknowledge that this acceptance might be some time in arriving), the Spaniards were allowed, even encouraged, to wage war until the Indians yielded. Bluntly, either the Indians surrendered or the Spaniards would kill them. This, remember, was a reflection of the proper order of things.

Let us retrace the steps taken to arrive at this juncture. First, "Indian resistance to conversion is a cause of war, because it violates not the divine law but the jus gentium administered by the sovereign."[53] Second, barbarians, although recognizably human and, therefore, equally governed and governable by natural law, have not achieved the full possession of reason necessary to discern and guide the law of nations. Third, because the law of nations can only be administered by a sovereign, and the barbarian lacks the knowledge to do so, not only does the law of nations reflect and reify Christian Europe but the sovereign can only be of those Europeans. And, as Antony Anghie argues, if the highest expression of sovereignty is the right to wage and determine a just war, and the barbarian lacks that which is definitive of sovereignty, then the barbarian can never wage a just war.[54] Moreover, if the sovereign is not only he who wages war but, significantly, he who retains the right to decide exemptions from war, then the barbarian is he who lacks the right to decide and to grant immunity from war.[55]

Why is this so? First, because the barbarian lacks reason and, second, because the barbarian lacks the sovereignty to judge, "The victor must think of himself as the judge sitting in judgment between two commonwealths."[56] James Brown Scott argues that, in Vitoria's view, "each and every ruler had the power of a judge only if his cause were just, and that his support of an unjust cause stripped him at once so far international law was concerned, of any power to pass on the right or wrong."[57] Ironically, Scott neglects to consider that this very claim can be read as the unqualified advocacy of the righteousness of the Spanish conquest because, within the logic of the Conquest, the cause of the Spanish was always already just.[58] Thus, once again, only the civilized sovereign can pass judgment on the reasons for and conduct of war. In this way, the difficulties posed by the just war concepts about the reasons for and conduct of wars of imperialism were resolved through the discourses of civilization.

To approach this point a different way, consider the emphasis on speech found in both the Requirement and in Vitoria. Speech, reasoning, persuasion, preaching, and communication were central to the process of conversion and submission. These were all attributes and privileges of the Spanish, not of the barbarians. What differentiated barbarians from the civilized was the power of speech—an attribute of the latter. Turning to Aristotle, to whom we owe our modern understanding of the relationship of speech to justice, we see the consequences of this characterization. In Aristotle's words, the "power of speech is intended to set forth the expedient and inexpedient and, therefore, likewise, the just and the unjust."[59]

Vitoria's writings, for all his protestations to the contrary, were indebted to the structure and the logic of the Requirement. Regardless of his aspirations, Vitoria substituted the right of conquest held by Christian states for that held by civilized states. Immunity remained premised on conversion, understood now as encompassing both an acceptance of Christianity and, through the work of Vitoria, civilization. Immunity was an effect of Christian mercy, which, as captured so complexly in Vitoria's writings, is the point of departure for the conceptualization of immunity as an effect of civilization. The logic of this transcription is manifested beautifully in Vitoria's insistence that the Spaniards were the "ambassadors of Christendom" and, therefore, inviolable as were all ambassadors within the law of nations.[60] The law of nations recognized and responded to the privileges and power of Christendom, transcribing the determination of immunity from a right of the Christian sovereign to a right of the civilized sovereign.

Thus, in Vitoria's view, immunity remains the privilege and exercise of civilized states. These civilized states, as a condition of recognition, extend their mercy as a writ of exemption from an "inevitable and endless war."[61] The condition of immunity is one of inequity. It is subject to the logic of charity and mercy, and it is formulated within and through the logic of the Conquest; "From its beginnings the imperialist mission is, in short, one of translation: the translation of the 'other' into the terms of the empire, the prime term of which is 'barbarian' or one of its variations such as 'savage' which, ironically, but not without a precise politics, also alienates the other from empire."[62] Immunity is caught by and in an imperial order—perhaps most brutally articulated in the Requirement but no less powerfully repeated by Vitoria, one of its most learned critics.

* * *

It is at this intersection of Christianity and civilization that innocence is transfigured. I read the writings of Vitoria and Francisco Suarez, his fellow Scholastic and intellectual peer, as evidence of a struggle to stabilize and reconcile the distinctions of immunity and innocence articulated in natural law and the law of nations.[63]

Recall that the etymology of *innocence* refers not only to an absence of culpability but also to ignorance and harmlessness (see chap. 2). The innocence of the Indians was defined in Vitoria's first disputation (*On the Indians Recently Discovered*) as stemming from their ignorance of the law of nations; it was the ignorance of an untutored child and the result of insufficient reason. As Aristotle would say, the Indian, like the child, is "imperfect."[64] This imperfection, not "relative to himself alone, but to the perfect man and to his teacher," initially spared the Indian at the behest of the Spaniard.[65] Consequently, the discourses of civilization invest ignorance with a particular meaning *vis-à-vis* the Indian, explaining why the Indian would be spared in war and also who would spare him. Indians were to be spared because they were like children. This is a reasonable claim in the traditions of war within which Vitoria wrote; however, it does little to defend his claim. Children, as discussed in chapter 2, are not always innocent and are certainly not consistently harmless. Indeed, Vitoria himself first notes that children should be spared in war because they are "obviously innocent," but he is forced to elaborate this point because the innocence of children is bounded, not absolute.[66] Recognizing this boundedness, he suggests that children are innocent and should be spared because they have *yet* to commit evil, not because they are incapable of committing evil. Likewise, the Indians should be spared because they had yet to commit evil; but, like children, the Indians bore the constant potential to "pose a threat in the future."[67]

Indians could also be considered innocent because they were ignorant of the laws of which they were in violation. Only when the Indians were no longer ignorant of the proper comportment and acceptance of the law of nations were they no longer innocent of their transgressions of that law. The reasoned arguments, persuasion, tutelage, and education provided by the Spaniards corrected the ignorance of the Indians. Thus, according to Vitoria, "if the barbarians deny the Spaniards what is theirs by the law of nations, they commit an offence against them," and the "laws of war against really harmful and offensive enemies are quite different from those against innocent or ignorant ones. The provocation of the Pharisees are to be met with quite a different response from one appropriate to weak and childish foes."[68] What is significant in this transformation is that any limitations that Vitoria placed on the practice of war against ignorant Indians were relinquished in a war against the invidious Indians.[69] There is a temporal instability in the assignation of innocence, in part because of the constant potential of both Indians and children to transform innocence into threat.

Recognizing this, it is difficult to agree with the claims made by both Richard Hartigan and Johnson that Vitoria was responsible for instituting a "material, objective fact" on which judgment of innocence and guilt can be made. They argue that participation in unjust activity—defined as "lack of any direct contribution to the war effort"[70] or, more specifically, "determined by the bearing or non-bearing of arms"[71]—is the objective material fact by which innocence is judged. But Vitoria was writing about lack of knowledge and lack of reason—neither of which are objective or material facts. Indeed, this is exactly what makes potential threats so difficult to identify and complicates the granting of immunity. Moreover, the ignorance (as lack of either reason or knowledge) of the American Indians is an effect of discourses of civilization—the bearing of arms does not appear in Vitoria's first disputation on the American Indians. This is why it is so crucial to follow Vitoria's instructions and read his second disputation, *On the Laws of War,* in conjunction with *On the Indians Recently Discovered.*

Victoria's work reveals the lack of a stable foundation for the distinction between innocence and guilt on which to map immunity. The distinction is both indeterminate and in flux because, even though innocence is presumed, the potential for guilt is ever present. Children may be innocent now, but will always pose a potential threat; likewise, Indians may be ignorant now, but they can become invidious. But, if innocence is not absolute and harmlessness cannot be always secured, how does one decide who may be killed (i.e., who is guilty) and who may not be killed (i.e., who is innocent)? How can the two be distinguished? The persistence of this question and the historical attempts to resolve it are remarkable in their consistency, arising not only during attempts to codify war but also during the practice of war. The desire to stabilize and materialize a distinction led Vitoria, and others after him, to rely on visible racial and sexual markers, which were held to correspond to internal dispositions and traits—in the case of the laws of war, to innocence and guilt. The need for a visible difference between the guilty and the innocent enters the laws of war when the temporality and indeterminacy of innocence are directly considered.

Vitoria resolved this *temporal* indeterminacy of guilt and innocence by instituting the visible distinction of sex, which allowed for the axiom that, whereas men may or may not be guilty, women should be considered innocent as a rule. He held that "in reality all adult men in an enemy city are to be thought of as enemies, since the innocent cannot be distinguished from the guilty, and therefore all may be killed."[72] What I find fascinating in this statement is that innocence or guilt, which is traditionally held as the foundation of the distinction, becomes irrelevant because it is impossible to tell who is guilty and who is innocent; thus, except for children, all males may be killed when it is otherwise impossible to distinguish among them. Likewise, Francisco Suarez, relied on the certainty of age and sex to distinguish among those who may be killed when it was "scarcely possible to distinguish the innocent from the guilty."[73] According to him, it was entirely permissible to "slaughter all whose innocence is not clearly evident for reasons of age or sex."[74] In contrast to men, women retained the presumption of innocence unless it could be proved otherwise, and in contrast to children, women retained the constancy of their sex, which identified them as innocents. Here the exception proves the rule.

Colm McKeogh argues that Vitoria and Suarez endeavored to link the "powerful moral concepts of guilt and innocence to the material facts of combatancy and non-combatancy...yet they can only link them by presumption."[75] Although I agree with McKeogh's assessment of the tensions of their arguments, what he overlooks is how Vitoria and Suarez link the concepts not only by presumption but also by explicitly relying on sex and sex difference. In part, McKeogh's mistake arises from his paying insufficient attention to the importance of natural law (and its relationship in Vitoria's work to the law of nations) and, significantly, to the discourse of gender found therein. Within the metaphysics of divine social order manifested within natural law, the discourses of gender identify particular categories of individuals as innocent according to age and sex.[76] As Suarez writes, "it is implicit in natural law that the innocent include children, women, and all unable to bear arms; by the *ius gentium*, ambassadors, and among Christians, by positive canon law religious persons, priests, etc."[77]

Drawing from the Scholastic tradition, Suarez holds that natural law "assumes the existence in a given act or object, of the rectitude which it prescribes or the depravity which it prohibits." In contrast, canon law and the law of nations "render evil what they prohibit." In the first, the characteristic is inherent within the act or object, whereas in the second the characteristic is ascribed to the act or object through the law. Hence, women and children are innocent according to natural law because innocence exists in women and children just as women and children exist as innocent. If it is "through the natural law that we participate in eternal order [and]...it is a standard of good and evil," then the innocence of women and children is not only derivative of eternal order, but is itself a standard of good and evil.[78] Furthermore, differences of age and sex provide visible markers that are taken to correspond with internal traits (e.g., innocence and guilt) and thus, in turn, identify who is to be spared and who is not.

What are the consequences of this? For these early theorists, the sacerdotal and social, the natural law and law of nations, bore a remarkable resemblance and had a special relation. Moreover, for both Vitoria and Suarez, the order among between nations was indebted to the proper natural order (understood in the most comprehensive sense of what is right) articulated in natural law. Thus, discourses of gender in the law of nations, which took arms bearing as instituting a distinction between men and women (those who were not to be spared and those who were), intersected with those found in natural law: women and children were named innocents. This is why innocence remains a gendered concept even when women are found to be guilty (i.e., to be bearing arms). Moreover, because Vitoria presided over the emergence of civilization as the binding identity of sovereign states, we may now understand why states identify themselves as civilized through the sparing of women and children—it is the standard by which they judge and are judged. Even Grotius, who otherwise believed that the Spaniards were the barbarians against which civilization needed to defend itself, accepted this form of reasoning and, significantly, in his effort to secularize the laws of war continued with this standard.

* * *

Hugo Grotius's *The Laws of War and Peace* (*LWP*) shares in the broad political and theoretical purpose of his earlier work, which was to establish and regulate international commerce and order by developing and systematizing the laws of nations among distinct nations.[79] But the emphasis of *LWP* is on the formation, through a synthesis of divine law, natural law, and the law of nations, of a legal order that should and could serve to moderate and restrain the ways and means of waging war: "a common law among nations, which is valid alike for war and in war."[80] This common law, said to regulate war, relies on a threefold distinction among potential sovereign entities and individuals engaged in war. *LWP* contrasts what is permissible for Christians with what is permissible for non-Christians and with, as its ultimate comparison, what is permissible for barbarians.

As Johnson explains, the difference among these entities lies in their capacity and exercise of moderation in war and, for Christians, the practice of moderation is facilitated by their familiarity with the concept of charity toward others. He writes, "Grotius notes that in spite of the comparative license granted in natural law and the law of nations, Christian countries proceed more mildly against their enemies because of the force of charity."[81] As a result, however possible it is for sovereign entities and individuals to act with the necessary requisite of moderation through the exercise of reason, it is Christian sovereigns and individuals who are, by virtue of this identity, most able to discern such restrictions and to act in accordance with the tempering influence of charity or, as *LWP* often terms it, love. This, too, follows the reasoning found in Vitoria.

LWP sets forth a hierarchy of moderation that is mapped on a hierarchy of religions; this mapping reiterates the common formulation of barbarians as lacking reason and control, and thus lacking the self-discipline and self-mastery intrinsic to nonbarbaric peoples. According to *LWP*, barbarians are "more animals than human beings." A syllogism emerges in which moderation is to charity is to Christians as excess is to barbarism is to barbarians, with the "better nations," presumably neither barbarous nor Christian, existing in between.[82] Significantly, in *LWP* Grotius does not argue that Christians, or even these better nations, must or will display moderation when confronted with barbarians, and it is certainly possible to war against those who so "offend against Nature" by practicing cannibalism, piracy, or parricide—which indigenous peoples were consistently described as doing by their more enlightened brethren. Therefore, *LWP*, quite "neatly legitimated a great deal of European action against native people around the world."[83] But this exclusion, and the violations it legitimates, it is not its only result.

As *LWP* argues for moderation and temperance, as both imagined and implemented, to be used in accordance with the distinctions among Christian, better, and barbarous entities, those distinctions must be evident.[84] Yet even as the argument in *LWP* presupposes those distinctions, taking them as proof of the possibility of moderation, Grotius presents these distinctions as without a meaningful difference. The imperative to moderate and temper war directly arises from the condemnation in *LWP* of the conduct marking the wars of Grotius's time. Yet what is most notable about these wars is that they were primarily waged among and by Christians. As Grotius most famously decries, "throughout the Christian world I observed a lack of constraint in relation to war, such as even barbarous races should be ashamed of."[85] The Spanish colonization of the Americas, known colloquially as the Black Legend, was primary among these wars that Grotius decried.

I agree with the many scholars who argue that the opposition between Christian and barbarian is a central presence in *LWP* and a sign of its influence on Grotius's conception of social order. But what should hold our interest is not only the appeal to this difference but also the lamentation of its erasure. Christians are acting like or, even more horrific, worse than barbarians—acting with "such utter ruthlessness" that it tempts one to despair.[86] Consequently, the fundamental distinction between Christians and barbarians on which the argument for moderation and temperance rests cannot be taken as given. Indeed, the atrocities of the wars proved it false. Thus, the *LWP* begins with a conundrum. Law is still possible and desirable, made more so because it provides the means to ensure a more peaceable order by establishing order in war. Its potential, however, is grounded in the distinctions rendered counterfeit by the wars of his time. How then is order to be accomplished? It is here that an analysis of discourses of gender, innocence, and civilization once again finds its imperative.

Opening the discussion of the law, *LWP* first sets forth the distribution and acquisition of rights and obligations that inform and maintain social order. Grotius proclaims, "by generation parents acquire a right over children—both parents, I mean, the father and mother. But, if there is a variance in the exercise of these rights the right of the father is given preference on account of the superiority of sex."[87] In addition, it is "deservedly the woman [who] ... is made subject for the male[,] for equality in rank produces strife."[88] The superiority of the male sex is posited as self-evident. Although there is an acknowledged potential that both sexes may very well be equal, asserting woman as subject avoids strife. As translated, woman is made subject for the man, not to the man, once again suggesting that to be made male is to have another made subject. Essential to the peace and order of domestic society is the proper distinction and distribution of power between the sexes.

It is not only domestic order that is founded on and arises from these hierarchical and gendered relations of power but also international order. After all, *LWP* sets the rights of individuals and the rights of states as comparable and, specifically, defined the power of the head of household as essentially similar to the power of the state.[89] For the seventeenth-century Dutch, "home...was both a microcosm and a permitting condition of a properly governed commonwealth."[90] Indeed, *LWP* further develops this analogy in reference to consent and rights over persons. In discussing marriage, Grotius collapses the fundamental distinction between rights derived from association and those derived from subjection. Men possess rights over women not only because marriage is, in Grotius's words, "the most natural association" but also because the woman submits through a "vow which binds herself to the man." The act of binding (in marriage) finds its parallel in the binding of men to a sovereign power; as by "the law of marriage" the husband is "superior," so by the law of nations is the sovereign superior.[91] But, by its own terms, association becomes subjection because, according to natural law, women are without the necessary reason to conclude a contract. Although the binding power of their vow derives from its voluntarily commission, in fact women possess no capacity, no authority, to actually vow. This has immediate effects on the conception of sovereignty and rights in war.

LWP also holds that the "maintenance of social order...is the source of the law so called," and that, indeed, "no association of men can be maintained without law."[92] Therefore, both the source and purpose of the law are to be found in the preservation of the proper social order, which, as we have seen, has as its foundation and as its model this arrangement between the sexes. Reasoning from this recursive relationship, it is fair to say that the peculiar position of women as both subject to and the property of men is not simply reflected and regulated in the social order but forms an integral dimension of the source and purpose of the law that governs that (domestic and international) social order. As *LWP* sets forth, the ideal order to which international and national entities should aspire is modeled by Christian nations.

There is a particularly illustrative example of the intersection of these multifarious hierarchies of relations, although, ironically, it is one for which *LWP* is frequently lauded, touted as evidence of Grotius's enlightened sensibility and, subsequently, the progressive potential of the laws of war he is said to have founded.[93] In deciding whether "rape is contrary to the law of nations," *LWP* declares there is an agreement among nations. First, nations that find the raping of women in war permissible reason that an injury done to another person, to the person of the enemy, is not "inconsistent with the law of war that everything which belongs to the enemy should be at the disposition of the victor."[94] But among the better nations, the rape of women in war is considered not solely on the premise of rightful acts of conquest. Better nations judge the rape of women according to two other principles: the "unrestrained lust of the act; also the fact that such acts do not contribute to safety or to punishment."[95] As one historian notes, "Grotius leans towards prohibition on the grounds that it could never contribute to attaining the purpose of war."[96] *LWP* holds that a hallmark of enlightened nations is to exercise restraint and moderation, to practice judgment and reason; accordingly, transparent displays of sheer physicality, prurient excitement, and poor judgment indicate barbarity. Thus, better nations conclude, "rape should not go unpunished in war."[97] In other words, it may be permissible, but it is unlawful. Moreover, among Christian nations the prohibition against rape is not merely punitive but also has the prescriptive authority of law: "Among Christians it is right that the view just presented shall be enforced not only as a law of military discipline, but also as a part of the law of nations."[98] Here, rape is not only impermissible and unlawful but also corrosive of the identity of Christian entities.

Notice that, for Grotius, the practice of and the response to rape distinguish nations according to a social hierarchy of reason, judgment, and comportment that, in turn, indexes barbarity, as it did for Vitoria and Suarez before him. The capacity to define rape as an error of strategic judgment and unappeasable appetites demarcates the better and, presumably, better-than-better Christian nations from each and all others. A discourse of gender animates and regulates the evaluation of intercourse among and identity of specific nations and, insofar as this carries with it presumptions of heterosexuality, it regulates a particular form of sex in the service of Christian nations. Indeed, a fundamental irony of the invocation of *LWP* as an enlightened or progressive source of the prohibition against the rape of women in war is that *LWP* is not at all concerned with the fate of women. Grotius is foremost concerned with creating and regulating a particular hierarchy of relations among nations in accordance with the modalities (divine, natural, and of nations) of law. Therefore, although it is tempting to also paint *LWP* as defending women, such strokes are too sweeping.

LWP admittedly acknowledges that rape is an "injury" done to another person, yet the actual person to whom that injury is done is unclear. If women are subordinate to men and categorized as possessions of the family, rape as causing an "injury to the person of another" could well be interpreted as injury to the family, to the husband, and, as it was the father and family who form the nucleus of the commonwealth, to the commonwealth.[99] Certainly, this interpretation is strengthened by the contention that rape is easily understood as sanctioned by the laws of war because everything that "belongs to the enemy should be at the disposition of the victor."[100] Women, then, are clearly *of* the enemy, property and possession, but are not clearly the enemy. In this sense, the formulation and understanding of war as a battle waged between and among men is produced and maintained within a very specific discourse of gender that takes the rape of women as its expression. Moreover, the comportment of men in war divides among that commonality.

LWP does not dispute the basic definition of the injury done, but identifies it as insufficient. It is not that rape qua rape is wrong—impermissible, unlawful, or unjust. Instead, it is the characteristic and the intent of the act that render it unlawful—it is an aberration of appetite and it is not an efficient or rational strategy of war (or of conjugal sex). Moreover, rape is also to be punished and prohibited because it injures not only those against whom it is committed but those who commit it. Most significantly, it denatures and dehumanizes men, preventing their ascension into progressively more civilized relations. The distinction of barbarism and civilization takes hold, is given substance, through this analysis of the effect of rape on men's capacity to govern themselves—in surrendering to their appetite, men surrender their humanity, becoming beasts. Men, unlike animals, have the capacity "to follow the direction of a well tempered judgment, being neither led astray by fear or the allurement of immediate pleasure, nor carried away by rash impulse. Whatever is clearly at variance with such judgment is understood to be contrary also to the law of nature, that is, to the nature of man."[101] Or, "lest by imitating wild beasts too much, we forget to be human."[102] *LWP* deems rape impermissible because it degrades the differences between men and animals, Christians and barbarians—differences and distinctions integral to the creation and maintenance of social order. Consequently, rape equally corrupts the strategic purpose of war—to seek and maintain an ever more progressive Christian social order. Although it may, in the gross sense, be permissible, it is destructive.[103]

We misread the power of this discourse if we read it only or primarily as a discourse of gender, one that is concerned with the treatment and protection of women. Rather, the discourses of gender and civilization converge, and the practice and prohibition of rape intimately constitute a particular international order by regulating intercourse among and identification of sovereign entities and individuals as enlightened Christian men. The disavowal of rape by Christians cites an authority to mediate temptation and transgression. Furthermore, the gradation of the permissibility of rape underscores the complex relations among the capacity for judgment, the potential to moderate actions in war (which, in turn, is intimately associated with Christianity and masculinity), and the understanding of what it means to be human. And, here again, we should be reminded of Vitoria's struggle to, at the same time, animate the Indians as humans and qualify their difference from the Spanish.

Ever careful to parse the degree of differences within the desired social order, and cognizant of the desirability of peace and the persistence of war, *LWP* remains intent on limiting the authority and right to wage war to those entities identified as public and sovereign. This is the first step toward instituting temperance and moderation, and ordering war. War, in his view, although possibly still taking the form of a duel or private feud, should be more or less emphasized as a contention by force among those who "hold the sovereign power in the state."[104] Or, as Karma Nabulsi puts it, "the thrust of Grotius' writings was to concentrate the legitimate recourse to war in public hands."[105]

As a result, the relationship imagined (as it was with his predecessors) between the right of war and the rights of (civilized) sovereignty is mutually constitutive. And, although it is tempting to deduce from this that the actual pursuit and practice of war should be limited to and by militaries, armies, and recognizable vested representatives of that sovereign power, it is difficult to find a consistent definition of *belligerents* or *combatants* in Grotius's work. For one, although the law of nations might so restrict the pool of combatants, the law of nature (the dictate of right reason) holds that "no-one is enjoined from waging war."[106] In other words, sovereign authority may indeed be the marker for legitimate recourse to war, but who may wage war and on whose behalf remains enigmatic.

This ambiguity is complicated by the position, in accordance with the contemporary customs of warfare and with natural law, that all inhabitants of a country against whom war is made may be warred against—"not only to those who actually bear arms, or are the subjects of him that stirs up war, but in addition to all persons who are in the enemy's territory."[107] The logic of this assertion is premised on the simple fact that "injury may be feared from such persons"; consequently, they may be defended against.[108] As Grotius states, "how far this right to inflict injury extends may be perceived from the fact that the slaughter even of infants and of women is made with impunity and that this is included in the law of war."[109] Thus, there is no clear differentiation between those who may kill and those who may be killed—to the degree that, as Grotius indicates, "neither sex nor age found mercy."[110]

LWP begins the task of developing a "remedy" to the unchecked virulence and "frenzy" of contemporary wars by establishing a mean between "nothing is allowable" and "everything is."[111] Moderation and temperance in war demarcated by the limitation on killing—the limitation of that fundamental right of war—establish the crucial mean through which war may continue to be waged. Significantly, when shifting from a discussion of the brutality of war, its random and excessive violence, to its potential moderation, Grotius also shifts from the conduct of war allowed by the law of nations to the law of nature and, as it is variously called, the law of love, mercy, and charity (a specifically divine and fundamentally Christian law). What underpins the potential for temperance, then, is not the actions or history of actions among sovereign entities but the desire and belief in a higher, perhaps more ephemeral but certainly more demanding law— divine law.[112] Thus, temperance in war evolves from distinguishing and discriminating among acts of war and individuals at war in accordance to precepts and principles best exemplified and articulated in Christianity. It requires, in essence, distinguishing between what is "permitted and what is right."[113]

Introduced within the category of permissibility, then, are further distinctions of what is right or what is just. *LWP* calls on both natural and divine law to discern the difference and demarcate the boundaries between acts done in war that are permissible—done with impunity under the law of nations—and acts that, although perhaps still permissible within the law of nations, are "devoid of moral justice."[114] This distinction of what is permissible and what is right also includes that which is "honourable."[115] The right of killing enemies is not simply a right, in the way that an individual possesses the lawful authority to do so, but must also be rightly done: "Consider not what you may do, but that of which the doing will honor bring."[116] Equally formative to distinctions of permissible and right violence is the concept of honor, what is just and good. This concept of honor is intimately associated, as it was in the chivalric codes of war, with the identification of masculinity because it is the honor of men that restrains them from lawful yet dishonorable acts.

LWP specifies the particular acts that fall under the rubric of lawful yet devoid of moral justice, concluding that it is the "bidding of mercy, if not of justice, that, except for reasons that are weighty and will affect the safety of many, no action should be attempted whereby innocent persons may be threatened with destruction."[117] Immediately after positing this principle, one that attests to the existence of and obedience to a "more just and better" law, *LWP* begins to outline the "special cases."[118] *LWP* employs a particular form of reasoning in which the rule is illustrated through examples. A general principle is posited, from which its proof is deduced through an analysis of specific particular cases.[119] On this move to special cases, the validity of the entire principle—that no innocent person can be threatened with destruction—rests. Accordingly, these special cases, through and by which the principle is exemplified and defined, illustrate the verity and legitimacy of the principle: "That children should always be spared; women, unless they have been guilty of an extremely serious offense; and old men."[120] With this, *LWP* contravenes the laws of nature and the laws of nations for they each allow the killing of children, women, and old men because all pose a potential harm and all have a potential right of self-defense.

How does Grotius reason this transgression? He does so in three ways. First, quoting Seneca, *LWP* straightforwardly states, "let the child be excused by his age, the woman by her sex."[121] At first, it seems that the *sex* of the woman refers to the sex had by a woman; recall that not all women are to be spared, only the virgins. Here *LWP* refers to the trial of the Midianites, arguing that, even in a war so just as to be ordained by God, all were not slaughtered. The virgins, "32,000 persons in all, who had not known a man by sleeping with him," were left alive, to be distributed among the Israelites. All others, every man and every woman who had known a man, were killed, as was the way in the wars against Canaanites; these were wars in which there "was not a single survivor left," and the practice was to "utterly" destroy "men, women, and children."[122] Virgins were excused because they, unlike other women, were innocent; they could not be accused of seducing the Israelites.

Second, continuing to trace this reasoning, we discover that it is not simply the lack of sex that sets certain women apart, to be spared among their kind. Sparing women during wars is equally grounded in the belief that women cannot "devise wars."[123] Recollect that "on account of the difference in sex the authority is not held in common but the husband is in the head of the wife...the woman under the eye of the man and under his guardianship."[124] Compare this with the contention, by no means unique among Grotius's interlocutors, that recourse to war should be employed primarily as a form of recompense against a violation of a right (and, thus, to recover property or to punish) or in the exercise of self-defense: "no other just cause for undertaking war can there be excepting injury received."[125] Now, because marriage is said to be "the most natural association" in which the husband rules over his wife, then especially within natural law the rights of the husband trump those of the woman. If husbands and fathers possess rights over their wives and daughters, as both property and subjects, and if, furthermore, wives are said to cede their rights first to their husbands and then, through him, to the sovereign, how exactly are women able to register a violation of rights? Finally, since "that power is called sovereign whose actions are not subject to the legal control of another, so that they cannot be rendered void by the operation of another human will," the least that can be said is that women are without the sovereignty necessary to register a violation of rights and a resort to self-defense.[126] In essence, women lack the authority and sovereignty necessary to devise war in a theory in which "the principle author of war is one whose right has been violated."[127]

Third, *LWP* holds that wars are to be waged solely for a just cause and for just purposes. As formulated, this contention erects another barrier against women being able to authorize or devise wars because women are among those who are constitutionally unable to adjudicate between "just and unjust, lawful and unlawful."[128] (And, in this we may trace the outlines of Vitoria, who believes barbarians to be equally unable to wage a just war.) Drawing from Aristotle, Grotius explains, "alike children, women and men of dull intellect and bad education are not well able to appreciate the distinction."[129] In this phrase, women are a problematic middle term—either like children or like stupid and poorly educated men or somewhat akin to both.[130] Therefore, although the exact analogy may be inconsistent, the consequences are not. Women are incapable of devising war.

Therefore, the substantiation of the first principle is as follows. Lacking deliberative and sovereign authority, and unable to tell just from unjust or to receive injury, women are to be spared because they are constitutionally and constitutively incapable of waging war. In addition to these definitional deficiencies derived from the matter of sex, women may be spared if they have not experienced sex itself outside of the proper boundaries of family and nation. We also now see how the earlier discussion of rape foreshadows this recursive relation among injury, rights, property, and sovereignty, made possible by the presupposition of heterosexual hierarchies of rule.

The power of this configuration of sex, in which differences attributed to materiality of the body are presumed to be the evident and natural foundations for the apparent opposition of sex, is made visible in the central role that material difference plays in the construction of the innocence of children and old men. I already suggested that *LWP* develops an analogy between children and women in which the absence of reason, authority, and capacity joins the two. Furthermore, children and women are without sovereignty. Innocence, then, is entangled with these absences and lack. Yet, whereas male children may grow out of, develop, and transform their inadequacies, either through education or by simply maturing (and old men may begin to fail), women are forever marked deficient in these regards.

Differences of sex are translated into moral, social, and political distinctions that, in turn, are taken as legitimating and demonstrating the existence of biological differences on which these putative distinctions are premised. The result is that innocence is not a descriptive characteristic borne by women, children, and old men equally, nor is it a corollary of occupational duties such as the clergy, merchants, farmers, or those "concerned with letters." Rather, innocence is inextricable from the female sex.

Although we have grown accustomed to thinking of children as natural civilians, it is in fact women who are made civilians by nature. It is only women whose innocence is not derived from the sequential and variable attributes of age; choice of religious, pastoral, or artistic occupation; and range of intellect and education. One grows into and out of these categories; the cycle of birth, maturity, senility, and death frame their span.[131] Furthermore, it is the very matter of their sex, this particular inscription of the meaning of sex and sex difference, that renders them innocent and excused—an understanding that we have now accepted as natural even though, as this reading of *LWP* reveals, it is decidedly unnatural. The governing discourses of gender do exactly what Judith Butler, feminist theorist, claims they do. They not only reflect and reify differences between the sexes, marking each as distinct; the discourses of gender are "also the discursive/cultural means by which 'sexed nature' or 'a natural sex' is produced and established." Discourses of gender both institute and stabilize the differences between those who should be spared and those who should not on which the hierarchies of moderation depend, and it is in women that innocence is substantiated.

This becomes particularly clear when we follow the attribution of guilt because women are innocent "unless they have been guilty of an extremely serious offense."[132] Elaborating on this prior claim, Grotius states that women should not be spared from war if "they commit a crime which ought to be punished in a special manner or unless they take the place of men."[133] This is a radical and disruptive claim for a text that holds that women are the "sex which is spared wars."[134] What, then, are the crimes for which women ought to be punished in a special manner? First, acts of seduction qualify because acts of seduction are not only serious offenses but, insofar as women acted, it could be said that they took the place of men.

Second, among those who wrote before Grotius and on whom *LWP* relies, the serious crime for which women should be specifically punished is taking the place of men.[135] For example, one of Grotius's most favored and honored predecessors, to whom he acknowledges a specific debt, is the Alberico Gentili.[136] Gentili argues that as a rule the "age of childhood is weak, and so is the sex of women, so that to both an indulgence may be shown," yet he, like Grotius, makes "an exception of those women who perform duties of men which are beyond the power of the sex in general."[137]

What is the substance of this crime that makes its commission so exceptional? As both authors intone, men are "not accustomed to wage war" against women. Quoting the same Roman authorities, both works underscore that women are a "sex untrained and inexperienced in war."[138] Thus, there is little honor to be gained in fighting against such callow foes. To the contrary, those who do fight women gain only the epitaphs of cruelty and savagery, the reputation for inhumanity and impiety, and the scorn of those to whom the difference between what is permissible and what is just is both apparent and applicable. Recall that a guiding principle of Grotius's argument is that "among good men even war has certain laws" and that "it becomes good men not to wage a war of annihilation."[139]

Consider, further, how this distinction among men founded on the pursuit and practice of honor, secured in the sparing of women, differentiates among the commonality of men who wage war. Again, this differentiation is not simply scored by differences of barbarism and Christianity but draws equally from the concept of honor. As with the chivalric tradition that preceded Grotius (a tradition with which he was by no means unfamiliar), the honor of men is intimately linked to their identity as men. Honor is not merely an elaboration of masculinity but its defining and distinguishing element. It may become good men to respect the strictures on war, but it is also the primary means by which men become good. For this reason, women's engaging in war confuses and contradicts the assignation of men as men and of men as good men, just men, among men. Women in war disrupt the order of things.

Thus, the crimes that so degrade the defense of women—both seduction and taking the position of a man—violate the regulation of sexuality, sex, and sex difference, as constructed in and through a hetero-normative hierarchy presumed to be integral to the proper order. Significantly, these acts destabilize the social order not only through their transgression of its boundaries but because they require and make manifest women's potential for agency—which, in the complicated logic of *LWP*, calls on and makes manifest sovereignty, a capacity that women are said not to possess. Consequently, the act of taking the place of men must be punished.

Yet notice how these works propose that this be done. *LWP* simply states that "when Nero in the tragedy calls Octavia a foe, the prefect replies: Does a Woman receive this name?"[140] Likewise, Gentili, also quoting Seneca, writes, "a woman does not take the name of the enemy," continuing in his own words, "for in so far as women play the part of men they are men and not women."[141] Therefore, he concludes, "if women are guilty, then it will be said that the guilt is destroyed rather than woman."[142] Or, as he elaborates, it will be that the "abomination" is destroyed—not the woman but her crime. Quite noticeably, both writers attempt to foreclose the potential disruption of the constitutive dichotomy of sex. In so doing, each defends the difference that founds the social order and betrays anxiety regarding its constitutive instability. That is, even when women transgress the boundaries of sex, it is they who are rendered suspect and not that boundary itself. It is not women who receive the name of foe, it is not women who play the part of men, and it is not women who are destroyed—it is the "guilt" and the "abomination" that are destroyed. Thus, *LWP* attempts to defend the essential opposition that girds its argument even as that opposition proliferates beyond its bounds.

It is fascinating to follow how Grotius reaches this conclusion after beginning from the premise that women are entitled, like all beings, to wage war in self-defense. Grotius writes that "we shall hold to this principle, that by nature every one is the defender of his own rights; that is why hands were given to us."[143] This claim is taken to be self-evident because it is founded in natural law, defined as that which reveals itself as "manifest and clear."[144] In addition, the law of nations does not distinguish between ages and sexes in the waging of war. For these reasons, LWP turns to divine law—to the commanding sentiments of love, justice, and charity—to produce reason and justification for a distinction among those against whom war waged; sex and sex difference are naturalized as the referents on which LWP measures the mean between "nothing is allowable" and "everything is," while simultaneously marking a distinction between what is permitted and what is right. Moderation in war is explicitly as an act of mercy and of charity, an act that refers the compassion of God, and it is introduced through the sparing of those who are, indelibly innocent—women. (It is no small wonder that the participation of women in war posed a threat of such degree.) Sex and sex difference found the fragile edifice of the laws of war.

As we have seen in this critical rereading of the canonical texts of the traditional history of the laws of war, Grotius, and to an appreciably lesser degree, Vitoria, both began with the premise that all may be killed in war. For Vitoria, this was expressed in the potential for guilt that both children and Indians bore and in the impossibility of distinguishing among men in accordance with their innocence or guilt. For Grotius, the indeterminacy of who should be killed and who should be spared was expressed in the belief that no one was enjoined from waging war and, therefore, no one should be automatically spared from war. Both of these publicists turned to discourses of gender and innocence to stabilize the distinction between those should be spared and those who should not, invoking this distinction as an index of civilization while establishing that it is only the civilized who may indeed make the distinction at all.

In the next chapter, I bring us forward to the nineteenth century, linking this genealogy of the principle of distinction to its modern articulation and, significantly, to its effects in practice.

GENERAL ORDERS 100, UNION GENERAL SHERMAN'S MARCH TO ATLANTA, AND THE SAND CREEK MASSACRE

Protection was, and still is, with uncivilized peoples, the exception.

—Francis Lieber, General Orders 100, 1863

In 1863, President Abraham Lincoln observed that "civilized belligerents...do all in their power to help themselves or hurt the enemy...except things regarded as barbarous or cruel...the massacre of vanquished foes, and of non-combatants male and female."[1] Regardless of the power of this sentiment and the significance of its orator, a year later Union General William Tecumseh Sherman's March to the Sea began and Colonel John Chivington led federal troops in a massacre of over one hundred Cheyenne and Arapaho Indians in Colorado. A contemporary editorial published in the *Rocky Mountain News* reported "that in no single battle in North America, we believe, had so many Indians been slain."[2] Although the American Civil War and the U.S.-Indian were nominally two different wars, during the American Civil War the western frontier wars against Native Americans were considered a secondary but significant front and both the Confederacy and the Union recruited particular Indian tribes to their cause. Not only was Stand Watie, the last Confederate general to surrender, a Cherokee chief, but as early as 1861 the Confederates sent emissaries to the Creek, Seminoles, Osage, and Cherokees to gain their loyalty.

The American Civil War is frequently invoked as the harbinger of modern warfare and as an exemplar of total war. But, when compared to the savagery of past European battles, as well as to the brutal tactics employed against the U.S. Indians, the American Civil war is more accurately, and now commonly, described using Mark Grimsley's concept of hard war.[3] In part, this is because the American Civil War degenerated infrequently into unalloyed violence, in which the distinction between combatant and civilian was disregarded.[4] However destructive the war became, the Union and Confederacy did not utterly trespass a set of mutually agreed-on limits to the violence.[5] In contrast, during the wars against the Indians, Unionists engaged in indiscriminate massacres. Although the principle of distinction held for the great majority of the American Civil War, the reverse was true for the U.S.-Indian wars.

Still, between 1861 and 1865 both wars were fought in many similar ways. Both initially involved many of the same officers in the Union and Confederate military, used the same weaponry, and began without the benefit of a coherent organized strategy beyond that of an offensive yet erstwhile conciliatory war. James McPherson, Civil War historian, writes that "the United States has usually prepared for its wars after getting into them. Never was this more true than in the Civil War."[6] According to Robert Wooster, another historian, the U.S.-Indian wars were fought in a similarly haphazard manner. Although the Indians primarily fought a different style of war, preferring tactical raids, small party engagements, and surprise attacks, it was a style not unlike that favored by both the Confederate and Union guerrillas who played a decisive role during the Civil War. "Many of the men who organized guerrilla bands presented as credentials for such service their experience as Indian fighters."[7] Finally, both wars sparked open debates over the proper norms for waging war. How should the war be fought? The tension of assimilation and extermination remained constant in the wars against the Indians, whereas in the American Civil War conciliation gave way to retaliation. As the strategies of both wars evolved to include wholesale devastation of the economic base of the South and appropriation of its resources, a tactic already in use during U.S.-Indian wars, the questions of who was to be spared and who was not, who was a combatant and who was a civilian, remained an unsettled, contentious element.

Initially, one answer to how the war should be fought and who should be spared was that women and children were outside of war and were not to be intentionally killed. The Indians chose their battlefields to separate their warriors from their families. The women and children remained, as far as possible, outside the sphere of combat unless attacked. Although many a story recounts Indian women fighting with equal brutality, the shared presumption of both the Civil War and the U.S.-Indian wars was that men were the primary combatants and women and children were not. For example, in 1862 General James Henry Carleton of the Union army, who had been originally sent to New Mexico to fight the Confederates, was given the task of fighting Indians. He ordered that "the men are to be slain whenever and wherever they can be found. The women and children may be taken prisoners, but, of course, they are not to be killed."[8] Similarly, in 1865, another officer instructed his men to "attack and kill every male Indian over twelve years of age."[9]

Women and children were similarly protected in the guerrilla warfare of the Civil War. Before his infamous raid on Lawrence, Kansas, to revenge the death of the women and girls of his family, William Quantrill, the feared bushwhacker, was said to have commanded, "boys...remember that in hunting us they gave no quarter. Shoot every soldier you see, but in no way harm a woman or child."[10] Further, Indian tribes, as a rule, considered the killing of women and children to be cowardly, preferring to capture and enslave them. Thus, common norms set aside women and children to be spared in war. This is not to claim that in all cases the norms were upheld—in both Sherman's March to the Sea and the Sand Creek Massacre (and in the 1862 Sioux uprising that preceded both), not all women and children were spared. A closer analysis the first modern code of warfare, known as General Orders 100 or the Lieber Code, authored by Francis Lieber, a Prussian immigrant, and issued by President Lincoln in 1863, may help us understand the reasoning behind such differences.

* * *

Issued in April 1863 as "Instructions for the Government of Armies of the United States in the Field," General Orders 100 was the definitive law for the American Civil War in its last two years. Expanding on the available work of European and U.S. publicists, Lieber produced the first integrative work of the codes of war on which future generations relied. It was the "undisputed basis for the so-called Law of The Hague," the first international treaties governing warfare.[11] In the opinion of many a commentator, not the least of whom was Frederic de Martens, the eminent nineteenth-century practitioner of international law after whom the Martens clause of the Geneva Conventions is named, it is a testimony to political conscience because of its careful calculation of the appropriate balance of humanity and brutality in war. It was first time in modern history that the laws of war codified the behavior, expectations, and obligations of all parties to the conflict. Significantly, it did so in the midst of an extant conflict.

Not formally replaced in the United States until 1956, General Orders 100 is taken by scholars of the laws of war to have done "away with the wide range of uncertainties and misunderstandings which at the time still governed relations between belligerents and which continued to provoke endless quarrels."[12] The correspondence between the commanding Union General Henry Wager Halleck, who authorized Lieber to undertake this project, and Lieber is filled with expressions of frustration regarding the minimal scholarship on the laws of war and the difficulties of answering how the Confederate soldiers were to be categorized and, consequently, how they were to be treated. Were they to be identified and treated as legitimate combatants of a contesting sovereign state or as seditious citizens subordinate to the permanent union of the United States? The debate over the exact relationship of the Confederacy to the Union was, in many senses, not dissimilar to the debate over the relationship of the Indians to the United States. Were each (the Indian tribes and the Confederacy) independent sovereign entities, with legitimate governance, engaged in sovereign wars? Or were they simply insurrectionists with no corresponding rights or recognition as belligerents? As the commissioner of Indian Affairs argued in 1862, it was debatable whether the Indian tribes were "quasi-independent nations" or, rather, lacking any "elements of nationality."[13]

Lieber previously had addressed questions of combatancy in his earlier treatise, *Guerilla Parties, Considered with Reference to the Law and Usages of War.* In this treatise, he recognizes that the institution of rules of combatancy is but an initial attempt to sort out, in this order, (1) combatants from all others; (2) combatants from all citizens, armed or unarmed; and (3) formal combatants from the myriad of other combatants (e.g., guerrillas, partisans, irregulars, and rebels). Guerrillas, partisans, and irregulars complicated combatancy because none fought according to the classic ideals but, instead, fought, according to Union and Confederate officers, like "the uncivilized Indian."[14] Moreover, it was common during the American Civil War for the irregulars of both sides to dress in the uniform of the other—or in no uniform at all. As one soldier wrote home, "I hate their [the guerrillas] getting the [Union] clothing worst of all for now we cannot tell them from our own men."[15] A Union commander rued that it was "impossible to come to grips with the guerrillas while protecting the civilians" because the two were blended into one.[16]

In General Orders 100, Lieber unequivocally states that those who fight in the uniforms of their enemies can expect no quarter, that the use of the enemy standard for deceptive purposes was perfidy, and that, those who engage in perfidy can expect no quarter. His laws of war do allow ruses and deceptions, however, and, although deceptions or ruses do not include passing as an unarmed citizen or wearing the uniform of the enemy, the mere admittance of these acts intensifies the uncertainty of the distinction between who may be killed and who may not be killed.

In General Orders 100, he repeats what eventually became the standard of identification for combatants—uniforms and arms. He even includes partisans in this standard. But he is still unable to come up with a means for distinguishing among unarmed citizens, and he was not so naïve as to claim that these unarmed citizens were either harmless or immediately identifiable. For example, sparing an "unarmed citizen," whom the soldier hopes will be one and the same as an "inoffensive citizen," poses a risk. This risk arises from the fact, as Grotius also pointed out, that "the citizen or native of [a] hostile country" is also an enemy and, as a result, even though unarmed may not be inoffensive.[17]

Therefore, Lieber argues that unarmed citizens must themselves be classified according to loyalty. Unarmed citizens can be loyal, disloyal ("known to sympathize without positively aiding"), or manifestly disloyal (giving "positive aid and comfort to the rebellious enemy").[18] Each class of unarmed citizens indicates the threat posed and dictates the appropriate response, with the full burdens of war thrown on the manifestly disloyal. Note, however, that the last two categories (the disloyal and the manifestly disloyal) come perilously close to undermining the conjunction of inoffensive and unarmed that was the initial premise; after all, one can be manifestly disloyal and not bear arms. Put another way, an unarmed citizen may be offensive, aiding and abetting the enemy in a way that poses a serious risk. Crucially, it is loyalty, and not arms bearing, that serves as the authoritative pivot on which the distinction turns. Consequently, an external sign (arms bearing) functions only insofar as the internal sentiment (loyalty) does not contradict. Indeed, it is not the arms one bears but the sentiment one carries that truly distinguishes combatant from civilian.

Let me restate this because it resonates with the struggles of past publicists to determine and justify the distinction of combatant and civilian. According to Lieber, the dictates of civilization demand the distinction between the combatant and all others, and although this distinction is indicated by the bearing of arms, one can never be certain that the unarmed civilian is, in fact, inoffensive; this civilian is also already an enemy, who may be giving "positive aid and comfort" to the armed enemy.[19] Furthermore, it is not a binary that he establishes (hypostasized categories of combatant vs. civilian) but a ternary one.

Consequently, Lieber concludes that the treatment of "inoffensive individuals" must be assessed in reference to the "overruling demands of a vigorous war" and should be practiced only insofar as the "exigencies of war will admit."[20] Thus, although he may have resolved one element of the distinction through the protocol of uniforms and arms, he was aware he did not do so fully. Lieber turns to the honor and discipline of the soldier to distinguish himself as a civilized man by identifying himself as a combatant, restraining the exigencies of war, and recognizing the demands of a vigorous war are to be gravely considered.

* * *

Lieber, shaken by the ferocity of the Civil War (his eldest son fought and died for the Confederacy, and another son was badly wounded serving the Union), imagined the code as a public code of moral and legal restraint that would prevent the excesses of violence threatening to undermine the righteousness of the war. For Lieber, an emphasis on discipline and a deference to authority could guarantee the proper progression of violence.[21] But Lieber did not hesitate to commend the strategic and necessary use of violence. In fact, he is one of the first authors to define exactly what is allowed under the rubric of military necessity—and, contrary to those who venerate him, it was considerable. He writes, "War admits of all direct destruction of life or limb of armed enemies and of other persons whose destruction is incidentally unavoidable....it allows the capturing of every armed enemy and every enemy of importance....it allows of all destruction of property...of withholding sustenance or means of life from the enemy."[22] In reading this, it is difficult to imagine how considerations of humanity are entered into the calibration of war; it would appear that Lieber accords the greatest worth to military necessity. Certainly, his correspondence with General Halleck evinces a thorough immersion in the details of the progress of the war and a keen desire to influence its success through the promulgation of law and policies decisively responding to the guerrilla sorties Halleck experienced as a commander. As a result, the code was, to say the least, "loosely framed"; it allowed a great degree of destruction and devastation.[23] In Lieber's own rather unfortunate description, it was "our little pamphlet...short but pregnant and weighty like some stumpy Dutch woman when in the family way coming with twins."[24]

Much like Machiavelli, Lieber was well aware of the perils of cruel deeds done poorly, proclaiming that "men who take up arms against one another...do not cease on this account to be moral beings, responsible to one another and to God." Military necessity, he continues, does not "admit of cruelty" merely for the sake of cruelty. Lieber's code depends on the moral strength of combatants to abide by the code, exercise careful discrimination, and be prudent in their use of violence. What is the source of this crucial moral strength that sheds the excesses of violence from its practice? From where does it arise?

For Lieber, as for many of his time, the source was the "principles of justice, honor, and humanity" to be found in their fullest expression in the men of civilized nations.[25] Like his chivalric predecessors, the soldier possessed a sense of honor that was as masculine as it was civilized. As one scholar of the Civil War writes, the "fear of personal dishonor, so rooted in social constructions of masculinity and in American culture, provided the motivation and much of the discipline of Civil War armies."[26] Another historian points out that white Southern men's capacity for honor was immediately linked to their "ability to exercise authority over others," most specifically his designated subordinates, "women, children, and African Americans, whether or not he owned slaves."[27] White Northern men were more inclined to valorize mobility and liberty and, consequently, identified slavery as a "blighting curse" on their honor.[28] For black men, not surprisingly, honor was to be found in self-governance, agency, and equality in treatment, to be gained through fighting in their own defense and for their own freedom. Although these permutations of honor are essential insights, the locus of honor still rests on discourses of gender, precisely as expressed through contests over the composition of a proper masculinity and the exalted ideal of the patriarchal family whose sanctity was protected by the magnificence of its men.[29] This honor was forged through conduct defined by of the priorities of civilization and civilized warfare, disciplined by the laws of war, and dependent on standards constitutive of good men. As Michael Fellman points out, as much as "proper Christian gentry leaders hated the…brutality of the guerrillas…but they also found them useful."[30] They found the brutality useful because it helped to confirm the righteousness of the Union cause by delineating the civilized belligerents (Union) from the uncivilized (Confederate). Thus, even though the soldiers of the Confederacy were awarded the rights of belligerency, the means by which they fought—namely guerrilla strategies—gave the Union cause to term them uncivilized and, in turn, use such uncivilized methods of warfare when needed.

Discourses of gender and civilization are most prominent in the reliance on masculine honor to uphold and enact the distinction (to refrain from perfidy and to discriminate among enemies), but are evident as well as in the repeated return of the code to "women and children" and "especially women and children" to categorize and identify unarmed and inoffensive citizens. Ironically, although the code codifies such categories, the practice during the American Civil War brought clearly to the fore the fact that neither uniform wearing nor arms bearing was a neutral distinction because women who fought during the war did so disguised as men—with the "beardless boy a universal favorite."[31]

It is somewhat puzzling that General Orders 100 draws on such a strong faith in those elements of chivalry, considering that only years earlier Lieber wrote, "if we ever we have civil strife, it will be the Middle Ages minus chivalry, little regard as I have even for that."[32] Perhaps he found nothing else to sustain his code and so he returned to the honor of men as the one source of justice and humanity that might withstand the force of necessity. As he intimates in the General Orders 100, the unarmed have little else to rely on than the honor of the combatant to check "the power of [the soldier's] arms." Yet Lieber also acknowledges that the laws and practice of war impose "many limitations and restrictions on principles of justice, faith, and honor" and that regretfully even these virtues are no promise.[33]

This was the exact critique forwarded by James Seddon, the Confederate Secretary of War. He wrote that, this code was "so vague" as to "justify conduct correspondent with the warfare of the barbarous hordes who overran the Roman Empire."[34] The Confederates dismissed the code as a mere legitimation of Union strategies, "mischief" made "code," and common soldiers seemed to know little of its existence.[35] This does not mean Lieber's code was insignificant—not at all. Its significance arises from its reflection on and constitution of the politics of distinguishing between combatant and civilian and, in turn, the justifications for the use of this distinction. If General Orders 100 invokes gender and civilization to serve the distinction in ways familiar from the past, the referents of *innocence* now also include loyalty as well as inoffensiveness or ignorance evident in prior uses.

* * *

During the Civil War, prominent Northern intellectuals actively deluged the public with speeches, sermons, letters, and manifestos describing the proper behavior for Union sympathizers. Furthermore, Lieber was himself a prominent spokesperson for the loyalists' publication societies that formed around the perceived need to draw together a sympathetic population, detail their proper comportment, and reward their unanimity. In Lieber's words, loyalty was "fidelity to one's homeland, as defined by geography, race and cultural tradition."[36] Moreover, as one historian writes, Lieber held that, once free institutions were established, "loyal citizens must resist all attempts to defy the laws and change the established order."[37] Considering his view that women should keep to matters of their sex and not stray into politics, specifically referring to suffrage, fidelity to one's homeland was also defined according to sex. As Lieber wrote to a colleague, "the woman must have her *proper* station: since different individuals, and more particularly, different sexes, are fitted to move in different spheres."[38] Moreover, during the war loyalty also came to connote not solely fidelity to one's homeland as defined by sex but also fidelity to one's sex. This point is significant because it helps us to better understand the logic and consequences of Sherman's March to the Sea. I contend that when discourses of gender and civilization articulate with that of loyalty, protection holds for those at its interstice.

Lieutenant General Ulysses S. Grant and Major General Sherman translated the Union public sentiment into a concentrated offensive against territories, armies, and individuals.[39] As General Halleck wrote to General Grant in March 1863, the "the character of war has very much changed within the last year. There is now no possible hope of reconciliation." The transformation in Union strategy was specifically designed to bring the war home to the civilian inhabitants of the South. "This may seem a hard species of warfare, but it brings the sad realities of war home to those who have been directly or indirectly instrumental in involving us in its attendant calamities."[40] Before this could be accomplished, however, a "shift in attitudes towards women" was required.[41]

Union militaries recognized that the civilians of the South were primarily women and children. Further, women and children were "especially" noncombatants, as dictated in General Orders 100. Even before the distribution of General Orders 100, Halleck had instructed his troops that "women and children, merchants, farmers, mechanics and all persons not in arms" must be spared.[42] (Observe how here, again, that women and children are a distinct category to be protected, separate from those of merchants and so on.) Moreover, paragraph 37 of General Orders 100 stated, "the United States acknowledge and protect, in hostile countries occupied by them, religion and morality; strictly private property, the persons of inhabitants, especially those of women; and the sacredness of domestic relations. Offenses to the contrary shall be rigorously punished."[43] This meant that warring against the inhabitants of the South, their private property and their persons, was in fact an offense against the code. Perhaps more crucially, Union soldiers were specifically enjoined against warring on women and children because such behavior was indicative of a barbarian people. Overall, warring against civilians and, thus, warring against women and children required special dispensation. This dispensation was granted through the construction of Southern women's culpability. As one historian states, Union acceptance of "the guilt of Southern women" was at the heart of this shift, facilitating the destruction of the South and its denizens.[44]

* * *

But exactly what were they guilty of? The answer to this question is complicated. First of all, by virtue of their support for the Confederate cause, these Southern women were guilty; the question of whether these women were bearing arms was immaterial. Writing in 1864, Captain Eugene Ware, a Union officer, commented, "The girls both North and South kept the soldiers feeling that their services were appreciated, and the boys in the ranks were bound that the girls should not be disappointed; and so, the war was long and severe. And the girls helped fight it."[45] What made Southern women's support so distasteful to Northerners, however, stemmed from their vehement public displays of this support—displays that betrayed women's customary modesty and decorum. In particular, their condemnation of the Union identified Southern women as manifestly disloyal to the Union and to their sex. As one writer at the time put it, "this [Southern] species of patriotism would not, even in barbarous times, have been considered appropriate in our sex."[46] Moreover, Southern ladies' treatment of slaves, slave women and children in particular, shocked and disgusted Union soldiers, further cementing the belief that Southern ladies were not ladies at all.[47]

Southern and Northern travelers and soldiers alike commented on Confederate women's anger, which was so disruptive and alien to the dominant discourse of gender, likening it to "flagrant prostitution."[48] This was no mere description; displays of insubordination or recalcitrance on the part of Southern women were legally codified as akin to prostitution. Indeed, in April 1862 General Benjamin Butler, having captured the largest city of the South, established martial law.

Once instituted, "there was no uncivil treatment received by our soldiers except from the upper class of women."[49] In response, Butler issued General Orders 28:

> As the officers and soldiers of the United States have been subject to repeated insults from the women (calling themselves ladies) of New Orleans, in return for the most scrupulous non interference and courtesy on our part, it is ordered hereafter that when any female shall, by word, gesture or movement, insult or show contempt for any officer or soldier of the United States she shall be regarded and held liable to be treated as a woman of the town plying her avocation.[50]

The phrase "plying her avocation" was drawn directly from the licenses granted to prostitutes by the Union army. Butler very effectively and, as it turned out, very successfully manipulated white Southern women's desire to be recognized according to their class and status in the community—to be accorded the dignity of ladies, not the familiarity of prostitutes. Ironically, in issuing this order, so effective in its formulation as to "execute itself," Butler caused a national and an international outcry.[51] Britain, which was attempting to remain neutral during the American Civil War, was sufficiently excised over the content of General Orders 28 to send a diplomatic message to the Union expressing "rebuke" and emphasizing that no such infamous act would be found in the history of "civilized nations."[52] Even President Lincoln's secretary of state worried that it could lead to soldiers' "having their way" with women, and in this the Confederacy did not disagree.[53] The Confederate Congress passed a resolution concerning the war in 1863, decrying "the conduct of the enemy has been destitute of that forbearance and magnanimity which civilization and Christianity have introduced to mitigate the asperities of war....helpless women have been exposed to the most cruel outrages and to that dishonor which is infinitely worse than death."[54] In the Confederacy, "Beast Butler" was vilified for his outrage on Confederate white women and the slur on their virtue. Jefferson Davis priced the head of Butler at 10,000 Confederate dollars.

Southern women's resistance to the occupation was equated with loose morals, wanton behavior, and public prostitution—all anathema to a society, both Confederate and Union, that created both the cult of true womanhood and the image of republican motherhood. The slur against Confederate women challenged Confederate men to restrain and retrain their women—to keep them off the streets.[55] As prostitutes, "hell cats who goaded half-crazed men," the women of the South were believed to be "more intensely bitter and malignant" than Southern men.[56]

Southern women were described by Northern presses as the "true warmongers of the Confederacy," and as "Eves goading their men for the fall...[with their] savage appetite...for secession and bloodshed."[57] Confederate women were described by no less than Elizabeth Cady Stanton, the renowned suffragette, as bowing to "mere pride of race and class" and were accused of "promoting war against the union."[58] By "showing their hatred of Federal soldiers," they imitated Lady Macbeth and "unsexed themselves."[59] As one Union soldier noted, "the *ladies* of the place allow no opportunity to pass, to insult our soldiers, and our flag....if I had the managing of the place I would burn the town....you women keep up this war. We are fighting you."[60] The presumptive civilian—the Southern white plantation woman—had become, as one Northern paper so vividly phrased it, a "venomous Southern virago...a female hyena."[61] No longer passive and apolitical but now public participants, these women were no longer guaranteed protection from the burdens of war. No longer acting their sex, warring against them was allowed.[62]

The conduct of Sherman's March to the Sea was conceivable and allowable when framed within this corruption of codes of gender.[63] As Halleck wrote to Sherman, "the conduct of the enemy, and especially of noncombatants and women," required "severe rules of war."[64] Emmerich de Vattel, influential scholar of the laws of war, writes, "if women wish to be spared they must keep to the duties of their sex" and refrain from war.[65] Halleck held that if "females so far forget...their sex as to take up arms, or to incite others to do so, they are no longer exempted from the rights of war, although always within the rules of humanity, honour, and chivalry."[66] Halleck's expansion on de Vattel further defines the duty of the female sex to not even voice an opinion but with "only charity and meekness...serve."[67] If women take up duties beyond their sex, stray outside their home and families, quite literally take to the streets, they will be treated as one who works the streets or, just as Gentili held, they will "cease to be women"—which, in the nineteenth century, "according to our Northern Creed," meant that "she becomes nothing or worse than nothing."[68] Thus, Sherman's march on Atlanta was militarily and morally conceivable because Southern women had, in the minds of the Union commanders, relinquished the protections owed their sex by not acting their sex. Indeed, the author of General Orders 100 was vehemently opposed to women's participating in public and in politics, writing that such participation would surely "unwoman her and her essential character...would be lost."[69]

Considering that women who betray their sex are no longer treated in accordance with their sex, sex differences can remain foundational for the distinction of combatant and civilian—women can be as easily dispatched as men when acting against their sex or, through their actions, becoming desexed. Thus, it is easy to see how General Sherman and Francis Lieber could at the same time identify women as "especially" civilians and hold, respectively, that for "the petulant and persistent secessionist, why, death is mercy and the quicker he or she is disposed the better" and that "the law of war, like the criminal law regarding other offenses, make no difference on account of the difference of sexes concerning the spy, the war traitor or the war rebel."[70]

* * *

Bearing this in mind, let us bring our attention to the conventional identification of Sherman's march to Atlanta as a turn toward total war. It is important to recognize the balance in my description: insofar as Sherman's march *did* result in widespread devastation and destruction, the burden of which fell on women, children, and those too disabled or debilitated to fight, his march did *not* result in atrocities or massacres of women and children. Thus, the discourses of gender that allowed for such devastation and destruction still prevented outright atrocities against white plantation women. Instead, General Sherman and his soldiers restricted their physical violence to the property of the planter class and moderated the actions taken in response to measures of loyalty among regional and state populations (e.g., South Carolina, the first state to secede, bore the greatest brunt of the violence). Certainly, they did deliberately destroy the infrastructure of the South on which primarily white women and children and the remaining male and female slaves depended for their economic and daily survival. But the Union soldiers did not massacre the women and children of the South. Joseph Glatthaar writes that not only did the Union army treat the civilians it encountered well but also that three Confederate generals left their wives in Sherman's care. What is more, it was well known that marriages between Southern women and Northern men occurred.[71]

The shift to hard war can be explained through an analysis of the articulation of discourses of gender and civilization, focusing on the discursive construction of the appropriate comportment for women. In addition, the discourses of gender and civilization also produced appropriate comportment for white men, whereby (as we have seen in the medieval codes, as well as the writings of Vitoria, Grotius, and Gentili) becoming a man—and, significantly, an honorable and civilized man—depended on the exercise of restraint. Furthermore, not only did the discourses of gender distinguish combatant from civilian, but the *valuing* of (particular) women in both the nineteenth and twentieth centuries demarcated the difference between civilized people and barbarians, and good men from all others. The moderation, control, and limitation of violence in the midst of a destructive war was much lauded as evidence of the self-mastery and true masculinity of Northern soldiers, in contrast to their effeminate Southern counterparts.

Although one Confederate observer inveighed, "the military authorities of the North seem to suppose that better success would attend a savage war, in which no quarter was to be given and no age or sex spared, than had hitherto been se-cured to such hostilities as are alone recognized to be lawful by civilized men in modern times," it was to little effect.[72] Sherman affectionately noted to General Halleck when discussing the occupation of Savannah, "A little loose in their for-aging, they did some things they ought not have done…yet, the behavior of our troops…has been so manly, so quiet, so perfect that I take it as the best evidence of true discipline and courage."[73]

When discourses of civilization and gender articulated, protection held. Yet discourses of gender also differentiated sufficiently that not all women were protected. Although the targeting of white women's property, livelihood, and families was deemed appropriate, and certainly Butler's order heightened the atmosphere of sexual and physical threat, there are few indications that white women were directly killed or physically violated. Black women were. Histori-cally, black women suffered great physical and sexual abuse throughout slavery, and this pattern was not noticeably interrupted in the chaos of the American Civil War. During General John Pope's occupation of Culpeper County, Virginia, "acts of the most beastly and infamous character were to have been perpetrated by Union soldiers against slave women."[74] In the wholesale destruction of Co-lumbia, it was black women who were "stripped, raped, and killed."[75] This prac-tice was not restricted to the Union military; Southern men, refining their slavery practices, specifically raped black women to "punish every black son of a bitch that they could find that had ever fought against them."[76] And, although this may seem a comparatively minor point, yeoman white women were often the targets of greater physical insults and violations than the white plantation women who were known by Union soldiers to be the most vocal of them all.

This differentiation in recognition and protection should not surprise us. After all, as we have seen, the laws of war descended from chivalric codes that differentiated among women as well, as did the earliest expressions of canon law. Recognizing this continued power of discourses of civilization and their inheri-tance from canon law, let us now examine the Sand Creek Massacre—an event in which neither Christianity nor civilization was sufficient to protect unarmed Indians—men, women, and children alike.[77]

* * *

Like the Confederates, the Indians in the United States were engaged in a strug-gle against the sovereign reach of the U.S. government. In earlier centuries, the Indians were granted recognition as a distinct, if different, sovereign entity encompassed within the sovereignty of the United States. Similar to Vitoria's un-derstanding of the American Indians, President Thomas Jefferson stated in 1792 that by the law of nations the Indians possessed the right of soil or occupancy.

But, although the Indian nations were characterized as equivalent, they were not yet equal to the United States. The 1831 decision of the U.S. Supreme Court on the right of the United States to implement the Indian Removal Act (which deported all the remaining Indians to west of the Mississippi River) exemplified this subordinate status.

President Andrew Jackson argued that the Indians must be moved for their own benefit, to save their own people and to "grow to be our equals in privileges, civil and religious."[78] Echoing the logic of the Requirement, the Indian Removal Act stated that Indian refusal would "necessarily entail destruction upon their race."[79] The Cherokee, who were one of the Five Civilized Tribes recognized by the United States, challenged the legality of this act, questioning why they should "be compelled by a civilized and Christian people" to leave their homes and land, relinquishing their sovereign, independent status that had hitherto been recognized.[80]

Ruling on their case, Chief Justice John Marshall spoke for the majority: the Indians were "domestic, dependent nation" and "wards" of the United States.[81] In effect, as with the American Indians centuries earlier, the Indians of the United States were legally and formally denied full sovereignty, and the war against them followed accordingly. In his travels in the 1830s, Alexis de Tocqueville noted that the conduct of the United States toward the Indians "was inspired by the most chaste affection for legal formalities" and it was nigh "impossible to destroy men with more respect for the laws of humanity."[82]

Thus, it is incorrect to argue that the customs and laws of war were not applicable to the U.S.-Indian wars because the right of the Indians to make war was acknowledged. Rather, as Vitoria first noted, the appropriate question was to what degree these laws could be applicable in a war against a foe at once dependent and dangerous—to be treated in "guardianship like a child" and as "maniacs or wild beasts"—who was at once like but less than his opponents.[83] Certainly, dominant perceptions of the Indians held them to be both inferior in every way, suffering from a "natural want of intellect," and like animals, "wild by nature."[84]

Discourses of civilization did distinguish the conduct of the U.S.-Indian war from that of the American Civil War. And just as the appropriate treatment of the Confederates was debated, so too was the appropriate treatment of the Indians. The death of over two hundred Cheyenne and Arapaho Indians at Sand Creek in November 29, 1864, was not the result of a unanimous advocacy of extermination. On the contrary, the country and its leaders were divided as to the best course of practice. The military officers in charge of waging wars varied in their appraisal of the Indians as equal belligerents deserving of respect or as rapacious criminals deserving of nothing less than devastation. If the Indians were not all "incorrigible savages," the "rules of civilized warfare" were applicable. Nevertheless, the argument went, these rules might "have to [be] modif[ied] in their application according to the character of the enemy."[85] Or, put more starkly by Governor John Evans of Colorado, "any man who kills a hostile Indian is a patriot."[86]

In the absence of unified military and public policy, these varying opinions were influential, if not diametrically opposed, for each was found in the ruling heuristic of Christianity and civilization. Indeed, the belief of the time was that it would never be possible to civilize the tribes unless they were first Christianized. In the end, the discussion focused primarily on the degree of military force necessary to convince the Indians that their salvation lay in their submission.[87] The committee formed to assess the state of Indian affairs concluded, "If the savage resists, civilization with the Ten Commandments in one hand and the sword in the other demands his immediate extermination."[88] Thus civilization and Christianity remained intimately bound to the purpose and practice of warfare, and as we have seen with the Requirement and the Crusades, wars for Christianity and for civilization were not necessarily fought as Christian civilized wars. In this sense, civilization and Christianity remained a gift given to the Indian— "civilization is in a most important sense a gift, rather than an acquisition"— which was to immunize them from the ravages of war, much as the Requirement was said to do for their forefathers.[89]

The polyvalent dimensions of civilization invoked—of civilized to savage, of civilized warfare against the warfare of savages, and of civilized men against savages—censured the military while simultaneously upholding the differences between civilized Christian men and the savages they desired to mutilate. Indians could not remain "bloodthirsty" savages if they were both like and unlike the settlers who sought their removal. The line of demarcation between the Indians and the settlers was therefore never absolute, and it was made all the more precarious by the practices of the federal militaries, which all too often reflected the (caricatured) image of the savage Indian rather than of the civilized settler.[90] The massacres of the Indians obliterated the distinction of civilization, the difference that putatively governed the right and obligation of the United States to exterminate or acculturate the Indians.

The disgust inspired by the Confederate bushwhackers testifies to the pride that the Union and the regular Confederate armies took in their conduct as members of a particular class of civilized Christian men. In fact, one scholar argues that a reason Confederates resisted incorporating guerrilla warfare into their own tactics was the fear that it would "turn the social order on its head by making coarse and uncivilized back country whites the leading actors in the drama."[91] But, as another scholar describes, it was also the association with Indians that made guerrilla warfare such a despicable and degraded strategy. One Union soldier vented, "the savage and brutal mode...waged by our enemies...is more barbarous than any waged by the savages who once inhabited this same country."[92] Still another opined, "they seemed determined not to carry on this war as civilized nations do, but in Indian fashion."[93] Thus, to employ such tactics was to further diminish the clarity of the hierarchical distinction between white men and Indians necessary to legitimize the forced removal and claims of superior dominion over the Indians.

Nevertheless, honorable restraint was not as uniformly valued in the wars against the American Indians as it was in the American Civil War, unless its absence denigrated the honor of the combatants. In 1862, General Henry Sibley ordered his men after a massacre to desist from mutilating Indian corpses, saying, "even savage enemies shall not be subjected to indignities by civilized and Christian men."[94] The U.S. Joint Select Committee on the Conduct of War wrote in response to the Sand Creek Massacre, "Wearing the uniform of the United States, which should be the emblem of justice and humanity [Colonel Chivington]...executed a foul and dastardly massacre which would have disgraced the veriest savage among them who were victims of his cruelty."[95] Thus, the permissibility of particular actions had more to do with upholding the honor of and difference of the white settler than it did with treating the Indians as honorable foes, equal belligerents, or fellow humans.[96]

In contrast, during the Civil War there is repeated mention of the great pride and honor taken by the Confederates and the Unionists in fighting a civilized war for civilization. In their letters and other writings, soldiers on both sides revealed that they considered the war a "Christian crusade of the 19th century."[97] In fact, as both Drew Gilpin Faust and Chandra Manning make clear, the meaning of fighting and dying for the Union cause was specifically and clearly found in a redemption narrative—one that included the liberation of those enslaved but also individual soldiers' Christian atonement.[98] There was no parallel redemption narrative in the war against the Indians.

Federal militaries organized against the Indians with the intent of forcibly bringing civilization to the savages or killing them to avoid contaminating civilization. The latter is a particularly interesting justification because it mimicked the argument of Confederacy as to why slavery must be upheld—abolition "worked like an infection."[99] Nevertheless, the broader discussion of liberty, honor, and freedom is difficult to find; the noble sentiments and passions that inspired Confederate and Union men to fight against one another are absent in the writings of those who waged war against the Indians. Noticeable, instead, is an almost rueful recognition of the brutality and injustice of their acts, a sentiment that did little to slow their course. Still, the concern with protecting their women and children, which was so apparent in the writings of Confederate and Union soldiers, did appear to directly influence the U.S. soldiers of the Indian wars and to lead them to choose revenge over redemption. For example, one officer pleaded in 1865 to be allowed to retaliate for the death of innocent white women and children: "the blood of the innocent and unoffending martyrs cries aloud for vengeance."[100] He was so allowed. Discourses of gender acted not to protect all women but to facilitate the choosing of which women and children were to be spared. In part, this is because discourses of civilization triumphed.

To understand why this is true, consider the Sand Creek Massacre. In November 1864, Colonel Chivington, an active abolitionist, preacher, and Union commander, attacked a Cheyenne village with a newly raised regiment of mostly volunteers and some professional soldiers. In his initial dispatch to headquarters, Chivington noted that his soldiers "all did nobly" and that he would continue to "catch some more" Indians.[101] By all accounts, Chivington was seeking greater political acclaim (a possible congressional seat once Colorado became a state) and angling for another military commission (he had acquitted himself marvelously in an early sortie against the Confederacy), and he believed success as Indian fighter might clinch his chances for both. He had sorely misjudged.

Congress instructed its Committee on the Conduct of War (CCW) to investigate the attack after hearing of its atrocity—one of two investigations authorized by Congress; a third was authorized by a military commission. The CCW was authorized in 1861 to review all aspects of Union military affairs, but its existence was controversial and its effect on the policies and practice of war was inconsistent. The CCW described its duty as "endeavoring to obtain such information in respect to the conduct of the war as would best enable them [the committee] to advise what mistakes had been made in the past and the proper course to be pursued in the future."[102] In this case, the CCW contribution was to publicize and document the massacre. As more information became public, it was made known that the Cheyenne and Arapaho band, following instructions of Governor John Evans of Colorado, had presented itself to the U.S. military at Fort Lyon as a friendly tribe seeking protection. In his proclamation of June 1864, Evans had promised that all Indians who turned themselves in would be given protection and recognized as loyal to the Union. The proclamation was addressed to those Indians who "have gone to war with the white people.... the Great Father is angry and will certainly hunt them out and punish them. But he does not want to injure those who remain friendly to the whites. He desires to protect and take care of them.... [But] the war on hostile Indians will be continued until they are all effectually subdued."[103] Suffice it to say, that this exchange of mercy, of protection and life, for subordination and surrender was offered on terms most generous to the militarily superior force and the white settlers.

Although very few bands were able to avail themselves of the terms of the proclamation (written in English and posted or read aloud by those Indian agents, interpreters, or traders who came into casual contact with the Indians), it was only two months before the offer was suspended. In August, Evans changed his mind and exhorted "all citizens...to kill and destroy...wherever they may be found, all such hostile Indians."[104]

The chiefs among the southern bands of Cheyenne and Arapaho had proven themselves to be loyal to the United States, upholding the terms of the treaty even when it was violated by incoming settlers, and had expressed their continuing desire to live in peace. It did not matter. The policy of 1864 was to fire first and distinguish later, while sufficiently detailed news of Indian attacks and depredations (albeit made in retaliation for wholesale attacks on peaceful villages and the murder of their chiefs by Colorado volunteers who would "kill anything in the shape of an Indian") made it appear to many a wise policy.[105] After all, how could you tell who was loyal among all the Indians when even the "squaws" were hard to identify? As Chivington preached, the only way to deal properly with the Indians was to "kill and scalp all, little and big" for "nits make lice."[106] General Sherman advised, "We must try and distinguish friendly from hostile and kill the latter...[but] it seems impossible to tell the true from the false....we cannot discriminate—they all look alike and to get the rascals, we are forced to include all."[107]

It was in this atmosphere of vitriol and "no gentle hand" that the Cheyenne and Arapaho band, led by Chief Black Kettle, did as initially requested—they essentially surrendered, becoming wards of the U.S. military under the protection of the U.S. flag.[108] But, at the behest of Evans, Chivington, and others—General Samuel Curtis, commander of the Department of Kansas, wished there to be "no peace till the Indians suffer more"—all promises were negated.[109] The commanders at the fort first disarmed the warriors of the tribe, but later returned the weapons, deciding that this tribe "could make but a feeble fight" if any at all, and sent the tribe to Sand Creek to await further command.[110]

Before launching the raid against the peaceable Indians massed at Sandy Creek, Chivington was confronted by two of his officers, who protested the imminent attack. Both Lieutenants Cramer and Anthony, later joined by others, argued that such an attack was a violation of the code of honor among combatants, especially as the Indians had been promised the protection of the military and, in situations past, had protected the lives of many of the officers gathered. These individuals attempted to invoke the terms of honor, the very same by which the Union military and Chivington conceptualized their own actions, to argue against the pursuit of the Indians.

Chivington was not convinced, responding to the threat of insubordination by declaring it "right and honorable to use any means under God's heaven to kill

Indians who kill and torture women and children."[111] For Chivington, the honor of men was the honor of civilized men, as so defined at the time, and civilized men revenged the murders of their women even if it required the massacre of other women. As one regiment volunteer wrote in defense of the attack, "we are men who proved our manhood by going out in defense of all we hold dear."[112] Furthermore, to defend the cause of the Indians was to be open to the charges of effeminacy, of "lacking masculine qualities of toughness and sound judgment" and being "soft-headed and emotional"—in short, of being an Indian lover, a disparaging term coined by General Sherman himself.[113] Indeed, Chivington rebutted any objections with the invective "damn any man that was in sympathy with Indians."[114]

Chivington called on the discourses of gender that also functioned so powerfully during the American Civil War to goad his men to battle. Here, it did not matter whether the actual Indians gathered were directly culpable in this crime (and from all investigations, it appears that the tribes that could be legitimately held accountable for warmongering were camped nearby), nor did loyalty to the Union or to peace seem to figure; it was sufficient that they were Indians. Indeed, the collection of unarmed peaceable tribes, composed in the main of women and children, would, by all other accounts, fulfill the requirements of civilian status. Chivington feebly gestured toward the sanctity of women and children in exhorting his troops, but it was not the Indian women and children whom he sanctified. "I don't tell you to kill all ages and sex, but look back on the plains of the Platte, where your mothers, fathers, brothers, sisters have been slain, and their blood saturating the sands."[115] As demonstrated in the differential treatment of women (black, white, yeoman, and plantation) in the American Civil War, the discourses of gender worked to distinguish among women and children and not to uniformly protect them.

Warriors, women, and children alike pleaded for mercy, some running toward the soldiers with their hands "raised as if begging for us to spare them."[116] Male prisoners were not taken; the few soldiers who did attempt to take women and children prisoners—a fact that alone points out the practical gendering of the principle of distinction—were overridden by their compatriots, who "killed and scalped" and mutilated the prisoners.[117] The killing, mutilations, scalping, and raping continued after any chance of Indian resistance was possible. Children and babies were shot point-blank, and women were horribly "cut into all sorts of pieces."[118] Of particular note was the murder of Jack Smith, the half-breed son of one of the interpreters, as he was held prisoner by the Third Regiment, as well as the murders of Indian women and children in the following days. Morse Coffin, discomfited by the stories of the attack in which he had participated, writes, "It was not easy to distinguish the sexes during the fight [but] ... I also know that it was on purpose during that battle to kill old and young of both sex."[119]

Regardless of these atrocities, the next day a newspaper editorial reported a "thousand incidents of individual daring" were had and "the Colorado soldiers have again covered themselves with glory."[120] The "bloodless" Third Regiment had become the "bloody" Third. Even as time passed, those who disagreed with the description of the battle as a massacre swore that the Indians "were a bad lot. They all needed killing, and the more they were fed and taken care of the worse they became."[121]

* * *

No such massacres occurred in the Confederate South, not even in 1864 at the very pinnacle of the hard war led by Sherman against the civilians and culture of the South. Individual soldiers of the Third Regiment had argued against the Sand Creek Massacre by calling on the self-same elements of civilization and combatancy by which their compatriots recognized themselves. These officers were dismissed, overridden both by the specter of dead white women and children and the insistence by their superiors that the Indians lay somewhere beyond the bounds of civilized warfare.

The text of the CCW is extensive. The horror is evident in the testimonies given over a period of several months. But, noticeably, as the testimonies also make plain, it was also the consequences of the attack that were worthy of horror. Indeed, one officer clarified that he had disagreed with Chivington about the attacks not because he objected to the "killing of Indians, as a matter of principle" but because it was poor policy. This officer also carefully noted that, although the only way to fight Indians is to "kill the women and children," it was with the understanding that "we" consider this a "barbarous practice." Not only was it barbarous, but "none but a coward" would fight women and children.[122] The ire heaped on Chivington was stoked by the disgrace he brought to the claims of civilization. Criticisms of the attack focused not on the killing of friendly unarmed Indians but on the killing of friendly unarmed Indian women and children.[123] Sex and sex difference remain as the foundation of the principle of distinction (not, it would seem, the bearing of arms), while the principle of distinction can simultaneously remain as a hallmark of civilization *and* be jettisoned in wars of civilization for civilization—after all what facilitated this savage cruelty was this very imposition and importance of civilization.

Both of these wars challenged the sovereignty of the United States. Both the Indians and the Confederates had a similar official status, in that neither were formally considered equal belligerents in their entirety; nevertheless, the overall conduct of these wars was appreciably different. The Union conceived of the Confederates as brothers who had momentarily stressed familial bonds, whereas the Indians were considered to have no such ties. Succinctly phrased, the goal of

the war against the Indians was extermination, which overruled even the majority of attempts at conversion, whereas the goal of the war against the Confederates was defeat and preservation of the Union. "To Southerners, terror meant the
destruction of economic resources and of the will to resist; to Indians it more
often meant death."[124]

The Civil War was fought with an acceptance of the distinction between combatant and civilian, whereas the U.S.-Indian wars were fought without an equal
acceptance of this distinction. Throughout these first chapters, the influence of
discourses of gender and civilization on adherence to the laws of war has been
underscored. For example, when the protection and treatment of white women
is compared with that of black and Indian women—a continuum of respect and
protection that is marked by degrees of civilization—the protection of women
and children as de facto civilians is shown to have been highly variable according
to race and class. Even though, as General Grant wrote in 1862, Southern women
and children were "worse rebels than the soldiers who fight against us," the white
plantation Southern women and children were treated with the greatest respect
given to Southern women and children in general.[125]

Interestingly, the question of loyalty that was so crucial to the construction of
General Orders 100 and to the transformation in tactics of the American Civil
War did not arise with the same fervor in the U.S.-Indian wars, even though
there were Indians loyal to the Union or the Confederacy (President Lincoln did
acknowledge the fealty of the Indians to his cause). The gradations of loyalty that
Lieber imagined were necessary to distinguish among unarmed citizens proved
unnecessary in the U.S.-Indian wars because they were waged against a population that was barely (if at all) accepted as equal belligerents, much less denizens
of the state.

Nevertheless, even in the U.S.-Indian war, participants debated the practice
and strategies of war, signifying a general uncertainty about their permissibility and legitimacy, and denoting the constitutive character of the civilian. But,
because the principle of distinction is at once reflective and productive of a desired social order, its implementation in the war against the Indians was abysmal.
The Indians were outside civilization and outside the scope of the law. Formal
recognition of the rights of war for the American Indians, much as for the Indians in the seventeenth century, appeared to do little to affect compliance with
the principle of distinction because formal recognition needs to be buttressed
by social recognition of individuals, a recognition that includes being treated
as fair and equal belligerents, privy to the rights and obligations of war. Clearly,
this was extended to the Confederates in the American Civil War. And, although
the Southern partisans and guerrillas were considered to be different from the

formal Confederate military, this difference became a matter of policy only as the war wore on.

* * *

General Orders 100, the code of war developed during the American Civil War, was the blueprint for the international conferences on the laws of war. The U.S. experience of *internal* armed conflict laid the groundwork for the formulation of war *among* states in the international system. Despite this history, as we see in the next two chapters, the applicability of the modern laws of war, premised on General Orders 100, to internal armed conflicts was all but rejected. Delegates to the 1949 preparatory conferences deemed the sovereignty of states, which is inextricably bound to the emergence and codification of the laws of war, too sacred to be subjected to international regulation. Instead, as has been the theme here, the benefits and protections of the laws of war were extended as a courtesy *of* civilized states *to* civilized states. General Orders 100 did not even provide a stable foundation for the distinction between combatant and civilian because it was based on a continuum of loyalty and, in fact, codified the principle that the "more vigorously wars are pursued, the better it is for humanity. Sharp wars are brief."[126]

THE 1899 MARTENS CLAUSE AND
THE 1949 IV GENEVA CONVENTION

Honor is a moral and social quality. The right to respect for his honor is a right invested in man because he is endowed with a reason and a conscience.

—Oscar Uhler and Henri Coursier, *Commentary on the IV Geneva Convention*

Although the particular purpose of the 1949 Geneva Convention was to rectify, in light of the past world wars, the neglect of the situation and status of the civilian in the laws of war, perhaps its avowed model, General Orders 100, was the wrong place to start.

Only after the express horrors of World War II did the international community willingly consider definite provisions for the protection of civilians. Recollect that, although *civilian* entered into common parlance (as a nonmilitary man or official) in the nineteenth century, it is not until the 1949 IV Geneva Convention that the category civilian is first formally introduced.

Until this juncture the formal laws of war, primarily the 1899, 1907, and 1929 Hague conventions, said very little about the definition, much less protection, of the civilian because the protections and standards of civilization were said to be sufficient— at least for wars conducted by the standardized armies among European states.[1]

The closest to codification these particular protections of civilization ever came was in the Martens clause. Should the formal laws of war prove incomplete, the authors of the 1899 Convention held that the expansive protections of the Martens clause would serve. Written by Frederic de Martens, an influential Russian lawyer and diplomat and a delegate to The Hague, the Martens clause conjures its "ancient antecedents in natural law and chivalry."[2] In its original formulation, the Martens clause held:

> Until a more complete code of the laws of war is issued, the High Contracting Parties think it right to declare that in cases not included in

the Regulations adopted by them, populations and belligerents remain under the protection and empire of the principles of international law as they result from the usages established between civilized nations, from the laws of humanity, and the requirements of the public conscience.[3]

The purpose of the 1899 Hague Conference, at which Martens introduced his clause, was to develop and codify to any extent possible the obligations of custom and law incumbent on civilized nations in times of war and, in particular, to limit the use and development of certain weapons of war. Significantly, it was the first conference not immediately proceeded by a war, and perhaps more significantly today, it remains one of the only conferences not immediately provoked by war.[4] Nevertheless, the failure to observe the Geneva Convention of 1864 during the Franco-Prussian War of the 1870s and the conduct of the Crimean War deeply disturbed prominent lawyers of the time. "A savagery unworthy of civilized nations" characterized the wars, betraying the hope that "undoubtedly civilized European nations" would conform as a matter of course with the laws of war.[5]

With the memories of these wars lingering, the Russian czar convened the 1899 Hague Conference to "humanize war, by which we mean that it must be regularized."[6] The significance of the regularization of war was twofold. First, wars must be made regular; that is, they must unfold as a predictable sequence of events, conforming to a particular pattern as practiced by professionals. Second, wars must be regulated. This required, much as the duels of old did,[7] precise standards of exchange and a clear choreography of engagement. If, as Maury D. Feld writes in regard to the seventeenth and eighteenth centuries, "the emergence of armed forces into their modern professionalized, disciplined form had the effect of transforming violence into a mode of order," then the atrocities of the past wars were catastrophic because they exposed the fragility of that order and the failure of discipline.[8] As was expressed by the delegates in attendance in 1899, warfare worthy of civilized nations was fighting governed and moderated by appropriate rules of engagement—rules that by the late nineteenth century included "the distinction between members of armed forces and civilians."[9] Gathered at the 1899 Conference, these men shared a considerable faith in the strength of the Martens clause. As one delegate vividly expressed it, warfare would hitherto be restricted "by the laws of the universal conscience, and no general would dare violate them for he would thereby place himself under the ban of civilized nations."[10] Furthermore, as another delegate proclaimed, among these civilized nations there was no "better watchman than the nation's honor. Let us believe it!"[11]

In other words, discourses of civilization not only identified the nations among whom these laws would arise and apply, but also identified the costs of their violation and the deterrents against it. The resonance of chivalric honor was also amplified in the writings of Francis Lieber, who fiercely defended honor and virtue as the distinguishing traits of civilized disciplined men. The echoes of this past clearly reverberate in the Martens clause as well. At each of those defining moments, the laws of war arose only from the uses established among civilized nations for both normative and strategic reasons. After all, it was only among civilized nations and men that the exercise of honor was in any way intelligible as a shared restraint. Considering the atrocities practiced by these same nations in wars of imperialism and colonialism, it makes perfect sense that no state would agree to be bound by those practices. As surveyed in the Martens clause, the laws of war were a means by which civilized nations and civilized men defined and defended their interests and identities.

Most delegates accepted the Martens clause as sufficient. In fact, many considered discussion of further regulations not only unnecessary but also insulting. Significantly, there was more to this sentiment than a desire to avoid being burdened unduly with regulations on weaponry and warfare. Rather, the delegates also interpreted the discussion of extensive protection during war or more detailed regulations as, for lack of a better word, unsporting.[12] Does the fact that the conference was convened, in light of the savagery of past wars, to address ways of preventing the recurrence of war and the escalation of its costs make these sentiments and faith all the more puzzling or all the more sensible? Perhaps both.

Indeed, no greater proof can be had of the dominance of these beliefs than the acceptance of Japan into the society of civilized states because of its conduct during the 1894–95 conflict with China. Gerrit Gong argues that the demonstration by Japan of its ability to "conform to the laws of war...in a manner worthy of the most civilized nations of Western Europe" guaranteed its inclusion into the vaunted society of civilized states.[13] But we should recognize that such conformance was by no means benign, as evidenced by the claim of one Japanese diplomat who wrote, "we show ourselves at least your equals in scientific butchery, and at once we are admitted to your table as civilized men."[14]

Note that this exchange allows us to observe, once again, the multiple effects of discourses of civilization. Discourses of civilization set boundaries, limits on to whom and among whom the laws of war apply. Yet discourses of civilization are also progressive and formative, as the case of Japan denotes. Japan distinguished itself as no longer barbarian by demonstrating its capacity and willingness to abide by the laws of war—although underscoring the performative contradiction of the distinction. Therefore, even as the discourses of civilization set and order an international hierarchy, they also expose the temporality of any such hierarchies.

In the discussion of the works of Vitoria and Grotius (see chap. 3), we have seen similar varying effects of the discourses of civilization. The discourses of civilization demarcate *static* differences, most frequently bounded by territorial distinctions. Yet they also denote *processes* of transformation—from barbarism to civilization—that immediately undermine the presumption of static or stable differences. Thus, for example, according to John Westlake, nineteenth-century legal scholar, the capacity of Japan to conduct itself in the war with China according to "western rules concerning war...presents a rare and interesting example of the passage of a state from the oriental to the European class"[15] (regardless or because of the publicized 1894 Japanese massacre of Chinese at Port Arthur?).

The tensions and ambiguities of discourses of civilization both set the limits of law (civilization vs. barbarism) and occasion the exercise of the law (from barbarism to civilization). Only individuals and nations that are defined as civilized are invested with the power to distinguish between combatants and civilians (see chaps. 2–3). Barbarians, by definition, lack the capacity to discriminate or to judge and, therefore, are unable to exercise this sovereign power. Consequently, as the Martens clause illustrates so well, the empire constructs the laws of war, especially the principle of distinction, and the barbarians are held to be (always already) in violation, regardless of actual practice. Indeed, what makes the final codification of the laws of war in 1977 so different from previous efforts is the widespread and vocal participation of previously colonized or "barbarian" entities. For the first time, "barbarians" dictated the laws of war.

* * *

The discourses of civilization fashioned boundaries. A perfect example of this is the way distinctions between civilized and barbarian, sovereign and savage, governed attendance at the 1899 Conference. Indeed, invitations to the conference were extended premised on these distinctions rather than on the possession of sovereignty. Consequently, no African nations were invited to the 1899 Conference, although six claimed sovereignty.[16]

This conscious, if unreflective, exclusion informed specific debates on the formulation of the laws with both a clear sense of the responsibilities of and affinities among these self-identified civilized nations and, in turn, the grand differences between themselves and, in the words of the British delegate, those "savages."[17] The (re)construction of a society of civilized states, readily identifiable in their pursuit and practice of international law, was a purposive and intentional goal of those gathered in 1899.[18] Considering that those nations gathered "controlled the resources and presided over the political destinies of three-fourths of the human race," the effects were substantial.[19] For instance, one of the major arguments expressed against limiting the use of the dum-dum bullet was voiced in these terms:

> In civilized war a soldier penetrated by a small projectile is wounded, with-draws to the ambulance, and does not advance any further. It is very different with a savage. Even though pierced two or three times, he does not cease to march forward does not call upon the hospital attendees, but continues on and before anyone has time to explain to him that he is flagrantly violating the decisions of the Hague Conference, he cuts off your head.[20]

In this view, the savage is not only physically but both psychologically and cognitively impervious to the dictates or demands of civilized war among civilized states. Subsequently, it was no fault of those civilized sovereign states that they were unable to include such savages within the realm of consideration and obligation. And, certainly, the conviction that the laws of war were necessarily suspended in colonial wars had already been well expressed in the 1894 text by Westlake, who held that "savages of half-civilised tribes" should be treated quite differently in combat.[21] Furthermore, in the United States, the ardent supporters of the 1899 Hague regulations were among those who most fervently advocated the torture and extermination of Filipinos during the Philippine-American War, accepting such extreme measures as the only possible response to the innate barbarism of the Filipinos.[22] As many have documented, in wars of barbarism few distinctions were made between those who fight and those who do not and temperance in war was found only within and among civilized states. To repeat, distinction is both the privilege and product of civilized states and sovereigns.

Although the barbarian was presumed to demarcate a clear opposite or absolute limit of civilization, the barbarian was, in fact, immanent to civilization. The barbarian was said to wage war unconstrained and without discipline; these were, in fact, some of the characteristics of barbarism. Yet, against the barbarian, civilized entities were allowed to wage a war unconstrained and without discipline. Consider the effects of this on the entire distinction between barbarian and civilized, which was believed to arise from the putative self-discipline, restraint, and moderation of civilized entities. Does this distinction disappear? Or was it simply never there? Answers to these questions underscore that the barbarian remained the constitutive outside, presupposed and prefigured by, civilization, a consistent theme in the development of the laws of war. To clarify, let us return to the impetus behind and origins of the 1899 Convention.

* * *

As indicated in the preamble to the 1899 Convention, the laws of war are animated by the "desire to serve, even in this case of war, the interests of humanity and the ever progressive needs of civilization." This formulation draws on the 1880 *Oxford Manual of the Institute of International Law* (one of the foundations of the 1899 Convention), which exhorts all "civilized nations to seek" a "positive set of rules" that do not hinder belligerents but "by preventing the unchaining of passions and savage instincts—which battle always awakens, as much as it awakens courage and manly virtues—it strengthens the discipline which is the strength of the armies."[23]

The laws of war qua laws produced civilization, just as conformance with these laws produced civilized men who had mastered the savage within. To their nineteenth-century authors, the laws of war were progressive and instructive— one manifestation of what Uday Mehta terms the "tutorial and pedagogic obsession" of empire.[24] As preoccupied as nineteenth-century Europe was with charting the stages of civilization, it is easy to see how the existence of and obedience to the laws of war became another marker of these stages. After all, the laws of war contributed to the ultimate intent of this grading. The intent was to identify collective and individual potential for progress and enlightenment, distinguish between those capable of self-rule and those to whom rule must be extended, and, subsequently, nominate European imperialism as a necessary and benevolent tutorial.[25]

Johann Bluntschli, an influential participant at the 1899 Conference, clearly argued for the laws of war as a progressive discipline of and for civilization. He was convinced that the laws of war refined "the fighting men's sensibilities so as to bring about those traits of character that were associated with civilized behavior."[26] Conformance with the laws of war distinguished individuals as restrained, moderate in their violence, making them "manly" men and distinguishing them from barbarians, who are "like children who allowed their passions to rule their behavior."[27] Almost a full century later, this argument was still compelling to some, such as John Keegan who writes, "A world without armies— disciplined, obedient, and law-abiding armies—would be uninhabitable. Armies of that quality are an instrument but also a mark of civilization, and without their existence mankind would have to reconcile itself either to life at a primitive level...or the lawless chaos of masses warring."[28]

What, then, does it mean to discipline? Foucault uses the concept discipline as a historical analytic to identify the elaboration (in the eighteenth century) of complex systems and tactics of power regimenting and producing selves and subjectivities. Specifically, he relies on military discipline as the paramount example of modern discipline. It formed and informed subjects both in the rote sense of regulation and repetition and in the productive sense of constituting a specific character. The laws of war discipline in this sense; they do not simply act to prohibit and restrain violence, but also to produce and train civilized men.[29]

As John Stuart Mill notes, well in advance of Sigmund Freud, "the first lesson of civilization [is] ...that of obedience."[30] This progressive and productive image of the laws of war as cultivating a civilized sensibility, the natural potential of men, permeated general writings on war.[31] Not unexpectedly, however, the natural potential of men was not considered the natural potential of *all* men. Just as with Vitoria, for whom all men possessed reason but not all men were equally reasonable, in the nineteenth century all men possessed the potential for civilization but not all men were equally civilized.

Recognizing the centrality of these distinctions and differences of civilization, it should come as no surprise that the author of the Martens clause also believed "that the peoples outside Europe were too uncivilized to meet the standards of his "'universalist' conception of international law."[32] This indicates that this clause, which now governs the interpretation and implementation of the laws of war, was premised on the nineteenth-century "intuition that restraint in warfare is an intrinsic part of European conscience."[33] Although we now recognize that the public conscience and principles of humanity to which Martens referred were those created and identified by the same European nations that unapologetically pursued brutal imperial rule and brutal imperial war, we have yet to reject the fundamental distinction of barbarism and civilization that informs the laws of war and still takes its referent from Europe. An echo of this nineteenth-century idea is heard in the words of Michael Ignatieff, who when describing the experiences of the ICRC in Sarajevo writes, "It was one thing to see the Geneva Conventions ignored in a non-European city, but to see how little their principles meant a few hours from Geneva was genuinely shocking."[34]

Acknowledging the influence of these discourses of civilization on the laws of war grants us an insight into contemporary arguments that stress the role of adulthood, specifically manhood and masculinity, in regulating war. After all, it is men who are disciplined by discourses of civilization and, in turn, it is men on whom the defense of civilization rests. To take a prominent example, Ignatieff writes, "in the manly bearing of many old Afghan warriors, or in the dignity of the Kurdish *pesh-merga,* there is a martial order that is also the proud vision of male identity." But the "particular savagery of war in the 1990s taps into another vision of male identity—the wild sexuality of the adolescent male."[35] Here Ignatieff claims to be describing the empirical reality that in contemporary wars (he is describing Africa) children are omnipresent combatants. Yet his description also conjures an understanding of brutality, savagery, and barbarism codified in the nineteenth century laws of war.

As we have seen so clearly in Vitoria and Grotius, as well as in the American Civil War, the laws of war, like most products of Enlightenment thinking, were premised on a vision of savages as children incapable of reason or self-control.

So, barbarians are children, and for Ignatieff, children literally are the barbarians, whose wild sexuality attests to their inability to gain mastery over themselves, to regulate their impulses, and to delay their pleasures. Again, this is contrasted with the full adulthood and manhood of civilized men. As Paul Gilroy observes in relation to contemporary wars, "government by terror has been associated once again with infrahuman blackness reconstituted in the 'half-devil, half-child' patterns favored by older colonial mentalities."[36] In other words, these contemporary discussions conjure the same metaphors and relations that structured the relations between sovereign and savage, civilized and barbarian, imperialism and colonization, on which the codification of the laws of war were premised. I do not mean to suggest by this that the past is a "sure and necessary road to an inevitable present."[37] Rather, these examples illustrate our indebtedness to the logic of the past, which continues to mold our standards of judgment about war and to inform our thinking about the laws of war. We need only review the history of the Martens clause to see that this is true.

* * *

The U.S. Military Tribunal at Nuremburg defended the Nuremburg trials against charges of retroactivity by arguing that the Martens clause was more than a "pious declaration" and that, therefore, crimes that transgressed its standards were prosecutable.[38] It was incorporated into both the 1949 Geneva Conventions and the 1977 Protocols Additional.[39] It was also invoked in the rulings of the ICTY as a lynchpin or measure of the expectations or prescriptions of the laws of war, which still hold even if practices of war violate them. Theodor Meron argues that the Martens clause attained primacy in the development and interpretation of the laws of war. In all cases of doubt, for example, the clause was used to support an interpretation "consistent with the principles of humanity and the dictates of public conscience."[40] Thus, although the clause may have limited, if any, influence on the battlefield, its "rhetorical and ethical code words" clearly exert a "strong pull towards normativity."[41] Therefore, he believes we must not ignore the challenge of formulating the public conscience, identified by Martens, as a predicate on which restraint in war continues to rely.[42] The strength of these code words, or the norms of war, was what the ICRC attempted to discern in its survey project "People on War" and in its later study on customary law.

But, let us not forget, this most influential statement of moderation and restraint not only demarcates such moderation as a privilege to be shared among civilized nations but also nominates it as a hallmark of that very identity. Paradoxically, then, one of the potentially most flexible and responsive standards of protection, accepted as customary law, is rooted in the discriminatory concepts of civilization from which the laws of humanity and the dictates of public conscience evolve. The Martens clause recites and relies on a distinction between barbarism and civilization to prohibit not all violence but only violence among civilized entities—after all, one of its code words is civilization. Yet, after the signal atrocities of World War I and II, "only a very few exceptionally blinkered inhabitants of Europe could talk with real confidence of the distinction between 'civilized' and 'barbarian' warfare—a distinction that had been granted in much previous discussion....The frequent use of the word *barbarian* to describe aspects of the hostilities had a special implication, that Europe was not superior (as it had previously thought) to the rest of the world."[43] How was it possible to distinguish between combatant and civilian after two world wars, when the distinction appeared obsolete, partly due to the logic and technologies of war; potentially dangerous in its observation; and indeterminate in its formulation? Was it possible to rescue the laws of war from charges of failure and obsolescence?

* * *

Those gathered at the conferences leading to the four 1949 Geneva Conventions were faced with this challenge and, like authors before them, turned to the Martens clause as a signal referent for their attempts to invest the laws of war with moral strength and progressive potential. Moreover, they found in discourses of civilization not only reasons for the continued codification of the laws of war but also reasons for the codification of the civilian. For the first time, the civilian was to be granted a status and a sanctity that relied not only on the dictates of public conscience but also on the dictates of public law.

In 1945, the Judge Advocate General of the U.S. War Department wrote that, even though humanity itself demands the preservation of a such a distinction between combatant and civilian, the distinction is one "more apparent than real."[44] Only a year earlier, Henry B. Wheaton, an eminent lawyer, had decried the very distinction as "illusory" and, as a result, any efforts to retain its use as "immoral."[45] Echoing this position, Hersch Lauterpacht, a legal scholar, dismissed it as a "hollow phrase."[46] Nonetheless, the destruction or dissolution of this distinction was said to betray the promise of civilization and to jeopardize humanity itself. As the Union Committee on the Conduct of (the American Civil) War had earlier found, so too did the Greek delegate conclude almost a century later: barbarity abounds when "belligerents strike army and civilian population alike without any distinction between the two."[47] Josef Kunz, a legal scholar, declared in 1951 that the two world wars exemplified the "the total crisis of Western Christian culture, a crisis which threatens the very survival of our civilization," because each demonstrated that the "cultured man of the twentieth century is no more than a barbarian under a very superficial veneer of civilization."[48] To repair the veneer, if not rehabilitate the man, the necessity of further developing international humanitarian law could not be denied. It guaranteed the "survival of our whole civilization."[49]

Once again, as with Hugo Grotius and Francis Lieber, the laws of war formed a pivotal and productive dimension of international and domestic order. In addition to regulating and legislating conduct among preconstituted entities, the laws of war constituted the subjects it was said to govern. Consequently, the task of the development of the laws of war in 1949 was similar to the task facing past publicists in the midst of their contemporary crises—to regulate and moderate war through the refinement of its rules and requirements while, simultaneously, producing the distinction between those who fight and those who do not on which the possibility of moderation depends.

Thus, the problem was not how to distinguish between combatant and civilian but how to produce the difference between the two. Moreover, because it is the observance of this distinction, the practice of moderation, that demarcates civilized nations from their barbarous brethren, men from a "savage horde," and honorable men from dishonorable, this distinction remains the means by which such differences may be indexed and identified.[50] Indeed, no better example of the resonance of this claim can be found than in the words of President George W. Bush when he held that he and his administration were determined to defend civilization against the existence of lawless violence, of barbarity itself, a primary measure of which was the violation of the principle of distinction or, in his phrase, the killing of the "innocent."[51] Earlier, President Bush had painstakingly contrasted barbarous violence with the measures taken by the United States in defense of civilization against "these outlaws and killers of the innocent."[52]

I draw my analysis here from both the final records of the preparatory conferences for the IV Convention and the official commentaries, produced under the auspices of the ICRC, which paraphrase and explicate the meanings of the treaties. These documents, often written by the participants in the preparatory conferences, are of utmost significance in interpreting the treaties of international humanitarian law and are highly "useful for clarifying the intended scope and operation of the provisions."[53] The commentaries state that if "the interpretation of the texts gives rise to some uncertainty, the opinions put forward are legal opinions, and not opinions of principle."[54] This is a significant contention. The commentaries are statements of legal opinions; therefore, it is not possible to dismiss or ignore the commentaries as merely the opinions of a few as these documents are employed by practitioners and lawyers to guide the interpretation and adjudication of international humanitarian law.

* * *

Reeling from two world wars in succession, the independence of new states, the collapse of former empires, and the specter of technological destruction, the states gathered in 1949 to discuss the future of the laws of war were intimately aware of the shocking transformation of the political landscape. Evaluated in terms of devastation and transformation, the end of World War II saw perhaps "fifteen million deaths in battle and another twenty-five as a direct result of war," marked the start of the Cold War, and began the "wholesale transformation of Western colonies into formally independent states."[55] The tactics of terror practiced by both Allied and Axis powers, from aerial and atomic bombings to concentration and internment camps, corrupted any facile distinctions between civilization and barbarism. In the midst of this ruin, the mission of those gathered at the preparatory conferences, some sixty delegations from Western, primarily European states, was to instantiate the distinction between those who fought and those who did not and, in so doing, rehabilitate some measure of civilization itself.[56]

This was not an easy proposition. First, the states agreed that the identification and determination of the civilian was intimately related to the identification and determination of the combatant. But the world wars had convinced most states that such determinations were obsolete, illusory, and immoral. The logic of total war, in which *all* individuals were implicated in service and support of the military, dominated the discussions in the preparatory conferences. In these discussions, it was agreed that every "enemy national" should be treated as a "potential soldier."[57] To those delegates, the civilian was in danger of disappearing. The guiding question, as posed by one scholar, was: "has the civilian, as liberal Europe used to know him, become extinct?"[58]

Second, the practices of occupation and resistance, as witnessed in both World War I and II, forced a controversial reconsideration of the conventional category of combatant to provide for the protection and treatment of partisans, or irregulars, upon capture. As one delegate from the United Kingdom forcefully stated in defense of a restrictive definition of combatant and of civilian: "The whole conception of the Civilians Convention was the protection of civilian victims of war and not the protection of illegitimate bearers of arms who could not expect full protection under rules of war to which they did not conform."[59] Underlying this controversy was the fear that any loosening of the standards of organization, appearance, or conduct by which combatants were identified would unfairly benefit irregulars, jeopardize the safety of both regular combatants and civilians, and degrade the standards of conduct because it would make it yet more difficult to distinguish between combatants and civilians. But the prominent and public role played by partisans in resisting Nazi occupation forced a reconsideration of the strict standards set by earlier Conferences of 1899 and 1907. "Not now to vindicate and legitimize…[resistance]…was unthinkable for those veterans of it who had survived and for the regimes who owed at least some [in the Yugoslav case, the whole] of their liberated existence to it."[60]

Recall that the development of the distinction between combatant and civilian in the late nineteenth century assumed the existence of professionalized standing armies engaged in set-piece battles with one another. At that time, wars of occupation, colonization, and resistance were addressed only tangentially (in the concept of *levee en mass*), if at all, and those who participated in such spontaneous uprisings were provided with insufficient protections and little legitimacy as combatants. The possibility of distinguishing between those who fight and those who do not was dependent on recognizing only a specific kind of fighting by a specific kind of forces with the exclusion of all others (e.g., "the people, the peasantry, the townsfolk" as de Vattel had argued in the eighteenth century). Those who were not directly engaged in the fighting forces, those "peaceful populations" to use the phrase of the 1940s British army manual, were to be protected or ignored because their labor was more usefully employed in supporting and nourishing the troops. "Humanitarianism chimed in nicely with official self-interest to recommend the observance of a distinction between combatants and non-combatants."[61]

The potential plasticity of the distinction between combatants and civilians served as a direct challenge to the standards of warfare that had developed over the centuries. Of course, Lieber had already struggled with this plasticity, suggesting a tripartite distinction rather than a misleading binary one, but the delegates did not heed his solution. (And, even now, a shadow category remains to haunt the laws of war.) Instead, after much heated debate during the preparatory conference, a less restricted definition of *combatant* was introduced that acknowledged the participation of partisans (as did General Orders 100) but that further stressed the distinction.

Third, as we can see in the debates over the wording of the Preamble to the 1949 IV Conventions (discussed next), the identification and determination of civilians rested on "much less solid ground."[62] The authors of this eminent commentary express their worries regarding the IV Convention, the "wounded and prisoners of war are human beings who have become harmless, and the State's obligations towards them are not a serious hindrance to its conduct of the hostilities; on the other hand, civilians have not in most cases been rendered harmless, and the steps taken on their behalf may be a serious hindrance to the conduct of war."[63] The authors also identify another potential source of confusion: whereas one could reasonably assume that the wounded and sick and prisoners of war were identifiable through their military regalia or presence in specific formations of war, civilians were but "an unorganized mass scattered over the whole of countries concerned."[64] Thus, the difficulties of identification and determination are compounded by the potential threat posed by this seemingly itinerant mass of individuals. Why, then, should civilians be protected at all?

The discussion about a potential Preamble to the IV Convention reveals some of the delegates' struggles to root the protection of civilians in a common identifiable ground. What was the justification for the IV Convention? Was it a statement of the "general principles on which civilization depended?" Or was it an "expression of universal human rights"?[65] Or was justification of the IV Convention, as the Holy See suggested in response to these proposals from Mexico and Switzerland, to be found in reference to God, the "source of absolute justice and charity, without which Conventions were valueless"?[66] Unable to reconcile these differing sources and foundations of the law or develop the "usual statement of motives" for the creation of the convention, the delegates took refuge in brevity and vagaries.[67] The Preamble to the IV Convention is notable for its brusque statement of purpose.

In responding to these three challenges of identification and determination, the delegates' first step, we might reasonably assume, would be to define the category under consideration. One delegate to the preparatory conferences did suggest that "since the Convention was concerned with the protection of 'civilians,' it would seem essential to define what was meant by the term civilian as opposed to 'military' and so avoid the use of the expression 'protected persons'"; nevertheless, the delegates did not in fact define *civilian*.[68]

Instead, the formal articles of the IV Convention refer only to the broader concept of "protected persons." *Protected persons* are individuals "taking no active part in the hostilities" as defined, for example, in Article 3 of the 1949 IV Convention. Prisoners of war, wounded and sick combatants, detainees and internees, and all others in the hands of the enemy were considered protected persons. Article 4 of the 1949 IV Convention attempts to distinguish more clearly among this mix of protected persons, to elucidate the differences among each type, and, subsequently, to specify to whom the protections of the IV Convention apply. As the commentary on this convention clearly states, "this article is, in a sense, the key to the Convention; for it defines the people to whom it refers."[69] Nevertheless, it also ruefully notes, "the meaning does not stand out very clearly," and even after distilling the definition, it may still "seem rather complicated."[70]

In Article 4, *protected persons* are defined as those who find themselves in the hands of an enemy of a *different* nationality and who are definitively not participating in "activities hostile to the security of the State" as members of a military organization. The problems with these definitions have already been well noted. As one respected commentator queries, "does this mean that all other persons are combatants and can be attacked?"[71] It was not until 1977 that activities hostile to the security of the state were formally defined and, even then, its definition is "regrettable" in its "ambiguities."[72] Thus, Article 4, on which the identification and determination of civilian rest, remains irresolute.

Moreover, as one scholar observes, the protection of civilians as defined in the IV Convention are "rudimentary and inadequate" and "of a somewhat abstract nature. It was difficult to say with any precision what it required."[73] The IV Convention—contrary to popular understanding—extends protection only "from arbitrary action on the part of the enemy, and not from the dangers of military operations themselves."[74] The majority of its provisions focus on the protection of civilians in three distinct localities: occupied territories, civilian medical establishments, and internment/detainee camps. Therefore, in international armed conflict the only people to be protected are

- *enemy nationals* within the national territories of each party to the conflict, and
- the population of occupied territories *excluding* the nationals of the occupying party.

As we can see, then, the 1949 IV Convention, a foundational text of the principle of distinction, is quite scant.

Defining the scope of protection is the deferral to sovereignty in that the relations of any state to its own nationals remains external to the Convention and the military necessity of the state (*raison d'etat*) takes precedence over a more complete refuge because enemy civilians are protected solely against arbitrary action and not against the dangers of military operations.[75] Finally, and highly significantly, these protections are offered only to those nationals of a state that agrees to be bound by the Convention. Here treaty ratification formalizes the reciprocal relations previously identified by membership in the society of civilized states, providing a means (strategically used by national liberation movements; see chap. 6) for states to gain entry into an otherwise closed society.

These days, we are accustomed to the nearly universal ratification of the 1949 Conventions. Thus, to the modern observer, the limitation of protection to only those nationals of a state that has agreed to be bound by the Convention may seem irrelevant. But consider its import immediately after the brutalities of the two world wars, when the question of whether states and which states would agree to be bound was unknown. Furthermore, it is important to recognize that the possibilities of protection to which the majority of the dictates of the IV Convention refer are dependent on nationality for identification and states for implementation.[76] Again, because we are so familiar with the possibility of international enforcement of international law by bodies other than states, we might not appreciate the limitations of this formulation. Yet remember that nationality and states provided only the most meager protection in war, and in the case of the German Jews after the passage by Germany of the 1935 Nuremberg laws, they provided essentially none.

Nonetheless, in the 1949 IV Convention, nationality and sovereignty are reca-pitulated as the final arbiters of the potential for protection, a formulation that would not have protected the Jews during World War II. The extension of the protection and rights of civilians is directly circumscribed by the acceptance of nationality and sovereignty.[77] The rights of protection were, in essence, the rights granted upon recognition of citizenship.

Ironically, the delegates to the preparatory conferences recognized the ex-tremely limited scope of the protections and refused to "accept the idea that these principles constitute the complete code of all the rights of civilians."[78] This limited scope of protections was no small tragedy considering the enormity of destruction wreaked on civilians during the last wars and the grossly evident necessity of their protection. It should also make us question the contemporary celebration of the 1949 IV Convention as establishing a "firebreak between civili-zation and barbarism"; after all, even those responsible for the 1949 Conventions did not consider the rudimental strictures of protection offered by them to be wholly acceptable.[79]

The delegates' inability to arrive at a cogent and coherent definition and, therefore, a broad scope of protection within the formal article itself, was one result of the contentious battles. These battles were over the preservation of state sovereignty to wage war as necessary, relatively unhindered by considerations of civilians and conscience and by the recognition, or at least admonition, of re-sponsibility to a common humanity. These tensions were most visible in the dis-cussions of the extension of protections of civilians to all civilians, not just those who were in the hands of the enemy, and to civilians in all wars, not just wars between sovereign states.

Fascinatingly, during the preparatory conferences, arguments for the greatest scope of protection of civilians were primarily voiced by the USSR and its allies against a coalition led by the United States and United Kingdom. In arguing for the application of all four of the 1949 Geneva Conventions to *all* wars and *all* civilians, and for the ban of atomic weaponry, the USSR took the lead. How-ever, in each case its suggestions were soundly rejected. Nevertheless, claiming the broadest extent of protections for civilians in the name of humanity and civilization proved to be an effective strategy for putting the United States and its allies on the defensive when justifying their more limited support for protection in these two areas. In response to the limitation of the IV Geneva Convention to those states that accepted its rule, the USSR strongly decried the expectation of reciprocity inherent in this rule: "the application of these humanitarian provi-sions…cannot be subject to criteria."[80] Indeed, the USSR accused states that sought to limit the definition and protection of civilians of being no less than the "enemies of humanity."[81]

The reliance on these discourses, reminiscent of the Martens clause, indicates how the formulation and observance of the laws of war continues to demarcate and define identities and societies of states, and it suggests that the discourse of civilization remains operative even when it is layered with that of humanity. An example of this is the promotion by the USSR of an expansive scope for and application of what is now Common Article 3 of the IV Convention.

* * *

Common Article 3 outlines the essential standards for the protection guaranteed to participants in internal wars (and indeed Common Article 3 is the one agreed-on element of the laws of war, for both the Obama and the Bush administrations, taken to govern the war on terror). The formulation of Common Article 3 was perhaps the most fiercely debated article within the IV Geneva Convention because it violates the sovereignty of a state by regulating conflict within its borders. And, although such a move may now appear relatively conventional with the newfound understanding of the responsibility to protect, at the time it sparked quite a furor.[82] In fact, as a result of this outcry, the initial proposal to specifically mention civil and colonial wars, which the ICRC had highlighted in its drafts, was dropped (to be revisited with greater success in the 1977 Protocols).[83] Moreover, for all its significance as the first legal regulation of internal wars, Common Article 3 in its present form is itself a significantly weakened version of the initial proposal made by the USSR.

The USSR proposed extending the full protections and detailed regulations of all four 1949 Geneva Conventions to internal armed conflicts, not simply the most elemental considerations, which was the final result. The delegate from France had already remarked that it was "impossible to carry the protection of individuals to the point of sacrificing the rights of States," while that of the United Kingdom remarked that "careful consideration of the provisions of the Convention...left little room for doubt that their application in civil war would strike at the root of national sovereignty and endanger national security."[84] The newly independent states were equally resistant to the broadening of application of the Conventions, fearing, as Burma did, that there were suspect motives on the part of other states: "I do not understand why foreign governments would like to come and protect our people."[85] Clearly, these delegates accepted some recursive relationship between the laws of war and the constitution of sovereignty; otherwise, their concerns about applying the laws of war within their own territories would not have been as great.

Common Article 3, for all its radical potential, was reduced to the minimum humanitarian standards for protection, limiting the application of the Conventions in internal armed conflicts to only the principles and expectations laid out in Article 3. Nonetheless, the ICRC delegate noted that Article 3, even though a difficult compromise and limited protection, grants "the application of the humanitarian rules which are recognized by all civilized peoples."[86] Once again, we notice the minimal expectations for protection and treatment advocated for and by civilized peoples, and the reliance on civilization to extend these protections when positive law is absent. Would the very experience of World War II not suggest that such formulations were, in fact, fraught with failure?

The debate over Common Article 3 suggests that the formulation and observance of the laws have been difficult for states not simply because of the importance of defending sovereignty but also because temperance in war is a significant dimension of the formulation of state identities and state sovereignty.[87] In fact, the USSR decried the limitation on the scope and definition of *protected persons* found in Article 4, taking it as a betrayal of the promise of "conscience and honour of nations, and the traditional standards of conduct generally recognized throughout the civilized world."[88] What precisely were those generally recognized standards? What exactly did the civilized world require? Once again, the laws of war replied in the discourses of gender and innocence.

* * *

Part II, Article 13, of the IV Geneva Convention attempts to restore the conscience and honor of the civilized world by broadening the definition of those protected under the IV Convention to all populations in the countries of conflict. In its short formulation, Article 13 simply states that general protections outlined in Part II cover the "whole of the populations of the countries in conflict." In Article 13, nationality and being in the power of the enemy are no longer the necessary markers for the protections, as they are in Article 4.

The commentaries inform us that the extension of protection to all populations is premised on binding the "belligerents to observe certain restrictions in their conduct of hostilities by erecting protective barriers to shield certain categories of the population who, by definition, take no part in the fighting."[89] Grotius would agree—temperance in war is the responsibility of those who wage it, and the practice of such prudence demands the determination of who should be spared. And he would happily assent to the proposed selection of those who shall be spared; according to the commentaries, those "certain categories that, by definition, take no part in the fighting" are "children, women, old people, the wounded and the sick."[90]

Note two moves. First, the extension of protection to *all* populations has just been reduced to only specific categories. It is not difficult to imagine the consequences of limiting protection to only children, women, old people, the wounded, and the sick because we have far too many examples. Most starkly, we saw it in 1995 in the round up and disappearance of men from the safe haven of Srebrenica; in that case, all men were considered combatants regardless of the fact that they were taking no part in the fighting.[91] This type of presumption is common to armed conflicts from Chechnya to Israel-Palestine. More recently, the United States has repeated this selective logic in the 2002 requirement that "virtually all male non-citizens" from eighteen countries, "mostly Muslim and Arab," who are in the United States register with the U.S. immigration authorities.[92]

The limitation of protection to specific categories may have appeared sensible in light of the almost universal conscription of men during the two world wars. Even at that time, however, it was contradictory on at least two counts. First, *women* took part in these wars—most notably in the Soviet Union, where the proportion of women was estimated to be in excess of 8 percent of the total armed forces.[93] That translated to at least 800,000 women serving in the army and many thousands in partisan forces. Moreover, in Greece, Italy, France, and Britain, women were active and public partisans and members of resistance movements, and in the German and British forces, women worked in reserve and support units. Second, women as combatants were specifically recognized by the ICRC and in other Conventions. The status of women as combatants is specifically addressed in the 1949 III Convention on Prisoners of War. The only time the ICRC was "able to invoke the provision of the 3d Geneva Convention" was after one of its delegates visited a prisoner of war camp in Poland where both men and women were being held.[94] Thus, the argument that the limitation in the IV Convention only reflects state practice, which was to selectively (as opposed to universally) conscript women, and that therefore its designation of women as civilians is logical does not hold. If the laws only reflect state practice, how can we reconcile the III and IV Conventions? How can we say that women by definition take no part in the fighting? The evidence suggests other possibilities are at play.

The logic of total war dispenses with discrimination between those who fight and those who do not. Everyone is considered a combatant—that is what makes it so horrifying. There is no exact "outside" to the fighting, as the commentaries regretfully acknowledge, and women are decisively "inside" the fighting. So, just as Grotius did, the commentaries are compelled to produce a distinction that did not exist at the time they were written.

This brings us to the second move. At the same time that the Commentary on the IV Convention institutes a distinction between those who take part in the fighting and those who do not, it substantiates the definition of the *civilian*. Keep in mind that this definition is not formulated in the formal articles of the IV Geneva Convention but is consistently referred to in the body of the commentaries.[95] In the commentaries, *civilians* are those who "by definition do not bear arms," are "outside the fighting," and "take no active part in the hostilities."[96] Thus, civilians are children, women, old people, and the wounded and sick. This is no small triumph because the essential challenge of the IV Convention was to isolate and identify a category of civilian that is distinguishable from that of combatant. Therefore, the nomination of these individuals, who by definition take no part in the fighting, institutes the distinction between combatant and civilian that the IV Convention fails to do. And recall that, given the role of the commentaries, this is no mere opinion but, rather, a statement of legal principle.

Furthermore, because this distinction is confirmed by the shared "suffering, distress, or weakness" of those who take no part in the fighting, the anxious concern of the commentaries over the potential threat posed by civilians is easily relieved.[97] In fact, we can identify a similar supposition for the protection of combatants; here, protection results from physical liabilities (wounds and sickness) and incarceration (being a prisoner of war). Physical liabilities and incarceration force combatants into situations of dependency and vulnerability because "once a solider is wounded or sick, he may be said to be no longer a combatant…but simply a suffering, inoffensive, human being."[98] As this statement shows, the basic justification for the protection of civilians has been grafted on that for the protection of wounded, sick, and captured combatants. In each case, the defining characteristics of harmlessness are dependency and vulnerability. For combatants, these are contextual or contingent characteristics; however, for children, women, and old people, these are essential characteristics. In terms of their shared suffering, distress, and weakness, there are now three distinct categories of individuals that function as a synchedoche for civilian; these categories secure the possibility of the distinction on the premise of harmlessness and victimhood.

There is a familiar logic of equivalence posited by the commentaries among these disparate and otherwise distinct categories of individuals. Most immediately it reminds us of Grotius. Like him, the commentaries argue that only women, by virtue of their sex, can be assumed always to possess the attributes of not bearing arms, remaining outside of the fighting, being weak, and suffering or being in distress. The others (children, old people, the wounded, and the sick) all bear these essential attributes as a result of unfortunate circumstances and transient conditions—that is, temporally or chronologically. And, in fact, the debates in the preparatory conferences were over the precise ages by which the categories children and old people would be defined and by which their "faculties" of judgment and strength could be assessed.[99] There were no corresponding inquiries into the exact criteria by which women would be known. Their sex alone (it is only women that appear to be marked by sex) is sufficient.

It is a fundamental principle of all four of the 1949 Geneva Conventions that "women shall be treated with all consideration due to their sex." In fact, the

III Geneva Convention Relative to the Treatment of Prisoners of War gives us a definition of *women* that is, simultaneously, our only definition of sex. The sex of women is defined on the basis of weakness, honor, and modesty, whereby pregnancy and childbirth are akin to weakness, and honor and modesty are articulated only in terms of sexual vulnerability to "rape, forced prostitution, and any form of indecent assault."[100] Women are both desired for and made vulnerable by their sex.

Unlike Grotius, the commentaries do not argue that women, like children, suffer from diminished powers of reasoning and discrimination that render them unfit to wage war. Nor do the commentaries agree with de Vattel, who believed that it is simply inefficient and inconvenient for women to be combatants because they can bear neither arms nor the hardships of the war.[101] Instead, the commentaries hold that it was the matter of women's sex itself—defined as reproductive capability and sexual vulnerability—that places women outside the fighting. As a result, it is only the category women, not the other distinct categories (children and old people), that both materializes and stabilizes the distinction between combatant and civilian as a matter of sex. Therefore, women, like children, old people, and the wounded and sick, are harmless; but unlike children, old men, and the wounded and sick, women pose no potential harm. Only the suffering, distress, and weakness of women, derived from reproductive capability and sexual vulnerability, are the constant and natural markers of their very sex and, thus, of sex difference. Consequently, the relations of protection and the corresponding (inequitable) relations of power that they require are consolidated through recourse to the seeming immutability of (fundamentally heterosexual) sexual difference.[102]

The chorus of appeals to a warrior's honor, a "proud vision of male identity," as a primary means of protection could be heard only within this orchestration.[103] Yet, contrary to common presumptions, the very weakness and harmlessness of the civilian do not necessarily result in an assurance of protection. It certainly did not during World War I or II. As David Forsythe argues, because the "civilian is frequently viewed as nothing: weak...old...female[,]...there is nothing to command respect" and, consequently, combatants have less reason to abide by injunctions to protect and respect civilians.[104] Among combatants, protection and respect derives from a sense of collective recognition and collective honor—a sort of old boys network of equals, which is absent between combatants and civilians. Moreover, even though women are put forward as the paradigmatic civilian, the protections afforded to them are couched in prescriptive rather than prohibitive language.[105] Thus, even if the discourses of gender produce the distinction between combatant and civilian, the civilian as constructed is not worthy of much protection at all!

Consequently, to accept, as the commentaries wish us to do, that these interpretations of sex and sex difference are "normal and natural" is to fail to inquire about the productive discourses of gender that achieve this effect.[106] Recognizing that appeals to what is normal and natural consolidate and legitimate specific historical and social norms should encourage us to trace the production of these ostensibly natural distinctions in the service of other interests. The formulation of the distinction between combatant and civilian draws on and contributes to a particular vision of a gendered domestic and international order, as we have seen vividly in Grotius, Lieber, and the commentaries.

* * *

There are at least two ways in which this vision of a gendered domestic and international order becomes evident. First, the observance of this distinction persistently sorts states according to degrees of barbarism and civilization (as it did in the work of earlier publicists). The observance of the distinction, specifically the treatment of women with all due consideration of their sex, remains the hallmark of "every civilized country," whereas its transgression conjures the "worst memories of the great barbarian invasions."[107] The recursive relationship between the combatant and civilian distinction, and sex and sex difference, generates and regulates a particular international order.

As the IV Geneva Convention and its commentary make clear, this international order has as its foundation and future the heterosexual family—the "natural and fundamental group unit of society."[108] It is on this foundation that an international order can be said to arise. If you think that the idea of "women" as equivalent to "family" is outdated, think again. In October 1999, the director of the ICRC told the UN General Assembly, "when one thinks of women, one also naturally tends to think of the family."[109]

Indeed, a large part of post–world war reconstruction was occupied with the reconstruction of a highly particular vision of a heterosexual nuclear family. After World War II, states as varied as the USSR, United Kingdom, and United States emphasized the re-creation of "'traditional' gender relationships, the familiar and natural order of families, men in public roles, women at home."[110] The promotion and defense of the conventional family—challenged by the widespread participation of women in the work of war—shaped postwar policies and politics. In both the United States and France, for example, "the short lived affirmation of women's independence gave way to a pervasive endorsement of female subordination and domesticity."[111] Indeed, during the last year of war in Britain, women auxiliaries were "given time off for mothercraft lessons, in order to prepare them for and remind them of their peacetime role."[112] There was a particular concern with returning to an ideal hetero-normative order, supposedly overturned during the wars.

These initiatives positioned and governed women as heterosexual wives and mothers, as sexually available but not sexually adventurous, and instituted men as husbands and providers, the defenders of home and hearth. Therefore, the reconstitution and reaffirmation of the heterosexual family, and the placement of women within that family and in need of male protection, were of utmost importance for a secure domestic order that, in turn, informed the international order. Within these social and juridical discourses of gender, reproductive capability and sexual vulnerability serve as clear markers of sex and sex difference. And these distinctions of sex, which make possible the distinction between combatant and civilian, are themselves neither normal nor natural but are instead produced by historically particular discourses of gender. Just as sex and sex difference ensure the self-evidence of the distinction between combatant and civilian, so does that distinction in turn reaffirm the naturalness of sex and sex difference.

* * *

In my reading of the 1949 IV Geneva Convention, we have seen that these supposedly natural interpretations of sex and sex differences, which serve as the paradigms of the differences between combatant and civilian, are actually effects of discourses of gender. This is where a genealogy of the laws of war serves its purpose and also where an understanding of discourse of gender as productive reveals its benefits. We have been able to identify the production of the distinction between combatant and civilian as what Wendy Brown calls an instance "in which differences that are effects of social power are neutralized through their articulation as attributes."[113]

The distinction between combatant and civilian, which governs international humanitarian law and contributes to its formative power, is an effect of particular, historically rooted philosophical and juridical formations of sex and sex differences. This is true even in the case of the 1977 Protocols, which formally defines the concept and category of the civilian in international humanitarian law. As I show in chapter 6, because this definition pivots on the distinction of those who fight and those who do not, it calls on the discourses of gender to legitimize this distinction. The contemporary characterization of women who fight as "de-sexed" (just as during the Civil War) is but one indication of the continuing force of gender in the maintenance of this distinction.[114]

Distinguishing among acts and individuals during war produces the distinctions of sex and sex difference that we are now accustomed to identifying as the basis for those actions. The discourse of gender at work in the 1949 IV Convention is pivotal not only to the establishment of the differences between and among men and women but to the production and governance of international (civilized) and domestic (familial) orders. The principle of distinction is one effect of the entanglement of the discourses of gender and civilization—civilization is marked by its regard for its women.

At the beginning of this chapter, I underscore some effects of the discourses of civilization—regulating entry into the European state system and legitimating an entirely different system of rules for those deemed outside the system. On one hand, the 1949 IV Geneva Convention formally holds treaty ratification as regulating the extension of the protections of war, ostensibly replacing the criterion of civilization. But, on the other hand, the IV Convention simultaneously reinvigorates the discourses of civilization, much as the Martens clause did centuries before, to ensure the extension of protection to wars within sovereign states; as evidenced in Common Article 3, the full application of the 1949 Conventions was expressly rejected. In the decades that followed, national liberation movements challenged and decolonization struggles exemplified the power and potential of the discourses of civilization to set the bounds of war.

THE ALGERIAN CIVIL WAR AND THE 1977 PROTOCOLS ADDITIONAL

When a bomb exploded "anyone was suspect. If you asked me at that point which Algerians were for or against the FLN, I would have found it difficult to answer you."

—Former French intelligence officer, quoted in Marnia Lazreg, *Torture and the Twilight of Empire: From Algiers to Baghdad*

The 1954–1962 French-Algerian War—its methods, its debates, and its consequences—altered the way in which wars of national liberation and decolonization were identified and understood, and introduced a new category of combatant (as well as a new category of war) into international humanitarian law. It occupies a "seminal place in the history of European decolonization," partly due to the self-appointed task undertaken by the leaders of the liberation struggle, the Algerian Front de Libération Nationale (FLN; National Liberation Front) in particular, to unify and exemplify the larger decolonization struggles of their time.[1] The FLN spoke of its "vocation" to lead postcolonial movements, specifically in Africa, and argued that the Algerian War had sounded the "toll of colonialism."[2] Among the many struggles for recognition and independence after World War II, including the influential Indochina War, the Algerian War was of pivotal importance because its participants were avid and successful advocates for the legitimacy of their struggle in both the United Nations and in the international community at large. "One of the consequences [of the long struggle of the Algerians for independence]...has been the development throughout the world of almost universal political support for a particular kind of war...the decolonization war."[3]

The 1960 UN Declaration on the Granting of Independence to Colonial Countries and Peoples was due in no small part to the intelligent efforts and consistent agitation by the Algerian FLN to influence the UN debates on Algeria and consequently to force a UN statement on the right to self-determination. For these reasons both the Algerian war and the UN declaration were particular references for the delegates in the 1970s, many of whom, engaged in the wars in Vietnam, Israel, and South Africa, took the Algerian war of independence as their guide.

Finally, the highly publicized and celebrated role that women played in the Algerian War presaged later national liberation wars throughout the 1960s and 1970s in which women fought, for example, in Mozambique, the Sudan, the Philippines, and Vietnam. After the Algerian War, could it again ever be said, as did the commentaries on the 1949 Geneva Conventions, that it was "normal and natural" to protect women in war? Tracing the discourses of gender in the Algerian War allows us to appreciate the continued significance of gender in the laws of war and the role of gender in determining combatant and civilian, which has thus far been overlooked in any analysis of the laws. Thus, the Algerian war illuminates not only the particular challenges faced by those representatives convened in the 1970s but provides a conceptual purchase on their proposed solutions.

* * *

The French-Algerian War was one of the most violent struggles for decolonization in the twentieth century; at least 350,000 Algerians were killed during the eight years of war (1954–1962).[4] The FLN, which formed from several nationalist groups in the early 1950s, began an offensive in 1954 with simultaneous bombings of rural French outposts and fought consistently for eight years. The French, reeling from their losses in Indochina, were quick to learn from their failures in Indochina and operated differently in Algeria. But the FLN and its Armée de Libération Nationale (ALN; Army of National Liberation) had learned as well. Insurgency and counterinsurgency tactics were the primary military strategies used on both sides. On the part of the French, this included strategic pacification, repopulation, forced displacement, directed killings, and torture; on the part of the FLN/ALN this included selective attacks, political organizing, assassinations, and torture. The military and political strategies of both sides purposively and fully politicized the entire population of Algeria, over whose support they fought.

The FLN considered every member of the Algerian population a potential combatant in some form. As Mohammed Bedjaoui, a highly influential Algerian jurist (who held the position of foreign minister of Algeria and ambassador to France during the Algerian War) writes, "every Algerian man or woman who is engaged in fighting for the objectives of the organization to which he belongs...and fulfills all obligation to that organization is a member of the FLN/ALN."[5] The French also approached the war in Algeria as unbounded, one in which the demarcation of friend or foe no longer corresponded to set battles or clearly identified fronts. The only boundary was a "non-physical, often ideological boundary."[6] All individuals were suspect at all times. Obviously, then, distinctions between combatant and civilian were troublesome to determine and dangerous to uphold because the "enemy was far more difficult to identify" in a war without spatial or temporal boundaries.[7] It takes little effort to see the parallels between this and the contemporary U.S-led war on terror, in which, according to President George W. Bush and his administration in 2001, one was either "with or against" us. The index of these differences—with us or against us and civilian or combatant—is reduced to crude ideology at best.

This is not to say, however, that during the Algerian War no attempts were made to fix its limits. The FLN decreed at various points in the conflict that civilians—by whom they meant women, children, and old people—were not to be killed, thus attempting in form (if not in function) to conform to the regulations they took to describe civilized warfare. The tactics of war, especially as the FLN attempted to confirm its own civilized potential and prowess, could not undermine the struggle for legitimacy. Nonetheless, the toll on the civilian population, as defined by the FLN, was devastating. As the war wore on, the FLN committed atrocities, although never as many as the French.[8]

Colonel Roger Trinquier guided the French counterinsurgency strategy. His disquisition on the proper means to fight this war (*Modern Warfare*), developed from his experiences in Indochina, was "seminal to the French army's response."[9] Central to his strategy was the belief that "the battlefield...is no longer restricted. It is limitless....the inhabitant in his home is the center of the conflict. Amidst the continuing movement of military actions, he is the stablest element."[10] Resettlement campaigns both physically and figuratively altered the familial and spatial arrangements of the Algerian home, placing them directly under the corporal authority and surveillance of the French. To secure the cooperation of the Algerian population, the French combined both political and military strategies, instituting assistance programs to win the hearts and minds of the Algerian people and to combat the sophisticated political organizing of the FLN. Trinquier believed these strategies should "enable the precise identification of the outlaw."[11]

Confronting these tactics, the FLN fought back not only militarily but also through a sophisticated political strategy. In 1954, the objective of the FLN was to internationalize all dimensions of its challenge to the French. To meet that objective, the FLN established political offices and media contacts outside Algeria, notably in New York City, to better influence the debates of the United Nations and to ensure the Algerian War was characterized as one between sovereign states. Moreover, in its campaign for international and domestic legitimacy, and to prove Algeria capable of self-rule, the FLN meticulously outlined its position regarding international law, specifically the laws of war.

In 1956, the FLN/ALN created a national congress. The congress developed both advisory and executive councils to oversee the war efforts. In 1958, the Provisional Government of the Algerian Republic was established in Tunis, after which its participation in the United Nations was accepted, although legal recognition was not extended. These efforts were specifically directed toward gaining international recognition of the right of Algeria to use force against the French and preventing the war from being considered an internal affair. In an influential treatise, Bedjaoui set out in fine detail the correspondence among the standards of international law, the organization and structure of the provisional Algerian government, and its army. The FLN strengthened its position as a legitimate authority in Algeria by its acceptance and application of the laws of war—a step since imitated by many national liberation groups, most notably at the start of the preparatory conferences for the 1977 Protocols.

Instructing its armed forces to comply with international humanitarian law, in 1960 the Algerian provisional government formally acceded to the 1949 Geneva Conventions. France had been a party since 1951. Eventually, recognizing the relative inadequacy of Common Article 3, the FLN also requested that the French agree to the implementation of further specific provisions or measures of international humanitarian law beyond Common Article 3. The French refused on the same principles by which they were conducting the war—the insurgency was domestic, internal, and thus privy only to the minimum standards of conduct outlined in Common Article 3.

France did not consider even Common Article 3, which governed internal armed conflicts, to be applicable to the war until 1956. The French insisted that the uprising was but a domestic disturbance because Algeria was part of France.[12] As we would expect, the FLN absolutely rejected this characterization. Instead, the FLN held that France conquered Algeria in the nineteenth century and that Algeria had been a sovereign nation before its colonization and annexation by the French in 1830. Since that date, Algeria had remained a resistant nation under occupation. According to the FLN, the war was to *restore*, not attain, sovereignty of the Algerian state, much as the resistance movements of World War II had struggled to achieve the same.

* * *

In 1960, in what is known as the *White Paper on the Application of the Geneva Convention,* the Algerian provisional government called on all states to enforce the terms of the 1949 Conventions by "respect[ing] and ensur[ing] respect" for the Conventions.[13] This, of course, was the fundamental obligation of all signatories to the Geneva Conventions, envisioned by its authors as a primary means of enforcing compliance with the laws of war. In an effort to demonstrate its commitment, notwithstanding the evident lack of commitment on the part of the French, the FLN had, in 1958, released some fifty prisoners of war; "it hoped that this gesture might lead to the progressive humanization of the war on the French side...and [reveal to]...the world at large that the laws of war took a high place of honour."[14] To further emphasize its commitment to international humanitarian law, the FLN also sent a permanent delegation to Geneva and continued to argue for the development of international law that would "take account of the sanction to the principle of self determination given by the United Nations Charter and United Nations resolutions."[15]

Collectively, these actions accomplished three ends. They (1) impelled the French to consider reciprocal observance, implicitly if not explicitly; (2) demonstrated the high standards of the FLN and its conformance with the accepted rules of engagement set forth in the international community; and thus (3) underscored that the French were the ones actually behaving like the savages that the Algerians were said to be whereas the Algerians were conducting themselves in accordance with the rules promulgated by civilized states. The official newspaper of the FLN discussed French tactics not only in terms of their barbarity but also in terms of the violation of international humanitarian law.

Contrasting its actions with that of the French, the FLN insisted throughout the war that the French disregard for international humanitarian law compromised the essential spirit and purpose of the law, threatening the international community that it bound. In so doing, the FLN nominated itself not only as an independent member of that community but also as one of its most faithful guardians. The acceptance of international humanitarian law facilitated the FLN claim that Algeria was competent, rational, and, most important, civilized enough to deserve and demand self-rule. When the French dismissed international humanitarian law as irrelevant to the conflict in Algeria, the FLN portrayed the action as contrary to the "humanitarian principles of justice and compassion" that must "govern and determine the treatment of man by man if *our* civilization is to be worthy of the name."[16] The debate during the Algerian War surrounding the interpretation and application of the laws of war evinces the highly strategic and productive role of international humanitarian law. The Algerian War was no less over the proper representative of civilization as it was about independence and liberation.

The political and military stalemate of the Algerian War was decisively shattered by increasing domestic and international opprobrium over the widespread use of torture and reprisals by French troops in Algeria. As evidence accumulated, especially about the commonplace practice of torture, it became almost impossible for France to maintain its claim to be the foremost representative of the Rights of Man, engaged in nothing more than a "civilizing mission" in Algeria to quell the uprisings of discontented people. Furthermore, the massive displacement efforts of the French were held to be in direct violation of the Genocide Convention by no less an authority than Raphael Lemkin, its conceptual author. The French, it seemed, lacked the discipline and moderation necessary to justify their sovereign claim to Algeria, as attested to by their violations of the laws of war. In contrast, it appeared that the FLN did possess such discipline and moderation. Franz Fanon proved himself attuned to the power of this difference when he observed that "an underdeveloped people must prove, by its fighting power, its ability to set itself up as a nation, and by the purity of every one of its acts, that it is, even to the smallest detail, the most lucid, the most self-controlled people."[17]

Contributing to the eventual settlement was the dramatic shift in international opinion, and specifically in the U.S. position, regarding the viability of retaining colonialism as a necessary dimension of international order. In 1956, President Dwight Eisenhower said, "All of these newly independent countries will turn from us to the USSR....win or lose, we will share the same fate of Britain and France...[and] the British and French would not win."[18] The wars of national liberation and decolonization were identified as central to the establishment of a new international order. They were no longer just internal matters.

* * *

The Algerian War was resolved in 1962, but its effects were felt throughout the rest of the 1960s and 1970s and informed the reasoning and strategies of Nelson Mandela and Yasser Arafat, two disparate leaders, each of whom has acknowledged his debt to the FLN/ALN. Most immediately, the FLN advocacy of the development of international humanitarian law to specifically address wars of national liberation and decolonization directly affected the formulation of Protocol I. Certainly, the results of its agitation were seen in the 1977 Conference at which wars of national liberation (now formally recognized as those in which peoples are fighting against "colonial domination and alien occupation and against racist regimes in the exercise of their right of self-determination"[19]) were invested with an international status. The FLN skillfully employed the normative and strategic resources of international humanitarian law to justify and legitimate their own claim to sovereign recognition, marshalling the evidence of civilized or barbarian tactics to discredit the French claim of being a superior civilization on which the Algerians depended and from which they learned.

Furthermore, the military (insurgency) strategies of both sides—by no means unique to the Algerian War—forced the preparatory conferences of the 1970s to grapple with the reconceptualization and redefinition of the combatant and the civilian in an effort to reconcile each with the methods of contemporary warfare. The spatial and temporal fluidity of combat and combatants undermined the premise of a bounded battle and clearly identified combatants on which the laws of war depended. Therefore, the Algerian War catalyzed many of the theoretical contests of the preparatory conferences, and it also bore witness to the refined military strategies of counterinsurgency and their effects.

But we would be in error if we read the Algerian War only in terms of its strategic and tactical effects. The Algerian War also catalyzed a profound skepticism toward the value of humanism. As Jean-Paul Sartre writes in his introduction to Fanon's *Wretched of the Earth*, "there is nothing more consistent than a racist humanism since the European has only been able to become a man through creating slaves and monsters."[20] The atrocities and torture of the Algerian War corroded faith in the existence of a universal human essence, the common dignity of humanity. In doing so, it also undermined a foundation for moral judgment and action. Could there be moral certitude? What was a clear course of action? The Algerian War confounded such presumptions for "if nothing can protect a nation against itself, neither its traditions nor its loyalties, nor its laws.... anybody at any time may equally find himself victim *or* executioner."[21] Just as the colonial wars of the eighteenth and nineteenth centuries betrayed the putative universality of the laws of war, so too did the wars of national liberation and decolonization of the twentieth century reveal the limits of the inalienable rights of the human person, said to be the center of the 1949 Conventions. The reaffirmation and development of the laws of war called for in the 1970s was deeply inflected by these crises as delegates sought to justify their efforts and, for the first time, directly negotiate colonized and imperial desires.

* * *

The preparatory conferences for the 1949 Conventions took place in a postwar peace, on the cusp of the Cold War, in the midst of reconstructing a viable international order, and at the end of a total war among sovereign states. The 1977 Protocols Additional were firmly rooted in the Cold War, were formulated in the midst of multiple wars, and confronted internal (albeit internationalized) armed conflicts characterized by guerrilla and counterinsurgent warfare. A simple comparison of the number and diversity of participants gathered for each of the preparatory conferences to draft these documents testifies to the rapid alteration and expansion of the international community. In the first case, approximately 62 delegations from Western, primarily European, states met over a period of three months in 1949; in the second case, more than 150 delegations, 11 national liberation movements, and 50 IGOs met over a period of four years in 1973–1977.[22]

The delegates to the conferences regarding the Protocols Additional did not have the same knowledge of and training in the laws of war as had their predecessors almost twenty-five years earlier. Many countries, especially the newly independent ones, lacked any experts on the subject. This was partially a result of the purposeful dismissal of the laws of war as an integral topic for both international lawyers and diplomats. From the 1940s to the 1960s, the study of the laws of war by international organizations and lawyers was interpreted as betraying the spirit and language of the United Nations Charter outlawing war.[23]

The absence of a common background in the laws of war was compounded by the differences in intent among the delegations. As one delegate described it, "Western delegations attended the session expecting to find an international law gathering and so tried to discuss the session's business, especially in regards to wars of national liberation, in legal terms. The other delegations saw it more as a political gathering with legal considerations taking second place."[24] Another scholar writes that the conferences were lit by an "inflamed Third World opinion against the existing legal order."[25]

The contest over the right of self-determination soon expanded to a debate over the laws of war. At stake was nothing less than the right of colonized peoples to decide on their own independence and the legitimacy of their use of force to do so. Members of national liberation movements from South Africa, Mozambique, Palestine, and elsewhere contended that the wars of self-determination in which they engaged were, in fact, international wars between contesting sovereign states and not treasonous disturbances or seditious struggles. Consequently, they argued, participants should be treated as *combatants* subject to international law and privy to international concern rather than as *criminals* subject only to domestic law. Recognized as combatants, rather than criminals, the participants in national liberation movements would be accorded the status of legitimate belligerents.

The importance of this cannot be underemphasized because "once one is accorded the status of a belligerent, one is bound by the obligations of the laws of war, and entitled to the rights which they confer. The most important of these is the right, following capture, to be recognized as a prisoner of war, and to be treated accordingly."[26] The primacy of this debate during the expert meetings and preparatory conferences indicates the challenges of conceptualizing and categorizing exactly who is a combatant.

By the mid-1960s, the possibility of creating a law that responded to the exigencies of wars of national liberation, or guerrilla wars, seemed more reasonable than it had at any earlier juncture. This was partly a result of the sheer proliferation of such wars, participation in the United Nations by formerly colonized states sympathetic to such struggles (as long as they did not occur within their territory), and, perhaps most important, the introduction of the concepts of self-determination and human rights into the lexicon of the laws of war. All of these invested these struggles with a newfound immediacy, if not legitimacy.

After World War II, the Soviet Union strongly advocated for the formalization and recognition of the right to self-determination, lobbying Western governments most effectively, and most slyly, with references to their own declarations of independence. Self-determination "as developed by Soviet backing for decolonization, and the original concept post First World War" meant self-determination for and of colonized people. And "a 'people' were no longer defined ethnically or racially—these factors were subordinated to a group of people being under 'colonial rule.'"[27] Moreover, the influential 1960 UN General Assembly resolution, the Declaration on the Granting of Independence to Colonial Countries and Peoples, specifically joined self-determination and decolonization, conceptualizing self-determination of colonized peoples both as a fundamental universal human right and as necessary to protect human rights. The declaration acknowledged the potential threat that decolonization posed to the maintenance of international stability and order, but concluded that a greater threat—manifested in the number of active conflicts—already existed. Therefore, it was only through decolonization that international order and stability would be assured.

Although it is tempting to see this as an absolute transformation of the logic that dominated the first part of the twentieth century (in which colonization was intrinsically linked to the establishment and maintenance of international order), the transformation was more complex; the formerly colonized nations strove to prove that they were capable of self-rule according to the standards *set* by the colonizers.[28] In fact, like the FLN in Algeria, participants in national liberation movements from the late 1950s to the 1970s appropriated discourses of civilization (barbarism and humanity) to legitimate their own claims to sovereignty—the sovereignty previously denied to them on the basis of those very terms. Although by the late 1960s and 1970s civilization was no longer the sole province of the Western European states, this was not because it had been dismissed as a standard of international order.[29] Rather, those peoples and entities hitherto barred from its purview successfully organized to re-signify and reassert civilization as a shared attribute. This facilitated their argument that self-determination was the province of civilized peoples. Therefore, at issue was not simply the practical failure of the laws of war to regulate internal armed conflicts but also the imperial history of the development and codification of the laws of war. Thus, the negotiation of the referents and meanings of these discourses was intense.

* * *

The claim for and foundation of the rights of protection and respect for combatants and civilians was also in flux throughout the 1960s and 1970s. Complicating matters was the problem that, insofar as the conduct of these wars was premised on securing the loyalty and complicity, if not participation, of the civilian population, by this logic alone the distinction between combatant and civilian on which the laws of war depend becomes (potentially) immaterial. Thus, the delegates debated the exact conception and categorization of the civilian and the combatant while the very existence of a distinction between the two was contested and, yet, still hailed as a referent of civilization.

In 1949, one can find within the commentaries on the IV Convention a certain respect for the human person, but the commentaries only tentatively refer to human rights. Indeed, a wistful passage within the commentaries on the IV Convention notes that:

> It is possible that a doctrine which is today only beginning to take shape may acquire authority in international law tomorrow and one day provide the basis for establishing the rights of the individual ... embody[ing] in law the original guiding principle of the Red Cross, that suffering should be relieved wherever it exists, without political considerations of any kind, in the name of the respect due to the human person.[30]

By 1973, the participants in the preparatory conferences accepted the concept of human rights as common currency, and the relationship between human rights and armed conflicts occupied the United Nations throughout the 1960s and 1970s.[31] A declaration from the 1968 Tehran Conference on Human Rights, held at the close of the UN International Year of Human Rights, captured the essential link: "Peace is the underlying condition for human rights and war is their negation." As might be expected from that time, the 1968 conference singled out minority racist and colonial regimes for particular condemnation and identified guerrilla warfare as worthy of particular study in further specifying the link between human rights and war. The debates at the United Nations—which, for the first time, directly affected the formulation of the laws of war—and at the preparatory conferences confronted the legacies of colonialism, which had historically denied both rights (human and sovereign) and recognition to specific peoples.

Later that year, the UN General Assembly passed a resolution requesting the secretary-general to report on three specific items: (1) the existing status of the implementation of the law of armed conflict, (2) the possible need for further instruments of this law, and (3) the possibility of outlawing certain methods and means of warfare. The secretary-general produced three reports in 1969, 1970, and 1971. Drawing from both human rights and the laws of war, these reports began to define the essential rights applicable in all armed conflicts, whether international or internal, and underscored the need for the further development of the laws of war as applicable to internal armed conflicts. These reports "rejuvenated" interest in the laws of armed conflict, which "had come perilously near to stagnation."[32] Consequently, the extension of protection and respect for combatants and civilians was linked directly to the concept of human rights, formulated as "to protect the human person" and to "safeguard essential human values...in the interest of civilization."[33]

Reviewing this work, a delegate at the 1974 conference noted, "the General Assembly had thus reaffirmed the existence and primacy of the inalienable rights of the human person by dissociating them from political, military, and other considerations."[34] He also voiced a claim heard throughout the conference: "It should be borne in mind that the purpose of those [1949] Conventions was not to serve individual or national interests or to deal with economic, still less with political problems, but to protect human life in the interests of the entire international community."[35]

Yet human rights were not the only coin in circulation at the conference. In a hotly debated and highly strategic move, participants in national liberation movements purposely defined the wars they fought as "just wars," consciously invoking the medieval concept of just wars as fought by a legitimate authority in pursuit of justice and peace. In particularly strong statements, the delegate from China insisted that "the wars of national liberation were just" because they were waged against imperialist and colonialist domination and that all wars "were divided into two kinds, just and unjust, and imperialism was at the root of all wars of aggression."[36] By asserting that the wars of national liberation were just, their proponents, including the South West Africa People's Organization (SWAPO), Palestine Liberation Organization (PLO), and the Mozambique Liberation Front, invested themselves and their actions with a sovereign juridical stature otherwise denied to them by the formal laws of war as codified in the 1949 Conventions. In fact, the proponents of national liberation compared themselves to the World War II partisans who had fought to retain and regain independence from Nazi Germany, claiming that their struggles were no less worthy of collective acknowledgement. Combatants in the wars of national liberation were no mere rebels, to be delivered to arbitrary justice, but freedom fighters struggling to secure justice, "a struggle in line with the one waged in the Second World War by many peoples of the world [against]...the menace of Hitler."[37] Recall that this was *exactly* the same argument used during the 1949 preparatory conference that resulted in the recognition of irregular combatants.

Also remember, however, that just wars are those in which the cause of the war also authorized the terms by which it is fought. Therefore, if the delegates accepted that national liberation wars were just wars, then the concept of just wars would be the foundation of protection and respect for combatants and civilians, not human rights. The U.S. delegate disagreed, stating that, if "the essence of humanitarianism was its universal applicability," then the "treatment of people affected by armed conflicts" took precedent over the evaluation of the "rightness or wrongness" of such conflicts.[38] In his view, which was not an isolated one, the revival of the concept of just wars was a subjective, particular interpretation of the cause of the conflict, and this threatened to displace or at least undermine the strength of human rights as the foundation of protection and respect.

His statement did not satisfy the proponents of the concept of just war. They argued that the concept was necessary because it was exactly the rights deemed universal and intrinsic that were transgressed at will during wars of national liberation. As the delegate from Togo pointed out, the "plight of tens of millions of peoples[,] ... victims of colonialism and apartheid," could be attributed to regimes that "signed the 1949 Geneva Conventions" but that nevertheless had "continued to deny individuals their fundamental human rights."[39] At stake was no less than the foundation of and reason for the laws of war.

Yet these negotiations were also deeply influenced by the knowledge that the human or humanitarianism to which the laws of war refer implicitly and explicitly excluded the participants in national liberation movements. These delegates pointed to the way in which, historically, the articulation of humanity and human, which supposedly served as the foundation for the laws of war, was fully compatible with and, indeed, dependent on an imperialistic racial logic. Self-consciously grafted on discourses of civilization, discourses of humanity and human rights did not automatically displace those hierarchies of power and protection embedded in discourses of civilization. As radical as was this re-signification of discourses of civilization, it did not absolutely replace the primary terms of exclusion (barbarism) through which civilization emerges. As Johnson comments:

> The "principle of humanity" has become embedded in the international law of armed conflicts, and universally it is used to denote restraints on the use of force that are in principle accessible by moral reflection on the part of all segments of humankind, though at the same time (as ... [the] ... preference for the term civilization reminds us) a higher moral goal that *some cultures* may better reflect than others in their conduct of hostilities.[40]

The delegates to the preparatory conferences grappled with questions such as: What would justify the rights and protections of the combatant and civilian? What exactly were their rights and responsibilities under the laws of war? Who was a combatant, and who was a civilian?

Throughout the series of expert meetings during the 1960s and 1970s, as well as in the preparatory conferences for the 1977 Protocols, the actors involved in the process voiced their skepticism. It was, as one expert commented, "extremely difficult, in practice, to distinguish between civilians and persons engaged in military operations."[41] Another expert held that the "fluidity" between combatants and civilians rendered such distinctions suspect.[42] And a third warned that the principle was in "jeopardy."[43] In 1974, the Organization of African Unity (OAU), composed of liberation movements, stated that the line between combatant and civilian is consistently "blurred," if not erased—a statement most recently repeated by the UN secretary-general in 2008.[44] In 1977, David Forsythe expressed a common view that "the innocent civilian may in fact be part of the enemy, or in any event, indistinguishable from the enemy."[45]

As in the 1940s, there were influential individuals who at the various exploratory meetings and preparatory conferences argued that the laws of war were admittedly outdated and that attempts to regularize wars were both utopian and misguided. Some suspected that premising the affirmation or development of the laws on the principle of distinction would, inevitably, lead to its failure; "is it still possible to take...[the distinction between civilians and combatants]...as the root principle of humanitarian law....Is there anything left to affirm if such a distinction is adopted as a starting point?"[46]

But the hesitations and objections of these individuals seemed to have little effect. They were overpowered by a familiar refrain: developing and observing the laws of war is integral to safeguarding civilization and, consequently, humanity itself.[47] One delegate to the preparatory conferences remarked, "the distinction between armed forces and civilians was a basic element of the law of armed conflict and an essential principle of civilization," without which "there would be a return to barbarism."[48] His words echoed those of the representative of the UN Human Rights Division, who in 1972 opened a meeting of experts on international humanitarian law with the exhortation to "save civilization."[49]

These comments capture how the laws of war, specifically the principle of distinction, are invested with productive and prescriptive force—a force that remains regardless of the practical violation or irresolution of the dictates of the principle of distinction. Delegates described the distinction between combatant and civilian as "blurred," emptied of "substance," and "indistinguishable." Not only was its empirical existence subject to dispute but also its legitimacy as a foundation for the laws of war. Nonetheless, the delegates retained the distinction because it continued to mark the differences between civilization and barbarism.

The principle of distinction is integral to particular understandings of what it means to be civilized, which, as we have seen, is also a form of understanding what it means to be human. That is, the principle of distinction persistently produces the difference between combatant and civilian, setting forth what it means to be either one or the other; its observance indexes the differences of civilization and barbarism and contributes to the constitution of humanity.

* * *

After years of contentious negotiations, the preparatory conferences concluded their work in 1977, producing two new treaties of international humanitarian law, Protocol I and Protocol II. Protocol I explicitly states its applicability to armed conflicts "in which people are fighting against colonial domination and alien occupation and against racist regimes in the exercise of their right of self determination."[50] This protocol supplements and develops the entire 1949 Conventions. In comparison, Protocol II supplements only Common Article 3 of the 1949 Conventions and its scope is highly restricted. Protocol II only covers conflicts that occur within the territory of a signatory to the 1949 Geneva Conventions between "its armed forces and dissident armed forces or organized armed groups which, under responsible command, exercise such control over part of its territory."[51]

Protocol II was eviscerated during the preparatory conferences once it was determined that wars of national liberation were to be included in Protocol I, granted international status, and recognized as legitimate. After this was accomplished, the same delegations that had advocated this interpretation of wars of national liberation saw little reason to risk threatening their newfound and hard-won sovereignty by allowing nascent internal challenges equal recognition or status. In fact, George Aldrich, who participated in the preparatory conferences, argues that the wording of Protocol I was chosen because it was understood to be "self-limiting to wars against Western powers by oppressed peoples and would not apply to wars within newly independent states."[52]

The delegate from Pakistan expressed this belief quite clearly on introducing his own revised version of Protocol II. The Pakistani delegation noted that delegations from "developed and under privileged countries" felt that Protocol II "ventured into domains which they considered sacrosanct...[e.g., internal conflicts within/against sovereign states]...and inappropriate for inclusion in an international instrument."[53] Countering the arbitrary division of internal conflicts into (1) internationally recognized national liberation movements covered by Protocol I and (2) dissident or rebel activity covered by Protocol II, the delegate from Norway retorted that the "distinction drawn between international and non-international conflicts, and the elaboration of two different Protocols with two levels of protection for victims...[depending on those legal classifications]...only led to discrimination or what has been called 'selective humanitarianism.'"[54]

His words were met with little response from the gathered delegates, many of whom had only recently argued that wars of national liberation (including their own) should no longer be excluded from the purview of international humanitarian law. Instead, the delegates from the newly independent countries sought to protect their nascent sovereignty (held to be their right, as it was the right of all civilized peoples) from international intervention in the guise of international humanitarian law and from domestic challengers. Although the delegate from Norway was correct in referring to select humanitarianism, it is perhaps more accurate to say that this particular debate captured both the delimitation of humanity and its production through exclusion. The human person, whose respect and protection were said to be independent of political, economic, or social context, came into existence only once combatants and civilians in particular wars were afforded particular protections and rights.[55] In fact, the delegates deleted a more determinate definition of the protection of civilian and civilian objects from Protocol II for fear of encouraging rebellion.[56] In analyzing the fate of Protocol I, we see that the question of who is a combatant and who is a civilian remains enmeshed with the politics of sovereignty.

As newly independent countries decided the substance and scope of Protocol II, those seeking to liberate themselves from imperialism invoked, seemingly paradoxically, discourses justifying imperialism: sovereignty, right, and discrimination. This might appear puzzling, but as Partha Chatterjee, among others, explains this is not to a simple recitation but a re-signification of their scope, meanings, and referents. That is, the discourses may appear derivative, but their expansive transformation and political use can lead to new forms of power and thought.

Claiming sovereignty prior to formal recognition, newly independent nations and national liberation movements rearticulated its meaning, effectively gaining international recognition for their combatants and forcing the laws of war to accommodate wars of their own making. Thus, as the Algerian War exemplifies, their invocation of standards of European civilization (sovereignty and discrimination) included a transformation of some of its historical elements. In particular, the renegotiation of combatancy affected the principle of distinction.

* * *

Protocol I purports to lay down a "more rigorous definition" of *civilian*, and the distinction between combatant and civilian, than had hitherto been accomplished in positive international humanitarian law.[57] It is only in Protocol I that the *civilian* is formally defined, developing Article 13 of the 1949 IV Convention (see chap. 5). Protocol I also codifies the principle of distinction, designed specifically to protect the civilian population against the effects of hostilities and not simply, as in the IV Convention, against arbitrary action on the part of the enemy. Article 48 specifically articulates the principle of distinction: "In order to ensure respect for and protection of the civilian population and civilian objects the Parties to the conflict shall at all times distinguish between the civilian population and combatants, and between civilian objects and military objectives and accordingly shall direct their operations only against military objectives."[58]

Article 48 of Protocol I, as Judith Gardam explains, is an abstract formulation of the principle of distinction, requiring a substantive definition for its implementation, a "clear content."[59] As the authoritative commentary of the ICRC states, it demands "a definition of the persons to whom it applies."[60] That is, the "application of detailed rules of non-combatant immunity is dependent on the definition of civilian."[61]

Found in Article 50 of the 1977 Protocol I, this definition is essentially "declaratory of existing international law" and, as such, is operative in all armed conflicts.[62] Yet, although the ICRC commentary might lead us to presume that the essential attributes and characteristics integral to the identification of the civilian stand alone, that is not the case. Rather, Article 50 is a negative definition of the civilian in which *civilian* is defined in opposition to *combatant*. Civilians are what combatants, members of armed forces, are not. This shift in the definition of the civilian from a "strictly defined category of civilians" to a negative definition was intended, according to the ICRC commentary, to ensure the increased precision of the category civilian by expanding the breadth of its coverage to *all* those who are not combatants.[63] The ICRC delegate to the preparatory conference asserted that the "credibility of humanitarian law...had suffered greatly" because the rules were "not always clear and precise."[64]

Nevertheless, even though this definition is applauded in the commentary, which refers to Article 50 as the "only satisfactory solution," with a "clear definition of each category,"[65] this definition did not resolve the fundamental doubt voiced throughout the Conferences. Article 50 fails to answer the questions of who should be recognized as a civilian and who should be recognized as a combatant because, as stated in Article 50, neither category stands forth independently. To put it a different way, according to Article 50, the definition of the civilian fails when and if its opposition to the combatant breaks down—but, as evinced in the wars of the national liberation and decolonization, this opposition was already failing. Nevertheless, in the words of one delegate, "attempts to confine the civilian population within narrower limits [i.e., to define it more strictly]...was tantamount to providing the imperialists and colonialists with a pretext for attacking the civilian population during their wars of aggression."[66] That is, the difference between combatant and civilian must be produced to defend, in this case, against imperialist violence. Put slightly differently, indictment against imperialist violence depended on the existence of a difference between combatant and civilian.

To respond to the indeterminacy of the distinction between combatant and civilian found in wars of national liberation, Article 50 directs that in "cases of doubt whether a person is a civilian, that person shall be considered to be a civilian." As I first mention in chapter 1, doubt not only provides the grounds for extending the category, but also (as codified in Article 50) is an integral attribute of the category itself; definition and doubt are simultaneously codified into the positive laws of war.

So, then, how is the civilian to be identified? As civilians are "persons who are not members of the armed forces,"[67] this negative definition relies on a concrete and specific meaning given to the *armed forces*. The definition of *armed forces* found in the 1977 Protocol Additional I is exactly the same as found in the III Geneva Convention on Prisoners of War and in Articles 43 and 44 of Protocol I, which supplements the specific rules and regulations of combatant status found in the III Geneva Convention. Thus, the civilian is what the prisoner of war and the combatant are not.

But is this really so? Although Article 44 appears straightforward, legal scholars criticize it for rendering the distinction between combatants and civilians more subjective. During one of the most contentious article debates of the diplomatic conference, the formal rules governing the identification of a combatant were relaxed. This was done to (1) recognize the unique circumstances and strategies of guerrilla warfare; (2) encourage compliance with the laws of war (namely the principle of distinction) by creating a standard of identification that all combatants could meet; and therefore (3) provide combatants in national liberation movements with prisoner-of-war status upon capture, which would not only recognize the legitimacy of their fighting but also provide a further inducement to conform to the laws of war.[68]

Article 44, specifically paragraph 3, alters the conventional definition of *armed forces*. Combatants no longer have to carry arms openly or distinguish themselves from the civilian population *unless, and only for such time as,* they are militarily engaged. The formal requirements of carrying arms openly and of wearing a uniform designated to mark combatant status are abbreviated to a specific duration. "Formulated as an unambiguous exception" to the fundamental obligation of combatants to distinguish themselves at all times from civilians—allowable only in highly particular forms of conflict—this abbreviation arguably confuses and challenges who is a civilian and who is not.[69] Consequently, rather than bringing about a more rigorous definition of the civilian—which potentially could have been accomplished through a precise delimitation of the requirements of the combatant—Protocol I can be read as the reverse. Broadening the category of combatant to include guerrillas and amending the strictures governing arms and uniforms created a more, rather than less, nebulous distinction. Far from tightening the distinction, Protocol I risks loosening it further.[70]

Moreover, the clarity and oppositional coherency of the combatant and the civilian were further loosened in a related decision. Delegates also concluded that civilians who participate in hostilities lose immunity from attack during and for the time of their involvement. Ostensibly designed to elicit proper comportment by civilians during armed conflict, in effect, this decision introduces the possibilities that a civilian may both participate in armed conflict and, while doing so, lose protection. Consequently, there now exists a category of civilian who acts as a combatant sometimes and may be treated as such. The opposition between combatant and civilian that grants a definition to each category is, by the very terms of the law, indeterminate and in flux. The introduction of this *temporal* element into the distinction—whereby combatants and civilians may act as each other, during which time specific protections and obligations are suspended or enacted—radically undermines the underlying assertion that the combatant and the civilian are only "conceived in opposition to each other."[71] How is an effective distinction, now understood to "be more difficult," not made "impossible"?[72] The delegates turned to the concept of visibility.

* * *

In 1973, the ICRC commentary on the draft Protocols Additional stated that the injunction to extend the rights and protections of civilians is "only valid in so far as the appearance and behavior are such as might be generally expected of persons claiming to be civilians."[73] "Uncertainty about the true character of the civilian," which governed the earliest discussions of the draft protocols, is dispelled if an individual looks and acts accordingly.[74] Unless this distinction between civilian and combatant can become "perfectly visible," there is little chance for its enforcement.[75] This reliance on visibility is picked up in the preparatory conferences by delegates who wished for a "fixed, permanent, and clearly visible" means of distinction, one that would be "physically observable."[76]

Other delegates were suspicious, aware of the disadvantages of absolute visibility. In 1974, the delegate from Vietnam decried visibility as a standard for the distinction between combatant and civilian, noting that it is a "rule in all neo-colonialist wars in Asia, Africa, and Latin America that the condition known as 'visibility' has always been an excuse for reprisals."[77] The compromise, as noted, was to limit *when* combatants must make their presence known and to change the requirement of wearing a full uniform to wearing a fixed recognizable sign.

As the ICRC commentary holds, carrying arms openly when in the "range of the natural vision of his adversary" or when "visible to the naked eye" will avoid the "confusion" of combatant with civilian and make the "distinction between an armed combatant and an innocuous civilian…perfectly clear."[78] According to the commentary, a combatant becomes visible *as* a combatant when arms are carried openly while launching or returning from an attack. At that moment, the blurred distinction is presumed to become clear. But carrying arms openly when visible to the adversary (either by the naked eye or through technology) only momentarily resolves the confusion of combatancy. It does nothing to address the situation of a civilian who does *not* look or act accordingly, especially because what a civilian *looks* like is never discussed. Thus, the criterion of bearing arms openly does not make the distinction between the two categories "perfectly clear" nor does it provide a permanent or fixed means of distinguishing them.

Instead, the answer lies in the imposition of permanence, a stable and secure substrate, from which combatants and civilians go out and to which they will always return. What we have learned is that civilians who lose their civilian status while participating in hostilities resume that status on ceasing their participation. Although a guerrilla combatant can wear "purely civilian dress, if the nature of hostilities requires it," this does not mean that he has the "status of combatant while he is in action, and the status of a civilian at other times."[79] Rather, once a combatant always a combatant. There is this strange perpetuity, an inalienability, of combatant and civilian that is otherwise not found in the laws or practice of war. It is as if the difference is, in its essence, self-evident—there to see even if neither the combatant nor the civilian is, as the delegates acknowledged, acting or identified as such.

It is here, when visibility and permanence converge, that it is close to impossible to avoid returning to discourses of gender to trace their operation within the 1977 Protocol I. The very definition of the civilian in the 1977 Protocol I directly draws on Article 13 of the IV Convention, which relies on discourses of gender for its very possibility (see chap. 5).[80] And, because each treaty of international humanitarian law is cumulative and responsive, supplementing and developing that which precedes it, such that "every new instrument can only have a purely cumulative or supplementary (but no destructive) effect,"[81] by it own terms it would be impossible to negate the continuing influence.

For example, after observing that "there is no doubt that there is still confusion as to who is a combatant and who is a civilian," one scholar concludes there must be a "heavy presumption that women and children are protected civilians."[82] Another scholar confirms her assessment, but strengthens it by recalling Francisco de Suarez's injunction that we can still identify the "clearly innocent," or what he also describes as the "indelibly innocent," by reasons of age, sex, and capability.[83]

As early as 1969, the ICRC had already argued for the lawful limitation of certain weapons of war because they "strike those who should be left outside the fighting: wounded, sick, women, children etc."[84] The influential 1970 UN General Assembly report on human rights in armed conflicts employed a familiar and consistent logic, whereby the protection of civilians is parsed into two categories such that the protection of civilians is "protection of women, children, the elderly and the sick *and* those who do not participate in the armed conflict nor contribute in anyway to the pursuit of military operations."[85] In taking up issues of human rights and self-determination in this 1970 report, the UN General Assembly for the first time deliberated on the "protection of women and children in emergency or war time, fighting for peace, national liberation and independence."[86] But, not unsurprisingly, women and children figured in the debate solely as "particularly vulnerable" and in need of protection. Regardless of the great numbers of women participating in armed conflicts, women and children were articulated as always already civilians in the discussions of the day.

But there are also other reasons to consider the influence of gender, reasons that may in the end help us understand why a permanence of position—combatant and civilian—can be posited in the face of empirical and juridical recognition of its indeterminacy. First, we must take seriously the position articulated by the delegate from Vietnam, and others, who clearly linked visibility to imperial aggression. Their critique resonates with contemporary scholarship demonstrating that a crucial element of imperial strategies was the arrangement of space, order, and governance to best facilitate the surveillance and control of the colonized. Indeed, this strategy can be approached as a form of visualization, which John Rajchman describes as "a scheme through which things are given to be seen, belong[ing] to the 'positivity' of knowledge and power of a time and place."[87] The strategies of imperialism called on discourses of gender, in particular the relation imagined between visibility and appropriation figured by women. As Barbara Harlow writes, "more than an analogy links the imperialist project of colonizing other lands and peoples with the phantasm of appropriation of the veiled exotic female."[88] Visibility is not a neutral concept or an objective ground of determination; instead, it is a specific form and effect of imperial regulation, relying on what Friedrich Nietzsche calls a "value positing eye."[89] This complex relation of visibility, gender, and imperialism is exemplified in the Algerian War. I now turn to how these multifarious relations among visibility, gender, colonialism, and imperialism, arduously tracked by these scholars, inflect the principle of distinction.

* * *

National liberation struggles are replete with discourses of gender. As many scholars have proved, these discourses are crucial to the social, ideological, and cultural reproduction of the nation and are deployed to various (and often seemingly contradictory) effects during armed conflict. For example, "at the same time that it took women within its ranks, the FLN held on to images of women as guardians of Algerian culture and to conceptions of the kin group as refuge from the destructive effects of colonial domination."[90] Thus, Algerian women were simultaneously fighting within the ranks as combatants, attempting to destroy French colonialism, while also retaining their sanctity as the guardians of Algerian culture. Their active transformative role as combatants did not appear to alter the identification of women as a passive refuge or as bearing an untouched or autonomous (and, considering French colonization, fictional) tradition of distinctly Algerian culture. In contrast, for the French liberating Algerian women from their presumed subjugation in Islam symbolized both the triumph of French patronage and the ease of trespassing into the heart and home of French Algeria—a converse yet corresponding valuation of the importance of Algerian women and also testimony to the formative effect of gender on the colonial project. Winifred Woodhull holds that Algerian women became "living symbols of both the colony's resistance and its vulnerability to penetration."[91]

This positioning of Algerian women is written into the "precise political doctrine" advocated by Colonel Trinquier during the Algerian war, which made the home the center of colonization and conquest.[92] By the very logic of this strategy of taking the home as a central target, relations of gender and the position of women are crucial; both women and relations of gender are subject to colonial administration and oversight. According to Franz Fanon, the French believed that "If we want to destroy the structure of Algerian society, its capacity for resistance, we must first of all conquer the women, we must go and find them behind the veil where they hide themselves and in the houses where the men keep them *out of sight*."[93] Medya Yegenoglu explains, "the veil was seen as the concrete manifestation of the colonized resistance....wearing the veil really meant the colony's resistance to being colonized."[94] Consequently, unveiling became a central strategy of French military oversight because seizing hold of the Algerian resistance required that it first must be made visible. And, continuing in this logic, as women were the essence of Algerian resistance and French colonization, women were the ones who must first be made visible. For the FLN, reclaiming the veil was, then, a form of resistance and, significantly, a way of remaining hidden from sight.

In a particularly grotesque enactment of their desire, in 1958 the French forcibly unveiled Muslim women in front of a crowd of Muslim men, accompanied by singing of the "Marseillaise" and chants of "Long live French Algeria." One can read this event, in which the "sexed body was suddenly laid bare," as a modality of rape, made no less so by the participation of French women in the unveiling.[95] It is also an explicit enactment of the relationship between Algerian women and the Algerian nation. Fanon directs our attention to this when he writes, "every rejected veil disclosed to the eyes of the colonialists' horizons until then forbidden, and revealed to them, piece by piece, the flesh of Algeria laid bare....announc[ing] to the occupier an Algerian society whose systems of defense were in the process of dislocation, open and breached."[96]

The symbolic and strategic contest over the veil both brought women into the conflict and made the structure and relations of gender a site over which both sides fought. It also illustrated the importance of visibility within the precise political doctrine of counterinsurgency. Etymologically, *visibility* is both a condition or state of *being* visible and the capacity to be seen. And, even as the French denigrated the veil as the penultimate sign of Islamic subjugation and suppression from which they sought to liberate Algerian women, the veil demarcated the limit of their oversight—the French were unable to govern behind the veil. Thus, the act of unveiling Algerian women illuminated the French desire for possession and control, for visual authority, that marked the their pursuit of Algeria. It also testified to French recognition of the implicit and explicit threat to their authority that the veil represented; the veil made perfectly visible the constancy of a hidden threat.

Algerian women were no mere ciphers for the nation, their bodies passive and inert, concealed or revealed at the hands of another; they were also active participants in its liberation. This made them not only objects of infiltration for the French but also agents of danger. Their participation in the war of liberation was actively encouraged, even glorified, and celebrated by the Algerian FLN.[97] "Revolutionary war is not a war of men. It is not a war waged with an active army and reserves. Revolutionary war, as the Algerian people are waging it, is a total war in which the woman does not merely knit or mourn for the soldier. The Algerian woman is at the heart of combat."[98] Under their voluminous dress, veiled women ferried bombs, ammunition, and instructions for the FLN, and occasionally even men. Moreover, men masqueraded as women to move freely and unhindered within the cities and, particularly, from the Kasbah (the protective labyrinth of the Algerian quarters) to the European quarters. Unveiling was believed to expose, and thus end, these practices. Unfettered French surveillance would restore their comprehensive authority over Algeria.

Yet this insistence that visibility was a means of security and certainty had been proven to be but a desire approximately a year earlier in the Battle of Algiers. Although the French wished to portray "the falling veil" (the title of one of the films produced by the French for a U.S. audience during the war) as a sign of the French liberation of Algerian women and as evidence of the superiority of *la mission civilisatrice*, they failed. In fact, Algerian women unveiled themselves to pass undetected and unsuspected—they were hiding in plain sight. Indeed, a "striking feature of urban guerrilla warfare was that it attracted generally educated women who seldom wore the veil."[99] The three women who placed the bombs in public spots at the start of the Battle of Algiers were "chosen for the job because, with their feminine allure and European looks, they could pass where a male terrorist could not."[100] Algerian women played on the French assumption that visibility and surveillance of Algerian women, stripped of the veil, led to a certainty of knowledge, possession, and control. First hidden behind the veil and then hidden by sex, Algerian women initially escaped the full surveillance of the French. As one former combatant testified, "I had to go unnoticed, be taken for a French person, so as not to arouse any suspicions, since anybody who looked like an Arab was searched and arrested. So, I used to put on make-up and dress in the French way."[101] The Algerian War brought to the fore the contest over the meaning and significance of women as both a site of struggle and intrinsic to the struggle itself, and highlighted its reliance on visibility to demarcate and materialize the boundaries of the war. "Vision with its accompanying image of unveiling the truth is figured as the key instrument in knowledge."[102]

As Michel Foucault has identified, the relationship of power and knowledge finds its expression in particular strategies of sight, premised both on the possibility of perfect visibility and on a rational correspondence among visibility, truth, and control.[103] To identify the adversary exactly, either in the laws or practice of war, presumes perfect sight. Yet, as the Battle of Algiers evinced, at the height of French surveillance three women passed undetected. They did not look like combatants. They looked like their sex—that is, they looked like proper French women—and so were identified as civilians.[104] But, instead, they functioned as a military arsenal. How was this to be negotiated?

During the period preceding the opening of the preparatory conferences for the 1977 Protocols Additional, the UN Commission on the Status of Women prepared its own report and resolution on the experience of women and children in armed conflicts. It held several open debates on the subject. Linked to the general discussions in the United Nations, the open debates in the commission referred to the necessity of respecting human rights in armed conflicts and, specifically, in conflicts over national liberation and independence. Ostensibly held to discuss the experience of women and children, in truth, these debates addressed only "the *protection* of women and children in emergency and armed conflicts in the struggle for peace, self-determination, national liberation and independence" and made little reference too much else.[105] This was a noticeably narrow discussion, and one that belies its earlier, more sophisticated engagement with the concept of human rights. Years before, the commission had begun to advocate equal political and legal rights for women in the context of social and economic inequality—formalized in the development and promotion of a UN Declaration on the Elimination of all Forms of Discrimination Against Women, adopted in 1967—and was working to convene the first UN Conference on Women.

Delegates to the Generally Assembly and to the expert meetings on the laws of war expressed significant doubt about whether a special declaration on the protection of women and children was appropriate, given that it could grant "special privileges" to women.[106] In 1971, a delegate to one of the expert meetings, on reviewing the draft protocols, commented, "the civilian population as a whole should be protected without special rules and discrimination in favor of women and children."[107] A hesitation to extend what was termed special protections to women was also expressed in the preparatory conferences, either because it would intimate that the general provisions did not apply to women or because it would undermine the full equality of women.[108] But, as the ICRC representative argued, "since the civilian population, and especially women, were becoming increasingly involved in present day conflicts, it was necessary to give them greater protection in relation to that enjoyed by men placed in a similar situation."[109]

In both the expert meetings and the preparatory conferences, as well as the commission and General Assembly discussions, participants voiced simultaneously the recognition of women as combatants—"all citizens, whether men or women, young or old, were involved as combatants"—and the complete dismissal of this fact.[110] Primarily, women were consistently conceived of as civilians.[111] This was so to such a degree that, in the Commission on the Status of Women, when the United States proposed an amendment stating that when "women are acting in a combatant role, they cannot expect to be accorded the special protection as a non-combatant civilian," it was roundly dismissed without debate. Considering the consistent and celebrated participation of women in the wars of national liberation, what did such a rejection require?[112] Why was it that even when women were highly and publicly visible as combatants they were not seen as such?

The justificatory introduction to the 1974 General Assembly Declaration on the Protection of Women and Children in Emergency and Armed Conflict captures the construction of the debate. "Expressing its deep concern over the sufferings of women and children belonging to the civilian population[,]…aware of the suffering of women and children in many areas of the world[, and]…conscious of its responsibility for the destiny of the rising generation and for the destiny of mothers…bearing in mind the need to provide special protections of women and children," the General Assembly called for the prohibition of attack and bombings and of chemical and bacteriological weapons, which inflict "incalculable suffering" and "heavy losses" on the most "vulnerable" and "defenceless" populations—women and children.[113]

The suffering of women and children testifies to the inhumanity of the colonizer, those "colonial and racist foreign domination Powers" that inflict "serious harm" and commit "inhuman acts" against them.[114] Fanon, too, describes the violence done to women "arrested, tortured, raped, shot down" as specifically testifying to "the violence of the occupier and to his inhumanity."[115] Imperialism is condemned, is condemnable, because of the suffering of women and children. Thus, the discourses of civilization that privilege and cite protection of women and children are invoked against those who would claim to possess civilization. Moreover, this condemnation also gains its force, and requires for its force, the innocence or inoffensiveness of women and children.

* * *

In the 1949 IV Geneva Convention, innocence and inoffensiveness referred to sexual vulnerability and reproductive capability, which in turn designated women and children as outside the fighting (see chap. 5). In the 1970s, reproductive capability became the salient characteristic. In the rhetoric of national liberation, women become powerful symbols of the nation, of its violation and its victory, of its future and its past. In particular, as we have seen in my discussion of Algeria, this particular construction both draws from and contributes to the interweaving of the heterosexual family and the nation whereby the future viability of the nation rests on the reproductive capability and heterosexual proclivity of women. "Women's biological capacities [become] ... patriotic duties or, through campaigns of sexual violence and terror meant to denigrate those outside the nation, vulnerabilities to be exploited."[116]

Either way, reproductive capacity and nationalism converge. The new nation is founded on and finds itself in the couple and the family, in which "an iconography of familial and domestic space" mediated women's agency and political participation, and domesticated their combatancy.[117] One result of this, as formulated by Fanon, is that the "*couple* becomes the basic cell of the commonwealth, the fertile nucleus of the nation."[118] Consequently, the "couple is no longer an accident but something rediscovered, willed, built. It is, as we can see, the very foundation of the sexual encounter that we are concerned with here."[119]

Significantly, this sexual encounter is explicitly geared toward heterosexual reproduction in service of the nation. Indeed, during the 1960s and 1970s there was a noticeable shift in emphasis in the discourses of gender, whereby the referent of these discourses was on reproductive capability (again, a change from sexual vulnerability of the 1949 Geneva Conventions) and the relation of women and children was expressly conceived of as maternal. Put another way, the logic of sex and sex difference repeated itself, although the emphasis now fell on reproductive capacity—not unsurprising because the discourses of war promulgated by the national liberation movements interwove family and nation, and the future viability of the nation rested on the reproductive capability and heterosexual proclivity of women.

Given this knowledge, the delegates' desire for and attainment of a fixed permanent means of distinction, one that would be perfectly visible, begins to become intelligible. Not only do sex and sex difference function as that substrate, but also, as Donna Haraway reminds us, "motherhood is known on sight."[120]

As the commentaries on these draft protocols indicate, delegates agreed that the purpose of suspending the death penalty for a pregnant woman was to protect the "*child unborn* and not the woman herself; this is why no prohibition has been made on the *pronouncement* of the death penalty."[121] And later in the preparatory conferences, when delegates passed measures outlawing the death sentence for women, the intent was to protect children. Articles or discussions that were introduced suggesting these protections should equally apply to others who might care for children, such as fathers or other family members, were dropped without further discussion.[122] Thus, the special protections of women and children continued to be simply the special protection of children and of only a particular subset of children.

In other words, the presumption of the visibility, materiality, and determinacy of maternity, within a particular matrix of sex and sex difference, makes possible the distinction between combatant and civilian at a particular time when no distinction is discernible. This construction of sex and of sex difference is maintained in the drafts and debates of the preparatory conferences and informs the construction of the civilian. What is worth noticing is the construction of a highly particular and highly specific understanding of sex—female sex, that is— for the purposes of legitimating and founding independent national states in the period of decolonization. Therefore, the discourses of gender permeate the very production of the laws of wars directly responding to this political formation. Here, once again, it appears that sex difference contributes both to how we see and what may be seen; it also contributes to what is considered self-evident on sight. The interpretation of female sex as reproductive capability is a particular, specific historical-political interpretation that acts simultaneously to ground the permanence of difference between combatant and civilian, and women as mothers within the nation. And here it is the valuing of the unborn child that becomes paramount.

But, discourses of gender, innocence, and civilization operate in more ways than this. Notably, the 1972 preparatory meetings relied on background papers that incorporated presumptions of gender, innocence, and civilization, for example that, in African countries, boys of fourteen "would automatically be combatant[s] in time of war" whereas girls would "probably [be] married."[123]

This presumption of sex differences is repeated more vividly in the ICRC commentary, which paints the "harrowing spectacle of boys, who have barely left childhood behind them, brandishing rifles and machine-guns and ready to shoot indiscriminately at anything that moves."[124] Thus, gender and civilization, referenced in terms of race and innocence, further cohere in the Conventions and contribute to highly a particularized understanding of protection, one in which innocence is denied to specific children.

* * *

Another suggestive effect of discourses of gender, innocence, and civilization is found in the inducement for compliance with the condition of carrying arms openly. Guerrilla wars, as all the delegates agreed, were marked by the asymmetrical distribution of technological, economic, and military resources. Therefore, the advantage guerrillas held over their adversaries, who usually possessed all or the greater amount of the resources, was invisibility, literally the ability to see without being seen—the very advantage that the French feared and the Algerian veil signified. And, as we shall see in the next chapter, the cost of being seen was paid in life itself: "a guerilla seen is a guerilla dead," went the slogan of the Guatemalan military.[125] So, why would they be willing to relinquish that advantage—to move in and out of sight—even momentarily by carrying arms openly? The answer conjures up again the force of chivalry and its construction of masculinity.

To be sure, the delegates to the conference encouraged this compromise, foolhardy on its face, by granting combatants who fulfilled the requirements of visibility prisoner-of-war status if captured. As one delegate stated, the "preparedness to take the risk implies that person deserves prisoner of war status."[126] Thus, the incentive to comply was articulated in terms of protection and fair treatment upon capture, no small reward in light of the history of summary executions of captured rebels. Yet, amazingly enough, the delegates also provided separate but equal status for any combatant who failed to fulfill the requirements of visibility—who "relies on his civilian attire and lack of distinction to take advantage of his adversary in preparing and launching an attack"[127]—because, although such a combatant "loses his right to prisoner of war status," he "preserves the right to be treated as one."[128] Such combatants are not immune to prosecution for those acts, as a legitimate combatant would be, but their treatment must be equivalent, including all the judicial rights, to that of a prisoner of war.[129]

This is an incredibly fine line, one that both explicitly and implicitly draws on the persistent presence of honor to encourage conformance with its rule. As one expert to the 1972 meeting insisted, "as a preliminary step…the need for the concept of honourable conduct between combatants [must] be preserved."[130]

Appeals to chivalry were also interspersed with discussions of compliance, as seen in the notation from the delegate from Belgium that all combatants should be encouraged to transcend the limits of the law and engage in "chivalrous respect" toward fellow combatants.[131] Moreover, if combatants fail to reinforce the important distinction between themselves and civilians, they "necessarily jeopardize the protection of … [those] … they were attempting to serve."[132]

Thus, underlying the motivation and motives of combatants to distinguish themselves is a recognition of their mutual responsibility to one another as participants in a particular ritual of war, as well as their benevolent responsibility toward those who rely on them for care, protection, and good treatment—yet another interesting legacy of chivalry. Moreover, the reliance on honor as mutual respect, recognition, and regard for combatants is crucial in preserving the delicate and precarious difference between acts of perfidy and mere ruses of war. Acts of perfidy, which took on a greater emphasis in the 1977 Protocols Additional because of the loosening of the regulations for combatant identification, are those that "invite the confidence of an adversary to lead him to believe that he is entitled to, or is obliged to accord, protection under the rules" of international law. Understandably, it was the perfidious feigning of civilian status (a trick that Alberico Gentili attributed to a man who dressed as a woman) that was the subject of much worried discussion during the drafting of the 1977 Protocols.

Yet the restraint on perfidy was not originally understood as solely a legal rule (although it was later restricted to the rules of international humanitarian law) but also as a moral rule.[133] To preserve fairness in fighting, it was absolutely imperative that the ruses of war (fair strategies of deceit) did not prey on the trust or betray a "brother's confidence when their family's reputation for fair dealing is uniquely at stake."[134] The success of the distinction is "dependent upon the degree of compliance by combatants with their obligation to distinguish themselves" and restrain from "perfidious breaches of this obligation."[135]

In other words, the success of the distinction is premised on the moral resolve and professional expertise of the combatants to conduct themselves honorably and in accordance with international humanitarian law. Perfidy is the breach of personal and collective honor; it is, in Best's words, "a sin against the Holy Spirit,"[136] in that it both exposes and, in so doing, undermines the entire edifice of laws of war as balanced on nothing more fragile and nothing stronger than honor among men who recognize themselves as equals. Thus, the abrogation of this obligation—an obligation rooted in the chivalric valor of the warriors—is attributed to the disintegration or absence of militaries and of men that define and distinguish themselves accordingly. The inheritance from divine and natural law is easily evident in the principle of distinction between combatants and civilians found in the law of nations—it essentially remains understood as a grant of mercy among men of honor.

THE CIVIL WARS OF GUATEMALA AND EL SALVADOR

"You're a guerrilla."
I replied, "I don't know what a guerrilla is. Is it a man or an animal?"

—Richard Falla, *Massacres in the Jungle: Ixcán, Guatemala, 1975–1982*

* * *

The civil wars of Guatemala and El Salvador tell us much about the effects of the discourses of gender, innocence, and civilization and their roles in defining exactly who should be considered a civilian and who should be considered a combatant. These conflicts raise all the issues that were debated during the codification of the laws of war in the 1940s and 1970s. Each war was fought using a combination of conventional and unconventional strategies, and although the conflicts were internal, they were heavily internationalized. Moreover, the parties to the conflict possessed different commitments to and understandings of the laws of war, and the international community had a sufficient, if not considerable, stake in both the conduct and resolution of the wars.

Although the peace accords and monitoring missions of the United Nations are not my focus here, the inclusion of international humanitarian law in the monitoring agreements of both the United Nations Observer Mission in El Salvador (ONUSAL) and the United Nations Verification Mission in Guatemala (MINUGUA) was groundbreaking. ONUSAL was the first UN mission to include the observation and verification of international humanitarian law in an internal armed conflict, beginning with its first phase of monitoring a cease-fire. MINUGUA also addressed international humanitarian law in its duties, and the designation of captured Guatemalan revolutionary forces as prisoners of war occupied the representatives of both sides of the conflict in 1994. Thus, as the war progressed, the laws of war became a greater influence in the interpretation and evaluation of the conflicts. This is especially noteworthy in Guatemala, where the initial reference and recourse to the laws of war by international and national actors were severely curtailed in comparison to El Salvador.

The applicable laws of war to the conflict in El Salvador included customary law, Common Article 3 of the 1949 Conventions, and Additional Protocol II. In Guatemala, only customary law and Common Article 3 were applicable. The provisions of Protocol II are more detailed in scope than Common Article 3, although many of the essential provisions of the laws of war were applicable in both conflicts as customary law.

The questions here are exploratory as well. Although I certainly put forth explanations for compliance with and implementation of international humanitarian law, I do so within a rich narrative of events and elements, rather than suggesting a straightforwardly causal sequence. This complex configuration of realities demonstrates both the integral role of the principle of distinction in regulating international and domestic order, and underscores the powerful effects of the series of discourses on compliance with the principle of distinction. Since the definition of the civilian in these civil wars draws from Protocol I, the same essential problems plague its definition and the discourses of gender, innocence, and civilization set its possibilities. This may be an obvious conclusion—but *how* it matters is what is of interest.

In analyzing the distinction of combatant and civilian produced during these wars, I touch on the intensity of the anticommunist beliefs held by the Guatemalan and Salvadoran militaries. I consider the strength of the international community in both Guatemala and El Salvador, especially its networks in and its knowledge of each country. I also address the familiarity of the Guatemalan and Salvadoran governments with the laws of war, the role of the United States, the intensity of the conflict, and the geography of each country.[1]

The conflicts in El Salvador and Guatemala essentially were fought over similar divisions (e.g., social and economic inequities, and repressive and authoritarian governments) and, oddly enough, broadly similar goals (e.g., establishing democracy or, for the governments of each, preventing communism) that were understood in radically different ways—to put it mildly. Each conflict transpired over roughly the same decades (1970s–1990s); employed comparable weaponry (although land mines and aerial bombings were used more frequently in El Salvador); and were bound by a common international logic, the Cold War. The strategies of these wars (winning hearts and minds, as it was in the Algerian War) are now a leitmotif in the conduct of most contemporary wars, including, most recently, the contemporary U.S. war on terror. Furthermore, the fluidity of battle in these internal armed conflicts preceded the emphasis on nonlinear engagements or "battle spaces" presently favored by the U.S. military.[2] Thus, the construction of the civilian in these complicated internal wars becomes highly relevant in considering contemporary wars.[3]

In addition, the Guatemalan and Salvadoran conflicts are also sufficiently different to provide a comparative analysis. For example, the Guatemalan insurgent forces were far weaker militarily than those in El Salvador. The international solidarity and human rights networks were involved more closely and more consistently in advocacy and publicity in El Salvador than in Guatemala (where such efforts were almost nonexistent in the first four years of the 1980s and, even in 1985, foreigners were sternly warned that "foreign meddling in Guatemalan actions cannot be tolerated"[4]).

The decade I examine here, 1980–1990, was the decade of the highest concentration of massacred, displaced, and refugee people. It begins with the unification of the Salvadoran revolutionary forces into the Frente Democrático Revolucionario (FDR; Revolutionary Democratic Front)/Frente Farabundo Martí para la Liberación Nacional (FMLN) in 1980, includes the unification of the Guatemalan revolutionary forces into the Unidad Revolucionaria Nacional Guatemalteca (URNG) in 1982, and ends two years before the peace accords in El Salvador (1992) and six years before the peace accords in Guatemala (1996). I concentrate on the early years of the 1980s when debates over the civilian were incited and the deaths from the civil wars reached their pinnacle. The comparative analysis of these two conflicts provides us with exemplary knowledge of the interplay among the definitions of combatant and civilian and the laws and practice of war.

In Guatemala, over 200,000 people were killed or disappeared during the thirty-six-year conflict. Of those killed in the eighties, approximately 80 percent were Mayan and 20 percent were Ladinos. (In the earlier phases of the conflict, the majority of the victims were Ladinos.) Over 600 entire villages were eradicated, and approximately 200,000 children orphaned. In El Salvador, during the six years of the most intense violence (1978–1983), approximately 1 percent of the population was wiped out, and, by the end of the war, 75,000 individuals had been killed.[5] In both countries, NGOs and truth commissions decisively documented the responsibility of the military for the majority of these deaths and disappearances (approximately 91 percent in Guatemala and 85 percent in El Salvador). Yet, sadly, many of the perpetrators had more in common with their victims than they did with the men who commanded them to kill. The dead were Catholics, campesinos, journalists, priests, nuns, catechists, students, union organizers, union members, lawyers, teachers, professors, human rights activists, Ladino, Mayan, men, women, and children of all ages. What is striking about the descriptions of those who were killed is how an array of distinct social roles and identities was articulated into one subversive threat by the governments of both countries. The diversity of these individuals was collapsed into what all were said to be—communists and guerrillas. As one commentator noted in regards to El Salvador, the military "equate[d] the government's critics

with the enemy, repressing trade unionists, campesino leaders, oppositions poli-
ticians and student protesters with the same or more force than they use on real
insurgents."[6]

In Guatemala, under President Fernando Lucas García (1978–1982) and the
subsequent presidencies of General Efrain Ríos Montt (1982–1983) and General
Humberto Mejía Victores (1983–1986), the Guatemalan military annihilated the
very coalition that produced the insurgent URNG: unions, the peasantry (specifically the indigenous Mayan), Catholic priests and lay workers, students, and
development workers. In these killings, the Guatemalan government effectively
reversed centuries of conventional norms of distinction by targeting exactly
those individuals who, as we have seen, were to be set aside during war: priests,
students, and farmers. The negative definition of the civilian (i.e., as what a combatant is not), so favored by the authors of the 1977 Protocols for broadening the
definition of the civilian and ensuring no potential civilians would be left outside
of its boundaries, had the reverse effect in Guatemala; it left the legal definition
and identification of the civilian highly malleable and subject to the discretion of
the state, which could then exclude most from its scope.

The national revolts of the 1980s were fought by the Guatemalan and El
Salvadoran states as low-intensity, counterterrorist, counterinsurgent, or small
wars. Nonetheless, these small wars were considered pivotal fronts in a major
(U.S.-led) counteroffensive against the encroaching threat of communism. In
1981, the U.S. ambassador to Guatemala held that "Guatemala and the US were
in a common battle and shared a common enemy, the international communist
conspiracy, which had a beachhead in Nicaragua and was using El Salvador as a
way station on route to its real targets—Guatemala and the Mexican oil fields."[7]

The ferocity with which the Guatemalan and Salvadoran militaries attacked
their perceived enemies indicates the perception of risk posed by such a conspiracy of communists. In both Guatemala and El Salvador, the violent and swift
suppression of dissent had been a hallmark of state policy for decades. However,
the United States had financed the "professionalization" of the security (military
and police) forces in the 1960s, and so the repressive techniques used by these
security forces acquired new rationales and sophistication (and were also refined by individual commanders' experience in fighting other insurgencies—
such as the brother of President Lucas García, whose military strategies were
learned from fighting with the French in Algeria). The buildup of each military
to respond to internal rather than external threats remained constant through
the 1980s.[8] Indeed, even as the beneficiaries of the security training programs
of both countries explicitly shifted from the police forces to the military and
paramilitary forces, the underlying rationale remained the same: "The training
curriculum…combines police and military techniques to meet a threat which

combines guerrilla warfare with open criminality...respond[ing] to the quasi-military nature of the...terrorist threat."[9]

The counterinsurgency campaigns mounted by El Salvador and Guatemala followed a typical pattern popularly summarized in Chairman Mao Zedong's famous aphorism: guerrillas are fish and the people are the water they swim in; if the temperature of the water is right, the fish will thrive and multiply. To prevent the fish from thriving, counterinsurgency forces in Guatemala and El Salvador attempted to (1) "gain physical control of territory and populace," (2) "penetrate" authority throughout the country, (3) promote economic and social development, and (4) raise the direct and indirect costs of supporting insurgencies for both the populace and the insurgents.[10] Overall, the first three tenets form the strategy commonly known as "winning the hearts and minds" and were, in combination with the fourth tenet, the dominant approach employed throughout both conflicts.

The guiding assumptions of this strategy are that (1) the insurgents are an illegitimate force seeking to overthrow the legitimate, duly constituted authority of the state; (2) the popular base of insurgencies is created and held through threats, propaganda and terror and the "ability to coerce a passive and generally apolitical peasantry"; and thus (3) insurgents and insurgencies are fundamentally neither credible nor valid challengers to the incumbent authority, nor do they have a willing base of popular support.[11] In other words, the fundamental postulate of counterinsurgency is that there are no legitimate challenges to the state, only illicit threats to legitimate states.

As Michael D. Schafer points out, this founding principle of counterinsurgency negates a priori any evaluation of the legitimacy or illegitimacy of the sovereign state itself and the laws of war define very few forms of state sovereignty (in Protocol I) as illegitimate (see chap. 6).[12] The laws of war are sparse in regard to internal armed conflict, and the strictures that do govern internal armed conflicts are noticeably weaker and lack comparable enforcement mechanisms (see chaps. 5–6). Insurgencies do not pose an outright challenge to the laws of war insomuch as they expose its fundamental ambivalence in regards to the sanctity of state sovereignty. After all, as the 1949 IV Convention decreed, a civilian is one whose nationality can be identified and assessed, and state sovereignty is to be held sacrosanct if at all possible.

According to the logic of counterinsurgency doctrine, any attempts to engage in an analysis of the legitimate sovereignty of the state, much less debate the claim by the state to sovereignty, are defined as direct and immediate threats to the stability of the state itself. As such, analysis of or debates about state legitimacy are outside the normal purview of political engagement. In the case of Guatemala, "this interpretation reinforces the idea that unjustifiable violence occurs only outside state structures and, conversely, that violence by the state to defend itself is mandated and thus justifiable."[13] As I have suggested, the disquieting fact is that the laws of war do not confront this interpretation and, in fact, allow it to stand.

The positing of legitimate and illegitimate violence contributes to an environment, well captured by the concepts of *La Violencia* or *La Situacíon,* in which political engagement, agency, or debate risks death and in which innocence is attributable only to those who refuse to participate. Therefore, if counterinsurgency doctrine politicizes the entire nation (similar to the strategies during World Wars I and II), identifying all individuals as a potential combatants, and the civilian is what the combatant is not, then the very possibility of the civilian is premised on the existence of apolitical, private, passive individuals—conjured by the iconic image of women and children.

Adhering to the presuppositions of a "hearts and minds" strategy, the National Plan for Security and Development in Guatemala held that "the causes of the subversion are heterogeneous...but it can be controlled." Similarly, the 1982 army counterinsurgency plan (Plan de Campaña Victoria) stated that "subversion exists because a small group of people support it and a large number of people tolerate it....Hence the war must be fought on all fronts."[14] In El Salvador in 1981, U.S. General Fred Woerner (memorialized in the infamous "Woerner Report," the general's effort to devise a successful strategy for the Salvadoran military as requested by the Pentagon) took up the task of preparing the Salvadoran armed forces to fight against the insurgents. Both the Guatemalan and El Salvadoran security forces chose and deployed strategic tactics based on the "annihilation" and "elimination" of all support systems—physical, material, and psychological—necessary to the survival of insurgents.[15]

The regions most forcibly impacted in Guatemala, in addition to the capital city, by the imposition of the counterinsurgency plans were the central and western highlands—the departments of Quiché, Huehuetenango, Chimaltenango, Alta Verapaz, Sololá, and Peten. In total, eighteen out of the twenty-two departments were strongly affected.[16] In El Salvador, in addition to the capital city, the northern regions were primarily affected—in particular the departments of Chalatenango, Morazán, Cabañas, and La Union. These regions were the targets of focused counterinsurgency campaigns by the militaries because of the dense concentration of popular political and revolutionary organizing believed to be occurring in and orchestrated from there.[17] Thus, there were regional, in addition to individual, distinctions made between combatants and civilians.

These regional categorizations, a geographical combatancy, both indicate the recognition of the difference between combatant and civilian, and undermine the predicate (as found in Protocol I) of the visibility of this distinction as identified through the bearing of arms or the wearing of uniforms. Instead, *regional* categorizations—in which territories rather than individuals are designated as hostile—are founded on ideological and other invisible differences. The El Salvadoran military spoke of guerilla controlled zones, and free fire zones, where all individuals were considered insurgents: "in these zones...there are no civilians."[18] The Guatemalan military color-coded particular areas as guerilla redoubts, with red marking territory (as it did in El Salvador) where there were to be no distinctions made between combatant and civilian.

As the delegate from Vietnam inveighed in 1974, insurgency and counterinsurgency wars, in which loyalty is often the only demarcation, belie the very concept of a visible distinction between combatant and civilian.

Moreover, the security forces of each country shared a common philosophy during the initial armed conflicts. Essentially, these forces believed that the destruction and reeducation of the popular base would weaken the insurgencies. Just as the military identified distinct geographical regions along a continuum of (to use Lieber's phrasing) manifestly loyal, loyal, and disloyal, so too did the military designate individuals. The belief in the continuum of revolution (from popular support to armed insurgency), along with a geographical combatancy, further blurred the legal principle of distinction, which is juridically predicated on the binary of combatant and civilian, made visible through arms bearing. This blurring through geographical combatancy and the continuum of loyalty is by now an obvious point; nevertheless, it points to the construction and stabilization of this putative binary as all the more significant, contested, and powerful.

In both Guatemala and El Salvador, the years 1980–1983 were the worst. In Guatemala, 1981 was catastrophic, ending with 18,000 deaths. In El Salvador, during the same year, at least 16,000 people died. The levels of violence in El Salvador steadily declined after 1981 (with the exception of 1988–1989). But this was not the case in Guatemala, where violence continued to spike (although never reaching the same heights as in 1981). In considering the ebb and flow of violence in both countries, we must bear in mind that the declines in violence may partially, and tragically, be explained by the brutal fact that there were "just not as many people left to kill."[19]

There was an attempt by both governments to institute a "clean counterinsurgency," as the U.S. ambassador to El Salvador termed it in 1980.[20] In 1982, the Ríos Montt government began an attempt to rectify the incredibly negative international image of the country by altering its counterinsurgent strategy to "be more compatible with the democratic system."[21] Even *El Grafico*, the Guatemalan national newspaper, described the massacres in the highlands as a "type of genocidal annihilation," noting that while there was "much talk of improving our image abroad...this image will continue blacken itself more and more with this new resurgence of blind and absurd violence."[22] But, although the violence might have been absurd, it was not blind.

Beginning in 1982, both governments attempted to be more judicious in their strategies of war and selection of targets. This de facto acknowledgement of the importance of discrimination between combatant and civilian is significant. As both the postwar Guatemalan and Salvadoran truth commissions concluded, such acknowledgement attests to the premeditated military strategies of each government, governed by a coherent command structure. The recognition of the existence of a potential distinction between combatant and civilian necessarily required justifications for the deaths of hundreds of thousands. Thus, the process of negotiation of the identification and determination of the civilian and combatant was deliberate. The words of a U.S. advisor in El Salvador capture this nicely: "The repression was excessive at times, certainly overly brutal.... [but] I have no problem with the idea of identifying your enemy and going out and killing him."[23]

* * *

Discourses of gender were influential in distinguishing between combatant and civilian in the Guatemalan and Salvadoran conflicts. In 1982 in Guatemala, a senior official in the Ríos Montt government explained that "we knew all along that the government had a policy of going into villages, taking out all of the men above 14 years of age, tying their hands behind their backs and executing them."[24] Those males not killed were conscripted into either military service for the government or, beginning in 1982, forced to serve in the patrullas de autodefensa civil (PACs; civil defense patrols). Implemented by President Lucas García, and effectively refined by President Ríos Montt, the PACs placed Mayan men (who were one-quarter of the entire Guatemalan population) under the direct command of the army and in the direct service of its policy of mass murder.[25]

This further confused the distinction between combatant and civilian. First, service in the PACs translated into the militarization of even ostensible civilians. Second, this militarization of civilians intimated that members of the PACs were potentially legitimate targets for attack by both the URNG and the Guatemalan military. Third, the PACs generally reified the presumption that all Mayan males were combatants—the only question was with/against whom they were fighting. In El Salvador, the militarization of the rural male population was not as extensive in Guatemala. But the combatants in both armies were inducted and indoctrinated through gendered psychosexual rites of combat and training.[26] Sex (e.g., being male) was a proxy for combatancy while the discourses of gender invested that difference with particular meaning and power.

Although women were active members of the insurgent forces, the masculinization of combat and the presumption of male combatancy dominated in both Guatemala and El Salvador. In El Salvador, women were more active as direct combatants in the insurgent FMLN, probably a result of the higher percentage of women combatants overall (30 percent versus 18 percent in Guatemala). Whether a reason for, or a result of, this higher percentage, the FMLN paid greater attention to gender equality in both the processes and goals of revolution in El Salvador.[27] Still, participation of women in both insurgencies was widely known. Cable traffic from the U.S. embassy in Guatemala noted on several occasions the participation of women guerrillas, and on one occasion, a conflict was denoted a guerrilla attack because of the participation of over thirty women.[28]

Nevertheless, human rights violations and death rates for women were noticeably lower than for men in both wars. One immediate way of ascertaining this difference is the greater numbers of internally displaced and widowed women (as opposed to men) in both wars. In addition, figures from Guatemala suggest that, overall, women made up only 15 percent of the named dead. The statistics suggest that in these two wars the discourses of gender were protective—not only preventing women from participating in direct fire but also guarding them from direct fire from the military. For instance, in El Salvador, one female FMLN combatant recounted her experience under attack with four hundred other villagers she had been assigned to defend: with the army shouting at them to surrender, and mortars falling all around, she began to yell, "there are no guerrillas here, we're just women and children and old people."[29] The military then allowed them to surrender unharmed. This is similar to events during the American Civil War, in which women deployed the discourses of gender to ensure their own safety. Similarly, in the French-Algerian War, the discourses of gender were used to disguise women's combatancy.

The evocative phrase *women and children* was heard on all sides as NGOs sought to indict the militaries for their slaughters, while the governments defended their strategies by swearing that no women and children had been intentionally harmed. As one Salvadoran ambassador stated, "I reject emphatically that the Army of El Salvador was engaged in killing women and children. It is not within the armed institution's philosophy to act like that."[30] The protection of women and children was and remains a powerful incentive for international action, and the failure of that protection remains a powerful incentive for international condemnation.

A survey of Latin American organizing attests to the power of this discourse. Traditionally, women and widows were the first to successfully organize in the midst of state repression and violence. In fact, widows and the families of the disappeared founded the first domestic nongovernmental human rights organization in Guatemala in 1984, Grupo de Apoyo Mutuo (GAM); widows also began the second such organization in 1986, Coordinadora Nacional de Viudas de Guatemala (CONAVIGUA; National Coordination of Guatemalan Widows). Both were modeled after similar organizations in El Salvador. Yet, as the grue-some murder of two GAM founders illustrates, such efforts remained dangerous to initiate.[31] In a perverse reflection of the power of maternalism, the Guatema-lan military also posted women soldiers to specifically to assist in the pacification and nurturance of the rural population in its model villages.[32]

As we have seen in earlier discussions of Francisco de Vitoria, Hugo Gro-tius, and Francis Lieber, respect for and protection of women and children are a standard by which civilized nations are both judged and identified. In 1977, the discourses of gender both celebrated and indicted civilized states for their treat-ment of women and children. Consequently, it is not difficult to identify how the treatment of and respect for women and children in both Guatemala and El Salvador were used, by IGOs, NGOs, and all parties to the conflicts, as a standard of good and evil (to invoke Francisco Suarez's description of natural law).

Although the discourses of gender may have protected women (as widows and as mothers), they also striated the very particular modes of torture practiced in both countries against women. The militaries of both countries raped and gang-raped women, and they killed unborn children in their mothers' wombs. This practice was attributed only to the military. Indeed, one Guatemalan widow who lived in one of the provinces most devastated by the conflicts stated that, although she believed "sometimes there is no difference" between the military and the Ejército Guerrillero de los Pobres (EGP; Guerrilla Army of the Poor, one of the strongest insurgent groups predating the consolidation of the URNG), the one variable of note was that the "EGP does not rape women because it is prohibited."[33] Likewise, the FMLN in El Salvador did not engage in rampant sexual violence.[34] In both countries, a particularly malignant form of torture practiced by the military was to force women wash clothes, prepare food, and en-tertain before and after witnessing and experiencing mass slaughters and being publicly raped.[35] It also appears that the military killed women and children in more brute ways. Survivors in Guatemala who recounted the deaths of women and children led Americas Watch to conclude that the "army does not waste its bullets on women and children."[36]

I stress here the multiple effects of discourses of gender, and the negotiations over the meaning, to expose the fragility of the putative protection offered to women and children as ostensible civilians. As surely as the discourses of gender may protect women, they may also inform the parameters of a particular form of torture.

The conduct, strategies, and experiences of war were gendered in more ways than these in both Guatemala and El Salvador. Most generally, males between the ages of seven and sixty were presumptive combatants, whereas women and children of both sexes below the age of seven were presumptive civilians.[37] In fact, in Guatemala the victims of the massacres of 1982 were predominantly women and children; in El Salvador, the military massacred selected women and children too. Plausible explanations for these deaths include that men were more likely to flee, be engaged in combat, or be dead already and, thus, less represented in the death tolls. Certainly, this might explain the predominance of women and children as victims—but why, in light of this otherwise dominant construction of women and children as civilians, were they victims at all?

It appears that, insofar as the principle of distinction worked at all, sex and sex difference stabilized it. However, it did not work very well. It is here that an analysis of the discourses of civilization is helpful. We are accustomed to referring to massacres as indiscriminate, but this is misleading. The massacres in Guatemala and El Salvador were, in fact, highly discriminate, intentional killings; the victims were chosen. To understand this, we must focus on the discourses of civilization.

* * *

"The outlandish violence of foreign doctrines, alien to our Guatemalan idiosyncrasies and customs, is trying to destroy our Army," railed a Guatemalan colonel in 1984, at the graduation of the first class of the School of Ideological Warfare.[38] For the governments and militaries of both Guatemala and El Salvador the foreign ideology threatening their sovereignty, security, and way of life was a composite of Marxist-Leninist-communist-subversive-terrorist thought.[39] As Salvadoran Colonel Campos Anaya stated, "the Communists have only one formula which is to defeat and destroy capitalism and democracy. This is our worst enemy."[40] In the national context, "our" referred to the traditional governing elite and its role as the sanctified guardian of the state. The members of this elite believed the threat originated in a carefully orchestrated communist campaign of propaganda and proxy wars. The militaries of the two countries held themselves to be the ultimate and final defense against communism, which threatened the "Western Christian way of life."[41] Thus, both internal armed conflicts occurred within the larger Cold War and within a mindset bound by the specter of an imminent overthrow of "our" way of life.

The military of both countries claimed a specific historical and political (paternal) mission, one that invested each with residual or partial state sovereignty. This mission was to protect the "nation's traditions and its permanent values."[42] Consequently, the militaries of both countries believed they were fighting a historically ordained defensive war to preserve the proper and civilized order against a radically subversive and aggressive foe—one that sought to destroy the nation (as the military identified and defined it). "You are a subversive. You don't belong in our democracy," said one Salvadoran sergeant after destroying the testicles of his victim thus ensuring that no future subversives would be born of this man.[43]

Unsurprisingly, as we have seen in other chapters, these discourses of civilization introduce and make possible divisions between those who should live and those who should die, informing the methods by which this is accomplished. As Guatemalan President Ríos Montt told President Ronald Reagan in December 1983, he did not pursue a scorched-earth policy but, rather, "a policy of scorched communists."[44] Here we can begin to identify how the discourses of civilization trumped those of gender. Civilization requires the participation and submission of all to propagate its future. These discourses make no distinctions among those who threaten its existence. One U.S. military author, accepting the predicate that women and children are not to be killed, explains how such killing occurs: "The soldier who does kill must overcome that part of him that says that he is a murderer of women and children, a foul beast who has done the unforgivable.... He must believe that not only is this atrocity right, but it is proof that he is morally, socially, and culturally superior to those whom he has killed."[45]

In Guatemala, unlike in El Salvador, these discourses of civilization racialized and materialized in the indigenous Maya. If the weighted opposition of communism and democracy can be said to provide the meta-referent for discourses of civilization during the conflicts, the Maya of Guatemala provided a national referent and, significantly, a visible referent otherwise absent in the war of insurgencies. The Guatemalan military justified the killing of Guatemalan Mayans using logic reminiscent of the Spanish Requirement. Just as the Requirement offered the Indians the Faustian choice of slavery or death, so did Ríos Montt offer the Mayans the choice of submission or death. In a sequence not unfamiliar from earlier chapters, first Ríos Montt offered, in May 1982, a pardon. He called for a temporary cessation of military operations, giving the guerillas thirty days to surrender, and to be received as "prodigal sons." In a bizarre broadcast he said, "What I want to say is...the amnesty wants to offer pardon....He who pardons is noble and the person who accepts it is a noble person."[46] Not unsurprisingly, few guerillas took him at his word, and so he withdrew all reconciliation. "Listen well, Guatemalans. We are going to combat the subversion by whatever means we want....prison and death to those who plant [the seeds] of criminality, violence, and treachery."[47] As he most famously stated at the start of the worst repression, beginning in June of 1982, "The Indians are going to die. However, the army's philosophy is not to kill them, but to win them back, to help them."[48]

The distinctions of civilization, of the differences among and within states, not only legitimated the counterinsurgent war as defending the international and domestic orders but also informed the specific treatment of the Mayas as both children to be (re)educated and savages to be exterminated. Helen Fein, in her discussion of genocide, speaks of the dehumanization of entire collectives and individuals as the preparation for massacres.[49]

Yet in Guatemala, this binary of human/nonhuman was not in circulation. Rather, there was a gradation of differences, as we have seen in earlier chapters. This gradation recalls Vitoria's interpretation of the Indians (see chap. 3) and also the one posited by the U.S. government during the U.S.-Indian wars (see chap. 4). Vitoria argued that the Indians were like the children of the Spaniards and that only in resistance did they become a treacherous foe. Likewise, in the nineteenth-century United States, the Indians were considered the wards of the government; nonetheless, these gentle wards of the nation were to be exterminated so that civilization could progress.

Similarly, the Maya of Guatemala were conceived of as children who had been tricked by the guerrillas but who nonetheless could still be slaughtered as subversives. If they submitted and came down from the mountains to resettle in model villages, they could be saved—although at the cost of their independent lives and identity as Maya. When we understand the historical, particular (racialized) discourse of civilization, the seemingly paradoxical argument that the Guatemalan military needed to kill the Mayas to "rescue" them, as the 1982 Victory Plan suggests, becomes quite logical.

Informing these seemingly contradictory constructions was the promotion of one united and stable national Guatemalan identity (which Ríos Montt fondly called *Guatemalidad*) through the modernization and assimilation of the Maya. In Ríos Montt's view, the development of a national unity, and the economic development and modernization of the state, depended on the incorporation of the Indians. As we can see, these tired tropes of colonial and imperial Spain had remained active and powerful in Guatemala. The construction of the Maya "as both the 'same' in that they are Guatemalans and mestizos...and as primordially different, racially distinct, a frightening mass of savages always ready to revolt" informed and were enfolded in the contemporary models of counterinsurgency.[50] The Maya could be rescued or they could revolt; the possibility of national unity and progress depended on the outcome. As we have seen in previous chapters, the ascription to the barbarian an innate tendency to revolt against civilization, to derail the progress of modernity, and to revert to savagery has influenced the position of Indians in the laws of war since Vitoria; this threat of savagery, said to be inherent only in barbarians but a skill of civilized men, was a founding argument for the necessity of chivalric, personal, and military discipline because it helped institute a difference between barbarism and civilization. The capacity to discriminate was an effect of this discipline and, thus, a hallmark of the civilized state and civilized man—even if the principle of distinction must be jettisoned in wars for civilization.

* * *

In Guatemala, another equally powerful construction linked the strength of the state to withstand the threat or injury of communism, to the "health" of the Maya. This construction argued that the condition of the Maya—who were pagans, poor, and peasants—weakened the Guatemalan state from within. As Greg Grandin writes, "much of the anti-communist rhetoric that the military used to identify Maya culture as either the real or potential seedbed of insurgency closely parallels the disease metaphor: whether cholera or communism, indigenous culture and society bred virulent threats to the nation's well being."[51] The accuracy of his claim is borne out by a Guatemalan army officer who, referring to a model village, stated, "The people here are like patients who are convalescing; they've just come out of the hospital; they need to be taken care of. The moment the Army leaves, the sickness will strike them down again."[52]

The formative racism and paternalism of the Guatemalan military, combined with a defense of civilization against the specter of sedition, created a world in which *Maya* was always already synonymous with subversion and sickness. (Indeed, the military described service in the PACs as a form of cleansing or rehabilitation that would rid Mayan men of the sickness and corruption of subversion.[53]) Moreover, this racism and paternalism created a world in which the murder of the Mayans as actual or potential subversives was the only antidote for the disease that they bore. Consequently, killing those who refused to submit, quarantining those who showed signs of the disease, and inoculating all those who survived guaranteed the unification, health, progression, and development of the Guatemalan nation. The vitality of the nation was expressed in an assessment of the health of the social body for which the military was responsible. One of the model villages, all of which were funded in large part by the U.S. Agency for International Development (AID) program, was introduced as an "an ideologically new anti-subversive community," just one of the "very impressive laboratories" for the "Indians."[54]

Notice too that, according to this construction, the infirmity of a sick people or the vulnerability of a child—other legitimate and possible interpretations of the construction of the Mayas as ill or childlike—were trumped by the emphasis on the potential harm embodied by the Maya. Thus, the contention that certain individuals should be protected because they are weak, infirm, and vulnerable was actually invoked in Guatemala to *deny* the Maya the protection said to arise from this vulnerability. There is no natural link, as posited by the 1949 and 1977 treaties, between infirmity, sickness, vulnerability, and age, on one side, and protection, on the other. Instead, this link must be made, and in Guatemala, it was effectively unmade. Instead, vulnerability and weakness were taken as justifications for the severity of the state repression because they indicated the susceptibility of these individuals to disease and dissent. The negotiation of meanings of these discourses is paramount.

The construction of the Maya as diseased and hidebound had no parallel in El Salvador. Nonetheless, there was a horrifying similarity between the attitude of the Guatemalan government toward the Maya and the attitude of the Salvadoran government toward children—it deemed children to be compromised by infection and insurrection. From the moment of their gestation, the children of subversives, and subversive children, posed potential threats to national unity and health. Their murders prevented the spread of this subversion, an illness carried, it seemed, in the blood. As a member of the Organización Democrática Nacionalista (ORDEN; Nationalist Democratic Organization), the Salvadoran paramilitary force, explained, "They are all communists, even the children. They are all sick with communism. How did they get sick? They were indoctrinated by a priest."[55] Their deaths were part of the required protocol to protect the health of the nation because subversion was transmitted through the blood. In this counterinsurgent logic, children were not healthy, they were not immune, and they were not innocent. They had no resistance to the communist infection and were thus susceptible to it. In this particular manifestation, the line between who should live and who should die was drawn in blood, much as the colonial order had depended on caste and bloodlines to ensure its reproduction.

The formulation and articulation of a concept of immunity is both an antecedent to and a definitive attribute of the civilian. Moreover, we can see how sparing an individual (i.e., recognizing immunity) can too easily remain solely an expression of charity and mercy—an indulgence—granted by individuals and states invested with sovereignty through the discourses of civilization. If the elemental rule of war is one of barbarism, which the laws of war do not contest, then a civilian is one who is granted an exception, a particular privilege otherwise usually denied.

Note that discourses of civilization also operated to exclude Guatemala and, to a much lesser extent, El Salvador from the society of self-identified civilized states. Guatemala was a pariah state for many years due to its excessive violations of human rights, whereas El Salvador began its peace process after calls for a "Guatemalan solution" to the civil war ended with six dead priests, as well as their housekeeper and her daughter. In beginning a peace process, as well as in refusing earlier to engage in acts of repression to the same degree of Guatemala, El Salvador sought to differentiate itself from its barbarous neighbor.[56]

Yet, Guatemalan President Ríos Montt's shift of counterinsurgency tactics as he took over from President Lucas García was, in part, a result of Ríos Montt's desire to reintegrate Guatemala into the international community. President Lucas García stated that, although he wished for economic and security assistance from the United States, he refused to change his tactics to encourage such support. Lucas García held that he "was engaged in a war with subversive leftists' forces which would not follow the rules, and there was no possibility of defeating them in a clean and legal manner."[57] Ríos Montt avoided such absolutes and benefited from so doing (although even in 1984 Army Chief of Staff General Rodolfo Lobos Zamora congratulated Guatemala on resisting outside forces and inflicting a "substantial defeat on subversion" through "our own nationalist strategy"[58]). Testimony prepared for the U.S. House of Representatives to request economic aid in August 1982 explicitly mentioned Ríos Montt's orders to military commanders to "protect innocent civilians" as indicating a major transformation in Guatemalan government policy and opinion.[59]

Actually, what Ríos Montt stated in July 1982 to his commanders when introducing his plan to "rescue" the Mayas was that he would leave the details of implementation of Plan Victoria to their discretion but that he "expected results."[60] Moreover, although he wished "each commander to take special care that innocent individuals would not be killed," he was more concerned that "if such unfortunate acts did occur, he did not want to read about them in the newspapers."[61] Thus, although he clearly recognized the importance of the principle of distinction to the international reputation of Guatemala, his intention to enforce it was secondary to winning the war. To defend civilization against communism, confining himself to warfare recognized among civilized states as conforming to civilized practices was a risk he was not fully willing to take. Indeed, the massacres begun under the presidency of Lucas García were regularized under Ríos Montt with the systematic "inclusion of women, children, and the elderly," the protection of whom had long been taken (as we have seen) to be the hallmark of civilization.[62]

Here we can see how the discourses of civilization generate and are complicit with the barbarism they are said to oppose. Wars in defense of civilization are not necessarily civilized wars and, indeed, often expose the artifice of such distinctions. Moreover, the killing of women and children—otherwise held as antithetical to the standards of civilization—is made intelligible when those women and children pose an immediate and direct threat to civilization. But what, then, becomes of innocence?

* * *

Innocence is a polyvalent discourse within these wars, one that was invoked most consistently in the solidarity work of IGOs and NGOs. The innocence of those targeted, killed, and disappeared was difficult to adjudicate because discourses of innocence entangled with discourses of civilization and gender, making the formulation of innocence difficult to trace. By suggesting that innocence was difficult to trace, I do not mean that it was difficult to identify who was responsible for the majority of the murders, deaths, and repression. Accountability for the massacres was evident to most who were cognizant of the violence in Guatemala and El Salvador during the wars (except the U.S. embassy personnel in both countries, particularly in Guatemala, who wondered who was killing whom well into the middle 1980s).[63] The truth commissions in both countries ultimately confirmed who was responsible. The difficulty of tracing the discourses of innocence here is in untangling the process by which the innocence of the population, individually and collectively, was negotiated.

As previously mentioned, there was the construction of children as sick; intertwined with this illness and lack of immunity was the construction of children as guilty. What sin, asked the parents of the murdered children, had their children committed? The answers given conjure the slaughter of the innocents ordered by King Herod. As explained by several top army officers in Guatemala, the foundation of the guerrillas' organization was the family and, therefore, the extermination of the guerrillas required the obliteration of the family. In El Salvador, the three-year-old son of an editor of an independent newspaper was grabbed by a member of the National Guard, who threatened, "we are going to take him, we have to kill him because he is the seed and we have an order to stamp out the seed."[64] In almost the exact same locution, a Guatemalan women testified about the threats made by members of the military and the PACs: "they constantly threatened to kill the male children in our village, saying they should die because they were bad people: *semillas del mal* [bad seeds; seeds of the guerrillas]."[65]

The threat to state sovereignty began with the child, thus guilt was a condition of birth. Although this construction of children is not alien to the history of the laws of war, the practice of killing (barbarian) children who might pose a threat in the future was condemned in the influential writings of the sixteenth-century Scholastics and continued to be condemned, albeit with less force, throughout the history of the laws of war. In fact, a return to the Scholastics also reminds us to trace the construction of innocence as found in its relation to politics, in which harmlessness is equated with apoliticalness. One of the more striking characteristics of the conflicts in Guatemala and El Salvador was the production of political participation and, indeed, any participation in politics outside the realm demarcated by the military and the sovereign state as inherently seditious. The highly selective individual murders in both countries in the late 1970s and 1980s followed this logic. The military targeted human rights activists, priests, union organizers, and students for assassination and disappearance.

The cries of family members on identifying their dead—"no es politica [she's not political]!"—resonate in the testimonies from both wars.[66] As one survivor of the massacre of El Mozote in El Salvador explained, "I remember people saying, 'Don't get involved. Let's just live and work and not get involved.'"[67] In Guatemala, some of the families of the disappeared protested that their loved ones did not participate in politics, nor were they excessively religious. The insistence on the latter becomes intelligible in light of statements such as the one made by a Guatemalan colonel: "We make no distinctions between the Catholics and the Communist subversives."[68]

Here innocence is adjudicated according to actions, but these actions are only understood according to religious and political beliefs. Hannah Arendt captures the consequences: "Every thought that deviates from the officially prescribed...is already suspect, no matter in which field of human activity it occurs. Simply because of their ability to think, human beings are suspect by definition, and this suspicion cannot be diverted by exemplary behavior, for the human capacity to think is also the capacity to change one's mind."[69] The capacity to change one's mind made the minds of the population a direct target. Therefore, innocence was never a stable state. For example, it was the putative naiveté or political innocence of the Indians that encouraged the Guatemalan military to begin its reeducation program in the model villages. As Diane Nelson puts it in describing official policy in Central America, there was an interpretation of the mind as the "instrument of subversion."[70] A Guatemalan woman remembered, "The military commissioner asked my neighbor, 'Do you have good or bad thoughts?' And she said, 'I don't think anything bad.' But they took her away. I could hear her screaming as they took her away."[71]

Let us consider this understanding of the volatility of innocence within the customs and laws of war. In both Guatemala and El Salvador, innocence was adjudicated according to the imperceptible and invisible distinctions discussed by Augustine. Recollect that Augustine held that the attribution of innocence or guilt was incumbent on the state of the soul and heart; as such, it was primarily an interior (an assessment of the soul) rather than exterior (an assessment of action) ruling. For Augustine, it was "not what the man does that is the thing to be considered; but with what mind and will he does it."

This formulation of innocence as an interior state found a complementary expression in the strategies promulgated to combat the insurgency wars during the early 1960s and 1970s, notably those in which the Guatemalan generals had gained their experience. In Algeria, the military tactics and training contended that distinctions between combatant and civilian were "non-physical, often ideological boundaries."[72] Thus, even though many of the delegates at the 1977 preparatory conferences attempted to tie innocence in war to the bearing of arms, it escaped those bonds. The question remained: Is innocence a result of what one does, what one believes, or who one is? Ironically, even in their struggles to bind innocence to a physical, material, and visible action—the bearing of arms—the delegates to the 1977 preparatory conferences recognized the insufficiencies of this construction and were warned against it. Because they were unable to resolve this, the consequences were deadly.

The 1998 *Guatemala: Nunca Más!* report attempts to chart the innocence of the victims according to their physical involvement. It notes that the perceptions of culpability discussed by the survivors "allude to the involvement with one of the parties to the conflict" and "whether or not the victims were known to be active, armed agents of the conflict."[73] Nevertheless, on closer examination, this standard fails. In this report it becomes clear, instead, that the survivors understood innocence to be both the absence of arms and an abstention of involvement that ranged from beliefs to practices. Certainly, neither the Guatemalan nor Salvadoran military held that arms-bearing was the fundamental index of innocence. This belief was vividly captured in Ríos Montt's proclamation that anyone who belonged or had belonged to organizations that upheld the philosophy of Marxism-Leninism could be arrested without warrant, establishing a "crime of opinion."[74]

In Guatemala and El Salvador, entire geographical regions and villages were designated as culpable. "It is natural that in these subversive redoubts the armed men are not there alone.... it's natural that there were a series of people killed, some without weapons, including some women, and I understand, some children."[75] The model villages of Guatemala, much like the reservation system for the Native Americans in the United States, were where the "good" Indians both lived and remained. Also, in Guatemala, the military color-coded regular villages—from white to red—to indicate the villagers' conscious and unconscious loyalties and to guide military action. In contrast, the Salvadoran military refused to acknowledge the presence of civilians in any insurgent area. As a Salvadoran army spokesperson explained, "In the conflict zones, there simply aren't any civilians. The people who move in zones of rebel persistence are identified as guerrillas. Good people—those who are not with the guerrillas—are not there."[76] Consequently, to be recognized as a civilian by the militaries one had to not live, act, or believe beyond a certain set and space of circumscribed possibilities. Hegel writes that innocence can also be "merely non-action, like the mere being of a stone, not even that of a child."[77] As a child raised in one of the model villages put it, "You had to be silent, completely silent. You were not free."[78]

Taken together, the construction of innocence in both of these conflicts was predicated on apolitical and passive behavior, a silence of word and deed, for by either one could be found guilty—reminiscent of early constructions of women as fundamentally apolitical and, thus, subhuman. Indeed, the very conception of individual or collective action and independent thought is rendered suspicious even though those capacities, as Arendt is so careful to remind us, are what render us human.

In Guatemala and El Salvador, to be recognized as a civilian by the governments required the abandonment of both political agency and mobility. This was not contrary to the laws of war, which require that only those outside of and posing no threat in the hostilities should be protected as civilians. Although a tragedy in itself, the greater tragedy was that, even in attempting to conform to these predicates, survival was not assured. Once again, the testimonies of those who survived these conflicts tell us that, for all of its appeal, passivity was not protective and neutrality was not possible. According to the Guatemalan military, "neutrality...[was] not permissible."[79]

One of the fundamental contradictions of the construction of the civilian in the laws of war is that remaining neutral does not necessarily result in protection.[80] First, survival during war requires complex decisions and negotiations that demand a high degree of knowledge and agency in a world with few choices; second, neutrality is rarely allowed. As Americas Watch reported during the Guatemalan conflict, "No-one is permitted to remain neutral. Those who do not aid the government may not be allowed to live."[81] Demands for recognition as civilians articulated within the laws of war might, paradoxically, either endanger individuals or be impossible to fulfill. Therefore, "commentary that only portrays civilians as fully innocent bystanders in war situations misrepresents the ugly complexities of war and can lead to dubious conclusions and policy recommendations."[82] The testimonies and experiences of the civil wars of Guatemala and El Salvador suggest that innocence is an ambivalent discourse on which to premise protection, one that demands too much from its subjects in exchange for far too little.

* * *

I have discussed the constancy of model villages in internal armed conflicts as a strategy of civilization. The immobilization of a particular population, which, concurrently, allows the designation of this population as civilian, is a strategy that the modern laws of war rely on. The collection and restriction of individuals within a particular geographical area to facilitate their identification as civilians is promoted by the positive laws of war in Article 14 of the IV Geneva Convention to designate safe areas for those who are "taking no part in the hostilities and whose weakness makes them incapable of contributing to the war potential of their country" and by the work of the ICRC to establish places of refuge. In saying this, I am by no means arguing that the intentions or consequences of the formulation of Article 14 and the establishment of model villages are precisely the same; nevertheless, the laws of war do not naturally challenge the practices of war and, in some cases, the laws and practices may be frighteningly copacetic.

In the establishment of particular villages or refuges, the means of distinguishing between civilians and combatants—remember, the foremost concern of the authors of the 1949 IV Geneva Convention about identifying and protecting civilians was their scattered existence—are the same. That is, in situations of indeterminacy that mark the conduct of war, the immobilization of individuals in one particular spot allows the government to conclusively identify them as civilians or as combatants. It is not sufficient to invoke the principle of distinction against the conduct of conflict without carefully attending to the ways that it draws from and, also, allows practices putatively antithetical to its purpose.

Thus far, we have seen in these two conflicts that the indeterminacy of identifying the civilian allowed for a range of interpretations, produced by discourses of gender, innocence, and civilization. We have also seen how the negotiation and use of these discourses argue for and against the sanctity of the civilian. By tracing the productive power of these discourses, we can identify the service these discourses provide. The indeterminacy of the distinction between combatant and civilian does not translate into the impossibility or futility of determining the distinction; it heightens the significance of the domain of intelligibility in which these decisions are made and disputed. Consequently, we now turn to an analysis of the formal laws of war applicable to the conflicts, touching on international strategies used to pressure compliance with these laws.

* * *

Both Guatemala and El Salvador ratified the 1949 IV Convention in the early 1950s with no reservations. The Protocols Additional were ratified, with no reservations, by El Salvador in 1978 and by Guatemala in 1987. The latter ratification was rather amazing, considering it was done before the end of that civil war. This ratification is best explained by both the desire of the Guatemalan state to continue to mitigate its pariah status and by the fact that in 1987 there was little chance that the Protocols could formally apply to the conflict.

The conflicts occurred within sovereign territories of Guatemala and El Salvador, although each also had substantial and consistent international financial support, training, and participation. (In addition to financial support, there is ample evidence that the United States, Taiwan, Argentine, Chile, Nicaragua, and Cuba sent military advisors/commanders to both El Salvador and Guatemala at various times.) Nonetheless, because the range of the battles took place primarily within sovereign territory (although at times spilling over the borders with Mexico and Honduras) only Common Article 3 of the 1949 Conventions, Protocol II, and customary law were specifically applicable to the conflicts. In El Salvador, Common Article 3, Protocol II, and customary law governed the conduct of the war. In Guatemala, only Common Article 3 and customary law applied because the insurgent URNG was never able to hold and control territory or develop a solid chain of command. (As an indication of this, Victoria Sanford, an anthropologist, tells of hearing from an EGP commander that, by 1982, orders from the guerrillas were taking at least four months to filter through to their combatants in the field.[83])

The codification of the 1977 Protocols specified a fivefold differentiation of armed conflicts: (1) interstate armed conflicts as defined in the 1949 Conventions, Common Article 2; (2) national liberation armed conflicts as defined by Protocol I, Article 1(4); (3) noninternational armed conflicts as defined by Protocol II, Article 1 (1); (4) internal armed conflicts as defined by Common Article 3 of the 1949 Geneva Conventions; and (5) internal disturbances as defined by Protocol II, Article 1(2). Theoretically, the characterization of a conflict proscribed the scope of the obligations and protections afforded to all its participants. On the ground, the characterization of a conflict often alters because the intensity, parties to the conflict, and strategies change during the war and are highly disputed. As a result, the authority to define the conflict is of utmost importance. Obviously, this ability to characterize the conflict assumes greater importance in conflicts 2, 3, and 4 because these are conflicts in which the insurgent party benefits greatly from the extension of protections and the imposition of obligations and restraints on the sovereign state and, conversely, in which the sovereign state is most likely to resist incursions or critiques of its sovereign right.

The authority to characterize conflict is primarily invested in the sovereign states occupied with the conflict. Although Common Article 3 is applicable as soon as an armed conflict "objectively exists," it is the sovereign state that, de facto, decides whether such a conflict is indeed in existence.[84] Characterizations by NGOs, regional organizations, and IGOs are nonbinding, whereas the ICRC, preserving its neutrality, does not publicly characterize conflicts.

Nonetheless, the characterization of a conflict by the members of the international community does affect the construction and interpretation of the conflict. Decisions by insurgents to acknowledge the legitimacy of international humanitarian law (as did the FLN in Algeria and the FMLN in El Salvador) also influence the general evaluation of the conflict. In 1980, the United Nations recognized the applicability of Protocol II of the 1949 Geneva Conventions to the conflict in El Salvador. In 1981, Mexico and France recognized the FMLN-FDR as a representative political force. The Reagan administration was able to blunt the effectiveness of this recognition by "mobilizing nine Latin American allies to protest it as an interference in El Salvador's internal affairs."[85] Nonetheless, it was impossible to ignore the FMLN, and its political counterpart the FDR, because it had a permanent representative at the United Nations and the recognition by Mexico and France led to a concomitant recognition of the FMLN/FDR by the United Nations.

The very existence of this debate publicized the conflict and shifted the terms (and space) of the debate from a solely domestic conflict to an international one. Also contributing to this shift were the 1981 acceptance by the FMLN of the Geneva Conventions as applicable to the war and its request for the ICRC to monitor the behavior of both sides. These actions identified and legitimized the FMLN as an equal party to the conflict, brought it international attention, and demonstrated its acceptance of the rules of international society—much as similar actions had done for the Algerian FLN (see chap. 4). Notable among its decisions was the FMLN's taking and turning over of prisoners of war to the ICRC—a practice that the El Salvadoran military refused to engage in for a year (1981–82) of the war.[86]

In contrast, the Guatemalan insurgent forces never publicly ascribed to or allied themselves with the laws of war. Some suspect that this decision, rather puzzling considering that the Salvadoran (and Nicaraguan) insurgents did so, can be attributed to the relative lack of sophistication of the URNG.[87] Others disagree, arguing that the Guatemalan insurgent movements were simply overwhelmed by a military that was more willing to fight than the Salvadoran military. Both before and immediately after their unification into the URNG, the insurgents were not prepared to either incorporate the number of new participants or adequately fight a war against the Guatemalan military—particularly after the devastation of the Organización Revolucionario del Pueblo en Armas (ORPA; Organization of People in Arms, one of the insurgent groups)—much less engage in detailed strategic debates.[88]

In any event, while the FMLN was effectively wielding international humanitarian law and building its complex network of international representatives, the URNG was struggling to merely survive. The absence of the laws of war as a standard of reference and as an operating protocol for the URNG, denied it an effective instrument to detail and document the violations of the Guatemalan government. It was difficult to find a comparable instrument of accountability applicable during armed conflicts because human rights law permits some derogation during states of emergency. Moreover, neither the URNG nor the international solidarity network that eventually formed was as knowledgeable or, in the case of the network, as densely operative as the FMLN and its network. Further, although the United Nations began to express consistent concern in 1980 about the conduct of the hostilities, and the Commission on Human Rights requested a special rapporteur for Guatemala in 1983 (after the height of the violence), the work of Mark Colville, Viscount Colville of Culross, the appointee, was dismal and desultory.

Overall, international public perception, interpretation, and knowledge of the Guatemalan conflict were minimal compared to the conflict in El Salvador. Moreover, the absence of a declaration from the URNG gave the Guatemalan government greater control to characterize the conflict as being between a legitimate state and armed terrorists, and also denied the URNG the forum to negotiate (as did the FMLN) over the application and interpretation of the laws of war.[89] In addition, the specific decision of Americas Watch in 1980 to begin using international humanitarian law as a methodology for documenting abuses and assigning accountability was stymied in the case of Guatemala.

One reason for this was that information was more difficult to receive from Guatemala. The ICRC was not even present to document or assist in the conflict until 1988, and the one or two domestic NGOs (almost all the international NGOs had left) were located in the capital operating under obscenely dangerous conditions. Another reason was that Common Article 3, the applicable law to the Guatemalan conflict, is less fully detailed than Protocol II, which was applicable to the Salvadoran conflict. Protocol II contains explicit provisions for the protection of the civilian population, whereas Common Article 3 really provides little more than would be required by "'civilized' states in relation to the treatment of common criminals."[90] Consequently, Americas Watch had less specific standards by which to monitor and document the practice of the war. As one of the proponents of the international humanitarian law methodology noted, the lack of information from Guatemala and the scope of the conflict made it a poor test case.[91] The fact was that the military was committing most of the abuses. Consequently, Guatemala was a politically unwise test case for a methodology intended to demonstrate the neutrality and honesty of NGOs in evaluating and indicting abuses by all parties to the Central American conflicts.[92]

Finally, the conflict in Guatemala never consistently reached the necessary intensity to qualify as a Protocol II conflict; this also informed the lack of international debate, attention, and oversight. The bright line of internal armed conflicts is sufficiently difficult to draw, and states are sufficiently resistant to involving themselves, or allowing others to be involved, in domestic affairs that internal armed conflicts are easily ignored.

This fact, in combination with the lack of information, absence of NGO and solidarity networks, and a particularly recalcitrant president through the 1980s, led to the abandonment of Guatemala by the international community. Moreover, when the international community did indict the Guatemalan government for its conduct, this shaming had the unintentional effects of confirming to the Guatemalan presidents (Lucas García and, to a lesser degree, Ríos Montt) that they alone truly understood the threat that Guatemala faced; it also insulted them personally.[93] As one ambassador to Guatemala wrote in 1981, "even goons and scoundrel develop a sense of offended dignity. We must recognize this if we hope to shape their actions."[94]

* * *

The absence of clear lines among and between internal armed conflicts, in practice, the very lack of precision in the definition of armed conflicts, and the absence of an independent evaluative body to adjudicate—all flaws of the treaties on the laws of war—contribute to both the hesitation and outright refusal to either apply or acknowledge Common Article 3 as applicable to armed conflicts. As I have underscored throughout, during the preparatory conferences of both 1949 and 1977, states were loathe to hold themselves accountable for the conduct of internal armed conflicts for fear of encouraging greater (reciprocal) scrutiny of domestic affairs and constraints on the freedom of sovereign states to quell internal dissent. Thus, although all signatories to the Geneva Conventions have a responsibility to both respect and ensure respect for the Conventions, the openness and responsiveness of both the international community and the domestic state were greater in the case of El Salvador. The highly unfortunate recursive interaction among all the elements meant that those interested in pressuring compliance with the laws of war had a better chance, greater resources and, in the end, greater success with El Salvador than with Guatemala. The process of characterizing the conflict and the characterization itself are additional elements in considering compliance, as are the rules of Common Article 3 and Protocol II.

Recall that Common Article 3, which was applicable to both conflicts, sets out the minimum humanitarian standards. The definition of *armed conflicts* in Common Article 3 is sparse, and the term is undefined in the text. Simply put, the insurgents must be at least collectively and minimally organized against the legal government, and there must be a resort to armed force.[95] Common Article 3 states that "persons taking no active part in the hostilities, including members of armed forces[,] ...shall be treated humanely." Expressly prohibited are acts against personal dignity, executions, and violence to life and person (murder, mutilation, cruel treatment, and torture), and these strictures bind all parties to the conflict equally.

The implementation of Common Article 3 does not affect the legal status of parties to the conflict and does not trigger the application of the provisions of the 1949 Conventions. For example, the Guatemalan government was not obliged to grant prisoner-of-war status to the URNG members it captured and, if it desired, could initiate criminal proceedings under domestic law against combatants for acts committed in the course of an armed conflict. In 1994, however, during the peace negotiations, the URNG and the Guatemalan government reached an agreement to reciprocally abide by Protocol II for the duration of the conflict, without acknowledging its formal applicability to the conflict. This type of an agreement, allowed and indeed encouraged by Common Article 3, was sought by the URNG because of its concerns about the treatment of its combatants. It was the first time the Guatemalan government had acknowledged Common Article 3 since the 1954 overthrow, and it did so only during a period of great international pressure and interest in resolving the war (and, recall, under a president who was aware of and consciously sought international acceptance). Common Article 3 does not govern the means or methods of armed conflicts; therefore, it does not protect civilians from attacks or the effects of attacks. Its purpose is to ensure humane treatment of those in the power of an adversary; it specifies that they must be treated with the respect guaranteed by all civilized nations.

Note that Common Article 3 does not define *civilian*. Customarily, this definition is derived through reference to the definition offered in Protocol I and from the characterization of civilians as "persons taking no part in hostilities." Common Article 3 was a formative moment in the development of the laws of war, being the first international treaty to codify the terms of protection within internal armed conflicts. Nonetheless, Common Article 3 provides only the bare minimum of protection, relying on the standards of civilization to buttress its weaknesses. Such a reliance proved misguided in a war waged to defend civilization against any encroachment, and it does little to contest the absolute power of the sovereign to judge the distinction between combatant and civilian.

Protocol II supplements Common Article 3. Its provisions are more detailed, but its scope is slightly more limited. Protocol II requires that parties to the conflict must control part of the territory of the opposition forces, be capable of sustained and concerted military actions, and have the capacity to implement and abide by international humanitarian law. These requirements presuppose an operative and organized command structure and sufficient capacity for oversight and communications within the organized dissidents. The FMLN had all these characteristics, including standardized uniforms, whereas the URNG lacked consistent control of territory and the capacity to carry out sustained military operations. Moreover, the URNG command structure and capacity for oversight and communications were severely attenuated due to both the intensity of the government repression and its internal conflicts and divisions.

Interestingly, there was a point in 1981 when the Guatemalan military did believe that the EGP possessed sufficient control of the Quiché region and organized capacity to be recognized as a insurgent force and, thus, possibly to invoke Protocol II.[96] At this time in El Salvador, the FMLN had already secured recognition from France and Mexico, Protocol II had been triggered, the victory of the

Sandinistas appeared to be imminent, and the international community had decisively repudiated Lucas García.[97] Taken together, the first three of these events provided the Guatemalan military with incentive to pursue extreme strategies against the EGP in Quiché while the fourth event provided them with cover to do so relatively unnoticed. Thus, the Guatemala military acted preemptively to thwart any possibility that the EGP could claim control of territory.

This raises the interesting question of whether the threat of triggering Protocol II forced the military to react more strongly than it would have otherwise. It is possible that this is true; but, considering the consistency and continued ferocity of the military campaign after the EGP and, later, the URNG were weakened, it is doubtful. Nonetheless, as the *Guatemala: Nunca Más!* report attests, the Guatemalan government was aware of the potential of international humanitarian law to restrain its actions and did take measures to prevent Protocol II from applying—once again demonstrating that Guatemala was cognizant of the potential power of the laws of war and, also, of the potential restrictions these laws would place on military actions.

The most significant dimension of Protocol II and Common Article 3 is that neither provides a definition of the *civilian*.[98] Both Protocol II and Common Article 3 speak only of individuals who are hors de combat, unable or no longer able to participate in the hostilities. Such individuals include both combatants and noncombatants who find themselves in the hands of and at the mercy of the opposing power. The definition of *civilian* (purposefully deleted from Protocol II) is customarily drawn from the definition provided in Protocol I and, as I argue, implicitly and explicitly, relies on the discourses of gender, civilization, and innocence for its stability and possibilities (see chap. 6). Thus, although the principle of distinction was clearly applicable to both conflicts in accordance with Common Article 3, Protocol II, and customary law, the lack of a definition meant that the construction of the civilian was dependent, once again, on these discourses for its meanings.

These discourses become all the more pivotal in wars fought in defense of civilization and, arguably, by militaries completely untrained in the exact requirement of the law itself. Indeed, scholars of the laws of war argue that the complexity of the Protocols I and II essentially render them useless in wars that are not fought by highly sophisticated, well-trained, and legally advised militaries—such as the United States. (Interestingly, the much-maligned presence of U.S. military advisors in El Salvador may have actually improved the observance by the Salvadoran military of the laws of war compared to Guatemala.) One scholar, examining the bulk of the Geneva Conventions, noted that by "taking as a starting point the existing inadequate Geneva Conventions" the 1977 Protocols Additional resulted in a body of law that remains "inapplicable to guerrilla warfare," its intended goal, and is "now probably too detailed even for conventional warfare."[99] In the context of these two conflicts, this observation suggests that the diffusion of, as well as the complexity of, the laws of war may matter for their implementation. The FMLN did employ the complexities of the laws to its advantage in debating its responsibilities. Note, however, that any discussion of diffusion and complexity assumes that the laws of war are already in use. This was less true in Guatemala than in El Salvador.

In the case of El Salvador, U.S. Secretary of State Elliott Abrams testified in 1982 that "respect for human rights and proper conduct toward the civilian population has been a principal part of our training," yet Human Rights Watch estimated that no more than 3 percent of the training offered by the U.S. military to the Salvadoran military in the United States was devoted to human rights training.[100] Moreover, the U.S.-trained rapid deployment forces, such as the Atlacatl brigade, were responsible for the majority of the massacres. Nonetheless, there was a marked difference in knowledge of and attention to the laws of war between Guatemala and El Salvador. For example, in 1980, the Salvadoran armed forces printed a new code of conduct; in 1983, the FMLN agreed that civilians must be respected; and in 1984, General José Napoleón Duarte issued new rules of engagement for aerial sorties against Salvadoran civilians.[101] There was even a card in circulation, authored by the ICRC, setting forth the basic rules of international law.[102] This was a marked improvement over the initial characterization of the rural population, promulgated by the U.S. State Department as well, as "something more than innocent civilian bystanders."[103]

In contrast, the approach toward civilians in Guatemala during the 1980s can be summarized by the fundamental philosophy of the entire Beans and Bullets program: if you are with us we feed you, if you are against us we kill you. Thus, although the three Guatemalan presidents (Lucas García, Ríos Montt, and Mejía Victores) appeared aware of and conversant with the laws of war, they essentially rejected them. Unfortunately, when both Ríos Montt and Mejía Victores began their rehabilitation of the international image of Guatemala by invoking the laws of war, no independent actors (networks or NGOs) actually documented their accountability.

As mentioned earlier, Guatemala refused access to the ICRC until 1988. This translated into (1) the international availability of very little knowledge about the conduct of the conflict and (2) the inability of the ICRC to effectively cajole, persuade, and pressure the Guatemalan government to abide by international humanitarian law. By contrast, in El Salvador it is possible to argue that, even though the government never officially recognized the applicability of Protocol II to the conflict, it agreed to abide by its standards in 1987, not only because of international pressure but because the ICRC was able to convince the Salvadoran government of the benefits of doing so. The ICRC had representatives in every department during the Salvadoran war and in contact with both the military and insurgent forces. But in Guatemala the ICRC was essentially useless. Its official headquarters during the war was in Costa Rica, and the Guatemalan government was actively hostile to its overtures until the worst of the conflict had passed. Thus, in Guatemala, the military and insurgent forces had no neutral arbiter of the laws of war, nor did they have the resources to inquire (if they so desired) about the legitimacy of their actions and debate the applicability of the laws.

* * *

In the end, however, the construction of the civilian and the combatant in both conflicts relied on the series of discourses: gender, civilization, and innocence. The FMLN proved more successful than did the URNG in debating, discussing, and dissenting from the tactics of the military and the characterization of its supporters and the general population. In part, the range of interpretations made possible by this series of discourses was limited due to the debate and to the oversight of the international community. In El Salvador the commonsense understanding of the civilian was created and disputed, whereas in Guatemala the military simply determined it.[104] Arguably, the difference in openness and responsiveness (as much as these words can be used in the context of armed conflict without becoming utterly oxymoronic) of all parties to the conflicts to contest the characterization of the civilian and combatant, and the distinction between the two, in combination with the more detailed provisions of Protocol II, may have determined the difference in the death tolls in Guatemala and El Salvador. To trace the productive power of the discourses is to chart whom they serve. In the case of Guatemala, they served the state.

This comparative history of the insurgency and counterinsurgency campaigns in Guatemala and El Salvador reveals certain dimensions of the material and discursive production of the distinction. The pivotal tenet of counterinsurgency doctrine holds that the strength and success of any insurgency is directly tied to its ability to gain and maintain a broad popular base. This tenet, when translated into the military action in Guatemala and El Salvador, resulted in the classification by the state of the majority of the population—essentially all but the oligarchy—as possible and therefore probable subversives, terrorists, and enemies of the state. This categorization justified scorched-earth military tactics and validated state attempts to control, by whatever means necessary, the general population. In Guatemala and El Salvador, military means were accompanied and supported by disciplines of terror designed to immobilize and regulate the population, both physically and psychologically, including the development of systems of surveillance and regimentation of daily life. In both countries, the strategies of war included the violent depopulation of regions designated as sympathetic or supportive of the insurgency and the subsequent state-directed repopulation of those areas with individuals demonstrably loyal to the state. Focusing on the rural pacification strategies of the governments and the responses of the URNG and the FMLN, we can see the incredible texturing of the conflict that made it difficult to consistently determine who was a combatant and who was a civilian through recourse to arms bearing. The focus of the 1977 Protocols Additional in constructing a visible difference between combatant and civilian did not clarify the determination of either in Guatemala and El Salvador.

In both Guatemala and El Salvador, the state bore the primary responsibility for the brutality unleashed on the civilian population and, in particular, for the displacement of over one-fourth of the population in each country. Each state believed the majority of the population was a threat to its stability and was "something other than innocent civilian bystanders."[105]

Nevertheless, the URNG and the FMLN also bore some responsibility in confirming this belief through their advocacy of protracted popular wars. For example, an EGP document claims, "In Guatemala, the Indian and Ladino workers are standing together at war against the present regimes....the Indians are not only supporting the popular revolutionary war, they have also assumed in it the principal role."[106] In El Salvador, the invocation of and reliance on the aphorism "the mountains are the people" placed millions of individuals in the direct line of fire with but sparse protection from any source. In El Salvador, the majority of those who were killed or displaced during the war were considered by the government to be "collaborators with terrorists" and treated as such.[107]

But in both conflicts, the URNG and the FMLN could not fiercely disrupt this portrayal of the populace as their supporters, as, either explicitly or implicitly, part of the people's revolutionary army. If they had done so, the operational and ideological logic of their revolutionary campaigns would have been compromised. As one FMLN commander stated, "the incorporation of all the people into the revolutionary war was the principal arm of our revolution."[108] The struggles for allegiance and the retreat to the tired mantras of revolutionary ideology sacrificed entire populations and also imprisoned the guerrillas in a cell of their own design. To continue their struggles against the state, both the URNG and the FMLN had to involve the population on their side and against the state. The fluidity of identification with the parties to the conflicts was exacerbated by the perfidious strategies of both the guerrillas and the military, who donned unrepresentative uniforms or civilian dress during military operations.

As this analysis of Guatemala and El Salvador illustrates, the construction of identity "often meant the difference between living and dying."[109] In each conflict, both the state and the insurgents purposefully and strategically manipulated the identity of the civilian for different purposes and with distinct consequences. Tragically, this contest to construct the civilian was essentially uneven. For in both Guatemala and El Salvador, the state effectively rendered the majority of the population guilty by charging the people with subverting civilization—a charge with both material and discursive consequences that proved difficult to counter. In El Salvador, the FMLN was able to challenge, with sufficient assistance from abroad, this charge laid by the state; but in Guatemala, the URNG, lacking such assistance, failed to do so.

Overall, Protocol II and Common Article 3 suffer from essentially the same flaws: poor enforcement and implementation mechanisms, lack of definition of clear concepts, and bias toward state sovereignty. Nevertheless, these instruments do set out the basic standards for, customary law on, and essential dictates on the treatment of civilians and combatants during armed conflicts. Recourse to the laws of war (namely Protocol II) in El Salvador did appear to facilitate the work of the FMLN/FDR and to protect civilians. But whether that recourse to the laws of war was the source of or the result of the strength of the FMLN is difficult to determine. As we have seen, Protocol II is triggered only after insurgents demonstrate significant strength and command. The relationship is thus recursive and a key factor was the density and sophistication of the solidarity and human rights networks in El Salvador. Because of this, although it is tempting to conclude that Protocol II made the difference, I believe it is more accurate to claim that Protocol II provided a highly effective instrument that both sides played well.

Although both the insurgents and the militaries of Guatemala and El Salvador purposely obfuscated the distinction between combatants and civilians during the conflicts, the insurgents did so to create an opening for revolutionary activity and, correspondingly, to force the recognition of the illegitimacy of the sovereign state. In contrast, the governments and their militaries did so to justify their extreme and highly discriminate violence as well as to consolidate their sovereign reach. In the end, the most powerful incentive to comply with the principle of distinction appears to have been the desire to be recognized and respected as a member of the international community of civilized states, demonstrating the incredible pull of discourses of civilization.

Yet, as we have seen, membership in this community is not contrary to, and is often complicit with, savage warfare. The discourses of civilization, like those of innocence and gender, are unstable foundations on which to premise protection and identification. Therefore, in describing the negotiation and production of the combatant and the civilian in conflicts in which the latter is said not to exist, I have focused on the signal importance of the generative power of discourses. The discourses of gender, innocence, and civilization were not replaced in El

Salvador; rather, the insurgents and their supporters more successfully captured the negotiation over their meaning. The laws of war do not substitute for these discourses; rather, the laws are grafted on them. Moreover, these discourses can be just as dangerous to the principle of distinction as they are necessary to its existence. To quote David Reiff: "To accept people's humanity and respect their dignity as individuals should not entail spinning fairy tales about their innate innocence."[110]

RESPONSIBILITY

Why is it that posing a question about a term is considered the same as effecting prohibition against its use?

—Judith Butler, *Excitable Speech*

In 2003, voicing the concerns of some scholars and practitioners of the laws of war, Colonel Kenneth Watkin argued that, in a post-9/11 world, what "remains to be seen is whether the [principle of distinction] ... provides an accurate, relevant, and ultimately credible basis upon which to regulate modern armed conflict."[1] The United States and its allies have defined the war against terrorism as being unlike any other, potentially requiring radically new military strategies. Despite this, as I document in chapter 1, the Bush and Obama administrations, as well as their allies, have not dismissed the significance of international humanitarian law and, indeed, have specifically highlighted the principle of distinction as central to their operations. After all, as Admiral Michael Mullen, chairman of the Joint Chiefs of Staff, noted in August 2008, any collateral damage or loss of life "really does set us back."[2] But let us also not forget that the principle of distinction indexes the difference between success and failure in the war on terrorism as a whole. Fundamentally, the premise of this war will be partially vindicated, or not, to the degree that the U.S. military can confront one of Al Qaeda's most formidable powers, namely, the capacity to simulate the civilian. Whenever a civilian remains the target of a combatant pretending to be a civilian, the war on terrorism is lost; when a combatant pretending to be a civilian can be fought and guarded against as such, the war on terrorism can, in theory, be won.

* * *

In considering the principle of distinction, both its critics and advocates note that compliance with and the implementation of this principle are circumscribed by evaluations of military necessity and calculations of proportionality—each of which privileges the authority of the state and militaries to conduct the war as is determined imperative to its success. Moreover, the evolution of technologies and different techniques of war may also mar compliance and implementation, or may render the distinction ambiguous in practice. Another dilemma is that implementation of the principle frequently relies on a sober symmetry of judgment and action of individuals in the midst of chaos, violence, and immense personal threat. The laws of war are of most immediate relevance in contexts marked "by exceptional conditions" and an absence of absolute oversight.[3] This is what James Morrow highlights in his discussion of the noise of armed conflict, which overall might be better called, as has Clausewitz, the friction of war.[4] These challenges underscore the plague of the laws of war—they are at once an ideal developed and imagined outside of the war and, yet, must also be practical in war. This is why I hold that the laws of war might be best characterized as a strategic expression of morals and moral expression of strategies.

Each of these explanations of the stresses on compliance is persuasive, and each underlines the difficulties of encouraging compliance by states, militaries, and combatants and of developing mechanisms for enforcement. Nevertheless, each of these explanations overlooks evidence of the indeterminacy of the principle. "Honestly, I don't know who we are fighting," said Staff Sergeant Tim Carter. "If I see them placing a roadside bomb or firing at us, then that's who we are fighting, but otherwise there is no way to tell if he is a civilian or al-Qaida. Here, a kid can run up to shake your hand and then later throw a grenade at you."[5]

Further, although at each defining moment in the history of the laws of war weaponry has grown more sophisticated, the rudimentary decision about who to target has not. In the Iraq and Afghanistan wars, technological advances in targeting specificity have not necessarily clarified the choice of targets. As Marc Garalasco of Human Rights Watch notes, "Technology has leaped forward, but the ability to know precisely who's at your target hasn't."[6] Some now argue that robots are the future of war, but it remains that the fundamental decision of who to kill and who not to kill, who to spare and who not to spare, must still be made or, in this case, programmed.[7] Commenting on the use of drones by the U.S. Central Intelligence Agency (CIA), Jane Mayer explains, "defining who is and who is not too tangential for the U.S. to kill can be difficult."[8] Thus, the laudable efforts to increase compliance with and enforcement of the principle of distinction must consider the exigencies of the distinction itself. I propose that the way in which compliance is formulated and assessed when the fundamental categories of the principle of distinction are in flux requires explicit attention to the power of the discourses that stabilize the distinction. I also submit that the series of discourses—gender, innocence, and civilization—that brace the principle of distinction may, paradoxically, undermine its utility. An analysis of this relation-ship not only points to the constitutive power of the series but also underscores the complex and contradictory ways in which compliance can be understood and defined within their parameters. That is, indeterminacy does affect compli-ance, and one of the ways to identify *how* it does so is to document the produc-tive power of gender, innocence, and civilization.

* * *

I am not alone in thinking through the effects of indeterminacy; scholars of in-ternational law and politics have drawn direct links among determinacy, preci-sion, clarity, and specificity and its effects. For example, Judith Goldstein and her colleagues define *precision* as "unambiguous" definitions of the conduct required, authorized, or proscribed by a rule, theorizing that the higher the precision the more likely there will be compliance.[9] Similarly, Vaughn Shannon debates the role of ambiguity in affecting compliance, noting that the greater the ambiguity the greater the chance for competing interpretations of specific rules or norms.[10] Thomas Franck would describe such an ambiguous rule as "indeterminate";[11] he contends that the relationship between determinacy and compliance is, in fact, testimony of the legitimacy of the rule because a legitimate rule clearly commu-nicates its intent. Michael Byers, following Abram Chayes and Antonia Chayes, highlights "clarity and specificity" as the pivotal element in compliance, and so too does Jeffery Legro.[12] Without misrepresenting the detailed differences among these scholars, it is possible to say that all share a common presumption that compliance and indeterminacy are inversely correlated. Yet none holds that inde-terminacy will *always* result in violations. Rather, as Chayes and Chayes discuss, indeterminacy might eventually facilitate greater compliance. In fact, there may be a desired, or decreed, "zone of ambiguity," "zone of permissibility," or what Meron (in reference to the laws of war) calls a "deliberate ambiguity."[13] And, indeed, this discussion is found in the literature on compliance with the laws of war, in which the porosity of the laws is identified as both hindering and helping compliance. This notion was vividly captured in the preparatory conferences for the 1977 Protocols Additional.

Opening the preparatory conference in 1974, the chair of the first meeting ar-gued that the "possibility of alleviating the suffering of victims of armed conflicts, saving their lives and protecting their dignity would, in large measure, depend upon the clarity of each of the relevant legal provisions."[14] Although his opinion was a common one, many of the smaller, newly independent or decolonizing nations contradicted his claim. Those delegates argued that such an emphasis on clarity—here the subject was the definition of a legitimate *combatant*—put their own struggles for freedom at a disadvantage. For them, advocating clarity was little more than a poorly disguised attempt to defend imperialism. Although I have explained the complicated political debates surrounding the 1977 Protocols Additional (see chap. 6), I return to them here because they underscore how the concepts of clarity, determinacy, precision, and ambiguity are not just political *outcomes* but also political *concepts*.

To return to Hannah Arendt, the predicate of the former is a relation of means and ends that is endemic to fabrication, the techne of politics. First, determinacy (and its numerous correlates) is an imagined end. It is an outcome of the process of definition, debate, and disagreement occurring in an already extant world among preconstituted actors. Second, determinacy is also a means. As Arendt says, "The fabricated thing is an end product in the two fold sense that the production process comes to an end in it…and that it is only a means to produce this end."[15]

In fact, a central element of the managerial model of compliance put forward by Chayes and Chayes is the "deliberative process," or "jawboning," that occurs among interested parties and that sets the scope of the rule and, in turn, monitors acceptable compliance.[16] Determinacy, then, is both the desired end of jawboning and an effective means of governing compliance. As Shannon notes, the "more parameters a norm possesses and the more ambiguous those parameters are, the easier it is for actors to interpret them favorably to justify violation."[17] Consequently, persuasion, argumentation, and justification—the media through and by which interpretations of ambiguities may eventually converge, decisions may be made, and actions may be evaluated—become central.[18] Accordingly, the shared emphasis of this literature falls on resolving indeterminacy or, at least, restricting it to an optimal scope.

It should come as no surprise that it is precisely at this juncture that my work again diverges from this company of scholars. As Foucault observes, "it is a question of a movement of critical analysis in which one tries to see how the different solutions to a problem have been constructed; but also how these different solutions result from a specific form of problematization."[19]

In considering the relationship between the indeterminacy of the principle and compliance, I did not initially attempt to clarify the distinction or resolve its indeterminacy. Instead, I identified how the principle of distinction does not simply regulate the protection of civilians. It also possesses another equally powerful effect; it is productive. First, the principle produces the subjects it ostensibly protects; that is, because the principle of distinction defines exactly which characteristics render a civilian and a combatant as such, the principle of distinction itself generates the very subjects that it protects.[20] Second, it produces international orders organized according to differences of civilization and sex.[21] Indeed, the question of what civilization requires—of whom and in relation to whom—is one that lies at the foundation of international law. The very presence of indeterminacy, its continued instability *and* iteration, is evidence of a productive process. Consequently, I sought to understand the power and meaning of indeterminacy, its history, and its effects—the politics of the principle.

* * *

The concept of politics to which I refer is marked by the contingency, unpredictability, and fragility of action—the spontaneous praxis through and by which we ourselves and the world that we hold in common are produced. Politics, in this understanding, is uncertain and remains so regardless of the best intentions or efforts of individuals to order it in accordance to their wishes or intentions. To recognize this uncertainty, or contingency, does *not* undermine the possibility of action, nor does it refuse the potential for change. Rather, it calls into question the possibility of and, contrary to a common critique, underscores the critical importance and potential of engaged action in a world without certainty.

Indeed, what occupies both Arendt and Foucault is how we shall deliberate, decide, and act when confronted with an inconstant world in common. What is our responsibility and accountability to one another and to ourselves? Significantly, both underscore that it is part of our responsibility as self-reflexive critical subjects to imagine how to make "the future formulations of a 'we' possible."[22] My choice to use a genealogy, or what Arendt might approach as "pearl-diving,"[23] reflects the central importance of this question in my own work. I believe that a genealogy, a form of a historical investigation, prepares us to most thoughtfully and critically reply to violations of the principle of distinction. It does so because a genealogy explicitly responds to instability and indeterminacy as conditions of politics rather than two of its failings. Moreover, a genealogy intentionally exposes, rather than presupposes, who "we" are and to whom "we" are responsive.

Although there are many affinities, it is this particular dimension of politics, unpredictable and productive, that the paradigmatic study of norms and law neglects to fully engage in its merging of strategic and normative rationality, premised on a moderated positivism, in an effort to demonstrate that the logic of events is not solely reducible to material force. Certainly, the reliance on actors with a given identity and the assumption of a consensual liberal polity guides our attention away from the productive, contingent dimension of politics.[24] Thus, guided by my understanding of politics and political theory, I resist the implicit orientation of examining the principle of distinction—its existence and its transgression—as simply the difference between an *ought* and an *is* that can be resolved through the right "design" or the right action of an "entrepreneur."[25] In addition to inquiries into how the indeterminacy of the principle of distinction can be resolved, and how we might ensure compliance and enforcement,

I propose these: What is the role of the principle of distinction, its indeterminacy and its violations, in constituting a "we"? What do its histories and formulations reveal about its persistence and its transgression in international law and politics?

Interestingly, the significant study of norms is also often parsed in accordance with their "function rather than substance," and the core categories and concepts of the norms themselves are too frequently taken as self-evident—indeed, to the degree that some norms themselves are granted "intrinsic characteristics."[26] Once politics is presumed to include the constitutive and productive, as well as instrumental, it is impossible to presuppose, as conventional evaluations of international humanitarian law do, the value and utility of the basic elements— combatant and civilian—of the principle of distinction.[27] Because the series of discourses—gender, innocence, and civilization—are productive of the categories combatant and civilian, the difference between them, my effort had been to trace how these discourses affect the indeterminacy of the principle. In turn, these differences reflect and affect the international and domestic orders. My work illustrates that the principle of distinction remains an integral dimension of international politics in spite of its consistent, if not constant, transgression.

To recall an earlier example, in 1945, the Judge Advocate General of the U.S. War Department, responding the brutalities of the world wars, dismissed the principle of distinction as "more apparent than real." But he also held that humanity itself demanded the preservation of such a distinction.[28] His sentiments, both his dismay and his insistence, were echoed in the words of delegates to the preparatory conferences for the 1977 Protocols. As were the delegates convened in the wake of the world wars, those gathered in 1973 at the preparatory conferences on the proposed draft of the Protocols Additional to the 1949 Conventions were struck by the failure of the laws of war to adequately respond to patterns of war and, in particular, by the seeming futility or obsolescence of the principle of distinction.

At each moment, the laws of war, and specifically the principle of distinction, were invoked and instantiated as an explicit dimension of a reconstructed international order of civilized nations. This suggests that the principle of distinction is *productive* even if or even when its utility is questioned. Introduced, then, is the possibility that the principle of distinction potentially may fall short of its purpose; it may fail in protecting civilians, yet still succeed in producing international orders. Underscoring the productive potential (power) of the principle that remains beyond its empirical violations is no less than what Friedrich Nietzsche suggested in his admonition to examine more carefully the tangled relations presumed among the purpose or utility of the thing, its history, and its effects.[29] Ironically, the focus on resolving indeterminacy or restricting its scope overlooks the potential productive power of the indeterminacy of the principle and of the discourses on which its existence relies.

* * *

As we have seen, the question of indeterminacy has plagued the laws of war throughout its history. The chaos occurring today in attempts to distinguish between combatant and civilian is nothing new. (The introduction of the new FM-34 counterinsurgency manual both recites and reorganizes the relationship of internal armed conflicts and the distinction between combatant and civilian.) The emergence of internal armed conflicts, and the use of the tactics perfected therein, does not uniquely trouble the distinction between combatant and civilian.[30]

On the contrary, the modern distinction was produced in the context of an internal armed conflict (as exemplified by General Orders 100) and bears all of the fragility and indeterminacy of that context. Furthermore, at each of its defining moments (General Orders 100, the Martens Clause, and Protocol I) the principle of distinction was formulated as a strategic, pragmatic distinction as much as it was formulated as a moral distinction. Therefore, it is responsive to war as much as it a restraint on it. This, after all, is a principle whose first beginnings are to be found in the efforts of Augustine to absolve soldiers of murder and, therefore, allow Christians to participate in war. This means that the principle of distinction may be invoked to both facilitate and to restrain war—as it did during the U.S.-Indian wars, when the killing of white women and children became a reason for killing Indian men, women, and children. In recognizing this and also in mapping the complicated effects of the construction of the principle (e.g., in the American Civil War, in which only white plantation women benefited from the protection, and in the civil wars of Guatemala and El Salvador, in which infants were denied the protections of the principle), I challenge the conventional evaluations of the success or failure of international norms and law as reducible to an either/or.

In international relations scholarship, the transformative studies focused primarily on proving that norms matter for the conduct and character of international relations. As a result, other scholars criticized the first set of studies on international norms as lacking convincing counterfactual examples of norms that failed (contrary to the ones highlighted by the work of norms scholars). For example, Paul Kowert and Jeffrey Legro write, "in order to understand how norms work, studies must allow for more variation: the success or failure, existence or obsolescence of norms."[31] This demand, however, implicitly relies on an unequivocal conception of the character and purpose of a norm. Either the norm works or it does not; either it is a success or a failure.

Yet, as my overview of the principle of distinction illustrates, such unmistakable assessments are themselves mistaken for two reasons. First, the principle of distinction has multiple effects, even in its most conventional interpretation as instrumental to the protection of civilians. Second, whether the principle is judged a success or failure is predicated on our prior agreement as to its purpose or utility. Part of my critique of Michael Walzer is that he presumes the principle of distinction reflects "universal notions of right and wrong,"[32] whereas it is more accurate to say that the principle helps to create them. For example, just as the discourses of sex and sex difference ensure the self-evidence of the distinction between combatant and civilian, so too does the distinction reassert the naturalness of sex and sex difference, both of which recite and reaffirm a heteronormative political order that, simultaneously, confirms itself as civilized. It is only after we agree on the purpose of the principle that we can evaluate the principle according to those purposes and, in this way, generate counterfactuals. For example, if we take its purpose to be the protection of civilians, then we might compare situations in which the principle was applied to those in which it was not applied at all.

But, in meticulously tracing its beginnings and through particular case studies, I have discovered that the actual purpose of the principle is neither singular nor stable. Even its most transparent purpose, to protect civilians, is not necessarily supported by its own articulation. Recollect that this principle has, from its earliest expressions, allowed both the purposeful killings of infidels and the incidental killings of those who would otherwise be spared. Moreover, its latest incarnation repeats this, privileging military objectives over civilian objects.[33] Furthermore, at each moment that the principle of distinction is invoked as protecting civilians, it is simultaneously invoked as producing and protecting civilization. Indeed, I wonder, can the principle of distinction do either—protect civilians or protect civilization—without producing both?

By focusing solely on the binary of success versus failure and by measuring success in numbers of dead, evaluations of the purpose, power, and potential of the principle of distinction reduce a complex matrix of effects to a simple opposition when, in fact, at times there may be no opposition at all. After all, the principle of distinction "succeeded" in constituting the "civilized" in 1899 (e.g., the Philippine-American War) while it "failed" to protect civilians. And, insofar as the principle of distinction presupposes and posits itself against barbarians, it is itself discriminatory. Consequently, measures of the purpose and effects of the principle of distinction—both compliance with it and its success/failure—should be broadened to acknowledge, if not address, the possible complexities of such assessments. As my genealogy illuminates, the principle of distinction—its existence and its transgression—is a testimony to the histories of thought, techniques of power, and standards of judgment that bear on our current condition.

* * *

One of the strongest arguments for resituating and reassessing the principle of distinction is found in my analysis of the discourses of civilization in the historical codification of the laws of war, the U.S.-Indian wars, the wars of decolonization, and the Guatemalan civil war. Consistently, discourses of civilization were employed to legitimate the refusal of protection to those designated as outside its boundaries. Yet it was also the discourses of civilization that, simultaneously, informed the existence and observation of the principle of distinction because it was a characteristic by which civilized entities, states and men, were known.

I proposed a genealogy as one way to begin to comprehend and respond to these complexities because a genealogy specifically attends to the production of the principle, its multiple purposes, and its sometimes contradictory effects. By identifying historical junctures at which these discourses of gender, innocence, and civilization converged to produce and distinguish the categories of combatant and civilian, we have seen that both the emergence and intelligibility of these two categories function in their debt. Tracing the effects of these discourses also provides a unique understanding of the relationship between the principle of distinction and the establishment and histories of international orders. The continuing debate over the proper designation of the civilian (apparent throughout the book and especially in the comparative chapters) not only conjures the discourses on which the principle of distinction is grafted but also demonstrates the inevitable relationship between the interpretation of the law itself (or, perhaps more accurately, the decision of its interpretation) and the presence and possession of the power to do so. Certainly, the unilateral executive decisions made by President George W. Bush about the status of those detained in Guantánamo Bay after 9/11 recall the power of the sovereign to decide who is within the reach of, but outside the protection of, the laws of war.

Yet, surely what was so phenomenal about the deployment of the principle of distinction by the Algerian FLN, the Salvadoran FMLN, and the U.S. Southern white plantation women is that it was not simply *material* power that enabled their interpretation and use of the principle. Tracing the effects of these discourses not only provides a unique understanding of the relationship between the principle of distinction and the establishment and histories of international orders; it also illustrates significant transformations in those orders that were not directly tied to material power.

In 1977, national liberation movements (building on the successful efforts of the FLN) reconstituted the laws of war, recycling and re-signifying the hierarchy of civilized/barbarian for their own purposes. They were successful in doing so not only because of the major international shifts during that period, including the strength of regional movements, but because they capitalized on the intrinsic instability of the discourses of civilization.[34] As discussed earlier, discourses are open systems of signification and, consequently, change is a condition of their operation.

Thus, this genealogy helps us to see that the civilian and the combatant are neither natural nor inevitable identities. They are not just regulative categories of the laws of war, but are also performative. That is to say, the combatant and the civilian gain in substance through persistent and constant, imperfect and provisional, iteration. Neither exists before this citation, before this ritualized practice. In this way, the very indeterminacy and fragility of the distinction, the frangibility of the civilian, are precisely its power. This is so because the indeterminacy of the distinction requires recitation that, in turn, opens the possibility of re-signifying its reach. Although my rereading of the canonical texts and conventional interpretations of the emergence and development of the laws of war shows that this universal norm descends from exercises of differentiation and relations of inequity, it is the "promising ambivalence of a universal norm" that I emphasize.[35] As John Rajchman writes, "to question the self-evidence of a form of experience, knowledge, and power is to free it for our purposes, to open new possibilities for thought or action."[36] The ambivalence of the principle, its open texture, and its deliberate ambiguity confront us daily with the need to make decisions: Who is a civilian? Who is a combatant? What is a civilian? What is combatant? How do we know? Who is to judge and on what grounds? It is on these decisions that lives depend. Nevertheless, we cannot simply give an answer without also being answerable to its formulation—that is, the demands and determinants of such an answer.[37]

For example, the discourses of innocence mark like red threads the formulation of this distinction. From Vitoria to Ríos Montt, the innocence of those whom we spare is of central importance. Yet, innocence is, paradoxically perhaps, premised on passivity, an apolitical and dependent status that may be both impossible and dangerous to maintain in times of war. To be innocent is also to be without the freedom or agency to act in one's own defense and for one's own life. These discourses can be as dangerous to the principle of distinction as they are necessary to its existence. This is the dirty history of the principle that we are responsible for and must respond to in our decisions.

* * *

I underscore that my inquiring into the possibility of the distinction is "not the same as negating or dispensing" with it; rather, "it is to ask after the process of its construction and the political meaning and consequentiality of taking [it]...as a requirement or presupposition."[38] It is precisely due to the atrocities that asking what allows the civilian becomes obligatory. Moreover, I take from Arendt the suggestion that thinking, which is aimed at meaning, prepares for judging in such a way as to make any arbitrary definition of the *civilian* impossible, for a definition must arise from and correspond to, not replace, the common world of human affairs. She speaks of a "common sense," the experience of being an individual "in the plural," that allows for "measured insight" and comprehension of a shared world.[39] Common sense presumes that we are responsible and responsive to the world through and in which we find ourselves reflected and received.

Arendt also emphasizes the importance of understanding. Understanding turns back on itself to ask about the categories of thought by which it proceeds and, in this case, forces us to inquire after the very conceptions of combatant and civilian on which the principle of distinction depends and to which it refers. Consequently, this genealogy is tempered and directed by my reading of her concept of understanding because understanding assists in both recognizing and building a world in common.

The endeavor of understanding, for Arendt, preserves the capacity to judge and to act absent the comfort of received categories and conventional standards of judgment. Understanding is a dimension of both thinking and judging that remains intimately, and necessarily, engaged with the political events from which it arises and to which it is bound. It is directed toward, as she writes in the preface of the *Origins of Totalitarianism,* the "unpremeditated attentive facing up to, and resisting of, reality."[40] As such, understanding bears the potential for both reconciliation and imagination; it allows us to come to terms with the irrevocability of political events, as it equally prepares us to imagine and, potentially, act differently.

Significantly, in the unique lexicon of Arendt, reconciliation is not the passive acceptance of, or acquiescence in, the brutal events of politics. Rather, "to reconcile ourselves to a world in which things are possible at all" is to reject the futility of acting as if this brutality, or a response to this brutality, is inescapably beyond the capacity of individual intelligibility or judgment.[41] Atrocities may explode conventional "categories of thought and...standards of judgment" on which understanding and judgment intrinsically rely, but they do not render them impossible.[42] Even as understanding enables us to recognize and reconcile the absence of absolute certainty, the ruin of "pillars of the best known truths," and a "veritable rubble heap" of moral verities, it inspires us to think without them; in her most evocative phrase, it prompts "thinking without a banister."[43]

Following Arendt, I contend that it is the activity of understanding that may allow us "to think what we are doing"—to configure and construct possible horizons of judgment and action not condemned or constrained by the inheritance of past but illuminated by it.[44] This is because "to understand without preconceived categories and to judge without the set of customary rules" is itself a form of beginning.[45] If, following Arendt, understanding is the "other side of action," then it is in understanding that our potential lies to think what we are doing and, potentially, act anew.[46] In this work, then, to think without a banister is to critically engage violations of the principle of distinction, the ethical and practical challenges that they raise, without presuming the self-evidence of the distinction or the inevitability of combatant and civilian.

Most precisely, the emphasis of this book falls on restoring to the principle of distinction its original status and power as a set of questions: What is a combatant? What is a civilian? Who is a combatant? Who is a civilian? How do we know? Who is to judge and on what grounds? The history of the laws of war is a history of attempts to answer these still unresolved questions. Indeed, it is possible to say that anxiety over these questions is constitutive of the laws of war, if not also generative of its injunctions. It is in our attempts to answer these questions that we will find ourselves between past and future.

Notes

1. GENDER, INNOCENCE, AND CIVILIZATION

1. Richard Myers, interview with *This Week* on ABC TV, October 21, 2001, quoted in Adam Roberts, "Counter-terrorism, Armed Force and the Laws of War," *Survival* 44, no. 1 (spring 2002): 13.

2. Anthony Dworkin, "Excerpts from Interview with Charles Allen, Deputy General Counsel for International Affairs, U.S. Department of Defense," December 16, 2002, www.crimesofwar.org/onnews/news-pentagon-trans.html.

3. Quoted in Jim Garamone, "Directive Aimed at Minimizing Civilian Casualties," *American Forces Press Service,* September 16, 2008, http://www.defense.gov/news/news article.aspx?id=51201.

4. Translated excerpt from the Taliban code of conduct, CNN website, July 30, 2009, http://www.cnn.com/2009/WORLD/asiapcf/07/30/taliban.code.excerpt/index.html and http://english.aljazeera.net/news/asia/2009/07/20097278348124813.html.

5. Kofi A. Annan, "Report of the Secretary General to the Security Council on the Protection of Civilians in Armed Conflict," UN Security Council Report S/1999/957, September 8, 1999, http://www.un.org/Docs/journal/asp/ws.asp?m=S/1999/957. In this report, Annan states that the protection of civilians is fundamental to the central mandate of the organization, an assertion picked up almost yearly in UN Security Council debates on the protection of civilians.

6. Wesley K. Clark, *Waging Modern War: Bosnia, Kosovo, and the Future of Combat* (New York: Public Affairs, 2001), 238, 434. President George W. Bush's statement on September 20, 2001, that the "United States makes no distinction between the terrorists and those who harbored them" drew international criticism for this very reason. George W. Bush, "Address to a Joint Session of Congress and the American People," September 20, 2001, http://georgewbush-whitehouse.archives.gov/news/releases/2001/09/20010920-8.html. For a more thorough assessment of degrees of compliance with the distinction, see also Helen M. Kinsella, "Discourses of Difference," *Review of International Studies* 31 (2005): 163–85; Colin Kahl, "How We Fight," *Foreign Affairs* 85 (November–December 2006): 83–101; Adam Roberts, "Counter-Terrorism, Armed Force, and the Laws of War," *Survival* 44, no. 1 (2002): 7–32.

7. Alberico Gentili, "De jure belli libri tres [2 vols.]," in *The Classics of International Law,* vol. 16, ed. John Carew Rolfe and Coleman Phillipson (Oxford: Clarendon Press, 1933), 15.

8. See Lauri Hannikainen, *Peremptory Norms (Jus Cogens) in International Law: Historical Development, Criteria, Present Status,* (Helsinki: Finnish Lawyers Publishing, 1988), 685–87.

9. See International Court of Justice, "Legality of the Threat of Use of Nuclear Weapons," Advisory Opinion, ICJ Reports, July 8, 1996, 226, paras. 75–82, http://www.icj-cij.org/docket/index.php?p1=3&p2=4&k=e1&p3=4&case=95.

10. Claude Pilloud, Yves Sandoz, Christophe Swinarski, and Bruno Zimmermann, *Commentary on the Additional Protocols of 8 June 1977 to the Geneva Conventions of 12 August 1949* (Dordrecht: Martinus Nijhoff, 1987), 586. The principle of discrimination is

composed of three essential tenets: proportionality, distinction, and military necessity. The fundamental emphasis of this book is on distinction.

11. In international humanitarian law, conflict is classified into two basic categories: international and noninternational. Noninternational conflict is further subdivided into specific categories, each of which is governed by a distinct set of rules. The total number of categories of conflict in this classification are five. Applying this classification scheme involves a subjective element, and in the words of one prominent legal scholar, the scheme is "fundamental—though truly artificial." Georges Abi-Saab, "Humanitarian Law and Internal Conflicts: The Evolution of Legal Concern," in *Humanitarian Law of Armed Conflict—Challenges Ahead: Essays in Honour of Frits Kalshoven,* ed. Astrid J. M. Delissen and Gerard J. Tanja (London: Martinus Nijhoff, 1991), 209. See also chapter 8.

12. Mary Kaldor, *New and Old Wars: Organized Violence in a Global Era* (Stanford: Stanford University Press, 1999), 12.

13. Karma Nabulsi, *Traditions of War: Occupation, Resistance, and the Law* (Oxford: Oxford University Press, 1999), 1.

14. Reviewing the 2003 Iraq war, a *New York Times* report described the difficulties of counting the dead as complicated by the inability to decide who was an enemy combatant and who was a civilian; "A Nation at War: Inquiries and Casualties," *New York Times,* April 10, 2003, http://www.proquest.com.ezproxy.library.wisc.edu. This points to the outstanding problem of measuring casualties (civilian and combatants), particularly in small conflicts in which "there is no single reliable source." Nils Petter Gleditsch, Peter Wallensteen, Mikael Eriksson, Margareta Sollenberg, and Håvard Strand, "Armed Conflict 1946–2001: A New Dataset," *Journal of Peace Research* 39, no. 5 (2002), 625. The controversy over the *Lancet* study captures the difficulty of identifying and counting civilian dead; Les Roberts, Riyadh Lafta, Richard Garfield, Jamal Khudhairi, and Gilbert Burnham, "Morality before and after the 2003 Invasion of Iraq: Cluster Sample Survey," *Lancet* 364, no. 9448 (2004): 1857–64. The oft-cited increase in civilian deaths from 5 to 90 percent is not traceable to any single or reliable source; Esbjörn Rosenblad, *International Humanitarian Law of Armed Conflict: Some Aspects of the Principle of Distinction and Related Problems* (Geneva: Henry Dunant Institute, 1977). The United Nations Children's Fund (UNICEF) attributes similar findings—an increase in civilian deaths from 50 percent in World War II to 80 percent in present wars—to studies undertaken for the International Symposium on Children and War held March 24–27, 1983, in Siuntio Baths, Finland; UNICEF, December 1985, C1, Annex 1.

15. Michael Ignatieff, "Unarmed Warriors," *New Yorker,* March 24, 1997, 59.

16. The use of nuclear weapons, of course, is the most immediate example of the erasure of any distinction between combatants and civilians. Although some argue that the development of new technologies such as smart bombs actually increases the possibility of exact discrimination, these technologies are limited to a few nations and are used in a relatively limited number of wars. Furthermore, precision targeting often fails and is ineffective in confused conflicts in urban areas. Ironically, then, even as weapons are developed that specifically obliterate the distinction, what remains implicit and explicit in these debates over precision is the acceptance of the principle of distinction as a legitimate means of assessing and regulating the tactics and technologies of war. The principle is boundary of war.

17. Thomas Aquinas, *Summa Theologiæ: Latin Text and English Translation, Introductions, Notes, Appendices and Glossaries* [hereafter *Summa Theologiæ*], vol. 2, trans. Thomas Gilby (Cambridge: Cambridge University Press, 2006), Q64, A7, 226–27.

18. For a definition of *robustness,* see Robert Powell, "Review: Anarchy in International Relations Theory: The Neorealist-Neoliberal Debate; Neorealism and Its Critics: Neorealism and Neoliberalism: The Contemporary Debate," *International Organization*

48, no. 2 (1994), 313. See also Martha Finnemore and Kathryn Sikkink, "International Norm Dynamics and Political Change," *International Organization* 52, no. 4 (1998): 887–917; Jeffry Legro, "Which Norms Matter?: Revisiting the 'Failure' of Internationalism," *International Organization* 51, no. 1 (1997): 31–64. On the protection of civilians, see Alexander Downes, *Targeting Civilians in War* (Ithaca: Cornell University Press, 2008). See also Hugo Slim, *Killing Civilians: Method, Madness, and Morality in War* (New York: Columbia University Press, 2008).

19. Joan Scott, *Only Paradoxes to Offer: French Feminists and the Rights of Man* (Cambridge, Mass.: Harvard University Press, 1996), 4.

20. UN Security Council, SC/6847, April 19, 2000, http://www.un.org/News/Press/docs/2000/20000419.sc6847.doc.html.

21. See Judith Goldstein, Miles Kahler, Robert Keohane, and Anne-Marie Slaughter, "Legalization and World Politics: Introduction," *International Organization* 54, no. 3 (2000): 385–99.

22. Kal Raustiala and Anne-Marie Slaughter, "International Law, International Relations, and Compliance," in *Handbook of International Relations,* ed. Walter Carlsnaes, Thomas Risse-Kappen, and Beth A. Simmons (London: Sage, 2002), 548. See also Anne-Marie Slaughter-Burley, "International Law and International Relations Theory: A Dual Agenda," *American Journal of International Law* 87, no. 2 (1993): 205–39; Anne-Marie Slaughter, Andrew S. Tulumello, and Stepan Wood, "International Law and International Relations Theory: A New Generation of Interdisciplinary Scholarship," *American Journal of International Law* 92, no. 3 (1998), 367; Goldstein et al., "Legalization and World Politics"; Finnemore and Sikkink "International Norm Dynamics and Political Change," 906.

23. Koskenniemi, *Gentle Civilizer of Nations,* 485. See also Christian Reus-Smit, "The Strange Death of Liberal International Theory," *European Journal of International Law* 12, no. 3 (2001): 573–93.

24. Annan, "Report of the Secretary General." See also Richard T. Cooper, "As Combat Escalates, Sparing Civilians Gets Harder Too," *Los Angeles Times,* April 2, 2003.

25. Simon Chesterman, "An Altogether Different Order: Defining the Elements of Crimes against Humanity," *Duke Journal of Comparative & International Law* 10, no. 2 (2000): 322.

26. Hilaire McCoubrey, "Jurisprudential Aspects of the Modern Law of Armed Conflict," in *Armed Conflict and the New Law Aspects of the 1977 Geneva Protocols and the 1981 Weapons Convention,* ed. Michael A. Meyer (London: British Institute of International and Comparative Law, 1989), 48. As one historian of international humanitarian law notes, "'civilians' and 'belligerents' are the two most commonly used categories[,]...yet, what those terms meant in the past, when the laws were originally created, is still poorly understood." Karma Nabulsi, "Evolving Conceptions of Civilians and Belligerents: One Hundred Years after the Hague Peace Conferences," in *Civilians in War,* ed. Simon Chesterman and International Peace Academy (Boulder: Lynne Rienner, 2001), 9.

27. *Protocol Additional to the Geneva Conventions of 12 August 1949, and relating to the Protection of Victims of International Armed Conflicts (Protocol I), 8 June 1977.* Protocol I, Article 50.

28. Ruth Wedgewood notes a common outcome of this confusion: "If you don't know who the combatants are, it tempts the other side to assume civilians are combatants." Quoted in Adam Liptak, "When Letter of the Law Does Not Spell 'Clarity,'" *New York Times,* May 1, 2002.

29. The 1949 Geneva Convention Relative to the Protection of Civilian Persons in Time of War entered into force October 21, 1950; http://www.icrc.org/web/Eng/siteeng0.nsf/html/genevaconventions.

30. Pilloud et al., *Commentary on the Additional Protocols,* 610.

31. Michel Foucault, "The Subject and Power," in *Power,* ed. James D. Faubion (New York: New Press, 2000), 344.

32. For an analysis of the analytic and practical primacy given to the combatant in the development and codification of international humanitarian law, see Judith Gardam, "Gender and Non-Combatant Immunity," *Transnational Law & Contemporary Problems* 32 (1993): 345–370.

33. Michel Foucault, "Politics, Polemics, Problematizations," in *Ethics: Subjectivity and Truth,* ed. Paul Rabinow (New York: New Press, 1997), 118.

34. Hannah Arendt, *The Life of the Mind* (New York: Harcourt Brace Jovanovich, 1978), 5.

35. Michel Foucault, "Questions of Method," in *The Foucault Effect: Studies in Governmentality, with Two Lectures by and an Interview with Michel Foucault,* ed. Graham Burchell, Colin Gordon, and Peter Miller (Chicago: University of Chicago Press, 1991), 76.

36. For example, Hugo Slim wishes to rescue what he calls "ambiguous civilians" by countering the "fragility" of the civilian identity with its "importance" as a moral identity and as a moral precept; *Killing Civilians,* 8.

37. Hannah Arendt, "Reply to Eric Vogelin," in *Hannah Arendt: Essays in Understanding,* ed. Jerome Kohn (New York: Harcourt, Brace & Co., 1994), 403.

38. Michel Foucault, "The Order of Discourse," in *Untying the Text: A Post-Structuralist Reader,* ed. Robert Young (Boston: Routledge, 1981), 68. I understand discourse as generative of the categories of meaning and thought through which "reality" is produced and understood, and therefore as constitutive of our knowledge and practices. Discourses are neither static nor complete but are systems of signification and authorization.

39. Hannah Arendt, "Understanding and Politics," in *Hannah Arendt: Essays in Understanding,* ed. Jerome Kohn, (New York: Harcourt, Brace, 1994), 311.

40. Quoted in Virginia Garrard-Burnett, *Terror in the Land of the Holy Sprit* (Oxford: Oxford University Press, 2010), 90. Human Rights Watch played on this supposedly inviolable relationship by titling a 1995 report on the role of women in the genocide in Rwanda "Rwanda, Not So Innocent: When Women Become Killers" (Human Rights Watch—African Rights, London, 1995).

41. Quoted in Amnesty International, *Guatemala: The Human Rights Record* (London: Amnesty International Publications, 1987), 96.

42. Hanna Fenichel Pitkin, *The Attack of the Blob: Hannah Arendt's Concept of the Social* (Chicago: University of Chicago Press, 1998), 2.

43. Charlotte Lindsey, "Women and War," public lecture given at the World Civil Society Forum, International Committee of the Red Cross, Geneva, July 20, 2002, http://www.peacewomen.org/resources/Human_Rights/ICRCWomenandWar.pdf.

44. Simon Chesterman, "Introduction," in *Civilians in War,* ed. Simon Chesterman and International Peace Academy (Boulder: Lynne Rienner, 2001), 2.

45. Jean Pictet, *Humanitarian Law and the Protection of War Victims* (Leyden: Henry Dunant Institute, 1975), 14.

46. See Judith Gardam, "Women and the Law of Armed Conflict: Why the Silence?" in *Humanitarian Law,* ed. Judith Gardam (Aldershot, UK: Ashgate, 1999).

47. Richard M. Price, *The Chemical Weapons Taboo* (Ithaca: Cornell University Press, 1997), 10.

48. McCoubrey, "Jurisprudential Aspects," 27; Terry Nardin, *Law, Morality, and the Relations of States* (Princeton: Princeton University Press, 1983), 59. See also Gerrit Gong, *The Standard of Civilization in International Society* (Oxford: Clarendon, 1984).

49. In citing the Peace of Westphalia as a significant moment in the emergence of the laws of war, I take seriously the challenges against the disciplinary orthodoxy raised by David Blaney and Naaem Inayatullah regarding the significance and import of the Peace.

According to them, the false veneration of the Peace of Westphalia as "the beginnings of a more liberal and tolerant sensibility" found in the field of international relations obscures the ways in which the Peace "re-enforced rather than challenged the interpretation of difference as a dangerous aberration from the norms of stability, safety and order." David Blaney and Naaem Inayatullah, *International Relations and the Problem of Difference* (New York: Routledge, 2000), 2.

50. Judith Gardam, *Non-Combatant Immunity: A Norm of International Humanitarian Law* (Dordrecht: Martinus Nijhoff, 1993), 3.

51. "St. Petersburg Declaration Renouncing the Use, in Time of War, of Explosive Projectiles under 400 Grammes Weight" (1868), preamble.

52. Jean-Jacques Rousseau, "On the Social Contract," in *Basic Political Writings,* trans. Donald A. Cress (Indianapolis: Hackett Publishing, 1987), 22.

53. *Noncombatants* are those members of the armed forces who do not take an active part in the conduct of hostilities; *civilians* are those who are not members of the armed forces. A combatant has the right to participate in the hostilities. A civilian is always a noncombatant, but a noncombatant is not always a civilian. See M. H. F. Clarke, T. Glynn, and A. P. V. Rogers "Combatant and Prisoner of War Status," in *Armed Conflict and the New Law Aspects of the 1977 Geneva Protocols and the 1981 Weapons Convention,* ed. Michael A. Meyer and Geoffrey Best (London: British Institute of International and Comparative Law, 1989), 118.

54. Theodor Meron, "The Humanization of Humanitarian Law," *American Journal of International Law* 94, no. 2 (2000): 239–78; Daniel O'Donnell, "Trends in the Application of International Humanitarian Law by United Nations Human Rights Mechanisms," *International Review of the Red Cross* 324 (1998), http://www.icrc.org/web/eng/siteeng0. nsf/html/57JPGA; Louise Beck-Doswald and Sylvain Vité, "Origin and Nature of Human Rights Law and Humanitarian Law," *International Review of the Red Cross* 293 (1993), http://www.icrc.org/web/eng/siteeng0.nsf/html/57JMRT.

55. The ICTR has a more expansive jurisdiction in regard to international humanitarian law than does the Yugoslav tribunal because the ICTR is qualified to prosecute serious violations of both Common Article 3 of the IV Geneva Convention and Protocol Additional II. This is quite notable because, before the Rwanda statute, Protocol II was not universally accepted as reflecting customary law and violations of either Protocol II or Common Article 3 were not criminalized. See UN Doc. S/1995/134 § 12, http://www.ictr. org/ENGLISH/basicdocs/statute.html. The Tadić decisions of the ICTY further substantiates this expansion of international humanitarian law; http://www.icty.org.

56. Meron, "Humanization of Humanitarian Law," 253.

57. Hugo Storey and Rebecca Wallace, "War and Peace in Refugee Law Jurisprudence," *American Journal of International Law* 95, no. 2 (2001), 363. For an overview of this argument, see Tom Hadden and Colin Harvey, "The Law of Internal Crisis and Conflict," *International Review of the Red Cross* 833 (1999): 119–34, http://www.icrc.org/Web/Eng/ siteeng0.nsf/html/57JPT4.

58. Hugo Grotius, *De jure belli ac pacis libri tres* (The Laws of War and Peace), trans. Francis W. Kelsey, reprinted in *Classics of International Law,* ed. James Brown Scott (New York: Oceana Press, 1964 [1646]), "Prolegomena," § 26, 18.

59. Price, *Chemical Weapons Taboo,* 10.

60. Hannah Arendt, *Between Past and Future: Eight Exercises in Political Thought* (New York: Penguin, 1968), 15. See also Jeffrey C. Isaac, *Democracy in Dark Times* (Ithaca: Cornell University Press, 1998), 41.

61. Maurice Keen, *The Law of War in the Middle Ages* (Routledge: London, 1965), 2.

62. "This is a new kind of evil [and] …this crusade…will rid the world of evil-doers." President George W. Bush, speech made at the White House, September 16, 2002. See also

James Carroll, "The Bush Crusade," *Nation,* September 20, 2004, http://www.thenation. com/doc/20040920/carroll. See also President Bush's statement on September 20, 2001, suggesting that the United States was the ultimate and final arbiter of justice: "[w]hether we bring our enemies to justice, or bring justice to our enemies, justice will be done." Bush, Bush, "Address."

63. Speech by President George W. Bush, March 11, 2002, http://www.pbs.org/news hour/terrorism/ata/bush_3-11-02.html.

64. Even though protection, as understood by the ICRC, consists of three components—diplomacy, development of the law, and direct enforcement of the law— the animating principles are charity and mercy.

65. Slim, *Killing Civilians,* 1.

66. Michael Walzer, *Just and Unjust Wars,* "The laws of war…[have] increasingly re- sorted to the concept of 'rights,' rather than sticking to the original concepts that priv- ileged persons shall be respected and protected." Asbjorn Eide, "The Laws of War and Human Rights—Differences and Convergences," in *Studies and Essays on International Humanitarian Law in Honors of Jean Pictet,* ed. Christophe Swinarski (Geneva: Martinus Nijhoff, 1984), 695.

67. For representative works on these points, see Michel Foucault, *Society Must be De- fended: Lectures at the College de France, 1975–1976,* (New York: Picador, 1997); Friedrich Hegel, *Elements of the Philosophy of Right,* Cambridge Texts in the History of Political Thought, ed. Allen W. Wood, trans. H. B. Nisbet (Cambridge: Cambridge University Press, 1991), 325.

68. Johnson, *Just War Tradition,* 133.

69. Alberico Gentili, "De jure belli libri tres [2 vols.]," in *The Classics of International Law,* vol. 16, ed. John Carew Rolfe and Coleman Phillipson (Oxford: Clarendon Press, 1933), 260.

70. *Oxford English Dictionary,* 2nd ed. (1989).

71. Koskenniemi, *Gentle Civilizer of Nations,* 9.

72. Ibid., 99.

73. Chapter 3 also serves as a preparation for my analyses of the 1977 Protocols Additional. These Protocols Additional to the 1949 Geneva Conventions return to and reformulate the relations between the laws of war and the discourses of civilization, reshaping the international order by granting recognition to formerly colonized states as fully sovereign entities privy to the rights and obligations of the laws of war. Finally, the characterization and conduct of the U.S.-Indian wars of the nineteenth century and the civil war in Guatemala, in my two comparison chapters, reflect the continu- ing power of the discourses of civilization to set the boundaries of immunity and sovereignty.

74. David J. Harris, *Cases and Materials on International Law,* 5th ed. (London: Sweet and Maxwell, 1983), 15.

75. See John Kelsay, "Islam and the Distinction between Combatants and Non Combatants," in *Cross, Crescent, and Sword: The Justification and Limitation of War in Western and Islamic Tradition,* ed. James Johnson and John Kelsay (New York: Greenwood Press, 1990). For an argument regarding the possible influence of Is- lamic law, via the Spanish Scholastics, on the work of Hugo Grotius, see Christo- pher G. Weeramantry, *Islamic Jurisprudence: An International Perspective* (New York: St. Martin's Press, 1988), esp. chap. 8. See also Nagendra Singh, "Armed Conflicts and Humanitarian Law of Ancient India," in *Studies and Essays on International Hu- manitarian Law and Red Cross Principles in Honour of Jean Pictet,* ed. Christophe Swinarski and International Committee of the Red Cross (Geneva: Martinus Ni- jhoff, 1984), 531–36; John Kelsay, *Arguing the Just War in Islam* (Cambridge, Mass.:

Harvard University Press, 2007); Mary Habeck, *Knowing the Enemy: Jihadist Ideology and the War on Terror* (New Haven: Yale University Press, 2006); Hisham Ramadan, *Understanding Islamic Law: From Classical to Contemporary* (Lanham, Md.: Rowman and Littlefield, 2006).

76. Luke Lea, commissioner of Indian Affairs (1869), quoted in Stuart Banner, *How the Indians Lost Their Land: Law and Power on the Frontier* (Cambridge, Mass.: Belknap Press, 2005), 231.

77. Quoted in Robert Allen Wooster, *The Military and the United States Indian Policy, 1865–1903* (New Haven: Yale University Press, 1988), 48. See also Jeffrey Ostler, *The Plains Sioux and U.S. Colonialism from Lewis and Clark to Wounded Knee* (Cambridge, UK: Cambridge University Press, 2004).

78. See, however, the more recent works by scholars of international law on the strengthening of the laws of war in internal armed conflicts through the work of regional tribunals, for example, Eve La Haye, *War Crimes in Internal Armed Conflicts* (Cambridge, UK: Cambridge University Press, 2008); Lindsay Moir, *The Law of Internal Armed Conflict* (Cambridge, UK: Cambridge University Press, 2002).

79. For the online version of the International Committee of the Red Cross Study of Customary Law, see http://www.icrc.org/customary-ihl/eng/docs/home.

80. M. L. R. Smith, "Guerrillas in the Mist: Reassessing Strategy and Low Intensity Warfare," *Review of International Studies* 29, no. 1 (2003): 37.

81. Stathis N. Kalyvas, "Wanton and Senseless?: The Logic of Massacres in Algeria," *Rationality and Society* 11, no. 3 (1999): 243–86.

82. Michael T. Kaufman, "What Does the Pentagon See in 'Battle of Algiers'?" *New York Times,* September 7, 2003.

83. Quoted in Linda D. Kozaryn, "Baathist Opposition Organized, Coalition Faces 'Guerrilla-type Campaign,'" *American Forces Press Service,* July 16, 2003), http://www.defense.gov/news/newsarticle.aspx?id=28715.

84. I am indebted to Mary Dietz for highlighting this phrase of Arendt; *Turning Operations: Feminism, Arendt, and Politics* (New York: Routledge, 2002).

2. MARTIAL PIETY IN THE MEDIEVAL AND CHIVALRIC CODES OF WAR

1. James Turner Johnson, *Just War Tradition and the Restraint of War: A Moral and Historical Inquiry* (Princeton: Princeton University Press, 1981), xxxiv, 47.

2. Ibid., xxx. Italics in quote.

3. James Turner Johnson, *Morality and Contemporary Warfare* (New Haven: Yale University Press, 1999), 123.

4. Louise Doswald-Beck and Sylvain Vité, "Origin and Nature of Human Rights Law and Humanitarian Law," in *Humanitarian Law,* ed. Judith Gardam (Aldershot, UK: Ashgate, 1999), 482.

5. Robert C. Stacey, "The Age of Chivalry," in *The Laws of War: Constraints on Warfare in the Western World,* ed. Michael Howard, George J. Andreopoulos, and Mark R. Shulman (New Haven: Yale University Press, 1994), 27–39, quotation on 39.

6. Theodor Meron, *Bloody Constraint: War and Chivalry in Shakespeare* (New York: Oxford University Press, 1998), 204; see also Theodor Meron, *Henry's Wars and Shakespeare's Laws: Perspectives on the Law of War in the Later Middle Ages* (Oxford: Clarendon Press, 1993), 78–79.

7. Adam Roberts, quoted in Meron, *Bloody Constraint,* 3.

8. Johnson, *Just War Tradition,* 6.

9. Hannah Arendt, *The Origins of Totalitarianism* (New York: Harcourt Brace Jovanovich, 1976 [1951]), ix.

10. Gerald I. A. D. Draper, "The Status of Combatants and the Question of Guerilla Warfare," in *The British Yearbook of International Law*, vol. 45 (London: Oxford University Press, 1971), 177.

11. The list of sources for this is enormous. See, for example, Michael Walzer, "Regime Change and Just War," *Dissent*, no. 54 (summer 2006), http://www.dissentmagazine.org/article/?article=663; Jimmy Carter, "Just War—or Just a War?" *New York Times*, March 9, 2003, http://www.nytimes.com/2003/03/09/opinion/09CART.html; George W. Bush, quoted in Darlene Superville, "Bush Thanks Military for Undertaking 'Just' Work," *Washington Post*, January 6, 2009.

12. I take the term *publicists* from Geoffrey Best, who uses it for the select group of individuals involved in the theorization, practice, and implementation of the law; Geoffrey Best, *War and Law since 1945* (Oxford: Oxford University Press, 1994). Although Best is speaking of later centuries, I employ the term here to indicate the general community of these individuals, not bound by a particular era.

13. Part III, HSMO, 1958 *Manual of Military Law*, para. 3, quoted in A. P. V. Rogers, *Law on the Battlefield* (Manchester: Manchester University Press, 1996), 3. See also Meron, *Bloody Constraint*.

14. See Meron, *Bloody Constraint*, 14–15.

15. *U.S. Army Field Manual* (FM 3-21.75), "Warrior Ethos and Soldier Combat Skills," Department of the Army, Washington, D.C., January 28, 2008. Stacey, "Age of Chivalry," 39.

16. Michael Bothe, Karl Josef Partsch, and Waldemar A. Solf, eds., *New Rules for Victims of Armed Conflicts: Commentary on the Two 1977 Protocols Additional to the Geneva Conventions of 1949* (The Hague: Martinus Nijhoff, 1982), 229.

17. Joseph Canning, *A History of Medieval Political Thought, 300–1450* (London: Routledge, 1996), 114–15; James Brundage, *Medieval Canon Law* (New York: Longman, 1995), 68.

18. Brundage, *Medieval Canon Law*, 118.

19. *Oxford English Dictionary*, 2nd ed. (1989).

20. David Bederman, *International Law in Antiquity* (Cambridge, UK: Cambridge University Press, 2001), 267.

21. Ibid., 265.

22. Deuteronomy 20:14–18, *The New Oxford Annotated Bible* (New York: Oxford University Press, 1994) [hereafter *NOAB*].

23. Deuteronomy 21:10–14, *NOAB*. The full text is "Suppose you see among the captives a beautiful woman whom you desire and want to marry, and so you bring her home to your house, she shall shave her head, pare her nails, discard her captive guard, and shall remain in your house for a full month, mourning for her father and mother; after that you may go in to her and be her husband and she shall be your wife."

24. Deuteronomy 20:17.

25. Numbers 31:13–19, NOAB.

26. Michael Walzer, *Just and Unjust Wars: A Moral Argument with Historical Illustrations*, 2nd ed. (New York: Basic Books, 1992), 135.

27. Ibid., 134.

28. Ibid., 135 Furthermore, as Harold Washington, a religious scholar, points out, "the fact that the man must wait for a month before penetrating the woman does not make the sexual relationship something other than rape unless one assumed that by the end of the period the women has consented." Harold Washington, "'Lest He Die in the Battle and Another Man Take Her': Violence and the Construction of Gender in the Law of Deuteronomy 20–22." In *Gender and Law in the Hebrew Bible and the Ancient Near East*, ed. Victor Harold Matthews, Bernard M. Levinson, and Tikva Simone Frymer-Kensky (Sheffield, UK: Sheffield Academic Press, 1998), 206.

29. Walzer, *Just and Unjust Wars*, 146. Walzer sketches a distinction between those who feed the "belly" of the army (what soldiers need to live on) and those who assist the "arms" of the army (what soldiers need to fight). Participation in the latter, he argues, does involve the loss of rights of immunity; these civilians are then no longer "innocent."

30. "Difference of religion is not a cause of just wars." Francisco de Vitoria, "De Indis et De Juri Belli Relectiones," sec. 10, in *Vitoria: Political Writings*, ed. Anthony Pagden and Jeremy Lawrance (Cambridge, UK: Cambridge University Press, 1991). Walzer is well aware of the difference between the treatment of individuals in the holy wars commanded by God against the seven Canaanite peoples and in those wars permitted by God. Thus, the rights or respect for personhood that Walzer discerns from the passage in Deuteronomy is clearly delimited by belonging to a particular people. In this sense, then, Walzer's conception of personhood is, itself, marked by a division—it is not a universal category in the sense that he employs it; rather, it was a gradation of possession. Michael Walzer, "War and Peace in the Jewish Tradition," in *The Ethics of War and Peace: Religious and Secular Perspectives*, ed. Terry Nardin (Princeton: Princeton University Press, 1996); Aviezer Ravitzky, "Prohibited Wars in the Jewish Tradition," in *The Ethics of War and Peace: Religious and Secular Perspectives*, ed. Terry Nardin (Princeton: Princeton University Press, 1996). Moreover, the conduct that appeared to be most significant in assuring protection, and remained so throughout the centuries, was when, given the opportunity, one left a city or fortress under siege.

31. Walzer, *Just and Unjust Wars*, 135.

32. Ibid., 133; see also 137.

33. In fact, Walzer does not really ever define his theory of human rights. It remains the unquestioned foundation of his argument.

34. Ibid., 133

35. Ibid., 120.

36. Ibid., 195.

37. John Keegan, *A History of Warfare* (Toronto: Vintage Books, 1994), 76.

38. The just war tradition is perhaps the most well known of the historical approaches to and interpretations of war. The essential elements of the just war tradition are that the war is waged (1) for a just cause, (2) with/by right of authority, (3) with proper intention, (4) as a last resort, (5) so that it does less harm than good, and (6) to achieve peace. The just war tradition underwent a significant revival during the late 1970s as theorists and theologians debated the validity of the Vietnam War, specifically, and of nuclear weapons, generally. For a recent feminist rewriting of the just war tradition, see Laura Sjoberg, *Gender, Justice, and the Wars in Iraq: A Feminist Reformulation of Just War Theory* (Lanham, Md.: Lexington Books, 2006).

39. Robert L. Holmes, "St. Augustine and the Just War Theory," in *The Augustinian Tradition*, ed. Gareth B. Matthews (Berkeley: University of California Press, 1999), 323.

40. Gareth B. Matthews, "Post-Medieval Augustinianism," in *The Cambridge Companion to Augustine*, eds. Eleonore Stump and Norman Kretzmann (Cambridge, UK: Cambridge University Press, 2001), 271. See also Paul Weithman, "Augustine's Political Philosophy," in *The Cambridge Companion to Augustine*, eds. Eleonore Stump and Norman Kretzmann (Cambridge, UK: Cambridge University Press, 2001), 247.

41. Quoted in Weithman, "Augustine's Political Philosophy," 247.

42. Philippe Contamine, *War in the Middle Ages* (Oxford: Basil Blackwell, 1984), 265.

43. Johnson, *Just War Tradition*, xxxi.

44. Thomas Aquinas, "Summa Theologica II/II," Q. 40 A.1, in *From Irenaeus to Grotius: A Sourcebook in Christian Political Thought*, eds. Oliver O'Donovan and Joan L. O'Donovan (Grand Rapids: William B. Eerdmans, 1999), 135. The paragraph in Letter 189 to Boniface is one of the few writings that fully lays out Augustine's understanding of

war: "Peace should be the object of your desire; war should be waged only as a necessity, and waged only that God may by it deliver men from the necessity and preserve them in peace....war is waged in order that peace may be obtained. Therefore, even in the waging of war cherish the spirit of the peacemaker, that by conquering those whom you attack you may lead them back to the advantages of peace."

45. Johnson, *Just War Tradition,* xxx.

46. Ibid., xxxiv, 47.

47. Holmes, "St. Augustine," 338. He states, as well, that "Insofar as the just war theory is thought to provide moral criteria by which to judge whether to go to war (jus ad bellum), and how to conduct a war once in it (jus in bello) there is, I maintain, little of such guidance in Augustine, hence little ground on that score for representing him as the father of the just war theory" (324).

48. Richard S. Hartigan, "Saint Augustine on War and Killing: The Problem of the Innocent," *Journal of the History of Ideas* 27, no. 2 (1966): 203.

49. Augustine, quoted in Holmes, "St. Augustine," 325. One vivid way of understanding Augustine's emphasis on interiority, or the virtue of the heart and soul, is his belief that chastity is a quality of the soul, not the body, and thus that rape only impugns the bodily integrity of a woman (so long as there is no "fleshly satisfaction"). Rather, the woman who kills herself in shame over rape violates both the integrity of the soul and the body because she commits murder. Augustine, *City of God,* trans. Gerald G. Walsh, Vernon J. Bourke, and Etienne Gilson (Garden City, N.Y.: Doubleday Image Books, 1985) 53.

50. Frederick H. Russell, *The Just War in the Middle Ages* (Cambridge, UK: Cambridge University Press, 1975), 19.

51. Ibid., 20. See also Hartigan who argues that Augustine admits there may be innocents among the enemy populace but does not think this "will regularly be the case." Hartigan, "Saint Augustine on War and Killing, 202.

52. Thomas Aquinas, "Injustice," Q. 64 A. 6, *Summa Theologiæ: Latin Text and English Translation, Introductions, Notes, Appendices and Glossaries* [hereafter *Summa Theologiæ*], vol. 38, trans. Thomas Gilby (Cambridge, UK: Cambridge University Press, 2006), 37. This statement heightens the importance that wars, such as the Crusades, be understood as commanded by God; without this sovereign command, the Crusaders would be committing vile and sinful murders.

53. Thomas Aquinas, "Consequences of Charity," Q. 40 A. 1, *Summa Theologiæ,* vol. 35, 83.

54. Russell, *Just War,* 275.

55. See Holmes, "St. Augustine"; Richard Shelly Hartigan, *The Forgotten Victim: A History of the Civilian* (Chicago: Precedent Publishing, 1982). See also Judith G. Gardam, "Gender and Non-Combatant Immunity," *Transnational Law & Contemporary Problems* 32 (1993): 345–70.

56. Augustine, "Letter 138 (to Marcellinus)," sec. 14 in *Political Writings,* trans. E. Margaret Atkins and Robert Dodaro (Cambridge, UK: Cambridge University Press, 2001), 38.

57. Thomas Aquinas, "Mercy," Q. 30 A. 4, *Summa Theologiæ,* vol. 34, 221.

58. Frederick H. Russell argues that the Isidore of Seville (in the seventeenth century) transmitted the concept of a just war to the Middle Ages, although without the complexity of Augustine's working; Russell, *Just War,* 27.

59. The concepts of order, right order, and peace are extensively set forth in Augustine's *City of God.* Order is explicitly hierarchical; "order is the arrangement granting to each of like things in a proper place." Peace, order, power, and hierarchy are intimately

related because peace remains "ordered concord." Augustine, *City of God,* chap. 13, XIX, 456. Order is also explicitly gendered, premised on the household (460).

60. Johnson, *Just War Tradition,* 127.

61. Russell, *Just War,* 186. See also Hartigan, *Forgotten Victim,* 204; ibid.

62. Contamine, *War in the Middle Ages,* 273–74.

63. See Russell, *Just War,* 183–86.

64. See Wilhelm Georg Grewe, *The Epochs of International Law,* trans. Michael Byers (Berlin: Walter de Gruyter, 2000), 115.

65. James A. Brundage, *Medieval Canon Law and the Crusader* (Madison: University of Wisconsin Press, 1969), 13. Brundage notes that the peace movement was definitively formed in Lateran Councils 1123, 1139, and 1179 in the twelfth century.

66. Thomas Head and Richard Allen Landes, eds., *The Peace of God: Social Violence and Religious Response in France around the Year 1000* (Ithaca: Cornell University Press, 1992), 2.

67. Quoted in Christian Rosaz-Lauranson, "Peace from the Mountains: The Auvergnat Origins of the Peace of God," in Head and Landes, *Peace of God,* 104–5.

68. Ibid., 114.

69. Matthew Strickland, *War and Chivalry: The Conduct and Perception of War in England and Normandy, 1066–1217* (New York: Cambridge University Press, 1996), 283.

70. John France, *Western Warfare in the Age of the Crusades, 1000–1300* (Ithaca: Cornell University Press, 1999), 11.

71. Johnson, *Just War Tradition,* 127.

72. Hans Werner Goetz, "Protection of the Church, Defense of the Law, and Reform: On the Purposes and Character of the Peace of God, 989–1038," in Head and Landes, *Peace of God,* 267–68. He also argues that the prohibition against harming peasants at their labor was more likely to be observed during famine, demonstrating that the peasants were not protected as people.

73. Amy Remensnyder, "Pollution, Purity, and Peace: An Aspect of Social Reform between the Late Tenth Century and 1076," in Head and Landes, *Peace of God,* 286. She writes that the prohibition on "secular weapons" might have reflected the regulations of the clergy as members of the "arms bearing noble class" of which many were a part.

74. Quoted in Richard W. Kaeuper, *Chivalry and Violence in Medieval Europe* (Oxford: Oxford University Press, 1999), 66. See also ibid.

75. In the twelfth century, the influential decretum "Concordance of Discordant Canons" specifically stipulated that a war would no longer be just if clerics became combatants. The *Decretum of Gratian* was a significant development in canon law because it systematically ordered, for the first time, the mass of canon law and teaching promulgated by the Catholic Church. It included the teachings of Augustine on the justice of war and related canonical teachings. See Canning, *History of Medieval Political Thought,* 116. See also Johnson, *Just War Tradition,* 157. Brundage notes Gratian's *Decretum* specifically prohibits indiscriminate killing in "The Limits of War-Making Power"; Brundage, *Medieval Canon Law,* 76. See also the masterful retelling of the Crusades in Christopher Tyerman, in *God's War: A New History of the Crusades* (Cambridge, Mass.: Belknap Press, 2006).

76. Contamine, *War in the Middle Ages,* 274–75.

77. Frederick Paxton, "History, Historians, and the Peace of God," in Head and Landes, *Peace of God,* 32.

78. Johnson, *Just War Tradition,* 127.

79. See Strickland, *War and Chivalry,* 29.

80. See, among others, Paxton, "History," 26. See also Maurice Keen, *Chivalry* (New Haven: Yale University Press, 1984), chap. 3.

81. The other infamous exception in the restrictions on warfare is the case of the crossbow, which was outlawed in the twelfth century—but only in battles among Christian warriors.

82. Tyerman, *God's War*, 50.

83. "Bless this sword...so it may be a defense for churches, widows, and orphans, and for all servants of God against the fury of the heathen." Quoted in Keen, *Chivalry*, 71.

84. Strickland, *War and Chivalry*, 285.

85. Keen, *Chivalry*, 70. In Keen's retelling of the specific instructions for those admitted to the order of chivalry—"spare his foe if he cries mercy, to keep counsel, to aid women in distress, to go to church and pray"—it is possible to see the still-present link of the concept of mercy and its attribute of power over a foe (70).

86. Richard W. Kaeuper, ed., *Violence in Medieval Society* (Rochester, N.Y.: Boydell Press, 2000), 34.

87. Kaeuper, *Chivalry and Violence in Medieval Europe*, 185.

88. Meron, *Bloody Constraint*, 204. "Without neglecting our existing system of international humanitarian law, we need to refocus on broad, simple, comprehensible principles of humanity." Ibid. Meron then reflects that these broad principles and norms may be found in the culture and values of chivalry. Here, the principles of humanity are the logical extension of the norms of chivalry, which were the principles of a specific class and founded in a Christian determination of humanity; Meron, *Henry's Wars and Shakespeare's Laws*. Meron concludes that "the medieval concept of mercy on which the dramatist [Shakespeare] drew evolved into the concepts of obligation of humanity in the modern law of war. What, after all, are obligations of humanity if not the legally binding progeny of mercy?" (216).

89. Meron, *Bloody Constraint*, 204.

90. See Maurice Keen, *Nobles, Knights, and Men-at-Arms in the Middle Ages* (London: Hambledon Press, 1996), chap. 1.

91. Contamine, *War in the Middle Ages*, 272.

92. Keen, *Nobles*, 33.

93. Kaeuper, *Chivalry and Violence in Medieval Europe*, 226;

94. Quoted in Kaeuper, *Violence in Medieval Society*, 34. Strickland, comments that the "overwhelming masculine, aristocratic, and martial milieu in which a man's standing rested directly on his feats of arms in war" that is, his standing as a man; Strickland, *War and Chivalry*, 102.

95. Quoted in Strickland, *War and Chivalry*, 24.

96. Johnson, *Just War Tradition*, 137.

97. Ibid.

98. Peter R. Coss. *The Lady in Medieval England, 1000–1500* (Mechanicsburg, Pa.: Stackpole Books, 1998), 73.

99. Rosalind Brown-Grant, *Christine De Pizan and the Moral Defence of Women: Reading beyond Gender* (Cambridge, UK: Cambridge University Press, 1999), 219.

100. James Brundage, "Domestic Violence in Classical Canon Law," in Kaeuper, *Violence in Medieval Society*, 184.

101. Ibid.

102. Neil A. R. Wright "The Tree of Battles of Honoré Bouvet and the Laws of War," in *War, Literature, and Politics in the Late Middle Ages*, ed. Christopher Thomas Allmand and George William Coopland (Liverpool: Liverpool University Press, 1976), 13–14. Wright notes that the treatise was available in at least four languages in addition to the original French and "quoted in legal disputes," and states that "there can be no doubt that the Tree was a popular and widely read book during the late medieval and early modern period." Ibid., 13.

103. Honoré Bonet, *The Tree of Battles,* trans. George W. Copeland (Liverpool: University Press, 1949), 184–85. In *The Tree of Battles,* he also clearly admits, however, that the innocent do suffer with the guilty, especially in the "false usage of war." Ibid., 125.

104. Ibid., 167–68.

105. Ibid., 143–45.

106. The work of de Pisan deserves more attention than I have granted it here. Suffice it to say that she writes a phenomenal chapter in *The City of Ladies,* trans. Rosalind Brown-Grant (New York: Penguin Books, 2006), entitled "Refuting Those Men Who Claim Women Want to Be Raped," in which she imagines a city in which, rather than women committing suicide due to the violation of their chastity, men are executed, a solution that Augustine neglected to consider.

107. Bonet, *Tree of Battles,* 184–85.

108. Meron, *Henry's Wars and Shakespeare's Laws,* 95.

109. Johnson, *Just War Tradition,* 133.

110. John A. Flynn, *Women, Armies and Warfare in Early Modern Europe* (Cambridge: Cambridge University Press, 2008), 117.

111. Johnson, *Just War Tradition,* 136.

112. Strickland, *War and Chivalry,* 286.

113. Bonet, *Tree of Battles,* 144.

114. Ibid., 185.

115. Contamine, *War in the Middle Ages,* 296. The Crusades can also be seen as the outgrowth of the pilgrimage tradition of early Christian life and thought; see Brundage, *Medieval Canon Law and the Crusader,* 11.

116. Thomas S. Asbridge, *The First Crusade: A New History* (London: Free Press, 2004), 168. Further, "the crusade was designed first and foremost to meet the needs of the papacy. Launched as it was just as Urban began to stabilize his power-base in central Italy, the campaign must be seen as an attempt to consolidate papal empowerment and expand Roman sphere of influence"(21).

117. See Keen, *Nobles,* 21.

118. See ibid., chap. 1.

119. Maurice H. Keen, "Chivalry, Nobility, and the Man-at-Arms," in *War, Literature, and Politics in the Late Middle Ages,* ed. Christopher Thomas Allmand and George William Coopland (Liverpool: Liverpool University Press, 1976), 40.

120. Asbridge, *The First Crusade,* 35.

121. Meron, *Bloody Constraint,* 6.

122. France, *Western Warfare,* 11.

123. Ibid., 233.

124. Strickland, *War and Chivalry,* 337.

125. Tyerman, *God's War,* 914.

126. Meron, *Bloody Constraint,* 118.

127. Johnson, *Just War Tradition,* 149 (emphasis added).

128. Russell, *Just War,* 308.

3. CIVILIZATION AND EMPIRE

1. Emory Heyward, quoted in Bernard Augustine De Voto, *The Course of Empire* (Boston: Houghton, Mifflin, 1952), 2. See also Stephen Greenblatt, *Marvelous Possessions: The Wonder of the New World* (Chicago: University of Chicago Press, 1991).

2. Philip Allott, "The Concept of International Law," in *The Role of Law in International Politics: Essays in International Relations and International Law,* ed. Michael Byers (Oxford: Oxford University Press, 2001), 78.

3. Wilhelm Georg Grewe, *The Epochs of International Law*, trans. Michael Byers (Berlin: Walter de Gruyter, 2000), 195.

4. James Turner Johnson, *Just War Tradition and the Restraint of War: A Moral and Historical Inquiry.* (Princeton: Princeton University Press, 1981), 222–23.

5. Hedley Bull, Benedict Kingsbury, and Adam Roberts, eds., *Hugo Grotius and International Relations* (Oxford: Oxford University Press, 1990), 26.

6. Johnson, *Just War Tradition,* 176 (emphasis added).

7. Charles H. Alexandrowicz, "Foreword," in *Alberico Gentili and the Development of International Law: His Life, Work and Times,* ed. Gesina H. J. van der Molen (Leyden: A. W. Sijthoff, 1968), ix.

8. Grewe, *Epochs of International Law,* 153.

9. Ibid., 154. For a discussion of "no peace beyond the line" in reference to these lines of amity and friendship, see Heinz Duschhardt, "War and International Law in Europe, Sixteenth to Eighteenth Century," in *War and Competition between States,* ed. Philippe Contamine (Oxford: Oxford University Press, 2000), 283.

10. *Oxford English Dictionary,* 2nd ed. (1989).

11. Ibid.

12. Grewe, *Epochs of International Law,* 450. See, among others, Peter Malanczuk, *Akehurst's Modern Introduction to International Law* (New York: Routledge, 1999), 2.

13. Gerrit W. Gong, *The Standard of "Civilization" in International Society* (Oxford: Clarendon Press, 1984), 36.

14. Henry Wheaton, *Elements of International Law,* 8th ed. (Boston: Little, Brown, 1866), 17–18.

15. Anthony Pagden, *The Fall of Natural Man: The American Indian and the Origins of Comparative Ethnology* (Cambridge, UK: Cambridge University Press, 1982), 16.

16. Yasuaki Onuma, "Eurocentrism in the History of International Law," in *A Normative Approach to War: Peace, War, and Justice in Hugo Grotius,* ed. Yasuaki Onuma (Oxford: Clarendon Press, 1993). "The modern European international order started with the formation of permanent international relations on a global scale under the hegemony of Spain and Portugal" and debates over the colonization of the Americas (382).

17. Grewe, *Epochs of International Law,* 187.

18. Quoted in Robert A. Williams, *The American Indian in Western Legal Thought: The Discourses of Conquest* (New York: Oxford University Press, 1990) 74. "Law, which Europeans have long revered as their instrument of civilization, became the West's perfect instrument of empire" (93).

19. Patricia Seed, *Ceremonies of Possession in Europe's Conquest of the New World, 1492–1640* (Cambridge, UK: Cambridge University Press, 1995), 70; Lewis Hanke, *The Colonial Experience* (Boston: Little, Brown, 1973), 123.

20. Seed, *Ceremonies,* 70.

21. The Requirement (1513), reprinted in Charles L. G. Anderson, *Panama and Castilla del Oro: A Narrative History of the Discovery* (Boston: The Page Company, 1911) 505–7, 505.

22. Ibid, 506.

23. Ibid.

24. Ibid., 507.

25. Ibid.

26. Ibid.

27. See Anthony Pagden and Jeremy Lawrance, eds., *Vitoria: Political Writings* (Cambridge, UK: Cambridge University Press, 1991), xv.

28. Ibid. See also Grewe, *Epochs of International Law.*

29. See Pagden and Lawrance, *Vitoria*. See also Peter Fitzpatrick, *Modernism and the Grounds of Law* (Cambridge, UK: Cambridge University Press, 2001).

30. Anthony Pagden, *Lords of All the World: Ideologies of Empire in Spain, Britain and France c. 1500–c. 1800* (New Haven: Yale University Press, 1995), 52.

31. Grewe, *Epochs of International Law*, 244. Both disputations, *On the Indians Recently Discovered* and *On the Laws of War*, provide the textual reference for this section. Vitoria did not envision that these works would be considered distinct disputations. His closing words clearly indicate that *On the Laws of War* is his second statement on the American Indians. His theories on the laws of war, for which he is well remembered and received, are deduced and developed from the particular case of the conquest of the Americas, an event that he decried but nonetheless sought to justify and legitimate.

32. Both Pagden and Seed underscore the complexity of reading the Requirement; Pagden, *Fall of Natural Man*; Anthony Pagden, "Dispossessing the Barbarian," in *The Languages of Political Theory in Early-Modern Europe*, ed. Anthony Pagden (Cambridge, UK: Cambridge University Press, 1987); Seed, *Ceremonies*. First, as a protocol of war, it was a hybrid of Islamic and Christian declarations and so, Seed argues, a derivation of the "Islamic summons to surrender to Allah." In fact, she argues that part of the fervor of de las Casas's famous attack on the Requirement and the conquest of the Americas stemmed from his recognition of the "Islamic-inspired ways of conquering and justifying the conquest of the New World." Seed, *Ceremonies*, 93. For background on Seed's claim, see John Kelsay, *Arguing the Just War in Islam* (Cambridge, Mass.: Harvard University Press, 2007).

33. The importance of this quest was central because Vitoria believed that, even though Spain had been granted a mandate through the Papal Bull of 1493 as the "spiritual head of Christendom" to "expand the Christian faith in America," this mandate was neither a sufficient nor legitimate basis for war undertaken against the Indians. Pagden and Lawrance, *Vitoria*, 284–85. Briefly, Vitoria challenged the idea that the pope could retain temporal as well as religious authority, much less any authority over the pagans. Regardless, then, of the actual reading of the Requirement informing the barbarians of the existence of this mandate, the Spanish claim to the legal possession of the Americas was invalid.

34. Ibid., 275–76.

35. Ibid., 276–77.

36. Ibid., 233.

37. Antonio de Montesinos (a Spanish Dominican who first decried the treatment of the Indians in his oft-quoted Advent sermon of 1511), quoted in Hugh Thomas, *Rivers of Gold: The Rise of the Spanish Empire* (London: Weidenfeld & Nicolson, 2003), 294.

38. Pagden and Lawrance, *Vitoria*, 332.

39. Two contemporary examples of scholarship that demonstrate that humanism, enlightenment, and empire are not mutually exclusive but, instead, draw on one another in multiple ways to order both colonial and imperial societies are Sankar Muthu, *Enlightenment against Empire* (Princeton: Princeton University Press, 2003); Jennifer Pitts, *A Turn to Empire: The Rise of Imperial Liberalism in Britain and France* (Princeton: Princeton University Press, 2003).

40. Pagden points out that, because the "situation in America possessed as self-evident reality…it had to be explicable in terms of…natural law." Pagden, *The Fall of Natural Man*, 65. Because Vitoria was writing his disputation not "to argue about the truth but explain it," he must draw on natural law to do so. Pagden and Lawrance, *Vitoria*, xvii.

41. Ibid., xviii, 238.

42. Peter Fitzpatrick, "Colonialism's Legacy," in *Law, History, Colonialism: The Reach of Empire*, ed. Diane Kirby and Catherine Coleborne (Manchester: Manchester University Press, 2001), 9. See also Antony Anghie, *Imperialism, Sovereignty, and the Making of International Law* (Cambridge, UK: Cambridge University Press, 2005).

43. Pagden and Lawrance, *Vitoria,* xiv-xv.

44. Ibid., xv.

45. Pagden, *Fall of Natural Man,* 67.

46. Pagden and Lawrance, *Vitoria,* 278.

47. The Requirement (1513), reprinted in Anderson, *Panama and Castilla del Oro,* 505–7.

48. James Brown Scott, *The Catholic Conception of International Law: Francisco de Vitoria, Founder of the Modern Law of Nations, Francisco Suarez, Founder of the Modern Philosophy of Law in General and in Particular of the Law of Nations: A Critical Examination and a Justified Appreciation* (Clark, N.J.: Lawbook Exchange, 2007), 130.

49. Antony Anghie, "Francisco De Vitoria and the Colonial Origins of International Law," *Social and Legal Studies* 5, no. 3 (1996), 328. See also Anghie, *Imperialism.*

50. Pagden, "Dispossessing the Barbarian," 17.

51. Greenblatt, *Marvelous Possessions,* 121.

52. Examine for a moment how this exchange of barbarism for civilization, through acceptance of Christianity, was formulated as a right of communication—a right of natural law and of the *jus gentium.* As defined by Vitoria, it was the right of the Spaniards to "advise" the barbarians about Christianity and the obligation of the barbarians to "listen" and, he continues, to "accept the faith of Christ." Pagden and Lawrance, *Vitoria,* 271. Each was owed to the other party. Recall the similar injunction found in the Requirement to "consent and give place" to the "religious fathers" to declare and preach the word of the Lord. Although it was purportedly a universal right established within and by the law of nations, the pope had entrusted this task of advisement to the Spanish and forbidden it to all others. We might well wonder how the Indians were to reciprocally exercise this right to communication as defined by the Vitoria. Attribution of the rights of communication was properly restricted to the Spanish, whereas the voice of the Indians remained inaudible. Thus, he continues, if the barbarians obstructed the Spaniards in their papal mandate, it was appropriate and permissible for the Spaniards to persist in preaching and "work for the conversion of that people against their will." Ibid., 285.

53. Anghie, "Francisco De Vitoria," 328.

54. At the time in which Vitoria wrote, the prevalent doctrine held that only one side in each war could have just cause because it was impossible that justice and rights, absolute in their formation, could come into conflict. Yet, due to what Vitoria describes in his second disputation as "provable ignorance" on one side and "true justice" on the other, it is possible for a war to be *perceived* as just by all parties. Thus, he acknowledges that an interpretation of the justice of a war may be both subjective and objective. In regards to the particular case that sparked this disputation, it is not difficult to decide to whom the definitive attribute of the "invincible error" of ignorance is assigned and to whom the possession of not only truth but also subjective and objective justice is accorded. Thus, for example, the Indians might believe themselves to be justified in defending themselves against the Spaniards when they first arrived, but this did not make their cause objectively just—it was not a true justice. Pagden and Lawrance, *Vitoria,* 313.

55. Ibid., 271.

56. Ibid., 327

57. James Brown Scott, *The Spanish Origins of International Law: Francisco De Vitoria and His Law of Nations* (New York: Lawbook Exchange, 2000), 212.

58. It is quite puzzling that Richard Hartigan insists that "nowhere is Vitoria's oft-noted humanism more evident than in these passages" without simultaneously recognizing its founding paradox: the humanism of Vitoria produces the barbarism of the Indians. Richard S. Hartigan, "Francesco de Vitoria and Civilian Immunity," *Political Theory* 1, no. 1 (1973): 79–91, 86.

59. Aristotle, *The Politics*, ed. Stephen Everson (Cambridge: Cambridge University Press, 1990), 3.

60. Pagden and Lawrance, *Vitoria*, 283.

61. The Requirement (1513), reprinted in Anderson, *Panama and Castilla del Oro* (Boston: The Page Company, 1911), 505–7, 507.

62. Quoted in Jill Lepore, *The Name of War: King Philip's War and the Origins of American Identity* (New York: Vintage Books, 1999), 250.

63. Suarez and Vitoria are frequently read in conjunction. Bernice Hamilton suggests that "when one comes to search for the best passage to illuminate a particular point, it is often on the more pedestrian Suarez that one lights." Bernice Hamilton, *Political Thought in Sixteenth-Century Spain* (Oxford: Clarendon Press, 1963), 8.

64. Aristotle. *The Politics*, 19.

65. Ibid.

66. Pagden and Lawrance, *Vitoria*, 315.

67. Ibid., 316.

68. Ibid., 282–83.

69. Vitoria contradicts his earlier insight that "war is no argument for the truth of the Christian faith" by allowing the Spaniards to "take up arms and declare war on them insofar as this provides the safety and opportunity needed to preach the Gospel." What, then, is the difference between this declaration of war and that found in the Requirement, in which the Indians are compelled to convert or suffer the ravages of war? Some might reply that the difference is found in the cautions inscribed in this right to war and that, in this example, the phrase carries the weight of that interpretation. This would not be a misguided view in that one of Vitoria's consistent concerns is that the Spanish observe "reasonable limits and do not go further than necessary." Ibid., 286.

70. James Turner Johnson, *Ideology, Reason, and the Limitation of War: Religious and Secular Concepts, 1200–1740* (Princeton: Princeton University Press, 1975), 196. In addition, Thomas Pangle and Peter Ahrendsdorf express concern that Johnson, although admitting that Vitoria erodes the rights of innocents whenever necessary, still "too constantly attempts to bend or to emend tacitly the stern Scholastic teachings in order to force them to comply with the late 20th century humanistic scruples." Thomas Pangle and Peter Ahrendsdorf, *Justice among Nations: On the Moral Basis of Power and Peace* (Lawrence: University Press of Kansas, 1999), 288.

71. Richard Shelly Hartigan, *The Forgotten Victim: A History of the Civilian* (Chicago: Precedent Publishing, 1982), 84.

72. Pagden and Lawrance, *Vitoria*, 317.

73. Francisco Suarez, *Selections from Three Works of Francisco Suárez, S.J.: De legibus, ac deo legislatore, 1612, Defensio fidei catholicae, et apostolicae adversus anglicanae sectae errores, 1613, De triplici virtute theologica, fide, spe, et charitate, 1621*, trans. Gwladys L. Williams, Ammi Brown, and John Waldron (Oxford: Clarendon Press, 1944), 847.

74. Ibid., 847.

75. Colm McKeogh, *Innocent Civilians: The Morality of Killing in War* (New York: Palgrave, 2002), 94.

76. Interestingly, Hartigan does not dispute this attribution, but he also does not locate it in natural law. Rather, he seems to locate it in the self-evidence of civilized societies. He argues, "even if practice and custom did not include women and children in the immune category, their status as innocents would be self-evident." Hartigan, *Forgotten Victim*, 89. He is careful to point out that it is the other classes of innocents that require explanation.

77. Francisco Suarez, *Selections from Three Works*, 843.

78. Hamilton, *Political Thought in Sixteenth-Century Spain*, 24.

79. Richard Tuck, *The Rights of War and Peace: Political Thought and the International Order from Grotius to Kant* (Oxford: Oxford University Press, 1999).

80. Hugo Grotius, *De jure belli ac pacis libri tres* (The Laws of War and Peace), trans. Francis W. Kelsey, reprinted in *Classics of International Law*, ed. James Brown Scott (New York: Oceana Press, 1964 [1646]) [hereafter *LWP*], "Prolegomena," 20.

81. Johnson, *Ideology*, 225.

82. Grotius, *LWP*, book 3, chap. 4, § XIX, 657.

83. Tuck, *Rights of War and Peace*, 103.

84. As Grotius reveals, it is the "The New Testament I use in order to explain—and this cannot be learned from any other source—what is permissible to Christians." Moreover, in writing his treatise on war his wish is to "inscribe these teachings on the hearts of those who hold sway over the Christian world." Grotius, *LWP*, "Prolegomena," 27; book 3, chap. 25 § VIII, 862.

85. Grotius, *LWP*, "Prolegomena," 20.

86. Ibid.

87. Ibid., book 2, chap. 5 § I, 231. "The right of the father" is a plangent phrase, evoking in some sense the supremacy of the father in Roman law, that implies that the laws of war have roots far deeper and more tangled than the conventional acceptance of *LWP* indicates.

88. Ibid.

89. Onuma Yasuaki notes that "the basic constituent unit of society was the household, with its head (paterfamilias) having governing power over his wife, children, and slaves." Yasuaki Onuma, "War," in *A Normative Approach to War: Peace, War, and Justice in Hugo Grotius*, ed. Yasuaki Onuma (Oxford: Clarendon Press, 1993), 60. See also See Tuck, *Rights of War and Peace;* Simon Schama, *The Embarrassment of Riches: An Interpretation of Dutch Culture in the Golden Age* (New York: Vintage Books, 1997), chap 6; Grotius, *LWP*, book 2, chap. 5 § XII, 240. As feminist theorists have often underscored, consent to the formation and formulation of the sovereign power of the state is predicated solely on the association and subjection of men, yet it fundamentally relies on the prior (hetero-normative) relation as imagined and naturalized between husbands and wives. For a classic analysis of this, see Carole Pateman, *The Sexual Contract* (Stanford: Stanford University Press, 1988). See also Christine Di Stefano, *Configurations of Masculinity: A Feminist Perspective on Modern Political Theory* (Ithaca: Cornell University Press, 1991); Jacqueline Stevens, *Reproducing the State* (Princeton: Princeton University Press, 1999); Wendy Brown, *States of Injury: Power and Freedom in Late Modernity* (Princeton: Princeton University Press, 1995), esp. chap. 6.

90. Schama, *Embarrassment of Riches*, 386.

91. Grotius, *LWP*, book 2, chap. 5, § VIII, 234.

92. Ibid., "Prolegomena." "This maintenance of the social order, which we have roughly sketched and which is consonant with human intelligence, is the source of law properly called" (12, 17).

93. Kelly Dawn Askin, *War Crimes against Women: Prosecution in International War Crimes Tribunals* (The Hague: Martinus Nijhoff, 1997). See also Meron, *Henry's Wars and Shakespeare's Laws*, 112n. 180; Meron, *War Crimes Law Comes of Age*, 129.

94. Grotius, *LWP*, book 3, chap. 4 § XIX, 656–57.

95. Ibid.

96. Kasai Naoya, "The Laws of War," in *A Normative Approach to War: Peace, War, and Justice in Hugo Grotius*, ed. Onuma Yasuaki (Oxford: Clarendon Press, 1993), 260.

97. Grotius, *LWP*, book 3, chap. 4 § XIX, 657.

98. Ibid.

99. Ibid. Feminist scholars have commented on the power and persistence of this framing, wherein the injury of rape is translated and interpreted as an injury done to the

family, community, or the nation rather than to the person violated. Indeed, the strategy of public rape, in common areas or in communities, is specifically intended to violate the community through the violation of the female body, and the interpretation of rape as a crime against (familial) honor, rather than a war crime, evinces this construction.

100. Ibid.

101. Ibid., "Prolegomena," 13.

102. Ibid., book 3, chap. 25 § II, 861.

103. The formation of an ethical self, its imbrication in the proper governance of sexual relations, desire, and the soul, precedes a specifically Christian theology as laid out by Michel Foucault in *The Use of Pleasure*. Its appearance here, however, cites these relations, a form of an "art of the self." The shift said to occur in the seventeenth century from the woman to the body as the locus for "moral reflection on sexual pleasure," as Foucault describes it, is not yet visible in *LWP* in the same way that the workings of power, at least as captured in the concepts of dietetics and economics, can be identified in *LWP*. Michel Foucault, *The Use of Pleasure: The History of Sexuality*, vol. 2 (New York: Vintage Books, 1986), 250–52.

104. Grotius, *LWP*, book 1, chap. 4 § IV, 97.

105. Karma Nabulsi, *Traditions of War: Occupation, Resistance, and the Law* (Oxford: Oxford University Press, 1999), 157.

106. Grotius, *LWP*, book 1, chap. 10 § IV, 165. Grotius has no doubt that by nature "all subjects may be used for purposes of war." And, although certain classes may be exempt from doing so, it is by "special enactment" (165). It is "in the first principles of nature, there is nothing which is opposed to war; rather all points are in its favor. The end and aim of war being the preservation of life and limb, and the keeping or acquiring of things useful to life, war is in perfect accord" (book 1, chap. 3 § IV, 53).

107. Ibid., book 3, chap. 4 § VI, 646.

108. Ibid.

109. Ibid., § IX, 648.

110. Ibid.

111. Ibid., "Prolegomena," 20.

112. Divine law is drawn from the Gospel and the Old Testament as well as from the law of nature and corresponds, but is not limited, to the duty of Christians. See Tanaka Tadashi, "Grotius's Concept of Law," in *A Normative Approach to War: Peace, War, and Justice in Hugo Grotius*, ed. Onuma Yasuaki (Oxford: Clarendon Press, 1993). See also Johnson, *Ideology*. Note, however, that Grotius also derives the law of nature in part from the practice of civilized Christian nations. Grotius, *LWP*, book 3, chaps. 10-11, 716–44.

113. See Grotius, *LWP*, book 3, chap. 4 § II, 643.

114. See ibid., book 3, chap. 11 § I, 722.

115. See Ibid., 634.

116. Ibid., book 4, chap. 10, § I, 716.

117. See Ibid., book 3, chap. 10 § I, 716, 734.

118. See Ibid., book 3, chap. 11 § VII–VIII, 734–35.

119. "Just as mathematicians customarily prefix to any concrete demonstration a preliminary statement of certain broad axioms on which all persons are easily agreed, in order that there may be some fixed point from which to trace the proof of what follows, so shall we point out certain rules and laws of the most general nature, presenting them as preliminary assumptions which need to be recalled rather than learned...with the purpose of laying a foundation upon which other conclusions may safely rest." Grotius, *De jure pradae;* Hugo Grotius, *Commentary on the Law of Prize and Booty*, ed. Martine Julia van Ittersum (Indianapolis: Liberty Fund, 2006), chap. 1[2], para. 54, http://oll.liberty fund.org/title/1718/77218/1870612.

120. Grotius, *LWP,* book 3, chap. 9 § I, 734.

121. Ibid.

122. Joshua, *The New Oxford Annotated Bible* (New York: Oxford University Press, 1994), 10, 11, verse 38, 283.

123. Grotius, *LWP,* book 3, chap. 9 § IX, 734n. 1.

124. Ibid., book 2, chap. 5 § VII, 234.

125. Ibid., book 2, chap. 1 § I, 170.

126. Ibid., book 1, chap. 3 § I, 102.

127. Onuma, "War," 99. Let me be clear: women would be barred from waging both private and public war, if even considered in the latter. In natural law, women possess at best limited rights due the most natural form of association, marriage. Because women are configured primarily as a form of property, it would seem difficult for women to wage a war to regain property. Finally, in the law of nations, it is "essential that it [a public war] should have the support of the sovereign power." Grotius, *LWP,* book 3, chap. 3 § IV, 633.

128. Grotius, *LWP,* book 2, chap. 20 § XXXI, 497. The power of discrimination is one of the fundamental characteristics distinguishing men from animals, as Grotius discusses in the "Prolegomena."

129. Ibid.

130. "Again, that which is always the rule in respect to children who have not yet attained to the use of reason is in the most case valid with regard to women." Ibid., book 3, chap. 11 § IX, 735.

131. The third category that Grotius focuses on consists of those who "also should be spared" because their occupations are solely religious or "concerned with letters," because their occupations are farming or mercantile, and, finally, because they are prisoners of war. Ibid., § X, 736. Note that this is occupational protection, a protection that does not determine an absolute difference, as do sex and sex difference.

132. Ibid., § IX, 734.

133. Ibid., 735.

134. Ibid., 736.

135. Crimes of perfidy (of disguise) were consistently decried within the larger tradition of theorizing on war. Specifically, the cross-dressing of the sexes was frowned on. In this, we need think only of the treatment and speculation regarding Joan of Arc and the crime for which she was executed—that of dressing as a man. In fact, the difference between an acceptable ruse of war and a crime of perfidy pivots on an understanding of honor; although it may be honorable to trick in war (use a ruse), it is not honorable to deceive.

136. For Grotius's acknowledgement of his debt, his "profit" from "the painstaking" of Gentili, see Grotius, *LWP,* "Prolegomena," 22. The relationship between the two scholars is discussed in Gesina H. J. van der Molen, *Alberico Gentili and the Development of International Law: His Life, Work and Times* (Leyden: A. W. Sijthoff, 1968); Peter Borschberg, *Hugo Grotius "Commentarius in Theses XI": An Early Treatise on Sovereignty, the Just War, and the Legitimacy of the Dutch Revolt* (Berlin: Peter Lang, 1994); Meron, *War Crimes Law Comes of Age,* 120–30.

137. Alberico Gentili, "De jure belli libri tres [2 vols.]," in *The Classics of International Law,* vol. 16, ed. John Carew Rolfe and Coleman Phillipson (Oxford: Clarendon Press, 1933), 252. Similarly, Vitoria suggests that there are crimes for which particular women should be explicitly punished, although all women should be presumed innocent. The nearest that Vitoria comes to defining such a crime is fighting in the war. Pagden and Lawrance, *Vitoria.*

138. Grotius, *LWP,* book 3, chap 11 § IX, 735.

139. Ibid., § VIII, 734.

140. Ibid., 735.

141. Gentili, "De jure belli libri tres," book 2, chap. 21, 253.

142. Ibid. 256–57.

143. Grotius, *LWP*, book 2, chap. 5 § I, 164.

144. Ibid., "Prolegomena," 23.

4. GENERAL ORDERS 100, UNION GENERAL SHERMAN'S MARCH TO ATLANTA, AND THE SAND CREEK MASSACRE

1. President Abraham Lincoln, letter to James C. Conkling, August 26, 1863, http://millercenter.org/scripps/archive/speeches/detail/3510.

2. "The Battle of Sand Creek," *Rocky Mountain News,* 1864, http://www.pbs.org/weta/thewest/resources/archives/four/sandcrk.htm. The massacre of Bear River, which occurred a year earlier under the leadership of Union Colonel Patrick Connor, did slay more Indians and was fully as brutal.

3. Mark Grimsley, *The Hard Hand of War: Union Military Policy toward Southern Civilians, 1861–1865* (Cambridge, UK: Cambridge University Press, 1995).

4. Edward Hagerman, *The American Civil War and the Origins of Modern Warfare: Ideas, Organization, and Field Command* (Bloomington: Indiana University Press, 1988). The debates over the description of the American Civil War as the harbinger of a total war are captured quite descriptively in Stig Förster and Jörg Nagler, eds., *On the Road to Total War: The American Civil War and the German Wars of Unification, 1861–1871* (Cambridge, UK: Cambridge University Press, 1999). Most well known is Mark Neely's essay "Was the Civil War a Total War?" in which he argues that the American Civil War was not a total war but a formative, ideologically driven, technologically sophisticated, and violent war. It was not waged with the intent of the total destruction of the Southern economy (which, as Neely points out, did not have any true essential industries—"determined men with rifles was the real problem" [42]), nor did it consistently violate the distinction of combatant and civilians, which is conventionally considered the essential hallmark of a total war. Furthermore, as the majority of authors in the volume note, the term total war is an anachronism and absent from the military strategies of the time. Mark Grimsley convincingly documents the evolution of the war from conciliatory to hard, but never to total; *Hard Hand of War.* See also the review of Mark Neely, *The Civil War and the Limits of Destruction* (Cambridge, Mass.: Harvard University Press, 2007), James McPherson, "Was It More Restrained than You Think?" *New York Review of Books,* February 14, 2008.

5. Brooks D. Simpson and Arthur Stanley Link, *America's Civil War* (Wheeling, Ill.: Harlan Davidson, 1996), 4.

6. James M. McPherson, *Battle Cry of Freedom: The Civil War Era* (New York: Oxford University Press, 1988), 312.

7. Daniel E. Sutherland, *A Savage Conflict: The Decisive Role of Guerrillas in the American Civil War* (Chapel Hill: University of North Carolina Press, 2009), 28.

8. Quoted in Dee Alexander Brown, *Bury My Heart at Wounded Knee: An Indian History of the American West* (New York: Bantam Books, 1972), 21.

9. Quoted in ibid., 103.

10. As recounted by one of his scouts, John McCorkle, quoted in T. J. Stiles, ed., *Civil War Commanders* (New York: Berkley Publishing, 1995), 185.

11. Arthur Eyffinger, *The 1899 Hague Peace Conference: "The Parliament of Man, the Federation of the World"* (The Hague: Kluwer Law International, 1999), 259.

General Orders 100 provided the basis for the Brussels Conference of 1874, a conference that produced the nonbinding International Declaration Concerning the Laws and Customs of War; see Richard S. Hartigan, *Lieber's Code and the Law of War* (Chicago:

Precedent, 1983). In addition, the code was adapted by the Prussian army and influenced the 1880 *Oxford Manual of the Institute of International Law,* all of which became the principal sources of the 1899 and 1907 Hague regulations governing war.

12. Arthur Eyffinger, *The 1899 Hague Peace Conference: "The Parliament of Man, the Federation of the World"* (The Hague: Kluwer Law International, 1999), 259.

13. Stuart Banner, *How the Indians Lost Their Land* (Cambridge, Mass.: Belknap Press, 2005), 247.

14. Quoted in Michael Fellman, *Inside War: The Guerrilla Conflict in Missouri during the American Civil War* (New York: Oxford University Press, 1989), 104.

15. quoted in ibid., 165.

16. A commander in St. Louis, quoted in ibid., 163.

17. General Orders 100 § 21.

18. Ibid. §§ 155, 156: "All enemies in regular war are divided into two classes—that is to say, into combatants and noncombatants, or unarmed citizens of the hostile government. The military commander…distinguishes between the loyal citizen…and the disloyal citizen. The disloyal citizen may further be classified into those citizens know to sympathize with the rebellion without positively aiding it, and those who, without taking up arms, give positive aid and comfort to the rebellious enemy without being bodily forced thereto."

19. General Orders 100 §§ 21–22: "the principle has been more and more acknowledged that the unarmed citizen is to be spared in person, property, and honor as much as the exigencies of war will permit." Also § 24: "The almost universal rule in remote times was and continues to be with barbarous armies, that the private individual is destined to suffer every privation of liberty and every disruption of family ties. Protection was and still is with uncivilized people, the exception."

20. Ibid. § 23.

21. See Francis Lieber, *Manual of Political Ethics* (Philadelphia: J. B. Lippincott, 1892).

22. General Orders 100 § 15.

23. Frank B. Freidel, *Francis Lieber, Nineteenth-Century Liberal* (Baton Rouge: Louisiana State University, 1948), 336. Note that this was essentially the criticism voiced by the Confederate secretary of war as well. See Freidel, *Francis Lieber;* James Turner Johnson, *Just War Tradition and the Restraint of War: A Moral and Historical Inquiry* (Princeton: Princeton University Press, 1981). This did not stop the Confederates from employing the code to condemn the actions of the Union soldiers.

24. Quoted in Richard Shelly Hartigan, *Lieber's Code and the Law of War* (Chicago: Precedent Publishing, 1983), 21.

25. General Orders 100 § 4. See Martti Koskenniemi, *The Gentle Civilizer of Nations: The Rise and Fall of Modern International Law, 1870–1960* (Cambridge, UK: Cambridge University Press, 2002).

26. David W. Blight, *Beyond the Battlefield: Race, Memory and the American Civil War* (Amherst: University of Massachusetts Press, 2002), 60.

27. Chandra Manning, *What This Cruel War Was Over: Soldiers, Slavery, and the Civil War* (New York: Alfred A. Knopf, 2007), 37–38.

28. Ibid., 43.

29. See, among others, Doris Kearns Goodwin, *Team of Rivals: The Political Genius of Abraham Lincoln* (New York: Simon & Schuster, 2005), chap. 21. See also Manning, who writes, "while slavery was necessary to white Southerns' conception of manhood…it was antithetical to manhood among black men" because it robbed black men of the capacity to protect, shelter, and preserve their families. Ibid., 12. For the relationship of black and white women in the plantation household, see Thavolia Glymph, *Out of the House of*

Bondage: The Transformation of the Plantation Household (Cambridge, Mass.: Cambridge University Press, 2008).

30. Fellman, *Inside War,* xviii.

31. Thomas P. Lowry, *The Story the Soldiers Wouldn't Tell: Sex in the Civil War* (Pennsylvania: Stackpole Books, 1994), 119. Ironically, cross-dressing was common in the war by both Confederate and Union soldiers; women disguised themselves as men to fight, and men disguised themselves as women for social entertainment. In both cases, the template of gender was revealed as imperfect, if present at all. Elizabeth D. Leonard, *All the Daring of the Soldier: Women of the Civil War Armies* (New York: W. W. Norton, 1999), 165; see also Catherine Clinton, *Public Women and the Confederacy* (Milwaukee: Marquette University Press, 1999). The woman who fought as a soldier wrote a memoir, published in 1864, entitled "Unsexed; or, The Female Soldier"; in Leonard, *All the Daring of the Soldier,* 179.

32. Lieber, letter to James H. Hammond written April 18, 1860, quoted in Thomas S. Perry, ed., *The Life and Letters of Francis Lieber* (Boston: James R. Osgood, 1882), 309. Grimsley (1995) comes to the same conclusion, arguing that the range of permissible actions was so broad as to facilitate rather than restrain the 'hard war' policies of the General Sherman; *Hard Hand of War.*

33. General Orders 100 § 4: "As martial law is executed by military force, it is incumbent upon those who administer it be strictly guided by the principle of justice, honor, and humanity—virtues adorning a soldier even more than other men, for the very reason that he possesses the power of his arms against the unarmed." General Orders 100 § 30: "the law of war imposes many limitations and restriction on principles of justice, faith and honor."

34. Scott Reynolds Nelson and Carol Sheriff, *A People at War: Civilians and Soldiers in America's Civil War, 1854–1877* (New York: Oxford University Press, 2007), 155.

35. Burrus Carnahan, "Lincoln, Lieber, and the Law of War: The Origins and Limits of the Principle of Military Necessity," *American Journal of International Law* 92 (1998), 218.

36. George M. Fredrickson, *The Inner Civil War: Northern Intellectuals and the Crisis of the Union* (Urbana: University of Illinois Press, 1993), 134.

37. Ibid., 134–35. For example, in 1863 a twice-reprinted pamphlet—30,000 copies of which were distributed to the army—exhorted the soldiers and citizens of the North to express their "unconditional loyalty" because only possessed of that could the North win the war. Notably, it advocated, "Let our women and children become the propagandists of unconditional loyalty" and the men its "missionaries." George M. Fredrickson, *The Inner Civil War: Northern Intellectuals and the Crisis of the Union* (Urbana: University of Illinois Press, 1993), 135. See also Henry W. Bellows, "Unconditional Loyalty," in *Union Pamphlets of the Civil War, 1861–1865,* ed. Frank B. Freidel (Cambridge, Mass.: Belknap Press, 1967).

38. Francis Lieber, *Letters to a Gentleman in Germany,* (Philadelphia: Carey, Lea & Blanchard, 1834), 69. See also his reaction to women voting, or women's rights, in Freidel, *Francis Lieber,* 385–86, 416.

39. Gary W. Gallagher, "Blueprint for Victory," in *Writing the Civil War: The Quest to Understand,* ed. James M. McPherson and William J. Cooper (Columbia: University of South Carolina Press, 1998), 21. Note that Royster is not as confident of a shift in strategy, arguing that the vindictiveness of the war was always the vindictiveness of enemies not fellow citizens; Charles Royster, *The Destructive War: William Tecumseh Sherman, Stonewall Jackson, and the Americans* (New York: Knopf, 1991).

40. "Major General W. T. Sherman to Lieutenant General US Grant, 1 January 1865," in U.S. War Department, *The War of the Rebellion: A Compilation of the Official Records*

of the Union and Confederate Armies, (Washington, D.C.: Government Printing Office, 1902) [hereafter *OR*], series 1, vol. 36, 157. See also William T. Sherman, *General Sherman's Official Account of His Great March,* (New York: Rennie, Shea, & Lindsay, 1865), 84.

41. Reid Mitchell, *The Vacant Chair: The Northern Soldier Leaves Home* (New York: Oxford University Press, 1993), 101.

42. General Orders 46, St. Louis, February 22, 1862, in *OR,* series 8, 563–64.

43. General Orders 100 § 37.

44. Mitchell, *Vacant Chair,* 101.

45. Eugene F. Ware, *The Indian War of 1864* (Lincoln: University of Nebraska Press, 1994), 109.

46. "A Few Words on Behalf of Loyal Women of the United States by One of Themselves," in Frank B. Freidel, ed., *Union Pamphlets of the Civil War, 1861–1865* (Cambridge, Mass.: Belknap Press, 1967), 775.

47. See Glymph for a description of white plantation women's violence toward their slaves. She refers to a "warring intimacy" that "tempered the very meaning of womanhood in the South." *Out of the House of Bondage,* 61.

48. See Nina Silber, "Intemperate Men, Spiteful Women, and Jefferson Davis: Northern Views of the Defeated South," *American Quarterly* 41, no. 4 (December 1989), 616, 623. Furthermore, "the North repeatedly cast aspersion on the sexual purity of women who gathered intelligence for the Confederacy, branding them as loose women, Jezebels, and secess harlots." Catherine Clinton, *Tara Revisited: Women, War and the Plantation Legend* (New York: Abbeville, 1995, 90.

49. Benjamin F. Butler, *Autobiography and Personal Reminiscences of Major-General Benj. F. Butler; Butler's Book* (Boston: A. M. Thayer, 1892), 417. The recognition of class is key because throughout the war the depredations of property and person were actively channeled in response to class differences. Edwards argues that, although white-upper class Southern women protested most publicly, it was the lower classes of white yeoman women that bore the brunt of physical degradation; Laura F. Edwards, *Scarlett Doesn't Live Here Anymore: Southern Women in the Civil War Era* (Urbana: University of Illinois Press, 2000). This is supported in the general literature as well. See also Victoria Bynum, *Unruly Women: The Politics of Social and Sexual Control in the Old South* (Chapel Hill: University of North Carolina Press, 1992).

50. General Orders, No. 28 (Butler's Woman Order), http://www.civilwarhome.com/butlerorder.htm.

51. Drew G. Faust, *Mothers of Invention: Women of the Slaveholding South in the American Civil War* (Chapel Hill: University of North Carolina Press, 1996), 210. See also Benjamin F. Butler, *Autobiography and Personal Reminiscences of Major-General Benj. F. Butler; Butler's Book* (Boston: A. M. Thayer, 1892), 419.

52. Mary P. Ryan, *Women in Public: Between Banners and Ballots, 1825–1880* (Baltimore: Johns Hopkins University Press, 1990), 130.

53. Catherine Clinton, "'Public Women' and Sexual Politics," in *Battle Scars: Gender and Sexuality in the American Civil War,* ed. Catherine Clinton and Nina Silber (Oxford: Oxford University Press, 2006), 66.

54. Congress of the Confederate States of America, "Address of Congress to the People of the Confederate States. Joint Resolution in Relation to the War," Documenting the American South, http://docsouth.unc.edu/imls/address/address.html.

55. The publicness of the Southern women both here and in the Richmond Bread Riots was enough to render them suspect. See Clinton, *Public Women and the Confederacy;* Clinton, *Tara Revisited;* Ryan, *Women in Public;* Nina Silber, *The Romance of Reunion: Northerners and the South, 1865–1900* (Chapel Hill: University of North Carolina Press, 1993).

56. Quoted in Mitchell, *Vacant Chair*, 97.

57. Clinton, *Tara Revisited*, 59. See also Royster, *Destructive War*, 86, 87; Mitchell, *Vacant Chair*.

58. Royster, *Destructive War*, 86–87.

59. Ibid.

60. Quoted in Royster, *Destructive War*, 87.

61. Ibid., 86.

62. In contrast, Southern men were mere mockeries—effeminate patrons of a licentious system unprepared and unable to recognize the potency of Northern capitalism and industrialization. This discourse of gender was present in the frequent popular characterization of the South as feminine and the North as masculine that became more frequent during the Reconstruction; Silber, "Intemperate Men, Spiteful Women." The centrality of gender to the explanations of the Union victory and Southern defeat was crystallized in the capture of Confederate President Jefferson Davis dressed in his wife's skirt and bonnet. This image was circulated throughout the North and "drew on a pervasive hostility among Northerners and a widespread desire to…make a mockery of southern manhood." Nina Silber, "Intemperate Men," in *Divided Houses: Gender and the Civil War*, ed. Catherine Clinton and Nina Silber (New York: Oxford University Press, 1992), 629.

63. Mitchell, *Vacant Chair*, 101.

64. Quoted in Sutherland, *Savage Conflict*, 254.

65. Emer de Vattel, *The Law of Nations or the Principles of Natural Law: Applied to the Conduct and the Affairs of Nations and of Sovereigns* (Washington, D.C.: Carnegie Institution of Washington, 1916), 283.

66. Quoted in ibid., 283 § 145; Henry W. Halleck, *International Law or Rules Regulating the Intercourse of States in Peace and War* (New York: D. VanNorstrand, 1861), 428.

67. *New York Herald*, April 30, 1861, quoted in Ryan, *Women in Public*, 142.

68. "Few Words in Behalf," 775. See also Faust, *Mothers of Invention*, 232; as Faust mentions in her introduction, the concern over "unsexed women" was pervasive (6).

69. Freidel, *Francis Lieber*, 385.

70. General Orders 100 § 102.

71. Joseph T. Glatthaar, *The March to the Sea and Beyond: Sherman's Troops in the Savannah and Carolinas Campaigns* (New York: New York University Press, 1985), 71–75. See also "Letter to Halleck Dec 1864 from JG Foster," in *OR*, series 1, vol. 44. For a more expansive rewriting of this debate, see Neely, *Civil War*. See also, the critical review of Neely's book, McPherson, "Was It More Restrained?"

72. Edward Alfred Pollard, *Southern History of the War: Second Year of the War* (New York: C. B. Richardson, 1866), 88.

73. "Letter to Halleck from WT Sherman on the Occupation of Savannah," in *OR*, series 1, vol. 44. See Herman Hattaway, *Shades of Blue and Gray: An Introductory Military History of the Civil War* (Columbia: University of Missouri Press, 1997), 194; Glatthaar, *March to the Sea*. See also Grimsley, *Hard Hand of War*, chap. 9. Grimsley also mentions the similarity of identities—the recognition of the face of the enemy as pivotal to the restraint practiced during the American Civil War. The discipline, external and internal, so desired by Lieber and much celebrated by both Northern and Southern society, lay also in the skill (as the war progressed) of veteran soldiers, no longer amateurs but now professionals of their trade. The majority of combatants in Sherman's campaign were the veterans of many campaigns, particularly in the western theater.

74. Daniel E. Sutherland, "Introduction to War: The Civilians of Culpeper County, Virginia," *Civil War History* 37, no. 2 (1991), 126. He quotes a British journalist as writing that in 1862 General Pope waged war against Culpeper County "in a way that cast mankind two centuries back toward barbarism" (128). This journalist also alluded to deeds

of violence "perpetrated upon respectable ladies…which are without parallel, save in the annals of the infamous Yankee race." Sutherland makes clear that women who responded to the "insults" of soldiers were arrested and jailed. Rapists, when caught, were punished severely by hard labor or hangings. Nonetheless, "sentencing was capricious and black soldiers seemed much more likely than whites to receive the death penalty." Thomas P. Lowry, *The Story the Soldiers Wouldn't Tell: Sex in the Civil War* Mechanicsburg, Pa.: Stackpole Books, 1994), 131. Clinton notes that there is still scant information regarding rape and that, overall, "little or no research has been conducted on this topic"; still, "both armies determined that rape would result in court martial and convicted rapists might be executed.…the rapes of black women were publicly revealed in the Northern press during this period." Clinton, *Tara Revisited,* 129. The significance of white Northern men raping black women is also an implied threat of what these men could do to white women but did not. Thus, sexuality during war is integral to the mastering and organization of the conflict.

75. Royster, *Destructive War,* 23.

76. Quoted in Mitchell, *Vacant Chair,* 110. See also Joseph T. Glatthaar, *Forged in Battle: The Civil War Alliance Black Soldiers and White Officers* (New York: Free Press, 1990).

77. Mark E. Neely compared these two exact cases in 2007, a few years after my initial work, and although our conclusions are similar, he does not focus on particular discourses in his discussion of identity. Neely, *Civil War.*

78. Quoted in Robert Vincent Remini, *Andrew Jackson & His Indian Wars* (New York: Viking, 2001), 227.

79. Ibid.

80. Ibid., 225.

81. *Cherokee Nation v. Georgia* (1831). Note that one newspaper later referred to this decision, arguing that "these gentle 'wards of the nation' must be exterminated." Quoted in Richard N. Ellis, *General Pope and U.S. Indian Policy* (Albuquerque: University of New Mexico Press, 1970), 134.

82. Alexis de Tocqueville, *Democracy in America,* ed. Jacob P. Mayer, trans. George Lawrence (New York: Harper & Row, 1988), 339.

83. Julius Seeyle, "Introduction," in *A Century of Dishonor: A Sketch of the United States Government's Dealings with Some of the Indian Tribes,* ed. Helen Hunt Jackson, Henry Benjamin Whipple, and Julius Hawley Seelye (New York: Harper, 1864), 3. General Pope in 1862, quoted in Philip Weeks, *Farewell, My Nation: The American Indian and the United States in the Nineteenth Century* (Wheeling, Ill.: Harlan Davidson, 2001), 109.

84. Thom Hatch, *Black Kettle: The Cheyenne Chief Who Sought Peace but Found War* (Hoboken: John Wiley & Sons, 2004) 93, 91.

85. John M. Schofield, "Notes on the Legitimate in War," 1881, quoted in Robert Allen Wooster, *The Military and the United States Indian Policy, 1865–1903* (New Haven: Yale University Press, 1988), 142. General Schofield was the initial commander of the Military Department of Kansas, within which the Colorado territory was administered, to whom Governor John Evans pleaded for more troops; Schofield was replaced by General Samuel Curtis.

86. Quoted in David Svaldi, *Sand Creek and the Rhetoric of Extermination: A Case Study in Indian-White Relations* (Lantham, Mass.: University Press of America, 1989), 170.

87. The reformers who believed that the Indians could be saved from savagery were composed of Quakers, abolitionists, and sympathetic pacifists.

88. "Report of the Commission on the Conduct of the War," quoted in Duane P. Schultz, *Month of the Freezing Moon: The Sand Creek Massacre* (New York: St. Martin's Press, 1990), 27.

89. Seeyle, "Introduction," 2. See also Jeffrey Ostler, *The Plains Sioux and U.S. Colonialism* (New York: Cambridge University Press, 2004), 15.

90. The line of demarcation between Indians and settlers, just as between white plantation owners and slaves, was further blurred by intercourse between the two peoples, leading to mixed-race families, children, and relationships.

91. George M. Fredrickson, *Why the Confederacy Did Not Fight a Guerilla War after the Fall of Richmond* (Gettysburg: Gettysburg College Press, 1996), 29.

92. Quoted in Sutherland, *Savage Conflict*, 34.

93. Quoted in Fellman, *Inside War*, 167.

94. Brown, *Bury My Heart at Wounded Knee*, 57.

95. Joint Committee on the Conduct of War, House of Representatives, Senate Reports: 38th Congress, 2nd Sess., vol. 4, #1214, January 10, 1865), reprinted in George Emory Fay, ed., *Military Engagements between United States Troops and Plains Indians: Documentary Inquiry by the U.S. Congress*, vol. 26 (Greeley: Museum of Anthropology, University of Northern Colorado, 1980), 76.

96. Robert Wooster mentions individual commanders, such as George Crook, who stood out for their expressions of both sympathy and respect for the Indians. Eventually even Sherman, writing in 1878, believed that the Indians had behaved as any would when an entire mode of life was destroyed: "Could anyone expect less?" Quoted in Wooster, *Military*, 49.

97. Oliver Wendell Holmes, letter of 1864, quoted in James M. McPherson, *What They Fought For, 1861–1865* (Baton Rouge: Louisiana State University Press, 1994), 43.

98. Drew G. Faust, *This Republic of Suffering: Death and the American Civil War* (New York: Knopf, 2008). Manning, *What This Cruel War Was Over*.

99. Manning, *What This Cruel War Was Over*, 35.

100. Colonel T. Moonlight, January 17, 1865, quoted in McPherson, *What They Fought For*, 202.

101. Dispatch to Commanding Officer of November 29, 1864 from Colonel Chivington, reproduced in Schultz, *Month of the Freezing Moon*, 4.

102. Quoted in Bruce Tap, *Over Lincoln's Shoulder: The Committee on the Conduct of War* (Lawrence: University Press of Kansas, 1998), 34.

103. Proclamation of June 1864, reprinted in U.S. Congress, House Committee on the Conduct of the War, *Massacre of the Cheyenne Indians* (Washington, D.C.: Committee on the Conduct of War, 1865), 47.

104. Dee Brown, *Bury My Heart at Wounded Knee: The Illustrated Edition* (New York: Sterling Publishing, 2009), 92.

105. *OR*, series 1, vol. 34, part 4, 402–4.

106. Quoted in Schultz, *Month of the Freezing Moon*, 90.

107. Quoted in Royster, *Destructive War*, 397.

108. Schultz, *Month of the Freezing Moon*, 107.

109. Quoted in ibid., 115.

110. Ibid., 117.

111. Ibid., 131.

112. Sergeant Stephen Decatur, quoted in National Park Service, "The Aftermath," *Sand Creek Massacre* (Washington, D.C.: U.S. Department of the Interior, 1864), http://www.nps.gov/sand/historyculture/upload/newest.pdf.

113. Ostler, *Plains Sioux and U.S. Colonialism*, 47.

114. Quoted in Hoig, *The Sand Creek Massacre*, 143.

115. Quoted in Schulz, Month of the Freezing Moon., 134.

116. Testimony from Lt. Cramer, quoted in ibid., 135.

117. Testimony from the reports, quoted in ibid., 139.

118. Testimony of Mr. John Smith, March 14, 1865, in U.S. Congress, *Report of the Joint Committee on the Conduct of War,* vol. 6 (Wilmington, N.C.: Broadfoot Publishing, 1989), 9.

119. Morse H. Coffin, *The Battle of Sand Creek,* ed. Alan W. Farley (Waco, Tex.: W. M. Morrison, 1965), 29.

120. Quoted in Hoig, *Sand Creek Massacre,* 161.

121. Ware, *Indian War of 1864,* 424.

122. Captain Silas Soule, quoted in National Park Service, "Aftermath."

123. See the testimony of Mr. John Smith of March 14, 1865, replying that the women and children were slaughtered indiscriminately and not because any of the soldiers believed they were warriors; Fay, *Military Engagements,* 79.

124. Wooster, *Military,* 138.

125. Quoted in Grimsley, *Hard Hand of War,* 100.

126. General Orders 100 § 29.

5. THE 1899 MARTENS CLAUSE AND THE 1949 IV GENEVA CONVENTION

1. The International Red Cross acknowledged the paucity of protections and actively tried to address the concept of protection for individuals during the Spanish Civil War. It was, to a limited degree, successful in arguing that those detained and interned should be considered analogous to prisoners of war—certainly an interesting analogy considering the later attempt to distinguish between combatant and civilian. ICRC activities during the Spanish Civil War further convinced the ICRC of the importance of establishing a convention to comprehensively address the status and treatment of civilians during armed conflicts. The ICRC had prepared a draft, the Tokyo draft, outlining just such a convention in 1934, which was adopted at the International Conference of the Red Cross the same year. This draft, however, had no international legal authority. In 1938, the ICRC once again attempted to draw attention to the "revolting and needless slaughter" of civilians that marked the new warfare. What was clear at the 1938 meetings was that civilians were equated with "innocent women and children" and "helpless women and children" whose "bodies...are being shattered and destroyed" and maimed. Indeed, the 1938 meeting expressly concerned itself with the protection of women and children, although nothing was concluded—so much for the call that "something must be done to restore civilization to a sanity which will at least stop the killings of the helpless and the innocent." Andre Durand and Pierre Boissier, *From Sarajevo to Hiroshima: History of the International Committee of the Red Cross* (Geneva: Henry Dunant Institute, 1984), 384. Not surprisingly, the performance of the ICRC during World War II is still roundly criticized, and the ICRC issued formal apologies for its failure to do more to prevent the slaughter in concentration camps.

2. Theodore Meron, "The Martens Clause, Principles of Humanity, and Dictates of Public Conscience," *American Journal of International Law* 94, no. 1 (2000): 79.

3. Preambles to the 1899 Hague Convention II and the 1907 Hague Convention IV.

4. As one participant wrote, "in the history of the world, it will be the first time, I think, that representatives of almost every civilized country are seen to meet peacefully, without a dispute to settle, without complaints to be redressed...in the two fold and liberal purpose of perpetuating harmony and softening the evils of war, or of regulating it for the day when it cannot be avoided." Senator A. Beernaert, May 26, 1899, quoted in Arthur Eyffinger, *The 1899 Hague Peace Conference: "The Parliament of Man, the Federation of the World"* (The Hague: Kluwer Law International, 1999), 218.

5. Martti Koskenniemi, *The Gentle Civilizer of Nations: The Rise and Fall of International Law, 1870–1960* (Cambridge, UK: Cambridge University Press, 2002), 39, 84. The codification of international law, specifically the laws of war, was facilitated by the

founding in 1863 of the International Red Cross Movement, which was responsible for the first formal conference on the laws of war held in 1864. In 1864, representatives from sixteen Western states produced the First Geneva Convention for the Amelioration of the Condition of the Wounded in Armies in the Field. During this conference, the International Red Cross underscored that one of its main organizing tenets was the distinction between combatants and all others.

6. A French military jurist, quoted in Karma Nabulsi, *Traditions of War: Occupation, Resistance, and the Law* (Oxford: Oxford University Press, 1999), 4.

7. The importance of the duel is great. It was after this war that the French returned to the ideals of chivalry and duels to restore their national honor: "what was needed was a revival of the idea of honor along with skills and ritual practices that sustained it." Richard Cohen, *By the Sword: A History of Gladiators, Musketeers, Samurai, Swashbucklers, and Olympic Champions* (New York: Modern Library, 2003), 182.

8. Maury D. Feld, *The Structure of Violence: Armed Forces as Social Systems* (Beverly Hills: Sage Publications, 1977), 16–17.

9. Gerrit W. Gong, *The Standard of "Civilization" in International Society* (Oxford: Clarendon Press, 1984), 75.

10. Quoted in Eyffinger, *1899 Hague Peace Conference,* 304.

11. Quoted in ibid., 222–23.

12. Likewise, Richard Price underscores how conformance with the ban against poison (also initiated at the Hague conference) both constituted and regulated the "common identity among the great powers as civilized nations." Richard Price, *The Chemical Weapons Taboo* (Ithaca: Cornell University Press, 1997), 37.

13. Gong, *Standard of "Civilization,"* 62.

14. Quoted in Koskenniemi, *The Gentle Civilizer,* 84.

15. Quoted in Alexis Dudden, *Japan's Colonization of Korea: Discourse and Power* (Honolulu: University of Hawai'i Press, 2005), 70.

16. In addition to the European countries, sixteen Latin American countries, Siam, China, Mexico, Japan, and the United States were in attendance.

17. Eyffinger, *1899 Hague Peace Conference,* 227.

18. Influential participants in the 1899 Conference were also members of the Institute de Droit International—which self-consciously styled itself as the "scientific organ of the common legal consciousness of the civilized world." For a lengthy discussion of the socialization of those at the 1899 Conference, from which these descriptions arise, see Koskenniemi, *Gentle Civilizer of Nations,* 42. See also Martha Finnemore, *The Purpose of Intervention: Changing Beliefs about the Use of Force* (Ithaca: Cornell University Press, 2004).

19. Quoted in Gong, *Standard of "Civilization,"* 71.

20. Eyffinger, *1899 Hague Peace Conference,* 227.

21. Koskenniemi, *Gentle Civilizer of Nations,* 86.

22. Roxanne L. Doty, *Imperial Encounters: The Politics of Representation in North-South Relations* (Minneapolis: University of Minnesota Press, 1996), 40–43.

23. Preface of the *Oxford Manual of the Institute of International Law* of 1880, reprinted in Dietrich Schindler and Jirí Toman, *The Laws of Armed Conflicts: A Collection of Conventions, Resolutions, and Other Documents* (Dordrecht: Martinus Nijhoff, 1988), 69, 37.

24. Uday Singh Mehta, *Liberalism and Empire: A Study in Nineteenth-Century British Liberal Thought* (Chicago: University of Chicago Press, 1999), 81–82.

25. Ibid., 83. Because the laws of war were codified in the great age of liberalism and enlightenment, in which philosophies and practices of imperialism literally ruled the day, the way in which these liberal presumptions of progress informed the creation of the laws of war is highly significant. Furthermore, the central importance of the capacity for self-governance as characterizing civilized sovereign states remains influential throughout the

laws of war. Indeed, it is exactly this capacity that liberation movements insist is theirs, and to demonstrate this capacity they accept and obey the laws of war. As we have seen in earlier chapters, sovereignty, war, and the laws of war are articulated in the discourses of civilization.

26. Quoted in Koskenniemi, *Gentle Civilizer of Nations*, 85.

27. Quoted in ibid., 214, 70, 76.

28. John Keegan, *A History of Warfare* (Toronto: Vintage Books, 1994), 384.

29. Michel Foucault, *Discipline and Punish: The Birth of the Prison* (New York: Knopf, 1995). Here, Max Weber's discussion of the importance of discipline (both as compulsory or "mechanized drill" and as an appeal to "firm ethical motives") is particularly relevant; *Economy and Society: An Outline of Interpretive Sociology* (Berkeley: University of California Press, 1978), 1150. Of particular note is Weber's argument that it is the former element of discipline that is the "irreducible residue in all situations in which the ethical qualities of duties and conscientiousness have failed" (1150). Thus, if honor no longer holds, perhaps rote memorization will do.

30. John S. Mill, *Considerations on Representative Government* (New York: Prometheus Books, 1991), 85.

31. Koskenniemi writes that within the "cosmopolitan" order imagined by these publicists of international law "no essential distinction existed between matters internal and international; a humanitarian order that focused on communities and individuals alike." *Gentle Civilizer of Nations*, 53. The progressive belief in the relation of education to civilization accords with the fervent belief in that century, perhaps best exemplified by John Stuart Mill, that through education the progressive talent of men would be encouraged and realized. Of course, the exceptions to this rule were the barbarians and, to many others, women, who required benevolent tutorials. For the convergence of education, rule, and civilization, see Mill, *Considerations on Representative Government*. Mill argues that in certain cases of "weak civilization" the best form of government is not representative but foreign rule by "superior civilization" that may shepherd the weak "through several stages of progress...clearing away obstacles to improvement which might have lasted indefinitely" (91).

32. Nabulsi, *Traditions of War*, 164. Moreover, Martens argues that agreements can only exist between "nations which have achieved more or less the same level of civilization and which do not significantly differ in their conceptions of law and morality."

33. Koskenniemi, *Gentle Civilizer of Nations*, 87.

34. Michael Ignatieff, *The Warrior's Honor: Ethnic War and the Modern Conscience* (New York: Henry Holt and Co., 1998), 140.

35. Ibid., 127.

36. Paul Gilroy, *Against Race: Imagining Political Culture beyond the Color Line* (Cambridge, Mass.: Belknap Press, 2000), 26.

37. Wendy Brown, "Genealogical Politics," in *The Later Foucault: Politics and Philosophy*, ed. Jeremy Moss (London: Sage Publications, 1998), 36.

38. Quoted in Meron, "Martens Clause," 80.

39. Shigeki Miyazaki, "The Martens Clause and International Humanitarian Law," In *Studies and Essays on International Humanitarian Law and Red Cross Principles in Honour of Jean Pictet*, ed. Jean Pictet, Christophe Swinarski, and International Committee of the Red Cross (The Hague: Martinus Nijhoff, 1984).

40. Meron, "Martens Clause," 89.

41. Ibid.

42. Ibid., 85.

43. Adam Roberts, "Land Warfare," in *The Laws of War: Constraints on Warfare in the Western World*, ed. Michael Howard, George J. Andreopoulos, and Mark R. Shulman (New Haven: Yale University Press, 1994), 126.

44. Lester Nurick, "The Distinction between Combatant and Noncombatant in the Law of War," *American Journal of International Law* 39, no. 4 (1945): 680–97, reprinted in Judith Gardam, ed., *Humanitarian Law* (Aldershot, UK: Ashgate, 1999), quotation on 680.

45. Quoted in ibid., 682.

46. Quoted in Esbjörn Rosenblad, *International Humanitarian Law of Armed Conflict: Some Aspects of the Principle of Distinction and Related Problems* (Stockholm: Stockholms Universitet, 1977), 57.

47. Greek delegate to the preparatory conference, quoted in Geoffrey Best, *War and Law since 1945* (Oxford: Oxford University Press, 1994), 103.

48. Josef L. Kunz, "The Chaotic State of the Laws of War and the Urgent Necessity for Their Revision," *American Journal of International Law* 45 (1951): 37–61.

49. Ibid., 59.

50. Ibid.

51. George W. Bush, "President's Remarks to the Nation," White House Archives, September 11, 2002, http://georgewbush-whitehouse.archives.gov/news/releases/2002/09/20020911–3.html.

52. George W. Bush, "Remarks to the United Nations General Assembly," White House Archives, November 10, 2001, http://georgewbush-whitehouse.archives.gov/news/releases/2001/11/images/20011110–3-4.html.

53. Judith G. Gardam and Michelle J. Jarvis, *Women, Armed Conflict, and International Law* (The Hague: Kluwer Law International, 2001), 258. Although they argue for a revision of some of the "outdated" interpretations found therein, it is more important to recognize that these interpretations are not simply inaccurate descriptions of otherwise neutral laws but are intricately involved in creating the meanings of those laws. Therefore, they cannot be so easily dismissed as outdated descriptions, but must be read as significant and powerful interpretations.

54. Claude Pilloud, Yves Sandoz, Christophe Swinarski, Bruno Zimmermann, and International Committee of the Red Cross, *Commentary on the Additional Protocols of 8 June 1977 to the Geneva Conventions of 12 August 1949* (Geneva: Martinus Nijhoff Publishers, 1987), xxv.

55. Charles Tilly, *Coercion, Capital, and European States, AD 990–1990* (Cambridge, Mass.: Blackwell, 1992), 198. Hobsbawm uses the phrase "inter-imperialist war" to describe WWII, "because until 1943 the great colonial empires were on the losing side." Eric Hobsbawm, *The Age of Extremes: The Short Twentieth Century, 1914–1991* (London: Michael Joseph, 1994), 216. India, Pakistan, Burma, and the Dutch East Indies (now Indonesia), among others, all gained their independence between the end of the war and the writing of the 1949 Geneva Conventions.

56. Max M. Petitpierre, "Opening of the First Meeting," *Diplomatic Conference for the Establishment of International Conventions for the Protection of Victims of War, vol. 2A: The Geneva Conventions of 12 August 1949* (Geneva: International Committee of the Red Cross, 1973), 9.

57. Oscar M. Uhler and Henri Coursier, *Geneva Convention Relative to the Protection of Civilian Persons in Time of War: Commentary* (Geneva: International Committee of the Red Cross, 1958), 232, see also 372.

58. Geoffrey Best, quoted in Adam Roberts, "Land Warfare," 136.

59. International Committee of the Red Cross, *The Final Record of the Diplomatic Conference of Geneva of 1949 for the Establishment of International Conventions for the Protection of War Victims* [hereafter *Final Record*], (Berne: Federal Political Department, 1949), vol. 2A, 621, http://www.loc.gov/rr/frd/Military_Law/RC-Fin-Rec_Dipl-Conf-1949.html.

60. Best, *War and Law since 1945,* 127. See also Nabulsi's discussion of the concerted organizing effort among French resistance groups to influence the position of the French delegation to the conferences on this very topic; Nabulsi, *Traditions of War,* 14.

61. Geoffrey Best, "Restraints on War by Land before 1945," in *Restraints on War: Studies in the Limitation of Armed Conflict,* ed. Michael Howard (Oxford: Oxford University Press, 1979), 27. Elsewhere Best writes that "in promoting and applauding developments of that part of the law which protected combatants, the manhood of the 'civilized countries' was in a strikingly real sense attending to its own interests and the womanhood was looking after its menfolk." *Humanity in Warfare,* 147.

62. Uhler and Coursier, *Geneva Convention,* 5.

63. Ibid.

64. Ibid.

65. *Final Record,* vol. 2A, 692.

66. Ibid.

67. Ibid., 692–97.

68. Ibid., 621.

69. Uhler and Coursier, *Geneva Convention,* 45.

70. Ibid., 46.

71. Louise Doswald-Beck, "Humanitarian Law in Future War," in *The Law of Armed Conflict: Into the Next Millennium,* ed. Michael N. Schmitt, Leslie C. Green, and U.S. Naval War College (Newport, R.I.: Naval War College, 1998), 54.

72. Michael Bothe, Karl Josef Partsch, and Waldemar A Solf, *New Rules for Victims of Armed Conflicts: Commentary on the Two 1977 Protocols Additional to the Geneva Conventions of 1949* (The Hague: Martinus Nijhoff, 1982), 302. The commentary on the IV Convention notes that "the idea of activities prejudicial or hostile to the security of the State is very hard to define"; moreover, even if what is "meant probably above all is espionage, sabotage and intelligence with the enemy," each of those elements is yet "harder to define." Uhler and Coursier, *Geneva Convention,* 258. See also Doswald-Beck, "Humanitarian Law in Future War."

73. Judith Gardam, *Non-Combatant Immunity as a Norm of International Humanitarian Law* (Dordrecht: Martinus Nijhoff, 1993), 20, 27.

74. Uhler and Coursier, *Geneva Convention,* 10.

75. In the preparatory debates, the exclusion of nationals of a state from protection by the laws of war was not articulated with regards to human rights laws. Rather, it was articulated solely in terms of the necessity of balancing the requirements of state sovereignty against the requirements of individual security. In the words of one Australian delegate, "both State and civilians had obligations and rights and that we must see that there was a fair balance between the two." Quoted in Best, *War and Law since 1945,* 106. Although human rights were mentioned, it was as a newly developing concept that could, potentially, be drawn in to the laws of war.

76. Only certain classes of individuals were entitled to protection; the exclusion of the nationals of a signatory state as well as the nationals of states that had not signed is significant. Reciprocity here was central for encouraging enforcement.

77. Therefore, during the Yugoslav war, the acts committed against Bosnian Serb civilians by the army of Bosnia-Herzegovina could not be considered grave breaches pursuant to 1949 Conventions because these civilians were of the same nationality as the adversary power whose hands they were in. This was the Tadić case; see case no. IT 94-I-T, May 7, 1997, http://www.icty.org/x/cases/tadic/tjug/en/tad-tsj70507JT2-e.pdf. This decision was then appealed and overturned, with nationality no longer being the pivotal formation of protection. The Appeals Chamber overruled these two interpretations and held that the

Bosnian Muslim victims were indeed protected in a widened interpretation of *protected persons*. The "chamber noted the inadequacy of the criterion of nationality in protecting civilians in contemporary interethnic armed conflicts." Marco Sassoli and Laura M. Olson, "Prosecutor v. Tadic (Judgement). Case no. IT-94-a-A. 38 ILM 1518 (1999)," *American Journal of International Law* 94, no. 3 (2000), 571, 574.

78. *Final Record,* vol. 2B, 457.

79. Roy Gutman, David Rieff, and Kenneth Anderson. *Crimes of War: What the Public Should Know* (New York: W. W. Norton & Co., 1999), 12.

80. *Final Record,* vol. 2B, 376.

81. Best, *War and Law since 1945,* 110.

82. Best describes the "two big and serious arguments" that dominated the preparatory conferences. There was "one rooted in political philosophy, and relating to the rights and duties of States and subjects; the other entangled with the ideological argument about the rights and wrongs of empires and colonialism." Ibid., 171.

83. In 1912, before the First World War (1914–1918), the ICRC presented a draft on its possible role in civil wars and insurrections. But, as Uhler and Coursier note, the "subject was not even discussed. *Geneva Convention,* 27. The ICRC attempted to inject such a consideration in 1921, but this attempt resulted only in a resolution affirming the rights of all victims of war, whether "civil wars, or social or revolutionary disturbances." Ibid. It was this resolution, then, that granted the ICRC some capacity for activity during the Spanish Civil War. Essentially, however, this was the right of succor and relief more than anything else. The success of the ICRC in providing some relief directly led to the further and focused consideration of the application of the Conventions to civil wars. Boldly, the Preliminary Conference of Red Cross Societies recommended, "in the case of armed conflict within the borders of a State, the Convention shall also be applied by each of the adverse Parties unless one of them announces expressly its intention to the contrary." See "Report on the Work of the Preliminary Conference of National Red Cross Societies for the Study of the Conventions and of Various Problems Relative to the Red Cross," from July 26–August 3, 1946, conference in Geneva (Geneva: 1947), 14, 51. But it was not until 1946 that the Conference of Government Experts agreed to consider the application of the principles of the law to civil conflicts, if not the law itself.

84. *Final Record,* vol. 2B, 10.

85. General Oung, delegate from Burma, quoted in Best, *War and Law since 1945,* 176.

86. *Final Record,* vol. 2B, 336–37.

87. As noted, the experiences of the two world wars seemed to shock states into collectively responding to the atrocities. Yet respect for and protection of state sovereignty continued to dominate even though it could be argued that it was exactly this aspect (after the conduct of Germany during the world wars) that should be reassessed. Certainly, the position of the newly independent countries, wishing to exercise sovereignty unencumbered by an excess of rules and the many vestiges of imperialism, deeply affected the strength and formulation of the laws. This, in turn, affected the willingness of states to be bound by them, as the debates over Common Article 3 illustrate. Moreover, the USSR-U.S. rivalry (with France, Australia, the United Kingdom, China, Spain, Canada, Greece, Italy, Switzerland, and the United States on one side and Denmark, Hungary, Mexico, Romania, and the USSR on the other), in which each side sought to portray the other as sacrificing civilization, certainly added to the mix.

88. *Final Record,* vol. 2B, 376. See also Best, *War and Law since 1945,* 112.

89. Uhler and Coursier, *Geneva Convention,* 118.

90. Ibid.

91. This has been the subject of innumerable commentaries. The ICRC released its "Special Report" in 1998 specifically detailing the events.

92. John M. Broder, "Threats and Responses: Facing Registry Deadline, Men from Muslim Nations Swamp Immigration Office," *New York Times,* December 17, 2002.

93. Mary-Louise O'Brien and Chris Jefferies, "Women and the Soviet Military," *Air University Review,* January–February 1982, http://www.airpower.maxwell.af.mil/airchronicles/aureview/1982/jan-feb/OBrien.html. Regarding female aviators/combat pilots, see Reina Pennington, *Wings, Women, & War: Soviet Airwomen in World War II Combat* (Lawrence: University Press of Kansas, 2002).

94. André Durand and Pierre Boissier, *From Sarajevo to Hiroshima: History of the International Committee of the Red Cross* (Geneva: Henry Dunant Institute, 1984), 548. See also the comment from the delegate to the 1949 preparatory conferences, vol. 2A, 490. He noted, "The position of women was a special one and in the last war all armies had women soldiers. Actual experience showed that the Germans and Japanese did not accord privileged treatment to women."

95. The U.S. Military Judge Advocate General (JAG) 2003 Deskbook, *The Military Commander and the Law,* http://milcom.jag.af.mil/, notes that although the IV Geneva Convention of 1949 "is devoted exclusively to the protection of civilians, it contains no definition of who falls within that category" (5).

96. Uhler and Coursier, *Geneva Convention,* 22, 296. Note also although the commentary cautions against internment simply because "a man is of military age," it allows internment if "there is a danger of [his] being able to join the enemy armed forces." Ibid., 258.

97. Uhler and Coursier, *Geneva Convention,* 119.

98. Ibid., 125.

99. "An age limit of fifteen was chosen because from that age onwards a child's faculties have generally reached a stage of development at which there was no longer the same necessity." Uhler and Coursier, *Geneva Convention,* 187, Article 24 § 1. As the commentaries note later, this was probably true only for "white countries" (ibid., 396).

100. Jean de Preux, Frédéric Siordet, and International Committee of the Red Cross, *Geneva Convention Relative to the Treatment of Prisoners of War: Commentary* (Geneva: International Committee of the Red Cross, 1960) Article 14, 147–48.

101. Besides, women are needed "for the other duties of society, and, in short, the mingling of the two sexes in armies would result in too many inconveniences." Emer de Vattel, *The Law of Nations or the Principles of Natural Law: Applied to the Conduct and the Affairs of Nations and of Sovereigns,* ed. Charles G. Fenwick (Washington, D.C.: Carnegie Institution, 1916), 238.

102. I say "seeming" because, although Grotius too called on sex and sex difference to constitute the distinction between the combatant and civilian, he relied on the possession of reason, discrimination, and sovereignty to demarcate the difference. The 1949 Conventions, instead, rely on reproductive capability and sexual vulnerability to demarcate these differences.

103. Ignatieff, *Warrior's Honor,* 117–18; see also 127.

104. David P. Forsythe, *Humanitarian Politics: The International Committee of the Red Cross* (Baltimore: Johns Hopkins University Press, 1977), 173.

105. Gardam and Jarvis, *Women, Armed Conflict, and International Law,* 109.

106. Uhler and Coursier, *Geneva Convention,* 119.

107. Ibid., 205.

108. Uhler and Coursier, *Geneva Convention,* 202. Earlier the commentary makes clear that these are the provisions on which the entire body of Geneva law rests. The exact formulation is drawn from the Universal Declaration of Human Rights, December 10, 1948, Article 16 (3).

109. "Statement by the ICRC on Items 109, 110" to the UN General Assembly, 54th Session, 3rd Committee, October 12, 1999.

110. There is an exacting body of research on this subject. The classic text is Margaret R. Higonnet, *Behind the Lines: Gender and the Two World Wars* (New Haven: Yale University Press, 1987), 27; see esp. "Introduction" and "The Double Helix." Note that this conservatism and erasure of women's wartime roles held during the American Civil War as well. See also Elizabeth Leonard, who argues that the postwar writings intended to "encourage women's silent retreat to their homes." *All the Daring of the Soldier: Women of the Civil War Armies* (New York: W. W. Norton, 1999), 277.

111. Elaine Tyler-May, *Homeward Bound: American Families in the Cold War Era* (New York: Basic Books, 1988), 86. Tyler-May also convincingly demonstrates that lesbianism and homosexuality were articulated fears during the war, when women's participation in the military was said to threaten her femininity and make her "act a man." She notes that the "marital-heterosexual imperative became even more intense, contributing to the increasing persecution of gay men and lesbians." (72). The racial/class character of these discourses (as I discuss in chap. 4 for the American Civil War) require further study because it was primarily to white women of a specific class that these injunctions were explicitly directed.

112. Gerard J. de Groot, "Sexual Integration in the Military before 1945," in *A Soldier and a Woman: Sexual Integration in the Military,* ed. Gerard J. De Groot and Corinna M. Peniston-Bird (Harlow, UK: Longman, 2000), 15.

113. Wendy Brown, *States of Injury: Power and Freedom in Late Modernity* (Princeton: Princeton University Press, 1995), 66.

114. Charlotte Lindsey and International Committee of the Red Cross, *Women Facing War: ICRC Study on the Impact of Armed Conflict on Women* (Geneva: ICRC, 2001), 24.

6. THE ALGERIAN CIVIL WAR AND THE 1977 PROTOCOLS ADDITIONAL

1. See George J. Andreopoulos, "Age of National Liberation Movements," in *The Laws of War: Constraints on Warfare in the Western World,* ed. Michael Howard, George J. Andreopoulos, and Mark R. Shulman (New Haven: Yale University Press, 1994), 200. Andreopoulos states that the Algerian war was a "test case for the relevance of the traditional distinction between international and internal wars" (200).

2. Robert A. Mortimer, "The Algerian Revolution in Search of the African Revolution," *Journal of Modern African Studies* 8, no. 3 (1970), 364.

3. Arnold Fraleigh, "The Algerian Revolution," in *The International Law of Civil War,* ed. by Richard A. Falk (Baltimore: Johns Hopkins University Press, 1971), 184.

4. The number of dead is sometimes quoted as 1 million, according to Algerian sources; Todd Shepard's most recent review suggests, at the very least, 250,000 and probably more Algerians. This does not include the French deaths. Todd Shepard, "After Deaths, after Lives," *History Workshop Journal* 66, no. 1 (2008): 243–53. See also Todd Shepard, *The Invention of Decolonization: The Algerian War and the Remaking of France* (Ithaca: Cornell University Press, 2006).

5. Mohammed Bedjaoui, "Humanitarian Law at a Time of Failing National and International Consensus," in *Modern Wars, the Humanitarian Challenge: A Report for the Independent Commission on International Humanitarian Issues,* ed. Independent Commission on International Humanitarian Issues (London: Zed Books, 1986), 80. He describes the FLN as a political party, although he also underscores the symbiotic relationship between the ALN and FLN: "the national liberation army forms an integral part of the FLN," and membership in one is equivalent to membership in the other (87).

6. Roger Trinquier, *Modern Warfare: A French View of Counterinsurgency,* trans. Daniel Lee (New York: Praeger, 1964), 26.

7. Ibid.

8. The French were, by far, the more brutal of the two forces; it has been suggested that the French targeted ten Algerians for every French person killed. The initial orders of the FLN to its fighters "strictly forbade violence against European civilians." But the 1955 Philippeville massacre, which "slaughtered…without regard to age or sex," marked a new FLN approach to war. John Ruedy, *Modern Algeria: The Origins and Development of a Nation* (Bloomington: Indiana University Press, 1992), 162. Nonetheless, Horne writes that in 1957, at the beginning of the Battle of Algiers, orders were given to "kill any European between the ages of eighteen and fifty four. But no women, no children, no old people." Alistair Horne, *A Savage War of Peace: Algeria 1954–1962* (London: Papermac, 1996), 184. See also Fraleigh, "Algerian Revolution." Horne notes that it was the Organisation de l'Armée Secrète (OAS; Organization of the Secret Army), the French anti-terrorist organization, that killed the majority of civilians during the war and did so in less than a year; the OAS killed "three times as many civilian victims as had the FLN from the beginning of 1956 onwards." *Savage War of Peace,* 531.

9. Rita Maran, *Torture: The Role of Ideology in the French-Algerian War* (New York: Praeger, 1989), 98. Trinquier was also an aide to and part of the "brain trust" of General Jacques Massu, who oversaw the response to the Battle of Algiers; Alf Andrew Heggoy, *Insurgency and Counterinsurgency in Algeria* (Bloomington: Indiana University Press, 1972), 242.

10. Trinquier, *Modern Warfare,* 29. "Like it or not, the two camps are compelled to make him participate in combat; in a certain sense, he has become a combatant also" (29).

11. Ibid., 33.

12. Until 1956, the French described their presence in Algeria as a police action. When the French forces multiplied, the French referred to their presence as a pacification operation. Neither of these characterizations would initiate the application of Common Article 3. Instead, by adopting specific legislation in 1956 to expand French administrative and legal powers to maintain order, France instituted "exceptional measures" to reestablish order, protection of lives and property, and territorial integrity. The ICRC pointed out that the size of the French military presence in Algeria indicated that the conflict clearly surpassed a police or emergency action. Agreeing with the FLN/ALN, the ICRC argued that Common Article 3 applied. In 1958, the ICRC formally held that Common Article 3 was applicable. See "Special Emergency Legislation Enacted by the Government of France," reprinted in Algerian Office, *White Paper on the Application of the Geneva Conventions of 1949 to the French-Algerian Conflict* (New York: Algerian Office, 1960), 12, 69.

13. Algerian Office, *White Paper,* 1. This is a highly sophisticated articulation of the applicability of the 1949 Geneva Conventions to the conflict. Produced in New York, this document no doubt was placed in the hands of the delegates of the United Nations.

14. Mohammed Bedjaoui, *Law and the Algerian Revolution* (Brussels: International Association of Democratic Lawyers, 1961), 214.

15. Fraleigh, "Algerian Revolution," 189.

16. Algerian Office, *White Paper,* 58.

17. Frantz Fanon, *A Dying Colonialism,* trans. Haakon Chevalier (New York: Grove Press, 1965), 24.

18. Matthew Connelly, *A Diplomatic Revolution: Algeria's Fight for Independence and the Origins of the Post-Cold War Era* (Oxford: Oxford University Press, 2002), 120.

19. Protocol Additional to the Geneva Conventions of 12 August 1949, and relating to the Protection of Victims of International Armed Conflicts (Protocol I), June 8, 1977, opened for signature December 12, 1977, Article 1, paragraph 4; for discussion, see Claude Pilloud, Yves Sandoz, Christophe Swinarski, Bruno Zimmermann, and the International Committee of the Red Cross, *Commentary on the Additional Protocols of 8 June 1977 to the Geneva Conventions of 12 August 1949* (Geneva: Martinus Nijhoff, 1987), 41.

20. Jean-Paul Sartre, "Preface," in *The Wretched of the Earth,* by Franz Fanon, trans. Constance Farrington (New York: Grove Press, 1963), 26.

21. Jean-Paul Sartre, "Preface," in *The Question,* by Henri Alleg (London: John Calder, 1958), xxviii.

22. Indeed, debates about the participation of international liberation movements, and about which national liberation movements at that, nearly derailed the entire preparatory conferences and wound up occupying the first third of the first session. Inviting national liberation movements, each recognized by a regional IGO, but denying them the right to vote resolved the matter. Due to U.S. pressure and the general exhaustion after the debate, the Provisional Revolutionary Government of South Vietnam was denied entry. The keynote speaker, the president of Mauritania, began the conference by roundly denouncing Zionist states and supporting national liberation movements—causing the Israeli representative to walk out, and it seems that this poor man was kept on his feet during the entire 1970s. See Keith Suter, *An International Law of Guerilla Warfare: The Global Politics of Law-Making* (New York: St. Martin's Press, 1984); Claude Pilloud, Yves Sandoz, Christophe Swinarski, Bruno Zimmermann, and the International Committee of the Red Cross, *Commentary on the Additional Protocols of 8 June 1977 to the Geneva Conventions of 12 August 1949* (Geneva: Martinus Nijhoff, 1987).

23. For example, in 1947 the UN International Law Commission decided that it "should refrain from taking up the question of the law of war, because if it did so, its action might be interpreted as a lack of confidence in the United Nations and the work of peace which the latter is called upon to carry out." James L Brierly, a member of the UN International Law Commission, quoted in Suter, *International Law of Guerilla Warfare,* 42.

24. Quoted in ibid., 128.

25. Geoffrey Best, *War and Law since 1945* (Oxford: Oxford University Press, 1994), 343.

26. Jean de Preux, Frédéric Siordet, and the International Committee of the Red Cross, *Geneva Convention Relative to the Treatment of Prisoners of War: Commentary* (Geneva: ICRC, 1960), Article 4, 46–47.

27. Joshua Castellino, *International Law and Self-Determination: The Interplay of the Politics of Territorial Possession with Formulations of Post-Colonial "National" Identity* (The Hague: Martinus Nijhoff, 2000), 21.

28. For a discussion of the complicated colonial inheritance of nationalism, see, for example, Partha Chatterjee, *Nationalist Thought and the Colonial World: A Derivative Discourse* (London: Zed Books, 1993).

29. After the world wars, the standard of civilization was criticized, both as a result of its referential incoherence and because of the grave (imperial) violence that had been enacted in its name, such that the "members of the International Law Commission agreed to refrain from using the expression "civilized countries"…because it dated back to the colonial era with its concept of the white man's burden." Gerrit W. Gong, *The Standard of "Civilization" in International Society* (Oxford: Clarendon Press, 1984), 90. As one scholar wrote in 1975, whereas considerations of civilization generally motivated the "progressive development of international law," "humanity, now, in our period of the peace loving nations, generally [is] regarded as decisive [rather than the value of civilization]." Bert V. A. Roling, "The Significance of the Laws of War," in *Current Problems of International Law: Essays on U.N. Law and on the Law of Armed Conflict,* ed. Antonio Cassese (Milan: A. Giuffrè, 1975), 141.

30. Jean S. Pictet, Oscar M. Uhler, and the International Committee of the Red Cross, *Geneva Convention Relative to the Protection of Civilian Persons in Time of War* (Geneva: ICRC, 1958), 373.

31. In 1966, the relationship between human rights and self-determination was strengthened by the codification of the International Covenants for Human Rights, both

the Covenant on Economic, Social, and Cultural Rights and the Covenant on Civil and Political Rights. The right to self-determination is found in Common Article 1 of both documents (and here the right to self-determination includes *all* peoples, not simply those who were colonized). In 1970, the Declaration on the Principles of International Law Concerning Friendly Relations and Co-operation among States in Accordance with the Charter of the United Nations further solidified self-determination as an essential human right of all peoples and called on all states to "bring a speedy end to colonialism" Declaration on the Principles, 2625 (XXV).

32. Quoted in Judith Gail Gardam, *Non-Combatant Immunity as a Norm of International Humanitarian Law* (Dordrecht: Martinus Nijhoff, 1993), 174. This was not a serendipitous event. Human rights were strategically used to focus attention on and increase interest in the laws of war. Interestingly, it was an international humanitarian scholar who introduced and reworded the essential tenets of customary international humanitarian law into the framework of human rights, recognizing the political leverage such wording would provide the laws of war. See Michael Bothe, ed., *National Implementation of International Humanitarian Law: Proceedings of an International Colloquium Held at Bad Homburg, June 17–19, 1988* (Dordrecht: Martinus Nijhoff, 1990).

33. 21st International Committee of the Red Cross (ICRC), Istanbul, *Reaffirmation and Development of the Laws and Customs Applicable in Armed Conflicts* (Geneva: ICRC, 1969) [hereafter Istanbul Conference], 21.

34. *Official Records of the Diplomatic Conference on the Reaffirmation and Development of International Humanitarian Law Applicable in Armed Conflicts, Geneva (1974–1977)*, 17 vols. (Bonn: Federal Political Department, 1978) [hereafter CDDH], SR.1: 21.SR.1: 10, vol. 5.

35. Ibid., SR.1: 11, vol. 5. The civilian population was described in terms of the "defenceless human being" (SR.13: 131).

36. Ibid., SR.12: 120, vol. 5.

37. Ibid., SR.41: 189-90, vol. 6. "The conspiracy of American and Soviet imperialism" was said to "strangle" national liberation.

38. Ibid., III, SR.16: 131, vol. 14. See also ibid., SR.11: 107.

39. Ibid., SR.13: 127, vol. 5.

40. James Turner Johnson, "Grotius' Use of History and Charity in the Modern Transformation of the Just War Idea," *Grotiana* 4, no. 1 (1983), 32

41. International Committee of the Red Cross (ICRC), *Conference of Government Experts on the Reaffirmation and Development of International Humanitarian Law Applicable in Armed Conflicts,* Report on the Work of the Conference (Geneva: ICRC, 1972), 142. Prior to the official start of the preparatory conference in 1973, the ICRC hosted a series of expert meetings on the reaffirmation of the laws of war. There were two conference reports written as well as available records from the conferences themselves.

42. Georges Abi-Saab, "Wars of National Liberation and the Laws of War," in *Humanitarian Law*, ed. Judith Gardam (Aldershot, UK: Ashgate, 1999), 170.

43. ICRC, *Conference of Government Experts,* 21.

44. Quoted in Antonio Cassese, "A Tentative Appraisal of the Old and the New Humanitarian Law of Armed Conflict," in *The New Humanitarian Law of Armed Conflict,* ed. Antonio Cassese (Naples: Editoriale Scientifica, 1979), 473. The OAU felt that not only was such a distinction "much more difficult to operate" but that freedom fighters and civilians fight side by side. Ibid. See also the series of reports by the UN Security Council on the issue of protection of civilians that sound similar themes, e.g., http://www.securitycouncilreport.org/site/c.glKWLeMTIsG/b.6354943/k.C7D2/CrossCutting_Report_No_3brProtection_of_Civilians_in_Armed_Conflictbr29_October_2010.htm.

45. David P. Forsythe, *Humanitarian Politics: The International Committee of the Red Cross* (Baltimore: Johns Hopkins University Press, 1977), 173.

46. Istanbul Conference, 39.

47. Marc Schreiber, "Opening Comments," in ICRC, *Conference of Government Experts, Report on the Work of the Conference,* 1972, vol. 1, 7.

48. Mr. Bindschedler, delegate from Switzerland, from "Opening Comments," in CDDH, SR.13: 137–38, vol. 5. In 1975, another scholar argued that the laws "lessen the danger that threatens the survival of our civilization." Roling, "Significance," 141.

49. ICRC, *Conference of Government Experts,* 7.

50. Protocol Additional to the Geneva Conventions of 12 August 1949 (Protocol I), June 8, 1977, Article 1(4).

51. Protocol Additional to the Geneva Conventions of 12 August 1949 (Protocol II), June 8, 1977, Article 1.

52. George Aldrich, "Some Reflections on the Origins of the 1977 Geneva Protocols," in *International Committee of the Red Cross: Studies and Essays on International Humanitarian Law and Red Cross Principles in Honour of Jean Pictet,* ed. Christophe Swinarski (The Hague: Martinus Nijhoff, 1984), 135.

53. Howard S. Levie, ed., *The Law of Non-International Armed Conflict: Protocol II to the 1949 Geneva Conventions* (Dordrecht: Martinus Nijhoff, 1987), 4.

54. CDDH, I. SR.23: 217, vol. 8. See also CDDH, II, SR.25: 147; See the reply from the delegate from Egypt, suggesting there was no such thing as selective humanitarianism but that, nonetheless, perhaps a human rights approach was superior (CDDH, I. SR.24: 104).

55. This is not to say that human rights were absent. Essentially, Protocol II, more than any other convention, pays special homage to the concept of human rights in its exposition of fundamental rights in Part II.

56. Michael Bothe, *New Rules for Victims of Armed Conflicts: Commentary on the Two 1977 Protocols Additional to the Geneva Conventions of 1949* (The Hague: Martinus Nijhoff, 1982), 669. The elimination of this article creates a "problem as to who the persons are who are entitled to the protections afforded by Articles 13–18 of Protocol"; Articles 13–18 form the substantive majority of protections for the civilian population (671).

57. Article 50. Pilloud et al., *Commentary on the Additional Protocols,* 610.

58. Protocol Additional to the Geneva Conventions of 12 August 1949 (Protocol I), June 8, 1977, part 4, § 1, chap. 1, Article 48.

59. Judith Gardam, *Non-Combatant Immunity as a Norm of International Humanitarian Law* (Dordrecht: Martinus Nijhoff, 1993), 146.

60. Article 50. Pilloud et al., *Commentary on the Additional Protocols,* 610.

61. Gardam, *Non-Combatant Immunity,* 147.

62. Ibid.

63. Pilloud et al., *Commentary on the Additional Protocols,* 610.

64. CDDH, III, SR.2: 13, vol. 14.

65. Pilloud et al., *Commentary on the Additional Protocols,* 610.

66. CDDH II, SR.7: 57, vol. 14.

67. Article 50. Pilloud et al., *Commentary on the Additional Protocols,* 611.

68. If guerrillas were forced to comply with standards of conduct that rendered guerrilla warfare useless or yet more dangerous to its participants, then guerrillas would be less likely to conform to these standards. In contrast, if these standards accepted and acknowledged the specific challenges of guerrilla warfare, then, so the logic went, those engaged would find it less onerous to conform to the rules. Note, however, that there is now the essential expectation that the conformance with the laws of war is absolutely necessary to be granted prisoner-of-war status; ICRC, *Reaffirmation and Development.* Along those lines,

the French delegate in 1974 proposed that "if standards were pitched too high they might be regarded as unattainable and consequently be ignored." CDDH, SR.13: 133, vol. 5.

69. Knut Ipsen, "Combatants and Noncombatants," in *The Handbook of Humanitarian Law in Armed Conflicts,* ed. Dieter Fleck and Michael Bothe (New York: Oxford University Press, 1995), 77; Hans-Peter Gasser, "Protection of the Civilian Population," in *The Handbook of Humanitarian Law in Armed Conflicts,* ed. Dieter Fleck and Michael Bothe (New York: Oxford University Press, 1995), 210.

70. My argument is that that the principle of distinction, and the corresponding definition of the civilian, each of which is said to be representative of customary law, are themselves fundamentally and intrinsically dependent on Article 44 for substance and clarification.

71. Pilloud et al., *Commentary on the Additional Protocols,* 511, 534. A combatant is identified by openly bearing arms when and for such time as engaged in attack. A civilian is denied protection as a civilian when participating in hostilities. But neither Protocol I nor Protocol II defines precisely what is meant by *hostilities* or *attacks.* The working committee that developed these paragraphs reluctantly decided to leave the terms undefined, stating that "as the interpretations of these terms may affect matters of life and death, it is indeed regrettable that the ambiguities are left for the resolution to the *practice of States* in future conflicts." Bothe, *New Rules,* 302.

72. "An effective distinction between combatants and noncombatants may be more difficult as a result, but not to the point of becoming impossible." Pilloud et al., *Commentary on the Additional Protocols,* 516. See also CDDH, SR. 40: 124, vol. 6.

73. International Committee of the Red Cross (ICRC), *Draft Additional Protocols to the Geneva Conventions of August 12, 1949, Commentary,* Diplomatic Conference for the Establishment of International Conventions for the Protection of Victims of War (Geneva: ICRC, 1973), 56.

74. *Report of the Conference on Contemporary Problems of the Law of Armed Conflicts, 1969* (Geneva: Carnegie Endowment for International Peace, 1971), 44.

75. Bedjaoui, "Humanitarian Law," 33. As an Algerian judge highly active in international and domestic politics, Bedjaoui's comment becomes all the more interesting when considered in light of the contested role of the veil in the Algerian Revolution.

76. CDDH, III, SR.33–36, vol. 14, annex: 462, 473.

77. Ibid.

78. Pilloud et al., *Commentary on the Additional Protocols,* 535.

79. Ibid., 516.; see also CDDH, III, SR.55: 160, vol. 15.

80. See ibid. See also ICRC, *Draft Additional Protocols,* 19; CDDH, III, SR.5: 35, vol. 15.

81. Christophe Swinarski, ed., *Studies and Essays on International Humanitarian Law and Red Cross Principles in Honour of Jean Pictet* (Geneva: ICRC, 1984), 276.

82. Ingrid Detter, *The Law of War* (New York: Cambridge University Press, 2000), 147–48.

83. Best, *War and Law since 1945,* 254–55. The confusion over the results of Protocol I is captured in the writings of Geoffrey Best, who at first goes so far as to write that the principle of distinction "perfects the classic combatant-civilian distinction by paring down to a minimum the combatant category and maximizing the civilian one." Best, *War and Law since 1945,* 255. Yet barely two pages later he suggests that the only way to substantiate the civilian is through recourse to the usual referents of gender, innocence, and civilization: "There were categories of nominally 'enemy' human beings whom it was possible and desirable not to hurt, persons who degree of non-involvement in the struggle or whose irrelevance to it commonly led to their characterization as 'innocent.' So many of them clearly could be innocent or utterly unthreatening—infants, disabled, ancients in all

circumstances; women, children, and old folks in many—that it has always been a matter of genuine regret for warrior working within the standards of civilization that the entire exclusion of civilians from wartime hurt and hardship can be guaranteed in only exceptional circumstances" (257). Thus, the concept of the civilian does not stand alone.

84. Istanbul Conference, 47.

85. UN General Assembly, "Respect for Human Rights in Armed Conflicts," Report of the Secretary General A/7720, New York, 1969, 48.

86. Ibid.

87. John Rajchman, "Foucault's Art of Seeing," *October* 44 (spring 1988), 91.

88. Malek Alloula, "Introduction," in *The Colonial Harem* (Minneapolis: University of Minnesota Press, 1986), xvi. See also Meyda Yegenoglu, *Colonial Fantasies: Towards a Feminist Reading of Orientalism* (Cambridge, UK: Cambridge University Press, 1998).

89. Friedrich Nietzsche, *On the Genealogy of Morals,* ed. Walter Kaufmann (New York: Vintage, 1967), sec. 10, 36.

90. Mounira Charrad, *States and Women's Rights: The Making of Postcolonial Tunisia, Algeria, and Morocco* (Berkeley: University of California Press, 2001), 186–87.

91. Winifred Woodhull, "Unveiling Algeria," *Genders* 10 (1991), 117.

92. Fanon, *Dying Colonialism,* 37.

93. Ibid., 37–38.

94. Yegenoglu, *Colonial Fantasies,* 142.

95. Marnia Lazreg, *The Eloquence of Silence: Algerian Women in Question* (New York: Routledge, 1994), 135.

96. Fanon, *Dying Colonialism,* 42.

97. In 1955, the Soummam Declaration set forth the goals of the FLN/ALN, referring to the "exalted revolutionary courage of the girls and women, the wives and mothers, of our sister *moudjahidates,* who actively participated and, occasionally, with weapons in their hands, sacrificed themselves in the struggle for liberation of the homeland." Quoted in Doria Cherifati-Merabtine, "Algeria at a Crossroads: National Liberation, Islamization and Women," in *Gender and National Identity: Women and Politics in Muslim Societies,* ed. Valentine M. Moghadam (London: Oxford University Press, 1994), 50.

98. *Résistance Algérienne,* 1957, quoted in Fanon, *Dying Colonialism,* 66. According to Fanon, the text "indicates the consciousness that the leaders of the National Liberation Front have always had of the important part played by the Algerian woman in the Revolution" (*64n. 17*).

99. Lazreg, *Eloquence of Silence,* 122.

100. Horne, *Savage War of Peace,* 185. Out of the approximately 11,000 women (registered) war veterans, about 16 percent were involved in direct fighting and at least 84 percent transported weapons, information, and medicines and acted as spies and lookouts for the FLN/ALN. Charrad, *States and Women's Rights,* 185–87. See also Djamila Amrane, "Algeria: Anticolonial War," in *Female Soldier—Combatants or Noncombatants?: Historical and Contemporary Perspectives,* ed. Nancy Goldman (Westport, Conn.: Greenwood Press, 1982); Lazreg, *Eloquence of Silence.* Lazreg notes that these figures are low estimates at best. She also brings out that approximately 78 percent of all women participated in the war. See Cherifati-Merabtine, "Algeria at a Crossroads." This should not be interpreted to mean that women's work was any less dangerous or less targeted by the French. Horne notes that the killing of women may have also radicalized other women to either join or support the FLN; *Savage War of Peace,* 407.

101. Cherifa Bouatta, "Feminine Militancy: Moudjahidates during and after the Algerian War," in *Gender and National Identity: Women and Politics in Muslim Societies,* ed. Valentine M. Moghadam (London: Zed Books, 1994), 27.

102. Yegenoglu, *Colonial Fantasies,* 109.

103. See John Rajchman, "Foucault's Art of Seeing," *October* 44 (spring 1988): 89–117.

104. Here we see again that the discourses of gender do not act alone to produce the distinction between combatant and civilian; rather, they are mutually inflected by other discourses, such as ethnicity and class. Recall the American Civil War and the U.S. Indian wars (chap. 4), in which yeoman white women, black slaves, and Indian women were not identified as civilians because the discourses of gender produced the civilian as white and plantation class.

105. Commission on the Status of Women, Resolution XXII, 1970. "Declaration on the Protection of Women and Children in Emergency and Armed Conflict" UN 3318 XXIX, 1974; see also report of the UN Secretary-General on protection of women and children (E/CN.6/561) and representative debates over protection of women and children in the UN, Commission on the Status of Women, e.g., E/CN.6/586, December 23, 1973, 1–40; and E/CN.6/SR. 620, 68–71; 84–96, January 28, 1974.

106. Ibid. See also ICRC, Conference of Government Experts, Conference Reports, 21, 71; and ICRC, Conference of Government Experts, 1971, vol. 3, 39.

107. ICRC, *Conference of Government Experts,* 86.

108. CDDH, I, SR.32: 195, 197.

109. CDDH, III, SR.44: 56, vol. 15.

110. Ibid., SR.7: 69; ibid., SR. 44: 58, noting women's "patriotism or political non-submission." Istanbul Conference, 141; see also Pilloud et al., *Commentary on the Additional Protocols,* 892.

111. See the 1969 meeting in which the work of the UN General Assembly and the Commission on the Status of Women is discussed solely in regards to the civilian population; Istanbul Conference, 141.

112. Women were active fighters in Mozambique, Zimbabwe, Sudan, Palestine, and Vietnam; all these nations later sent representatives to the conferences. For example, by the middle of the war for independence in Zimbabwe (1977) between one-quarter and one-third of the 30,000 combatants were women in the Zimbabwe national liberation army. See Mary Tetreault, *Women and Revolution in Africa, Asia, and the New World* (Columbia: University of South Carolina Press, 1994).

113. UN Declaration 3318 (XXIX), December 14, 1974.

114. Ibid.

115. *Résistance Algérienne,* 1957, quoted in Fanon, *Dying Colonialism,* 66.

116. Sita Ranchod-Nilsson, "(Gender) Struggles for the Nation: Power, Agency, and Representation in Zimbabwe," in *Women, States, and Nationalism: At Home in the Nation?* ed. Sita Ranchod-Nilsson and Mary Ann Tétreault (London: Routledge, 2000), 168–69.

117. Anne McClintock, *Imperial Leather: Race, Gender, and Sexuality in the Colonial Contest* (New York: Routledge, 1995), 357.

118. Fanon, *Dying Colonialism,* 114.

119. Ibid.

120. Donna Haraway, *Simians, Cyborgs, and Women* (New York: Routledge, 1991), 135.

121. Draft Additional Protocols, October 1973, 86, http://www.loc.gov/rr/frd/Military_Law/pdf/RC-Draft-additional-protocols.pdf. The delegate from Jordan repeated this presumption, noting that pregnant women who engage in hostilities should be protected "because two lives were at stake and the unborn infant should not have to suffer." CDDH, II, SR.12: 100.

122. CDDH, III, SR.44: 57, vol. 15.; see also Pilloud et al., *Commentary on the Additional Protocols,* 892.

123. ICRC, *Conference of Government Experts*, vol. 2, 86–87 (under draft instruments submitted to the ICRC).

124. Pilloud et al., *Commentary on the Additional Protocols*, 900.

125. Diane M. Nelson, *Reckoning: The Ends of War in Guatemala* (Durham: Duke, 2009), xvi.

126. CDDH, III, SR.33–36: 473, vol. 14.

127. Pilloud et al., *Commentary on the Additional Protocols*, 529.

128. Ibid., 538.

129. As was recently reaffirmed in the ICTY, there is "no gap" between the III Convention on Prisoners of War and the IV Convention Relative to the Protection of Civilians. 1988 Celebici Judgement (§ 271), http://www.icty.org/sid/7617.) As a result, combatants who are not prisoners of war become civilians for the purposes of the Geneva Conventions. Or, even more oddly, as articulated in Protocol I combatants who are not prisoners of war occupy a parallel designation—a status that is equal to, but not the same as, that of prisoners of war—entitling them to procedural and substantive protections.

130. ICRC, *Conference of Government Experts, Report on the Work of the Conference*, vol. 1, 28. See also CDDH, III, SR.36: 374–75, vol. 15.

131. CDDH, III, SR.36: 374–75, vol. 15.

132. CDDH, III, SR.56: 179, vol. 15; see also CDDH, SR.41: 150, vol. 6

133. ICRC, *Draft Additional Protocols*, 43.

134. Best, *War and Law Since 1945*, 292.

135. Bothe, *New Rules*, 295. See also Pilloud et al., *Commentary on the Additional Protocols*, 510–38.

136. Geoffrey Best, *Honour among Men and Nations: Transformations of an Idea* (Toronto: University of Toronto Press), 91.

7. THE CIVIL WARS OF GUATEMALA AND EL SALVADOR

1. El Salvador, the smallest and most densely populated Central American country, was not physically divided as easily as was Guatemala. In Guatemala, scorched-earth campaigns were restricted to the northwestern highlands, whereas in El Salvador the most intensive of these campaigns, the bombing and forced displacement of the Guazapa volcano, were visible from the capital; in addition, the FMLN was successful in its stated goal of bringing the war into the capital. Furthermore, in Guatemala the linguistic and cultural identities of the indigenous Mayas may have also contributed to their initial isolation, causing further difficulties in attracting and sustaining international attention. In other words, beginning with Efrain Ríos Montt in Guatemala, the war was effectively hidden in the northern highlands. For a discussion of the relationship of geography to insurgencies, see James D. Fearon and David D. Laitin, "Ethnicity, Insurgency, and Civil War," *American Political Science Review* 97, no. 1 (2003): 75–90.

2. Michael N. Schmitt, "The Principle of Discrimination in 21st Century Warfare," *Yale Human Rights and Development Journal* 2 (1999), http://papers.ssrn.com/sol3/JEL JOUR_Results.cfm?form_name=Pip_jrl&journal_id=589841.

3. Another example: Michael Sheehan, a U.S. military advisor to the Salvadoran government during the war, was the New York City Police Department counterterrorism expert after 9/11.

4. *Prensa Libre*, April 12, 1985, quoted in Americas Watch Committee, *Guatemala, The Group for Mutual Support, 1984–1985* (New York: Americas Watch, 1985), 49.

5. The exact death toll in El Salvador has not been calculated with the same precision as in Guatemala. The accepted documentation is from both Tutela Legal and Socorro Júridico Cristiano (SJC). The death toll of 50–70 percent comes from SJC and

William Stanley, *The Protection Racket State: Elite Politics, Military Extortion, and Civil War in El Salvador* (Philadelphia: Temple University Press, 1996). The UN 1993 report on El Salvador does not engage in a sustained comprehensive analysis but, instead, focuses on representative or illustrative cases; UN Secretary-General, "From Madness to Hope: The 12-Year War in El Salvador: Report of the Commission on the Truth for El Salvador," United Nations Document no. S/25500, New York, 1993, http://www.lemoyne.edu/Portals/11/pdf_content/ElSalvador-Report.pdf; the Catholic Archdiose of Gutaemala led one of the reports, Proyecto Interdiocesano Recuperación de la Memoria Histórica (REMHI), *Guatemala: Nunca Más!* (Maryknoll, N.Y.: Orbis Books, 1999). The UN-sponsored report for Guatemala by the Comisión para el Esclarecimiento Histórico (CEH; Historical Clarification Commission), "Memoria del Silencio," February 1999, http://shr.aaas.org/guatemala/ceh/mds/spanish/toc.html. Two days after the public presentation of the Catholic Church's report, which was more extensive in its assignation of responsibility than that of the UN report, Bishop Juan Gerardi, who supervised the report, was murdered by the Guatemalan military.

6. Quoted in Elisabeth Jean Wood, *Insurgent Collective Action and Civil War in El Salvador* (Cambridge, UK: Cambridge University Press, 2003), 127.

7. American Embassy in Guatemala to Secretary of State US, "Re: Ambassador Walter's call on President Lucas, Guatemala Collection, September 22, 1981, National Security Archive, Washington, D.C., no. 06366.

8. See George Black, *Garrison Guatemala* (New York: Monthly Review Press, 1984). The particular shape of state violence did change during the 1980s. In its study of the violence in Guatemala during the 1980s, the preeminent human rights organization Grupo de Apoyo Mutuo (GAM) wrote, "El recurso de la violencia, como forma de control social nunca había sido llevado a extremeos como en la década de los 80." Centro Internacional para Investigaciones en Derechos Humanos (CIIDH) and Grupo de Apoyo Mutuo (GAM), *Quitar el agua al pez: Análisis del terror en tres comunidades rurales de Guatemala (1980–1984)* (Guatemala: CIIDH y GAM, 1996). See also REMHI, *Guatemala*.

9. U.S. State Department justification for supplying military aid to El Salvador in 1982, quoted in Michael McClintock, *Instruments of Statecraft: U.S. Guerrilla Warfare, Counterinsurgency, and Counter-terrorism, 1940–1990* (New York: Pantheon Book, 1992), 398. See also Kate Doyle, "The Art of the Coup: A Paper Trail of Covert Actions in Guatemala," in *Getting Our Way: Inside Clinton's Latin American Policy, NACLA Report* 31, no. 2 (1997): 34–39.

10. Michael D. Shafer, *Deadly Paradigms: The Failure of U.S. Counterinsurgency Policy* (Princeton: Princeton University Press, 1988), 116. The fourth tenet is derived from a cost-benefit approach to counterinsurgency developed in the late 1960s by RAND Corporation. In 1985, Americas Watch called on the U.S. to condemn this approach in El Salvador as it had "vigorously" done in regard to Soviet practice in Afghanistan. Americas Watch, *Draining the Sea* (New York: Americas Watch, March 1985), 2.

11. Schafer, Deadly Paradigms, 107.

12. Ibid.

13. Jennifer Schirmer, "The Looting of Democratic Discourse by the Guatemalan Military: Implications for Human Rights," in *Constructing Democracy: Human Rights, Citizenship, and Society in Latin America,* ed. Elizabeth Jelin and Eric Hershberg (Boulder: Westview Press, 1996), 92.

14. Carol A. Smith, "The Militarization of Civil Society in Guatemala," *Latin American Perspectives* 17, no. 4 (1990), 12. It is in this plan that the plans to "rescue" and "recover" the Maya take hold.

15. "The Development of Anti-subversive Campaigns to the Victoria 82 Plan of Campaign," app. H, reproduced in Black, *Garrison Guatemala,* 179. Waging "total and

protracted warfare" to "win over the people or destroy them," the security forces of both countries focused primarily on poisoning the water in which the fish swam. Department of Social Sciences, Universidad de El Salvador, "An Analysis of the Correlation of Forces in El Salvador," *Latin American Perspectives* 14, no. 4 (1987), 434.

16. In 1986, the army commandant of the Ixil Triangle in Guatemala (a region where it is estimated that one out of every three Ixil Mayans was killed or displaced during the armed conflict) stated, "We believe the war against subversion is total, permanent, and universal....our aim is to drain the ocean to flush out the fish." Victor Perera, *Unfinished Conquest: The Guatemalan Tragedy* (Berkeley: University of California Press, 1993), 82.

17. In both countries, the regions that emerged relatively unscathed through the violent conflicts of the 1980s were those that had previously (in the 1930s for El Salvador and in the 1960s for Guatemala) been the sites of extreme repression by the governments in response to popular revolutionary activity. This suggests that the memories and consequences of that repression were enough to prevent renewed popular organizing, which could only strengthen the belief of the armies in the importance of wiping out all possibilities of resistance. If the armed forces of each country consciously recognized this fact, then, tragically, modern repression seems quite efficient in the long term in preventing future challenges to the state. See Tommie Sue Montgomery, *Revolution in El Salvador: From Civil Strife to Civil Peace* (Boulder: Westview Press, 1995); James Dunkerly, *The Long War: Dictatorship and Revolution in El Salvador* (London: Verso, 1985); Michael McClintock, *American Connection: State Terror and Popular Resistance in Guatemala* (London: Zed Books, 1985); Gabriel Aguilera Peralta and John Beverly, "Terror and Violence as Weapons of Counterinsurgency in Guatemala," *Latin American Perspectives* 7, no. 2–3 (1980): 91–113; Timothy Wickham-Crowley, *Guerrillas and Revolution in Latin America: A Comparative Study of Insurgents and Regimes since 1956* (Princeton: Princeton University Press, 1992).

18. Americas Watch, *Draining the Sea*, 25. Quoting Col. Ochoa of the El Salvadoran army.

19. Thomas Buergenthal, "The United Nation Truth Commission for El Salvador," *Vanderbilt Journal of Transnational Law* 27 (1994), 497. Buergenthal was one of the three commissioners responsible for the Truth Commission report. See also *United Nations and El Salvador: 1990–1995*, United Nations Blue Books Series, vol. 4 (New York: United Nations Publications, 1995). In Guatemala, the incidence of massacres increased during Ríos Montt's presidency. Indeed, some estimate that out of the 200,000 who died in Guatemala, 43 percent died during his time in office. Virginia Garrard-Burnett, *Terror in the Land of the Holy Spirit* (Oxford: Oxford University Press, 2010), 6.

20. Stanley, *Protection Racket State*, 213; The UN El Salvador report notes that in 1983–1987 the "number of violations fell, but was accompanied by a greater selectivity." UN Secretary-General, "From Madness to Hope," 31, see also 44 for a discussion of the indiscriminate violence in the early years. See also Montgomery, *Revolution in El Salvador*, 131.

21. General Hector Gramajo, one of Ríos Montt's chief officers in charge of developing this new strategy, quoted in Jennifer Schirmer, *The Guatemalan Military Project: A Violence Called Democracy* (Philadelphia: University of Pennsylvania Press, 1998), 23.

22. Jorge Carpio Nicolle, *El Grafico*, May 20, quoted in Americas Watch Committee, *Human Rights in Guatemala: No Neutrals Allowed* (New York: Americas Watch, 1982), 22. He was later assassinated.

23. Quoted in Stanley, *Protection Racket State*, 220–21.

24. "Faltan Mas," *Network in Solidarity with the People of Guatemala and Guatemalan News and Information Bureau: Report on Guatemala* 10, no. 2 (1989), 8. "They treat the boys as if they were animals." *Report on Guatemala* 13, no. 1 (1992), 14.

25. The introduction of the PACs was particularly insidious because it forced indigenous peoples to become informants and participants in the counterinsurgency wars. By turning neighbors against neighbors and kin against kin, the PACs successfully contributed to the deterioration of essential community networks of social trust and solidarity. This, in turn, heightened the general psychological dislocation and sense of fear created and cultivated by the state. "People were not free to come or go. They could not express themselves without fear of retribution. There were open agents of the army and hidden "ears" in every place, in every meeting. The entire rural area had become, in effect, a prison." Clark Taylor, *Return of Guatemala's Refugees: Reweaving the Torn* (Philadelphia: Temple University Press, 1998), 31. In counterinsurgency doctrine, the establishment of social control and the corruption of the local populace in the explicit service of the state are designed not only to increase direct military oversight but to mimic or match the strategies of the insurgents in their reliance on and cultivation of the civilian population. The PACs made it essentially impossible for civilians to choose neutrality or noncombatancy—they were either with the guerrillas or against them. In most cases, individuals in the PACs "serve[d] . . . as cannon-fodder." Americas Watch Committee, *Civil Patrols in Guatemala* (New York: Americas Watch, 1986), 2.

26. Accounts of one massacre in Guatemala included reports that the members of a civil patrol were exhorted to prove their masculinity by killing all the men from a neighboring village. See Americas Watch Committee, *Creating a Desolation and Calling It Peace* (New York: Americas Watch, 1983). The gendered training of the U.S. military was also a significant influence because many of the Salvadoran elite battalions, as well as some of the Guatemalan military, were schooled in the United States.

27. Ilja A. Luciak, "Gender Equality, Democratization, and the Revolutionary Left in Central America," in *Radical Women in Latin America: Left and Right,* ed. Victoria González and Karen Kampwirth (University Park: Pennsylvania State University Press, 2001), 189–211. The URNG did include women's equality in its initial manifestos and statements. See Guatemalan National Revolutionary Unity and Guatemalan Patriotic Unity Committee, *Unitary Statement from the Guatemalan National Revolutionary Unity* (San Francisco: Solidarity Publications, 1982). As Luciak points out, as was common in most insurgent movements, women's equality per se was set aside in the pursuit of overall social equality. The more expansive attention to gender equality in the Guatemalan peace accords is due to the work of women's movements outside the URNG as well (and, again, learning from the Salvadoran peace accords).

28. American Embassy in Guatemala (Taylor) to Secretary of State, "Re: Guerillas Attack Tecpan; Violence Grows in Quiche and Chimaltenango," November 18, 1981, National Security Archives, Washington, D.C., no. 07797. This assigns blame based on the participation of women. See also American Embassy in Guatemala to Secretary of State, "Re: Congressional Hearing on Guatemala," August 9, 1982, National Security Archives, Washington, D.C., no. 95655.

29. Olivia Bennet, Jo Bexley, and Kitty Warnock, *Arms to Fight, Arms to Protect: Women Speak Out about Conflict* (London: Panos, 1995), 184.

30. Ernesto Rivas Gallort, Salvadoran ambassador to the United States, quoted in Lawyers Committee for International Human Rights, *Justice Denied: A Report on Twelve Unresolved Human Rights Cases in El Salvador March 1985* (New York: Lawyers Committee for International Human Rights, 1985), 64.

31. Captured with one of the GAM founders were her two-year-old son and twenty-one-year-old brother. Neither was spared torture and murder. A Guatemalan archbishop admitted, "It is impossible for a human rights organization to exist in Guatemala at this present time." Americas Watch Committee, *Guatemala,* 2. The first GAM meetings were

held in the house of international Peace Brigades. In 1985, GAM invoked international human rights treaties to hold the Guatemalan government accountable for disappeared.

32. REMHI, *Guatemala.*

33. Quoted in Victoria Sanford, *Buried Secrets: Truth and Human Rights in Guatemala* (New York: Palgrave Macmillan, 2003), 105.

34. Wood, *Insurgent Collective Action,* 130.

35. Catherine Nolin Hanlon and Finola Shankar, "Gendered Spaces of Terror and Assault: The *Testimonio* of REMHI and the Commission for Historical Clarification in Guatemala," *Gender, Place and Culture—A Journal of Feminist Geography* 7, no. 3 (2000): 265–86. Analyzing the CEH statistics, they note, "Men outnumbered women approximately four to one in the categories of arbitrary executions, torture, forced disappearance, detention, and the category of 'other.' Women and men were found in equal numbers in the statistics of death by forced disappearance, while 99% of sexual violations were experienced by women" (275). "Almost 90% of cases of sexual violation were reported by Maya females, while a not insignificant 10% of the cases were reported by Ladinas" (277). See also, the testimony from the 2008 Genocide Trial against eight senior Guatemalan state officials, held in Madrid, Spain, http://www.gwu.edu/~nsarchiv/guatemala/genocide/round1/summary1.pdf.

36. Americas Watch Committee, *Creating a Desolation,* 14, quoted in Aryeh Neier, "Extermination in Guatemala," *New York Review of Books,* June 2, 1983.

37. The 1999 American Academy of Arts and Sciences (AAAS) report by Patrick Ball et al. employs this presumption of male = combatant and female = civilian to analyze the indiscriminate character of the killings in Guatemala. The authors assume that "if men were the main protagonists in the armed conflicts and...therefore...primarily responsible for the political orientations of their families," then we may analyze the difference in death rates of women, children, and men on this premise. Here, then, we see the construction of the civilian as both sexed and gendered in that the civilian is apolitical, passive, and dependent. Patrick Ball, Paul Kobrak, and Herbert F. Spirer, *State Violence in Guatemala, 1960–1996: A Quantitative Reflection,* 91, http://shr.aaas.org/guatemala/ciidh/qr/english/index.html.

38. Quoted in *Shadow Play: Central America's Untold Stories, NACLA Report* 19, no. 6 (1985), 21.

39. Representative statements capture this well. According to a field commander: "Perhaps they will wake up to our reality when 80 million Mexicans have been enslaved under the Soviet boot." Quoted in "Guatemala on the World Stage," in *Guatemala: The War Is Not Over, NACLA Report* 17, no. 2 (1983), 26. And according to a senior Salvadoran officer: "I studied in North Carolina. You taught me how to kill communists and you taught me very well." Quoted in "Middle Game," in *End Game: A Special Report on U.S. Military Strategy in Central America, NACLA Report* 18, no. 1 (1984), 35. See also Andrew J. Bacevich, *American Military Policy in Small Wars: the Case of El Salvador* (Washington, D.C.: Institute for Foreign Policy, 1988), 24.

40. Interview conducted in July 1987, in Max G. Manwaring and Court Prisk, *El Salvador at War: An Oral History from the 1979 Insurrection to the Present* (Washington, D.C.: National Defense University Press, 1988), 94.

41. Brian Loveman and Thomas Davies, *The Politics of Antipolitics: the Military in Latin America* (Wilmington, Del.: Scholarly Resources, 1997), 408.

42. Ibid., 401.

43. Quoted in Stanley, *Protection Racket State,* 231.

44. President Efraím Ríos Montt, "Guatemala Vows to Aid Democracy," *New York Times* interview, December 6, 1982, quoted in Americas Watch Committee, *Creating a Desolation,* 8.

45. Dave Grossman, *On Killing: The Psychological Cost of Learning to Kill in War and Society* (Boston: Little, Brown, 1995), 209.

46. Ríos Montt, quoted in Garrard-Burnett, *Terror in the Land,* 70.

47. Ibid.

48. Foreign Broadcast Information Service, Central America, June 2, 1982. "Ríos Montt's Views on Peasant Killings, Communism" (Washington, D.C.: June 2, 1982. U.S. Broadcast Information, 1982).

49. Helen Fein, *Genocide: A Sociological Perspective* (London: Sage, 1993).

50. Diane Nelson, *A Finger in the Wound: Body Politics in Quincentennial Guatemala* (Berkeley: University of California Press, 1999), 29.

51. Greg Grandin, "An Onerous Citizenship: Race, Disease, and the Realignment of Rule in Nineteenth-Century Guatemala," in *Reclaiming the Political in Latin American History: Essays from the North,* ed. Gilbert Joseph (Durham: Duke University Press, 2001), 223.

52. Sgt. Julio Corsantes, quoted in *Shadow Play,* 23.

53. "To be an Indian man is to be subversive unless one has in effect, cleansed oneself through participation in patrols." Americas Watch Committee, *Persecuting Human Rights Monitors: The CERJ in Guatemala* (Americas Watch: New York, 1989), 10.

54. George Black, "Shadow Play," in *Shadow Play,* 10, 18. The shift from security to development (also noted in the French-Algerian War) was not, fundamentally, a shift at all. Development required pacification, and assistance was premised on a simple matter—in the words of a military commander in Quiche: "one, help them. Two, slap them down." Ibid., 12.

55. Quoted in *NACLA Report* 15, no. 3 (1981), 15.

56. The role of the U.S. certification process, in which El Salvador had to demonstrate a decrease in human rights violations to garner more aid, also contributed to difference between El Salvador and Guatemala. Nevertheless, note that it was the bargaining in the U.S. Congress, among NGOs, and in the Salvadoran state that allowed the entities to reach an acceptable level of compliance with human rights norms. A corresponding engagement and process were absent in Guatemala. In part, this was because of the almost absolute refusal of the government (here Lucas García is paradigmatic) to consider changing its military strategies under U.S. pressure. Both Lucas García and, later, Ríos Montt held that the defense of civilization trumped any other concerns. Thus, there was no opening for pressure or incentives to really be effective.

57. American Embassy Guatemala (Melvin Sinn) to Secretary of State, "Re: Emissaries to President Lucas," August 18, 1980, National Security Archives, Washington D.C., no. 5263.

58. Quoted in *Shadow Play,* 13.

59. American Embassy in Guatemala (Taylor) to Secretary of State, "Re: Congressional Hearing on Guatemala," August 2, 1982, National Security Archives, Washington, D.C., no. 05655.

60. U.S. Department of Defense, Joint Chiefs of Staff, "Re: Guatemala/Mexico/Additional Information on Operations Plan 'Victoria 82,'" July 30, 1982, National Security Archives, Washington, D.C.

61. Ibid.

62. Sanford, *Buried Secrets,* 158. Thus, although Ríos Montt's campaign was not as deadly in the cities, his systematization of the massacres actually resulted in more deaths per massacre.

63. What is consistently amazing about this stance is that the testimonies of the survivors of massacres are clear and certain about who was killing whom—the killers were often easily identifiable by their boots (military issue) and weapons (Israeli). In contrast,

during this time the U.S. embassies were sending home reports of complete confusion, and indeed, it was not until 1985 that the embassy in El Salvador began to report deaths attributable to the Salvadoran army. Congressional Research Service, *Comparison of US Administration Testimony and Reports with the 1993 UN Truth Commission Report on El Salvador* (Washington, D.C.: U.S. Printing Office, July 1994). Regarding Guatemala, Chapin wrote, "as usual it remains difficult to sort out who is doing what to whom." American Embassy in Guatemala (Taylor) to Secretary of States, "Re: Massacres and Refugee Concentrations reported in the Press," June 16, 1982, National Security Archive, Washington, D.C., no. 00822. The embassies also consistently blamed insurgent strategies for making it impossible for the militaries of each country to discriminate between combatants and civilians.

64. Quoted in ACLU Report on Human Rights (ACLU: New York, 1982), 138

65. Testimony of Maria C. G., May 27, 2008, "The Atrocities in Quiché and the Strategies of the PACs," Summary of Genocide Proceedings before the Spanish Federal Court at the Guatemalan Genocide Trial (against eight senior Guatemalan governmental officials) Opened in Madrid, Spain, http://www.gwu.edu/~nsarchiv/guatemala/genocide/round2/may27.pdf.

66. *NACLA Report*, 15, no. 6 (1981), 40.

67. Mark Danner, *The Massacre at El Mozote: A Parable of the Cold War* (New York: Vintage Books, 1994), 19.

68. "All Change: No Change," in *Guatemala: The War Is Not Over, NACLA Report* 17, no. 2 (1983), 21.

69. Hannah Arendt, *Origins of Totalitarianism* (New York: Harcourt Brace Jovanovich, 1973), 430.

70. Diane M. Nelson, "Relating to Terror: Gender, Anthropology, Law, and Some September Elevenths," *Duke Journal of Gender, Law and Policy* 9 (2002): 204.

71. Testimony of Maria T. to the Guatemalan genocide trial in Madrid, 2008, Summary of Genocide Proceedings before the Spanish Federal Court, Round 2, http://www.gwu.edu/~nsarchiv/guatemala/genocide/round2/may28.pdf. See also Testimony of Maria C. G.

72. Roger Trinquier, *Modern Warfare: A French View of Counterinsurgency*, trans. Daniel Lee (New York: Praeger, 1964), 26.

73. REMHI, *Guatemala*, 24. The testimonies struggle to explain the violence. The question of what individuals did to deserve death as an appropriate response (for lack of a better term) is answered through references to a variety of sociopolitical and geopolitical explanations that are not limited to or arranged according to arms bearing.

74. Americas Watch, *Human Rights in Guatemala*, 41.

75. Col. Domingo Moterroso, 1982, commander of the U.S.-trained Atlactl battalion, quoted in Americas Watch, *Report on Human Rights in El Salvador*, Second Supplement, January 20, 1983 (New York: Americas Watch, 1983), 89. See also the January 23, 1984, embassy cable from El Salvador noting that "Masas do live in close proximity of and travel with the company of armed guerrillas. This intermingling with, and support of the armed insurgents makes them something more than innocent civilian bystanders when…under fire." Embassy cable quoted in United States Committee on Foreign Affairs, House of Representatives, *The Situation in El Salvador* (Washington, D.C.: U.S. Government Printing Office, 1984), 314.

76. An army spokesperson, quoted in Joe Fish and Cristina Sganga, *El Salvador: Testament of Terror* (New York: Olive Branch Press, 1988), 61.

77. Georg Wilhelm Friedrich Hegel, *Phenomenology of Spirit*, trans. Arnold V. Miller (Oxford: Clarendon Press, 1979), 289.

78. Summary of Genocide Proceedings before the Spanish Federal Court, Round One, February 4–8, 2008, http://www.gwu.edu/~nsarchiv/guatemala/genocide/round1/summary1.pdf.

79. *Guatemala: The War Is Not Over,* NACLA *Report* 17, no. 2 (1983): 23. see Americas Watch, *Human Rights in Guatemala;* Schirmer, *Guatemalan Military Project,* 82.

80. This comes through in both interviews with and the testimonies of women in the war zones; survival required a complex negotiation with the forces in the conflict and a form of agency/involvement that was both complicit with and subject to the violence. It is this that makes the binary of combatant and civilian so difficult to obtain given the complications of war. Furthermore, the insistence on apolitical dependency also points to the sheer erasure of the agency necessary for self-constitution. As Wood writes in regards to El Salvador, "the *campesinos* acted in *order to act:* this assertion of agency (and thus a reclaiming of dignity) was itself a reason for acting—a constitutive and expressive reason." Elisabeth Jean Wood, "The Emotional Benefits of Insurgency in El Salvador," in *Passionate Politics: Emotions and Social Movements,* ed. Jeff Goodwin, James Jasper, and Francesca Polletta (Chicago: University of Chicago Press, 2001), 268. As Arendt argues, "action is a political expression par excellence"; thus to be a civilian circulates around passivity in a way harmful to political engagement. Hannah Arendt, *The Human Condition* (Garden City, N.Y.: Doubleday, 1959), 9.

81. Americas Watch Committee, *Creating a Desolation,* 2.

82. Bruce D. Jones and Charles K. Cater, "From Chaos to Coherence: Toward A Regime for Protecting Civilians in War," in *Civilians in War,* ed. Simon Chesterman (Boulder: Lynne Rienner, 2001), 249.

83. Sanford, *Buried Secrets,* 106-107.

84. This was one of the highly debated and unresolved questions of the 1977 preparatory conference. As shown in earlier chapters, sovereign states were already invested with a self-recognized and self-perpetuating sovereignty (a sovereignty premised on the distinction between civilized and uncivilized) and were to be the judges of the threshold of the conflict. The reaction of the newly independent states to Protocol II confirms the general stance of both newly and traditionally sovereign states to retain as much power over the characterization as possible.

85. Hugh Byrne, *El Salvador's Civil War: A Study of Revolution* (Boulder: Lynne Rienner, 1996), 90.

86. Manwaring and Prisk, *El Salvador at War,* 324–28.

87. As in El Salvador, in Guatemala there was a clear interaction and interdependence among the membership of both popular and insurgent groups as well as a strong class component to all the organizing. Byrne notes that in El Salvador "More than 95% of the guerrilla combatants were from the peasantry by the end of the war, as were four out of every five intermediate military commanders." Ibid., 35. In both Guatemala and El Salvador, the influence of the Comunidades Eclesiales de Base (CEBs) also played an important role in the development and ideologies of the URNG and the FMLN. The CEBs were particularly crucial in the radicalization of the rural poor in El Salvador and of the indigenous poor in Guatemala. The URNG did contain intellectuals and urban workers, but its membership consisted primarily of rural peasant workers under the leadership and governance of both segments of society. The Comité de Unidad Campesina (CUC; Peasant Unity Committee), for example, was a primary feeder for the URNG, particularly among the highland indigenous people. The "leaders were all Mayan and if not engaged in agricultural work themselves were only a generation removed from it. All were educated either formally at the university or informally through religious and cultural study groups, and all were involved to some degree in the pastoral work of Acción Católica." Greg Grandin, "To End with All These Evils: Ethnic Transformation and Community Mobilization in Guatemala's Western Highlands, 1954–1980," *Latin American Perspectives* 24, no. 2 (1997), 15. The named leaders, however, of both the URNG and the FMLN were predominantly university-educated, middle- or upper-class individuals. For both the URNG

and the FMLN, the separate cadres that composed the unified groups were ideologically and geographically linked to specific segments of the radicalized population. For the distinctions in leadership within the FMLN, see George Vickers, "El Salvador: A Negotiated Revolution," in *NACLA Report* 25, no. 5 (1992): 4–8, 86. For further information on the membership and leadership profiles of each insurgency, see Wickham-Crowley, *Guerrillas and Revolution in Latin America.*

88. Although the temporary opening during Kjell Eugenio Laugerud García's reign, in combination with more sophisticated political organizing on the part of the popular sectors, initially proved fortuitous for the insurgency, that very fortune turned deadly. The insurgency, unfortunately, was not only unprepared to defend its supporters and members but also unable to launch any successful offensive campaign of its own. Scholars note that by time of unification, the URNG forces were already diminished and, by the end of the 1980s, numbered less than 2,000 active members. Furthermore, Lucas García was able to destroy (due to improved intelligence techniques and equipment) at least twenty safe houses in Guatemala City extensively used by ORPA, and his campaign to exterminate all subversives introduced the direct targeting of northern highlands.

89. The FMLN engaged in active debate with Americas Watch and the ICRC over its implementation of international humanitarian law and the interpretation of the law. See, for example, Jean-Marie Simon, *Closing the Space: Human Rights in Guatemala* (New York: Americas Watch, 1988); Robert Goldman, "International Humanitarian Law: America's Watch's Experience in Monitoring Internal Armed Conflicts," *American University Journal of International Law and Policy* 9, no. 49 (1993): 52–72.

90. Waldemar A. Solf, "The Status of Combatants in Non-International Armed Conflicts under Domestic Law and Transnational Practice," *American University Law Review* 33, no. 1 (1983), 64.

91. Goldman, "International Humanitarian Law," 52–72.

92. In other words, the lack of information undermined one of the core strengths of networking, the presentation of facts, whereas the inability to document the abuses on both sides gave the impression of a subjective methodology (actually, Americas Watch began its 1982 report by discussing violations by the URNG under customary law and Common Article 3). Subjectivity was to be avoided; the international humanitarian law methodology had been introduced to combat the supposed subjectivity of human rights reporting that focused on holding governments accountable.

93. In January 1983, Frederic Chapin warned against a visit by a senior U.S. military officer to Guatemala, stating that Guatemala was not El Salvador and, moreover, that such a visit would be interpreted as "American imperialism and the American raj." American Embassy in Guatemala (Chapin) to Secretary of State, "Re: Next Steps for Guatemala," January 13, 1983, National Security Archive, Washington, D.C., no. 00334.

94. American Embassy in Guatemala (Melvin Sinn) to Secretary State, "Re: Annual Human Rights Reports," March 2, 1981, National Security Archive, Washington, D.C., no. 01267.

95. See the Tadić 1997 appeal on jurisdiction for the definition of *armed conflict* in Lindsay Moir, *The Law of Internal Armed Conflict* (Cambridge, UK: Cambridge University Press, 2002), 35.

96. See Schirmer, *Guatemalan Military Project;* REMHI, *Guatemala.*

97. Comparatively speaking, the capacity of the FMLN to hold territory not only helped to trigger the application of Protocol II (in 1984, it controlled almost one-third of the territory of El Salvador) but supported the establishment of alternative institutions of government that radically undermined the Salvadoran government claim that the guerrillas were simply terrorists seeking violence and unbridled power. Instead, the FMLN (as it did in its decision to abide by international humanitarian law) identified itself using

conventional and customary means as a legitimate challenger to the existing state power. As with the Algerian FLN, the FMLN used the standards set by the society of states to garner international support and recognition for its actions against the brutal responses of the Salvadoran government. In contrast, without control of territory, among other elements, the URNG could not invest its own actions with these standards of civilized society, and as a result, its members were more easily branded as mere subversives.

98. Protocol II was severely attenuated during the 1977 Conferences (see chap. 6), primarily by the developing states, which resisted incursions in their domestic affairs. Judge Hussain of Pakistan, in literally a last-minute effort to preserve Protocol II in some form, introduced several compromises to ensure its acceptance. The definition of the *civilian* was one article that was cut from the final draft.

99. Keith Suter, *An International Law of Guerilla Warfare: The Global Politics of Law-Making* (New York: St. Martin's Press, 1984), 3.

100. quoted in Americas Watch, *Report on Human Rights in El Salvador,* 87.

101. See "External Activities," *International Review of the Red Cross* 242 (September–October 1984), 296, http://www.loc.gov/rr/frd/Military_Law/pdf/RC_Sep-Oct-1984.pdf. This documents the training of an estimated 3,800 members of the Salvadoran military. For a general discussion of civilian status, see Americas Watch Committee, *Protection of the Weak and Unarmed* (New York: Americas Watch, 1984); Americas Watch Committee, *El Salvador's Decade of Terror: Human Rights since the Assassination of Archbishop Romero* (New Haven: Yale University Press, 1991), 64–70.

102. See "The Report from the Sixth Annual American Red Cross–Washington College of Law Conference on International Humanitarian Law: A Workshop on Customary International Law and the 1977 Protocols Additional to the 1949 Geneva Convention," *American University Journal of International Law* 2, no. 2 (1987), 496. Jean Jacques Surbeck, "Dissemination of International Humanitarian Law," *American University Journal of International Law* (1983).

103. U.S. Embassy in Salvador cable to the U.S. State department in January 1984, quoted in Aryeh Neier and Juan Mendez, eds., *Protection of the Weak and Unarmed: The Dispute Over Counting Human Rights Violations in El Salvador* (New York: Americas Watch Committee, 1984), 2.

104. For a brief synopsis of this history, see Goldman, "International Humanitarian Law."

105. Quoted in Americas Watch Committee, *Guatemala: Slaying of Rights Activists, Impunity Prevail under New Government* (Washington, D.C.: Americas Watch, 1991), 53.

106. Documents from the EGP, in Marlene Dixon and Susanne Jonas, *Revolution and Intervention in Central America* (San Francisco: Synthesis Publications, 1983), 145.

107. Beatrice Edwards and Gretta Tovar Siebentritt, *Places of Origin: The Repopulation of Rural El Salvador* (Boulder: Lynne Rienner, 1991), 15.

108. Interview done by Marta Harnecker and published in *Con la mirada en alto: Historia de las Fuerzas Popular de Liberación Farabundo Martí* (1993) and FMLN documents, *El Salvador Vive,* both quoted in Byrne, *El Salvador's Civil War,* 83, 87.

109. Mark Danner, *The Massacre at El Mozote: A Parable of the Cold War* (New York: Vintage Books, 1994), 18.

110. David Rieff, *A Bed for the Night: Humanitarianism in Crisis* (New York: Simon & Schuster, 2002), 25.

8. RESPONSIBILITY

1. Colonel Kenneth W. Watkin, "Combatants, Unprivileged Belligerents and Conflicts in the 21st Century," background paper prepared for the Informal High-Level Expert

Meeting on the Reaffirmation and Development of International Humanitarian Law, Cambridge, Mass., January 27–29, 2003, Harvard Program on Humanitarian Policy and Conflict Research, http://www.ihlresearch.org/ihl/pdfs/Session2.pdf.

2. Quoted in "Collateral Killing—Too Many Innocent Afghans Are Dying in U.S. Airstrikes," *Washington Post*, August 31, 2008.

3. Theodor Meron, "Geneva Conventions as Customary Law," In *War Crimes Law Comes of Age*, ed. Theodor Meron (Oxford: Clarendon Press, 1998), 159.

4. James D. Morrow, "When Do States Follow the Laws of War?" *American Political Science Review* 101, no. 3 (2007): 559–72, quotation on 560. Carl von Clausewitz, *On War: The Complete Edition* (*Brooklyn, N.Y.: Brownstone Books,* 2009), 50.

5. Quoted in Phillip Roberston, "U.S Soldier Battling Hard in Iraqi City," Associated Press, September 21, 2008.

6. Quoted in Mark Thompson, "Afghan Civilian Deaths: A Rising Toll," *Time*, September 4, 2008, http://www.time.com/time/magazine/article/0,9171,1838778,00.html.

7. Cordelia Dean, "A Soldier, Taking Orders from Its Ethical Judgment Center," *New York Times*, November 25, 2008. See also Peter Singer, *Wired for War: The Robotics Revolution and Conflict in the Twenty-first Century* (New York: Penguin Press, 2009).

8. Jane Mayer, "The Predator War: What Are the Risks of the C.I.A.'s Covert Drone Program?" *New Yorker,* February 6, 2010, http://www.newyorker.com/reporting/2009/10/26/091026fa_fact_mayer.

9. Kenneth Abbott, Robert O. Keohane, Andrew Moravcsik, Anne-Marie Slaughter, and Duncan Snidal, "The Concept of Legalization," In *Legalization and World Politics*, ed. Judith Goldstein, Miles Kahler, Robert O. Keohane, and Anne-Marie Slaughter (Cambridge, Mass.: MIT Press, 2001), 29.

10. Vaughn P. Shannon, "Norms Are What States Make of Them," *International Studies Quarterly* 44 (2000): 293–316.

11. Thomas Frank, *The Power of Legitimacy* (Oxford: Oxford University Press, 1990).

12. Antonia Chayes and Abram Chayes, "On Compliance," *International Organization* 47, no. 2 (1993): 175–205; Michael Byers, *Positivism and the Power of International Law: Custom, Power, and the Power of Rules* (Cambridge, UK: Cambridge University Press, 1999); Jeffrey W. Legro, "Which Norms Matter?: Revisiting the 'Failure' of Internationalism," *International Organization* 51, no. 1 (1997), 31–63; 35.

13. Chayes and Chayes, "On Compliance," 189; Friedrich Kratochwil, "How Do Norms Matter?" In *The Role of Law in Politics*, ed. Michael Byers (Oxford: Oxford University Press, 2000), 63. Meron argues that as a "mixture of actual and desired practice" humanitarian law may "reflect deliberate ambiguity, designed to encourage broader compliance with the stated norms and to promote greatest possible acceptance." Theodor Meron, *War Crimes Law Comes of Age: Essays* (Oxford: Oxford University Press, 1998), 159.

14. *Official Records of the Diplomatic Conference on the Reaffirmation and Development of International Humanitarian Law Applicable in Armed Conflicts, Geneva (1974–1977)*, 17 vols. (Bonn: Federal Political Department, 1978), Summary Record of Committee Two, II, SR.1: 5.

15. Hannah Arendt, *The Human Condition* (Garden City, N.Y.: Doubleday, 1959), 143.

16. Chayes and Chayes, "On Compliance," 205.

17. Shannon, "Norms," 293–316, quotation on 294.

18. Harold H. Koh, "Why Do Nations Obey International Law?" *Yale Law Journal* 106 (1997): 2599–659.

19. Michel Foucault, "Polemics, Politics, and Problematizations," in *Essential Works of Foucault, 1964–1984, vol. 1, Ethics, Subjectivity, and Truth*, ed. Paul Rabinow, trans. Robert Hurley (New York: New Press, 1997), 118–19.

20. Here it is interesting to compare Alex Downes's and Hugo Slim's work on identity, specifically the identity of both combatant and civilian. For Downes, identity becomes the means by which to incite and legitimate harsher measures. "The more severe the conflict…the more likely that the enemy will come to be viewed as evil or barbarous." Alex Downes, *Targeting Civilians in War* (Ithaca: Cornell University Press, 2008), 177. In contrast, Slim believes identity to be causal through genocidal, dualistic, or collective thinking in which one individual stands for a group that has been identified as evil, inferior, and worthy only of death. Interestingly, however, the one identity that Downes does presuppose, that of the civilian, is the one identity that Slim argues is most ambiguous. In other words, Downes assumes exactly that which Slim believes underlies and facilitates civilian suffering and killing—the ambiguity of the civilian. Accordingly, I think that ultimately the concept of identity invoked by Downes is too simplistic to capture the work that identity does in armed conflict, whether it is the identity of the civilian or the combatant that is at stake. But I also believe that Slim's invocation of "we are all the same" is far too flimsy an understanding of identity to maintain, much less to name as a foundation for the protection and defense of civilians (as, paradoxically, his own scholarship demonstrates). See the review by Helen M. Kinsella, "Targeting Civilians in War, and Killing Civilians: Method, Madness and Morality in War," *Ethics and International Affairs* 22, no. 4 (2008), http://www.cceia.org/resources/journal/22_4/reviews/004.html.

21. For a superb exposition of this claim regarding different substantial evidence, see Ann E. Towns, *Women and States: Norms and Hierarchies in International Society* (Cambridge: Cambridge University Press, 2010).

22. Michel Foucault, "Polemics, Politics, and Problematizations: An Interview with Michel Foucault," In The *Foucault Reader,* ed. Paul Rabinow (New York: Pantheon, 1984), 385.

23. "Pearl-diving" draws from Walter Benjamin's image; Hannah Arendt, "Walter Benjamin: 1892–1940," in *Men in Dark Times* (New York: Pantheon Books, 1968), 205–6.

24. One example of this is found in the standard definition of *norms* offered throughout the international relations literature. Following Katzenstein, norms are appropriate standards of behavior for "actors with a given identity." Yet, simultaneously, they are also held to be constitutive (as well as regulative and prescriptive); Peter J. Katzenstein, Social Science Research Council, and Committee on International Peace and Security, *The Culture of National Security: Norms and Identity in World Politics* (New York: Columbia University Press, 1996), 5. This is an oxymoronic definition. If norms are indeed constitutive, as I believe they are, then the actors' identity can never be given or assumed in advance. Indeed, it is the process of normalization that both invests and identifies actors as subjects—that is, as Foucault writes, "the way in which the individual establishes his relation to the rule and recognizes himself as obligated to put it in practice." Michel Foucault, *The Use of Pleasure,* vol. 2 of *History of Sexuality,* trans. Robert Hurley (New York: Pantheon, 1978), 27. Norms are processual, not instrumental.

25. Martha Finnemore and Kathryn Sikkink, "International Norm Dynamics and Political Change," *International Organization* 52, no. 4 (1998): 887–917, 893; Alexander Wendt, *Social Theory of International Politics* (Cambridge, UK: Cambridge University Press, 1999), 377. For a similar functionalist approach to the work of political theory and international relations theory, see Anne-Marie Slaughter, Andrew S. Tulumello, and Stepan Wood, "International Law and International Relations Theory: A New Generation of Scholarship," *American Journal of International Law* 92, no. 3 (1998), 373. For a familiar reliance on a binary of instrumentalism (*is*) versus normativism (*ought*) in the study of international relations and international law, see Robert Keohane, "International Relations and International Law: Two Optics," *Harvard International Law Journal* 38 (1997), 487.

26. Margaret Keck and Kathryn Sikkink, *Activists beyond Borders: Advocacy Networks in International Politics* (Ithaca: Cornell University Press, 1998), 195.

27. Kratochwil underscores the difficulties of even identifying clarity simply by noting that, if a "prohibition seems clear and unambiguous," it is only "because it is embedded in a whole host of at first unarticulated shared understandings." Kratochwil, "How Do Norms Matter?" 40.

28. Lester Nurick, "The Distinction Between Combatant and Noncombatant in the Law of War," *American Journal of International Law* 39, no. 4 (1945): 680–97, 680.

29. Friedrich Nietzsche, *On the Genealogy of Morals,* trans. Walter Kaufman (New York: Vintage Books, 1989).

30. For example, in September 2003 the Pentagon assigned the film *Battle of Algiers* as necessary viewing for its analysts. The promo read, "How to win a battle against terrorism and lose the war of ideas. Children shoot soldiers at point-blank range. Women plant bombs in cafes. Soon the entire Arab population builds to a mad fervor. Sound familiar?" The idea came from the Directorate for Special Operations and Low-Intensity Conflict, which a Defense Department official described as a civilian-led group with "responsibility for thinking aggressively and creatively" on issues of guerrilla war. M. T. Kaufman, "What Does the Pentagon See in the 'Battle for Algiers,'" *New York Times,* September 7, 2003, http://www.nytimes.com/2003/09/07/weekinreview/the-world-film-studies-what-does-the-pentagon-see-in-battle-of-algiers.html. In 2007, Henry Kissinger recommended to George W. Bush that he read Sir Alastair Hornes's history of the Algerian war, and the author himself sent Donald Rumsfeld the same book on the recommendation of Rumsfeld's staff; Sir Alastair Hornes, *A Savage War of Peace* (London: Papermac, 1996).

31. Paul Kowert and Jeffrey Legro, "Norms, Identity, and Their Limit," In *The Culture of National Security: Norms and Identity in World Politics,* ed. Peter Katzenstein (New York: Columbia University, 1996), 485. See also Jeffrey T. Checkel, "Norms, Institutions, and National Identity in Contemporary Europe," *International Studies Quarterly* 43, no. 1 (1999): 83–114.

32. Michael Walzer, *Just and Unjust Wars: A Moral Argument with Historical Illustrations* (New York: Basic Books, 1992), 42.

33. Article 48, IV Geneva Convention.

34. The transformation and re-signification of these discourses are essential elements in my analysis. I reject the claim, made most famously by Alexander Wendt but presumed by others as well, that "constitutive analysis is inherently static." Wendt, *Social Theory of International Politics,* 185.

35. Judith Butler, *Excitable Speech: A Politics of the Performative* (New York: Rutledge, 1997), 91.

36. John Rajchman, *The Freedom of Philosophy* (New York: Columbia Press, 1985), 4.

37. Gayatri Spivak suggests that responsibility involves not only "respond[ing] to," as in "giv[ing] an answer to," but also the related answering to, that is, "being answerable for." Gayatri C. Spivak, "Responsibility," in *Gendered Agents,* ed. Silvestra Mariniello and Paul A. Bové (Durham: Duke University Press, 1998), 19–66, quotation on 20.

38. Judith Butler "Continent Foundations" in *Feminists Theorize the Political,* ed. Judith Butler and Joan W. Scott (New York: Routledge, 1992), 3–21, 4.

39. Hannah Arendt, *Origins of Totalitarianism* (New York: Harvest Book, 1973), 352, 475. See also Hannah Arendt, *The Life of the Mind* (New York: Harcourt Brace Jovanovich, 1978).

40. Arendt, *Origins of Totalitarianism,* viii.

41. Hannah Arendt, "Understanding and Politics," In *Hannah Arendt: Essays in Understanding,* ed. Jerome Kohn (New York: Harcourt, Brace, 1994), 308.

42. Ibid., 318, 321.

43. See Arendt, "On Humanity in Dark Times," 10. See Hannah Arendt, "On Hannah Arendt," In *Hannah Arendt: The Recovery of the Public World,* ed. Melvyn Hill (New York: St. Martin's Press, 1979), 336.

44. Arendt, *Human Condition,* 5.

45. Arendt, *Hannah Arendt: Essays,* 321.

46. Ibid.

Index

Abizaid, John P., 21
Abrams, Elliott, 182
Afghanistan, 1–2, 14, 20, 26, 188
Aldrich, George, 140
Alexandrowicz, Charles H., 55–56
Algeria, 127–33, 147–49, 176, 195
    discourse of gender, 163
    discourse of innocence, 172–73
Allen, Charles, 1
American Civil War. *See* United States, Civil
    War in
Americas Watch, 164, 174, 178
Anghie, Antony, 65
Annan, Kofi, 2
Arafat, Yasser, 132
Arbenz, Jacobo, 18
Arendt, Hannah, 7, 13, 26, 172, 174, 190, 191,
    197–98
Aristotle, 33, 66, 67, 68
Armée de Libération Nationale (ALN), Algeria,
    128, 130, 132
Arms, as standard identification of combatants,
    85–86, 143–45, 153
Asbridge, Thomas, 50
Augustine, 14, 24–25, 34–37, 50, 51, 172, 193

Barbarians. *See* Civilization, discourse of; Civi-
    lization and empire
Bederman, David, 29–30
Bedjaoui, Mohammed, 128, 130
Belgium, 154
Bentham, Jeremy, 56–57
Best, Geoffrey, 154
Black Kettle (Indian chief), 99
Bluntschli, Johann, 109
Bonet, Honoré, 14, 45–46, 48–49
Book of Deeds (Christine de Pisan), 46
Brown, Wendy, 125
Brundage, James A., 28, 45
Burma, 119
Bush, George W., 14, 26, 113, 119, 129, 195
Butler, Benjamin, 90–91, 94
Butler, Judith, 79
Byers, Michael, 189

Campos Anaya, Oscar, 165
Canada, 27
Canon law, 26–41
    distinguished from civil law, 28
    gender and immunity, 30–34
    just war and immunity, 34–37
    peace movement and, 37–41
Carleton, James Henry, 83
Carter, Tim, 188
Charity, civilization and empire, 59, 66, 70,
    76, 81
Chatterjee, Partha, 141
Chayes, Abram, 189, 190
Chayes, Antonia, 189, 190
Chesterman, Simon, 9
Children
    Algerian Civil War, 145–46, 149–51
    canon law, 30, 33
    chivalry, 46
    civilization and empire, 63, 67, 69
    El Salvador and Guatemala, 163–65, 168,
        171
    equivalence with civilian, 8–9, 16
    General Orders 100, 88–90
    Geneva Conventions, 120–26
    Grotius and colonialism, 76–77, 78
    Martens Clause, 110–11
    unborn, 151–53
    United States Civil War, 19–20
    Unites States–Indian Wars, 83–84, 97–98,
        100, 102
China, 137
Chivalry, 27, 41–49, 154
    modern wish to reinvigorate, 25, 43
Chivington, John, 82, 97–100, 101
Christine de Pisan, 14, 15, 45, 46–47
Cicero, Marcus, 29
Civil law, distinguished from canon law, 28
Civil wars. *See* Algeria; El Salvador; Guatemala;
    United States, Civil War in
Civilian
    definitions of, 5–6, 16
    root and history of term, 28–29
    use of term, 13–14

Civilization, discourse of, 7–9, 13–14
  Algerian Civil War, 127–33
  El Salvador and Guatemala, 165–70
  Geneva Conventions, 112–13
  Martens Clause, 107–12
  Protocols Additional, 135–45
  See also Civilization and empire
Civilization, eighteenth century definitions
    of, 56–57
Civilization and empire, 53–81
  charity and, 59, 66, 70, 76, 81
  Grotius, 55–57
  Grotius and gender, 71–81
  Grotius and innocence, 75–81
  military transformations and, 53–54
  Spanish Requirement, 57–66
  Vitoria, 54–57
  Vitoria and gender, 68–70
  Vitoria and innocence, 62–68
Clark, Wesley K., 2
Clausewitz, Carl von, 188
Clergy, peace movement and concept of immu-
    nity, 37–41
Coffin, Morse, 100
Colonialism. *See* Civilization and empire
Colville, Mark, 178
Combatant, use of term, 13–14, 29
Committee of the Conduct of the War (CCW),
    98, 101
Concept of discrimination, of Augustine, 24, 35
Concept of proportionality, of Augustine, 25, 35
Contamine, Phillipe, 34, 38, 40, 47
Coordinadora Nacional de Viudas de Guatemala
    (CONAVIGUA; National Coordination of
    Guatemalan Widows), 163–64
Coss, Peter R., 45
Council of Clermont, 15, 41, 50
Courtly love, 43–45
Crusades, 25–26, 41–42, 49–52
Curtis, Samuel, 99
Customary law, 27–28

Davis, Jefferson, 91
De indis noviter inventis (On the Indians Recently
    Discovered) (Vitoria), 55, 59, 67
De jure belli (On the Laws of War) (Vitoria), 55,
    59, 68
De jure belli ac pacis libri tres (On the Laws of
    War and Peace) (Grotius), 13, 55, 70–80
De jure pradae (On Prize Laws) (Grotius), 55
Decretrum of Gratian, 45
Doctrine of double effect, 36
Doswald-Beck, Louise, 25
Draper, Gerald, 26

Duarte, José Napoleón, 182
Dutch East Indies Company, 16

East India Company, 16, 29
Eisenhower, Dwight, 132
Ejército Guerrillero de los Pobres (EGP; Guer-
    rilla Army of the Poor), Guatemala, 164,
    180–81, 184
El Salvador, 155–86, 193, 195
  combatants' strategies and tactics, 155–62,
    183–86
  discourse of civilization, 165–66, 169–70
  discourse of gender, 162–65
  discourse of innocence, 160, 170–75
  Protocols Additional, 156, 158, 175–86
Elderly
  canon law, 33, 46
  Geneva Conventions, 120–26
  Grotius and colonialism, 76–77, 78
  as momentary civilians, 16
  Protocols Additional, 146
Evans, John, 96, 98–99

Fanon, Franz, 132, 133, 147, 148, 151
Faust, Drew Gilpin, 97
Fein, Helen, 167
Feld, Maury D., 105
Fellman, Michael, 88
Fitzpatrick, Peter, 62
Forsythe, David, 123, 139
Foucault, Michel, 6, 7, 8, 15, 109, 149, 190, 191
France
  Algerian Civil War, 127–33
  El Salvador and Guatemala, 176–77, 180
  Geneva Conventions, 119, 124
France, John, 39, 51
Franck, Thomas, 189
Frente Democrático Revolucionario (FDR;
    Revolutionary Democratic Front), El Salva-
    dor, 157, 176–77
Frente Farabundo Martí para la Liberación
    Nacional (FMLN), El Salvador, 157, 163,
    164, 176–77, 180, 182–85, 195
Front de Libération Nationale (FLN), Algeria,
    22, 127–32, 147, 148, 176, 195

Garalasco, Marc, 188
Gardam, Judith, 9, 142
Gender, discourse of, 7–9, 13–16
  Algerian Civil War, 128, 145–53, 163
  canon law and immunity of women, 30–34
  chivalry and courtly love, 43–49
  El Salvador and Guatemala, 162–65
  Geneva Conventions, 22, 120–26

Grotius and civilization and empire, 71–81
United States Civil War, 19–20, 88–94, 163
United States–Indian Wars, 83–84, 97–102
Vitoria and civilization and empire, 68–70
General Orders 28, of U.S., 91, 94
General Orders 100, of U.S., 18, 103, 193
Geneva Convention III Relative to the Treatment
of Prisoners of War, 123, 143
Geneva Convention IV Relative to the Protec-
tion of Civilian Persons in Time of War
(1949), 6, 11, 12, 21–22, 26, 112–26
Algerian Civil War, 130–31, 132, 133,
135–45, 149–54
Common Article 3, 18, 20, 119–20, 126, 130,
156, 175–76, 178–81, 185
deferral to national sovereignty, 117–20
protected persons and, 116–20
sociopolitical context, 20–21, 112–16, 133–35
women, children, elderly, sick and wounded,
120–26
See also Martens Clause
Geneva Conventions (1864), 105
Gentili, Alberico, 2, 15, 55–56, 79, 80, 92, 154
Gilroy, Paul, 111
Glatthaar, Joseph, 93
Goetz, Hans W., 39
Goldstein, Judith, 189
Gong, Gerrit, 106
Grandin, Greg, 168
Grant, Ulysses S., 89, 102
Greenblatt, Stephen, 64
Grewe, Wilhelm, 54, 60
Grimsley, Mark, 82
Grotius, Hugo, 13, 22, 55–57, 70–80, 85, 120, 121
Grupo de Apoyo Mutuo (GAM), Guatemala,
163–64
Guantánamo Bay detainees, 195
Guatemala, 12, 29, 153, 155–86, 193
combatants' strategies and tactics, 155–62,
183–86
discourse of civilization, 165–70
discourse of gender, 162–65
discourse of innocence, 8–9, 160, 170–75
Protocols Additional, 156, 158, 175–86
Guatemala: Nunca Más! report, 173, 181
Guerilla Parties, Considered with Reference to
the Law and Uses of War (Lieber), 84

Hague Regulations (1899 and 1907), 11, 18,
104–5. See also Law of the Hague; Martens
Clause
Halleck, Henry Wager, 84, 87, 89–90, 92, 94
Hamdan v. Rumsfeld, 20
Haraway, Donna, 152

Harlow, Barbara, 146
Hartigan, Richard, 35, 67
Hegel, G. W. F., 15, 173
Heterosexual family units, Geneva Convention
and, 124–25, 151–53. See also Marriage
Honor
canon law, 25, 26–27, 44
civilization and empire, 76, 80
General Orders 100, 86–88
Martens Clause, 105–6
Protocols Additional, 153–54
United States–Indian Wars, 97, 99–100
Human rights law, 11–13, 31–34, 136–37
Human Rights Watch, 182
Humanitarian law, use of term, 9. See also Inter-
national humanitarian law

Ignatieff, Michael, 110–11
Immunity
Crusades, 50–51
just war concept, 34–37
laws of war, 30–34
peace movement, 37–41
root and history of term, 29
Spanish Requirement, 59, 66, 68
See also Innocence, discourse of
Imperialism. See Civilization and empire
Indian Removal Act, 95
Innocence, discourse of, 7–9, 13–14
Algerian Civil War, 172–73
El Salvador and Guatemala, 8–9, 160, 170–75
Grotius and civilization and empire, 75–81
Vitoria and civilization and empire, 62–68
Vitoria and natural law, 62–68
See also Immunity
Innocent civilian, use of term, 8–9
International Committee of the Red Cross
(ICRC), 9, 20, 111, 113, 176
Algerian Civil War, 142, 144–45, 146, 150, 153
chivalry, 27
El Salvador and Guatemala, 177, 178, 182–83
Geneva Conventions, 119, 120
International Criminal Court (ICC), 2, 12, 20
International Declaration Concerning the
Laws and Customs of War, 18
International humanitarian law, 3–6, 9–13
International law, origin of term, 57
International Tribunal for Rwanda (ICTR),
12, 20
International Tribunal for the Former Yugosla-
via (ICTY), 12, 20, 111
Iraq, 1, 21, 188
Ius ad bello, 10, 30
Ius in bello, 10–11, 30

Jackson, Andrew, 95
Japan, 106–7
Jefferson, Thomas, 94
Johnson, James Turner, 14, 15, 138
  civilization and empire, 55, 67, 70
  medieval and chivalric codes, 24–25, 26, 38,
    40–41, 45, 47–48, 52
Jus in bello, 25, 35
Just and Unjust Wars (Walzer), 31

Kalyvas, Stathis, 21
Keegan, John, 33, 109
Keen, Maurice, 14, 26, 43–44, 49–50
Kellogg-Briand Pact, 9
Knights
  chivalry and courtly love, 42–49
  peace movement and, 38
Koskenniemi, Martii, 16
Kowert, Paul, 193
Kunz, Josef, 112

Las Casas, Bartolomé de, 60
Lauterpacht, Hersch, 112
Law of Geneva, 11. *See also Geneva Convention*
  entries
Law of the Hague, 11, 84. *See also* Hague
  Regulations
Laws of war
  history of, 10–13
  positive and customary distinguished, 27–28
  twofold purpose of, 29–30
  use of term, 9–10
Legro, Jeffrey, 193
Lemkin, Raphael, 132
Lieber, Francis, 18, 84–90, 92, 103, 106, 115
Lincoln, Abraham, 82, 83, 102
Loyalty
  General Orders 100 and, 85–86
  of U.S. Indians, 98–99
  of women to Confederacy, 89–93
Lubanga Dyilo, Thomas, 12
Lucas García, Fernando, 158, 162, 170, 178–79,
  181, 192
Lynn, John, 47

Mandela, Nelson, 132
Manning, Chandra, 97
Mao Zedong, 159
Marriage, Grotius and social order, 72, 77. *See
  also* Heterosexual family units
Marshall, John, 95
Martens, Frederic de, 84, 104–5
Martens Clause, 84, 193
  discourse of civilization, 107–12
  sociopolitical context, 104–7

Mayan people, of Guatemala, 166–69, 170
Mayer, Jane, 188
McKeogh, Colm, 69
McKiernan, David D., 1
McPherson, James, 83
Medieval law. *See* Canon law
Mehta, Uday, 109
Mejía Victores, Humberto, 158, 182
Mercy, 25, 37
  civilization and empire, 58–59, 66, 76, 81
  concept of rights and, 15
Meron, Theodor, 12, 14, 24, 25, 37, 43, 47, 48,
  51–52, 111, 189
Mexico, 176–77, 180
Military manuals, 27, 54
Mill, John Stuart, 110
Milosevic, Slobodan, 12
Model villages, in El Salvador and Guatemala,
  173–75
Modern Warfare (Trinquier), 129
Montesinos, Antonio de, 61
Morrow, James, 188
Mozambique Liberation Front, 137
Mullen, Michael, 187
Muslim women, Algerian War and visibility of,
  147–49
Myers, Richard, 1

Nabulsi, Karma, 75
Nelson, Diane, 172
Nietszche, Friedrich, 146, 192
Noncombatant immunity, of Augustine,
  24, 35
Noncombatants, Law of Geneva and, 11
North Atlantic Treaty Organization–
  International Security Assistance Force
  (NATO-ISAF), 1–2
Norway, 140–41
Nuremburg Tribunal, 111

Obama administration, 119, 187
Old Testament, laws of war and, 30–34, 36, 44
On Prize Laws (Grotius), 55
On the Indians Recently Discovered (Vitoria),
  55, 59, 67
On the Laws of War (Vitoria), 55, 59, 68
On the Laws of War and Peace (Grotius), 13,
  55, 70–80
Organización Democrática Nacionalista
  (ORDEN; Nationalist Democratic Organi-
  zation), 169
Organization of African Unity (OAU), 139
Origins of Totalitarianism (Arendt), 197
*Oxford Manual of the Institute of International
  Law*, 18, 109

Pagden, Anthony, 57
Pakistan, 140
Palestine Liberation Organization (PLO), 137
Patrullas de autodefensa civil (PACs; civil
    defense patrols), Guatemala, 162, 168, 171
Peace of God, 15, 26, 37–41, 43, 48
Peace of Westphalia (1648), 10, 53
Perfidy, Protocols Additional and acts of, 154
Permanence, Protocols Additional and, 145–46
Philippine-American War, 108, 194
Pictet, Jean, 9
Pinochet, Augusto, 12
Politics
    Guatemala, El Salvador, and sovereignty,
        171–74
    of principle of indeterminacy, 191–93
Pope, John (General), 94
Portugal, 56
Positive law, 27–28
Price, Richard, 13
Principle of discrimination, 2–3
Principle of distinction, 2–3, 6–9, 14–16
    conventional narrative of development of,
        24–26
    definition of civilian and, 5–6
    fragility, compliance, responsibility and, 3–5,
        187–98
    international humanitarian law and, 3–5
    value of genealogy of, 6–9, 191, 194–97
Prisoners
    Algerian Civil War, 131
    Geneva Conventions, 115–16, 121–23, 153
    Guatemala, 155, 177, 179
    Protocols Additional, 134, 143
    United States Civil War, 83, 100
Protected persons, Geneva Conventions and,
    117–20
Protocols Additional to the 1949 Conventions
    (1977), 11, 12, 21–22, 27, 111, 192
    Algerian Civil War, 132–44
    determinacy and, 189–90
    differentiation of armed conflicts, 176
    El Salvador and Guatemala, 156, 158,
        175–86
    Protocol I, 20, 132, 140–45, 156, 159,
        160–61, 176, 180–81, 193
    Protocol II, 18, 140–41, 156, 175–76,
        178–79, 180–85

Quantrill, William, 84

Rajchman, John, 146, 196
Rape, 45, 49, 73–75, 78, 94, 147–48
Reagan, Ronald, 166, 176
Refugee law, 12–13

Reiff, David, 186
Requirement, of Spain, 57–66
Rights concept, concept of mercy and, 15
Ríos Montt, José Efraín, 8–9, 12, 158, 161, 162,
    166, 167, 170, 173, 178–79, 182
Roberts, Adam, 25, 37
Rousseau, Jean-Jacques, 11
Russell, Frederick H., 35, 36, 38
Rwanda, 3, 12

Sand Creek Massacre, 17, 82, 94, 95–101
Sanford, Victoria, 176
Sartre, Jean-Paul, 133
Schafer, Michael D., 159
Scott, James Brown, 64, 65
Second Council of Elne (1065), 39
Seddon, James, 88
Seneca, 77, 80
Sepulveda, Juan Ginés de, 60
Shannon, Vaughn, 189, 190
Sherman, William Tecumseh, 19, 89, 92–94, 99
Sibley, Henry, 97
Sick and wounded, 120–26, 146
Smith, Jack, 100
Smith, M. L. R., 20
South West Africa People's Organization
    (SWAPO), 137
Sovereignty
    Algerian Civil War, 130, 135, 140–41
    civilization and empire, 53–54, 56, 65, 72, 75,
        77–78, 80
    defense of, 21
    El Salvador and Guatemala, 156–60, 165, 169,
        171–74, 185
    Geneva Conventions, 107, 117–20
    Protocols Additional, 141
    Requirement and power of, 58–59, 65
    United States Civil War, 101
    United States–Indian Wars, 94–95, 101
Soviet Union, 118–20, 124, 135
Spain, 56, 57–66
Stacey, Robert, 25, 27
Stand Watie (Cherokee chief), 82
Stanton, Elizabeth Cady, 92
Strickland, Matthew, 42, 51
Suarez, Francisco, 66, 68–69
Sudan, 3
Summa Theologiae (Thomas Aquinas), 36

Tehran Conference on Human Rights (1968),
    136
Thomas Aquinas, 4, 14, 34–37, 50, 62
Togo, 138
Tocqueville, Alexis de, 95
Tree of Battles, The (Bonet), 46

Trinquier, Roger, 129, 147
Truce of God, 26, 37–38, 41

Unidad Revolucionaria Nacional Guatemalteca
    (URNG), 157, 158, 162, 164, 176, 177–80,
    183–85
Uniforms, as standard identification of combat-
    ants, 85–86, 143–45
United Kingdom
    Geneva Conventions, 114, 118, 119, 124
    military training manuals, 27
United Nations
    Algerian Civil War, 127, 129–30, 136–38, 146
    Charter of, 9
    Commission on the Status of Women, 149
    Convention on the Rights of the Child, 12
    Declaration on the Elimination of all Forms
        of Discrimination Against Women, 150
    Declaration on the Granting of Independence
        to Colonial Countries and Peoples, 127,
        135
    El Salvador and Guatemala, 176–78
United Nations General Assembly
    Declaration on the Protection of Women
        and Children in Emergency and Armed
        Conflict, 150
    Resolutions of 1968 and 1969, 11–12
United Nations Observer Mission in El Salvador
    (ONUSAL), 155
United Nations Security Council, 1–2, 4, 5
United Nations Verification Mission in Guate-
    mala (MINUGUA), 155
United States
    El Salvador and Guatemala, 158, 182
    Geneva Conventions, 118, 121, 124
    military training manuals, 27
    UN Commission on the Status of Women, 150

United States, Civil War in, 17–20, 82–84, 193
    discourse of gender, 89–93, 163
    Lieber and General Orders 100, 84–90
    Sherman's March to Atlanta, 82, 92–94
United States–Indian Wars, 17–20, 82–84,
    94–103, 167, 193
Urban II (pope), 50

Vattel, Emmerich de, 92, 115, 123
Vietnam, 144, 161
Visibility, gender and Algerian Civil War,
    144–53
Vité, Sylvain, 25
Vitoria, Francisco de, 16–17, 54–70, 94, 95, 110,
    167

Walzer, Michael, 14, 15, 24, 30, 31–34, 45, 48,
    194
War on terror, 1, 12, 20, 119, 129, 156, 187–89,
    193
Ware, Eugene, 90
Watkin, Kenneth, 187
Westlake, John, 107, 108
Wheaton, Henry B., 112
White Paper on the Application of the Geneva
    Convention, 130
Woerner, Fred, 160
Women. See Gender, discourse of
Woodhull, Winifred, 147
Wooster, Robert, 83
Wretched of the Earth (Fanon), 133
Wright, Lawrence, 2

Yegenoglu, Medya, 147
Yugoslavia, 3, 12

Zamora, Rodolfo Lobos, 170

CPSIA information can be obtained at www.ICGtesting.com
Printed in the USA
BVOW02s2247280216

438430BV00001B/2/P